First published in Great Britain in 2007 by Reality Press Ltd.

'The Good Guys Wear Blue'™ is the trademark of Paul Browning.

ISBN 978-0-9557815-0-6

Cover Design by Dixie Press

Book Design by WordsWay Copyediting

Printed in Great Britain

The Good Guys Wear Blue

The Good Guys Wear Blue

Paul Browning

Published by Reality Press Ltd

Editorial Services by *WordsWay Copyediting*

Dedicated to

Police Officers

all over the World

Contents

Foreword

Geoff Thompson

I worked for a decade in an employ (as a nightclub doorman) that brought me into regular contact with the police, both uniformed and CID. I also trained in the martial arts with a few coppers, and count several as good friends. So as you can imagine, I thought I had a basic grasp of how the police worked.

Then I read Paul Browning's book about his former life as a bobby.

What a shock! What a revelation!

I thought I knew about the police, but realised I knew nothing at all. I'd like to tell you that I feel safer after reading it, that we have the best police in the world and that our enforcers of law are above reproach. But I can't because they are not.

And that is what I loved most about this book. It shows the police for what they really are. Not superhuman, but human beings. Funny, quirky, massively moral, more immoral than the worst criminals, above reproach, below contemptible, hugely courageous, massive cowards, wildly intelligent, thicker than a whale sandwich, altruistic and the biggest egotists on the planet. I could go on, but I think you get the gist; the human disparity within the force is gaping.

But then, if there wasn't such a colourful diversity of character, this, I am sure, would not be such a great read.

Before I read it I had a great respect for the police. After reading it I still have a great respect for them because theirs is a thankless job. But I have to tell you that I will never be able to see the police in quite the same light again.

I love this book, and I greatly admire the inspirational work ethic of its author. I hope it sells a million. Just the sheer honesty of the author deserves at least that.

Coventry
27 September 2007

Acknowledgements

I would like to express my gratitude to Geoff Thompson who shared some of his vast writing knowledge with me whilst writing this book. I would also like to thank Haydn Middleton for helping me edit this book down from the original 900-plus pages to something far more readable and professional-looking.

Prologue

If you'd told me that five minutes into my paper round I'd be running full pelt after a large violent skinhead who'd just mugged an old lady I'd have smiled at you politely and walked away. But here I was tearing down the road as fast as my 14-year-old legs would take me. The skinhead must've been about 6' 2" and his long legs made huge leaps as he sprinted down East Street in Coventry. I pumped my arms up and down and sprinted as fast as I could praying that I could keep him in sight.

In his right hand he was holding the bag belonging to the lady he'd just robbed. It was a slim plain black leather handbag and the strap flew up and down as his arms moved. Black was not his colour at all. Having mousy fair hair, he'd be better off with a very light tan colour handbag to go with his doc martin boots, or he could possibly have pulled off a light mauve, but no, not black.

He glanced over his right shoulder to see if I was still behind him, and as our eyes met I could see a look of hatred come over his face, it had a sort of 'You're fucking dead if you don't stop chasing me' ring about it. There was no way I was going to stop, though. He'd pushed an elderly Indian lady onto the ground and taken her bag, and I'm afraid that wasn't acceptable to me. Also, her property had to be returned.

His long legs bounded all the way along East Street and then across the road into a housing estate in Winchester Street. I knew my way around that estate like the back of my hand because I'd been the paperboy there for the past 12 months.

I was very fit because I'd been going to karate lessons since I was 11. My stepdad had made me go because he thought I needed toughening up. I hated it at first, but grew to love the lessons and now I was glad he'd sent me.

The guy I was chasing was running on pure adrenalin. It wasn't his first offence, and robbery meant prison time. At 19 years old, he'd have to serve his time in a juvenile detention centre, which isn't as bad as prison, but still bad enough to want to avoid.

As he turned into Colchester Street I lost sight of him for about 30 seconds. I was panting hard and my lungs had sucked air into rarely used areas; they felt like I'd been underwater for two minutes and were ready to burst.

I ran to the bottom of Colchester Street and spotted him two-thirds the way up, about a hundred yards ahead of me. He was just about to walk through a back gate into a garden and I shouted at him, 'Oi you, I want that bag back.' His head snapped 'round in my direction. He began to walk towards me, and for the first time I could see him from the front.

His hair was completely shaved off apart from a triangular patch at the front, the apex of the triangle pointed down towards his forehead. He was wearing skintight blue jeans with turn-ups at the bottom exposing his maroon doc martin boots, with a plain white tee shirt. His arms were long and muscular and covered in bulldog and Union Jack tattoos.

We walked towards each other. It was just like sundown at the Okay Corral, but without the guns or the music. The trouble is that I just realised that I'd no plan as to what to do if I actually caught up with him. We got to within about 20 yards of each other and I could see we were going to be fighting. He clenched his fists in readiness to smash into my spotty teenage face. I had to think fast. I'd never been in a fight in my life – unless you count the one I had in the school playground when I was 7 after 'Nitty' Nigel stole the curly wurly from my lunchbox during break time.

I shouted out to him, 'I'm a black belt in karate. Just give me the bag back, that's all I want.' I immediately cringed at what I'd said. He suddenly stopped in his tracks and said, 'Okay, I'll show you where I threw the bag.' He turned on his heel and walked up to the top of Colchester Street where there were some derelict garages with asbestos roofs.

He stood by one in the middle and said, 'I threw it on the roof. You'll have to give me a bunk up, mate.' I thought he might stab me if I got too close, but his hands seemed empty so I took the risk. I linked my hands together, he put his foot on them and I gave him a push up so he could reach the roof. He retrieved the bag and handed it to me. He looked at me one last time and waked away without saying another word.

I walked back to South Street which is where the chase had begun. I retrieved my paper bag from the pavement outside Southfields school which was one of my paper round stops and walked back to George and Rose Palmers newsagents whom I delivered papers for. Rose called the police and a nice police lady came. She told me I'd been very brave and had done a wonderful thing.

I heard that the owner of the bag burst into tears when she got her bag back with everything in it. She had photos of her family inside, and a piece of jewellery given to her by her mother when she was a little girl in India – irreplaceable.

I gave a statement to the CID officer who came to our house to collect me. DC Robin Jones took me to the Little Park Street police station in the city centre. He told me how impressed he was with what I'd done and that I should be very proud. I just shrugged it off. I gave my statement and a couple of weeks later I heard that the skinhead had been arrested. He pleaded not guilty, which meant I had to go to court to give evidence.

When I went I was accompanied by Robin Jones and another detective.

They looked after me until it was my turn to give evidence. The skinhead was sitting there in court looking very innocent, having grown his hair long and wearing a suit. His barrister said that I was mistaken and that I'd got the wrong person. I looked across the courtroom and pointed to the man I'd chased, saying that it was definitely him. He was sentenced to 18 months in juvenile detention centre.

He had done wrong and justice had been served. I was hooked, I knew now what I wanted to do with my life. I wanted to be a policeman and help other victims of crime, and I wanted to catch the bad guys and see them punished.

Year 1 – Initiation by Fire

It was my very first incident as a police officer, but all I could think about were my brand-new doctor martin boots which were crippling my feet. I'd spent my entire life wearing trainers, and to force my delicate feet into a pair of leather boots caused my achilles tendon to ache. Every step was painful. And you thought it was easy being a police officer!

Despite the fact that it was a cold crisp evening, cold enough in fact for me to wear my police-issue 'NATO' navy jumper, my male pride wouldn't let me put it on. All the policemen on my watch took pride in only wearing their short-sleeved shirts no matter how cold it became (unless you were on foot patrol). You weren't even allowed to wear a tee shirt or you were called a 'poof'. A pathetic macho gesture, I know, but I was eager to blend in as much as possible.

I'd been partnered up with Katie who was standing in as my tutor constable for a few nights until my actual tutor constable (Alan) came back from leave. Katie was an attractive woman, her police skirt hugged her slim waist and her toned arms hinted at the fact that she kept herself in shape. With sparkling green eyes and long chestnut blonde hair which was always tied up in a bun when she was on duty, she was certainly easy on the eye, but she was spoken for. She was married to a fireman who worked at a station in Coventry.

Katie was a very professional police officer, and perhaps due to the fact she was in her late 30s and wanted to have children but never had any, so had a tendency to mother the new recruits she was tutoring. She'd hover over you and make sure you'd done all your paperwork just right and ticked all the right boxes on the right forms. Not that I minded, of course, because I was completely clueless when I joined and was grateful for any advice I was given.

Our police Panda car crept slowly along in second gear behind the Pink Parrot nightclub which is in Silver Street in Coventry. We were there because this was the place where most of the fights took place over the weekend. The Pink Parrot is now closed, but in its day was one of Coventry's premier night spots (not that much to boast about, actually). Every builder, hairdresser, trolley-pusher and off-duty police officer would flock there in droves.

The girls would wear as little as possible no matter how bitterly cold the weather and how long the queue outside. The idea was that if the bouncers were engaged looking at how hard their nipples were sticking out or trying to guess if they had a G-string on or not, they wouldn't notice that they were only 14 and well past their bedtime.

I suppose that was one of the dangers of pulling a girl in a dark nightclub. Late one evening one of my mates had pulled a cracker in a nightclub in Birmingham. He took her outside to his car in the car park and shagged her rotten on the back seat. When he'd finished, she turned 'round to him and with a big dolphin-like grin asked, 'How does it feel to have fucked a 14-year-old?' He threw her out of the car and sped off home. For the next few weeks he prayed that the police didn't come to arrest him for shagging a kid. Dim disco lighting and five Bacardi Breezers would've been no defence. He'd have had to serve his time in the nonce wing in prison, always looking over his shoulder and sleeping with one eye open.

The boys would wear the best of their 'Buy One, Get One Free' suits for Ciro Ceterio and pray the bouncers didn't notice they were pissed as farts despite the fact their eyeballs were rolling into the back of their heads due to loss of muscle control. They had to get drunk in a city centre pub before going to the Pink Parrot because the drinks were so expensive you could only really afford one bottle and had to make it last all night long. Well, that and the fact that the queues for the bar were 10 persons deep so you had more chance of winning the lottery than getting served no matter how many tenners you waved in the air at the barman.

The Pink Parrot nightclub (or 'Sick Parrot' to its regulars) had fulfilled its role of intoxicating its patrons and letting them jiggle up and down on the dance floor for a couple of hours before spitting them out into the streets to either stagger home, fall into the back of a taxi and puke into the footwell or get a bag of chips with curry sauce. I know I sound really judgemental about all this, but this was back in the day and I am a really nice person nowadays and love everybody (even chavs, but not gippos).

We were the second patrol car in Bishop Street; Mike Zulu 1 were already lurking around there because their 'patch' was the city centre of Coventry. They also covered some of Radford, but apart from the occasional scuffle at the local bingo hall due to a false 'house' call there was rarely any trouble there.

The crew of Mike Zulu 1 were Zane and Rick. Zane was a 6' tall Coventrian (i.e., from Coventry) aged about 44. He had thinning gelled-back black hair combed from front to back in an attempt to cover the bald patch growing at the top of his head. Zane's complexion was pallid and greasy, probably due to his very poor diet. He was a few pounds overweight due to his propensity to eat curry or chips every evening on late shift (2 p.m. to 10 p.m.) or nights (10 p.m. to 6 a.m.).

Zane had what my mum would've called chubby chops – his cheeks were round and fat which reminded me of when a hamster stores food in its cheeks to eat later on. You just wanted to go up to him and pinch his cheeks like he was a cute little boy. Zane's second-most distinguishing feature was a thin moustache, which never seemed to fill out quite enough. It looked more like his eyebrow had come down for a drink than a moustache. His most distinguishing feature was his right eye which had no pigment, so was a bright silvery blue which contrasted with the hazel in his left eye.

Zane insisted on wearing his police-issue black leather gloves whenever possible, and especially when he was wearing his short-sleeved shirt because he thought it made him look 'well ard'. They also covered a gold ring he wore on the index finger of his right hand. The ring had his initials 'ZK' which stood for Zane King (not his real name, of course).

Although he was 44, Zane was pretty young in service at only two years, but had already managed to secure a seat in the fast-response Zulu car, which was good going for his service.

Rick with seven years' service was the advanced Zulu driver and more experienced than Zane. At 6' 2" he towered over most people. His albino-like bright blonde hair was cut into a spiky pattern at the top and shaved at the back. He was also a wee bit on the tubby side and showing the first signs of man boobs (or bitch tits), again due to a poor diet and lack of exercise. Rick (I was to discover very soon) had an extremely violent temper. He could be laughing and joking with you in the station and a few minutes later putting a prisoner's head through a window (without opening it first). Seconds before Rick snapped, his face would go bright red and his eyes would start to bulge.

But I'm getting ahead of myself here.

Zane and Rick had spotted a drunken man who'd just come out of the Parrot staggering down Bishop Street towards the double archways that lead to Silver Street which was the Mecca of all the city centre drunks. At the bottom of Silver Street sat the Parsons Nose chip shop which made possibly the best chips in Coventry (at least they tasted that way at that time of the morning). Next to it was Mr Porkys which was a vegetarians' nightmare because it sold pork and stuffing batches with gravy which probably tasted like manna from heaven at that time of the morning after a rake of beer.

Rick and Zane sat in the comfort of their 2-litre Austin Montego watching for signs of trouble. They loved a good 'knock' and the back of the Pink Parrot was a sure place to have one. The Zulu was always a nicer car than the Pandas and had extras such as electric windows and central locking which were not standard at the time. The Panda drivers had to lock every door with the key which was a pain when you had to dump your car and run after somebody.

The drunken guy was called Barry or Baz to his mates. Baz was a very slightly built man, probably about 5' 7" tall. He walked with a slight stoop as if he was carrying two heavy buckets which did nothing to improve the look of his already very skinny frame. He looked like a strong wind would've knocked him over. Baz was walking the walk of shame which is when a drunken person tries with every fibre of their being to walk in a straight line, but judging by the way he was taking two steps forwards and one back he was clearly very, very drunk. Baz had the standard town uniform on, which consisted of a Ben Sherman shirt (not tucked in), Kicker shoes and cheap black trousers from the market.

Baz's misses was walking just behind him. Aged about 19 but with more make up than Coco the Clown she didn't do herself any justice. Her jet black hair was tied into two long pigtails but one of the hairbands had fallen out so a large clump of hair was half sticking out and half draped over her shoulder. She was wearing a white boob tube and a jet black miniskirt which made a big spare tyre of fat she had wobble every time she took a step, like jelly on a plate.

The full-length mirror on her wardrobe door must've been covered in shit for her to think that what she was wearing was remotely attractive. She wore white stiletto shoes at the bottom of her blotchy white legs and was struggling to walk in them because every few steps her ankle would turn over. She kept stopping to pull the boob tube back up just before one of her tits spilled out over the top. She was singing (very badly) a tune from the nightclub; it was something like 'Everybody Everybody' by Black Box, but whatever it was, she was murdering it to death as they say.

As they were about 10 yards away from Zane and Rick's car Baz did something that was to have a profound effect on the rest of his evening. There must be some sort of script for drunk people that's handed out before they step out of the nightclub or pub because you'll hear the same tired old lines time and time again as a police officer. Baz saw the police car and one of the lines popped right into his drunken mind. He shouted over to Zane and Rick. 'Any chance of a ride home, mate?' Anybody who's lived in a reasonable-sized town knows that this is just about the funniest thing you can ever say to a police officer in a car – do you detect a hint of sarcasm? It's almost compulsory for any drunken idiot to shout it out, much to the delight of any passers-by.

Normally, this kind of comment would be ignored by police officers – but not by Zane and Rick. They used a particular tactic known as 'winding people up' which usually meant saying something to stir a reaction in a person and then arresting them. Rick shouted out through his open window, 'Fuck off you knob.'

Baz clearly didn't know who he was dealing with here. At some level in what was left of his rational mind, this was not supposed to happen.

It was a joke, and they weren't playing along. 'Come on, Baz,' slurred his girlfriend as she wiggled her boob tube a few inches higher; she was following her obligatory lines in the script used in city centres up and down the country on a weekend, 'It ain't worf it.' Although her words were uttered after a few too many Bacardi Breezers the sentiment behind them made perfect sense to anybody with a modicum of common sense.

Unfortunately, our drunken friend had no common sense left. He took umbrage to being spoken to like this and was having none of it. 'That's bang out of orda,' protested Baz to Zane and Rick. As Baz spoke, tiny globs of spit flew out of his mouth into the cold night air, he wobbled from side to side struggling to maintain his posture, but the effect of the fresh air mixed with the alcohol in his body was too much to fight. The piercing neon white light from the lamp post Baz was standing under illuminated a bald patch on the top of his head.

By now I could see that he was so drunk even his eyes were pointing in different directions; one was waiting for the number 32 bus and the other for the number 12. 'I wuz only 'avin a laff, mate,' said Baz indignantly. Zane and Rick stepped out of the car. Zane pulled his leather gloves further down his hands for dramatic effect and Rick clenched both his fists as he walked towards Baz.

I didn't know what was going to happen having only just met Zane and Rick for the first time on parade an hour earlier at the police station. Even though I was only 19 and had no experience as a police officer I felt that Baz was completely harmless and the best course of action would be to ignore him and let him go and get his bag of chips and fall asleep in front of a football match on Sky Sports.

Katie nudged me with her elbow and said, 'Let's get out of the car, Paul,' and I did, although I didn't know why we had to. I opened the car door and lifted up the outside handle while pushing the door lock stalk down on the inside of the window. It was the only way to lock your car doors without the key back then. As I slammed the door shut I looked up to the sky and was surprised to see that it was completely clear, not a cloud in sight. The only thing to be seen were thousands of stars glistening. It reminded me of when I was a little boy and I'd lie in bed looking up at the sky for hours hoping to see a shooting star so I could make a wish.

The click of the metal seg on the heel of Katie's shoes scuffing against the tarmac brought my attention back to the moment. The street was covered with discarded McDonalds bags, empty beer bottles and cans and over a thousand pieces of chewing gum spat out and left to stick to the ground and turn black. Katie slowly began to walk towards the four of them and I instinctively followed her, feeling the tension of anticipation slowly growing in my stomach.

I later realised that if any women need to be arrested or touched in any way it's better for a female officer to do it to avoid any accusations of 'touching them up'. Due to the boob tube it would've been easy for one of her tits to land in your hand whilst struggling with her, which would not look very good if a paparazzi happened to be passing at the time. I can imagine the headline now, 'Coppers in Knocker's Shocker "I was only trying to put them back in" claims shamed three in a bed love-rat PC'. It could've led to a nice career for Miss Baz with a series of interviews in *Take a Break* magazine followed by a month on 'I'm a celebrity: get me out of here' and then a career as a celebrity supermarket opener.

Katie obviously thought that Baz and his girlfriend were going to be arrested for something or other and wanted to be there when it happened.

It suddenly struck me that I was no longer in training school. Baz and his misses were not police officers in plainclothes pretending to be drunk. There weren't going to be any debriefs or sitting down watching videos of what had happened, no flip charts covering learning points and definitely no second chances. This was for real. I felt a burn in the pit of my stomach as the tension turned to fear, which was the gradual release of adrenalin getting me ready for a confrontation.

Zane and Rick walked up to Baz, both towering above him casting a shadow as they blocked out the bright light from the lamp post above. The way they stood and spoke indicated to me that they'd played this game many times before and that the outcome wasn't going to be pretty. Baz had absolutely no idea how much trouble he was in. I began to shout to him in my mind, 'Just go home mate, walk away and go home,' but he didn't. Zane lifted his arm with his glove-covered hand, poked Baz in his puny chest with his index finger knocking him back slightly, put his face down into Baz's face and said through clenched teeth, *'Fuck off cunty bollocks or you're nicked, and take your slag with you.'* Zane's chin was pointing forward well ahead of his body by now. Any decent fighter could've taken Zane's head off with a left hook, but that would've brought a world of pain to their door.

Baz's girlfriend began to tug at his arm, having quickly begun to sober up. She could sense impending danger (as only women can) and wanted to get her man away to the safety of the chippie. As she pulled in vain at Baz's arm a faint breeze blew towards Katie and me wafting the scent of her cheap perfume under my nose. Well, it was either cheap perfume or she was wearing WD40.

'You're bang out of ord…' Baz didn't get to finish his sentence. BANG. Zane sank a left hook into Baz's jaw and he fell to the ground like a sack of spuds, his skull smashed full force into the pavement and bounced off it once before coming to rest on a half-eaten bag of chips. I yelped out loud 'Aarrgghh' and sucked in a huge gulp of air and Katie shot me a stare as much as to say, 'Get a fucking grip of yourself.'

As Baz lay motionless on the floor Rick gave him a kick in the ribs like he was passing a football back to some nearby children. Baz's lifeless body just shook from the force. Miss Baz was screaming and crying by this point; there were no onlookers nearby to witness what was taking place and she was clearly and justifiably devastated by what had just happened. I have to say, I wasn't that impressed myself. There was no point in calling the police – because we were already there.

Zane kneeled on top of Baz who miraculously had begun to come 'round and wave his arms about in the air like a turtle who has rolled over onto the top of his shell and couldn't turn over. Zane began to handcuff Baz while Rick was consoling Miss Baz the only way he knew how, 'Fuck off you slag or you're next.'

I was lost for words, my feet were frozen to the ground at what I'd just witnessed. I thought we were supposed to be protecting the public, not kicking the living shite out of them. I looked to Katie to see if she was at least half as shocked and disgusted as I was. Katie shot me back a look of complete disdain, rolled her eyes at me, blew out a puff of air and said, 'Well aren't you going to help them then?'

≈ ≈

I spent 12 years of my life working for the West Midlands Police as a cadet, police constable, detective and eventually a sergeant (man and boy, man and boy). The vast majority of that was on the streets dealing with the sort of people you pray you'll never meet up a dark alley (so the moral is to stay away from dark alleys). As a police officer you've to expect anything to happen during your tour of duty. One minute you're telling somebody their mum is dead and the next you're rolling 'round on the floor with a crackhead shoving your fist down their throat or pulling their hypodermic needles out of your hand.

If you've come here wanting to hear stories of us helping old ladies across the road or walking up the street spinning our truncheon, whistling, speaking to the vicar about little Johnny stealing apples from the churchyard, you've come to the wrong place. This isn't the Bill, it's real life. Some of my story is going to be hard for you to hear just as it was hard for me to tell – but tell it I must. It contains scenes of dreadful violence, abuse, horrible deaths and stories about the sort of men your children have nightmares about. If you're sensitive or easily upset then please give this book away to somebody else. Seriously, you'll probably throw up over the pages when I get to the bits about rotting corpses.

My story also contains scenes of hilarity, joy, friendship, bravery, happiness and hope, but then this is the yin and yang of life. Sun and rain make rainbows and tears and laughter make wisdom and you can't have one without the other. I just want to present the truth to the best of my ability, and sometimes the truth hurts. The truth is that the only time I've ever heard the news report on how wonderful a police officer was is when they've been murdered. The rest of the time we're either ignored or put down without a voice to stand up for us.

I'm going to tell you what happened during the time I was in the police. Some of it was good and some of it was bad, but then you probably already have a clue as to what really happens behind the thin blue line. It would be an insult to every police officer past, present and future to tell anything other than the truth. Judge away if you will, but under extraordinary pressure people do extraordinary things. All I can do is tell you what went on. Clearly, I'm going to be biased in favour of the police, but bear in mind that I also worked with some police officers I was close to punching out myself. I came across more than a few prats during the 12 years I served.

≈ ≈

I really should introduce the main character of our story, and since I'm writing it, I guess it's me. Well, I certainly don't consider myself a hero, I'm just a normal bloke with a story to tell. Your past forms you whether you like it or not and many of the things that happened whilst you were growing up have a huge impact on your life as an adult and knowing about them may help you understand why I did the things I did and maybe why you do some of the things you do now, probably without even thinking about them.

I was born on 5 June 1970 in Walsgrave Hospital in Coventry. My mum's name is Angela McLaughlin and my dad's is Liam (short for William) John Kenny. My dad was one of 14 children (a good Irish family). He was born and bred in Ballinasloe which is in County Galway in Ireland.

My mum is one of four children including Gina, Pat and Tom. They were all born in Greenoch in Scotland. Their mum (my grandma) died from TB when they were all little children. Her dying wish was that her children all be kept together, but unfortunately for them my grandad was an alcoholic and compulsive gambler. He used to sell his work suit at the pawn shop on a Friday and with any winnings he had left, buy it back on Monday morning so he could go to work.

He did remarry after my grandma died but soon after, his new wife left and was never seen again by my mum. My mum tells me that she remembers seeing them both arguing and shouting and after that she never saw her stepmum again. My grandad decided he couldn't look after his children and be in the pub at the same time so they were divided between aunts and grandparents and split between Ireland, England and Scotland. As they were all taken away to live with relatives, the entire community came out to protest at their mother's dying wish being ignored. They grew up and fitted in the best they could, but were really just used as cleaners and free babysitters for the relatives they ended up living with.

When my mum was 18 she was married off to the first half-decent suitor who came to visit – and that was my dad. My dad wasn't the romantic sort, so when he came to call on my mum he brought with him photos of when he was in the army and some wild boar his unit had caught and slaughtered. Before she knew it, my mum was married and pregnant and nine months later my sister Cheryl was born.

Shortly after Cheryl was born she contracted meningitis and nearly died. It left her unable to use her right arm and with right leg disabilities. Cheryl also acquired some learning difficulties which meant she struggled with her communication. In the early 1970s if you had any disabilities you were labelled a 'spastic' (lovely term) and sent to the spastics' school. The authorities issued you with a calliper and often some sort of head guard even if you didn't need them. I swear it was so you could be recognised as handicapped. I came along two years later.

When Cheryl was a bit older she was given the opportunity to go to Lourdes with her special school. I guess they must've been hoping she'd come back cured, but she came back just the same as she went. Well, almost the same, the nuns always managed to flog everyone who went a load of bottles of holy water. The bottles were in the shape of the Virgin Mary and cost about a fiver each. The nuns must've been making a killing. Cheryl has been back again to Lourdes about six times since. Talk about persistence.

I don't know the full details, but I do know that my mum wasn't happy living with my dad. She met someone called Jeff who was really nice to her and so left my dad for him. Jeff was a real character. He grew up in the 1950s and 1960s and was a free spirit. He used drugs regularly and had travelled all over the world working and partying. Jeff could find work wherever he went because he was a master stonemason.

Jeff was only about 5' 7" tall, stocky and had a head covered with naturally wavy hair which bounced around as he moved or walked. He was a real earthy character with a natural gypsy sort of charm and rugged swarthy complexion so it's no wonder my mum fell for him. He was the complete opposite of my dad who (like me) is very strait-laced.

I remember the skin on Jeff's hands always being very rough from handling bricks and cement all day long. He was a free spirit and would often take off to another country without a plan or a penny in his pocket. Jeff was always laughing and joking and never seemed to have a care or worry in the world. The only problem was that he was a bit light-fingered and so was often in prison for theft. He never robbed houses but used to steal lead from roofs or brass fittings from houses under construction. The police and CID were always calling 'round the house looking for him so he'd have to run out of the back door to get away.

My mum was young and naive so it was easy to fall for Jeff's charms. Jeff had to change his name every now and again to avoid detection by the police or debt collectors. He changed his name to Browning at one point for some reason and my mum decided to change my surname from Kenny to Browning. My sister Cheryl's name remained Kenny.

I'd like to tell you that the name Browning was inspired by the famous poet or even the famous American inventor or perhaps one of the other famous Brownings. Well, I'm afraid that my name comes from off the side of a bag of cement. Jeff used cement browning for plastering and bricklaying and that's why he chose that name. I've carried the name ever since. I'd like to change it back to Kenny but to get my passports and bank accounts changed would be a bit of a nightmare. I think my name being changed really hurt my dad. I have very vague memories of him not being happy when he heard. Because I was his only son, when my name changed from Kenny, he knew that his name would not survive him.

I went to Cardinal Wiseman Roman Catholic School in Woodway Lane in Coventry when I was 11. At Wiseman, you were either a bully, or you were bullied. A few weeks into the first term people had decided which they were, and it stayed that way throughout the five years you were there.

The teachers at Wiseman were hard as nails. They'd realised that you had to put the fear of God into the students or they'd make your life a misery. While I was there several teachers cracked and had nervous breakdowns. One used to keep a bottle of vodka under his desk and drank from it throughout the day to keep himself going.

One day, a rumour spread around the school that we were going to have a riot. There'd been one on a TV programme called *Grange Hill* that week so people thought it would be fun to have our own. When the PT teachers got wind of what was planned, they armed themselves with baseball bats and carried out patrols of the school corridors. As they walked along the corridors they tapped the baseball bats on their palms and looked like they were more than prepared to use them on us. The riot never came.

As I got older I'd see a few friends I'd been to school with hanging around Hillfields dealing drugs. One was later shot dead by a competing drug dealer and another one arrested for drug dealing. I was working in the cell block at Little Park Street police station and he called me over to his cell hatch to say hello. We had sat next to each other in physics for three years and he was a great guy, always laughing and joking. The day after I saw him he was sentenced to eight years for supplying heroin. It was his third prison sentence.

There, but for the grace of God, went I. It could easily have been me if I'd chosen different friends, dropped out of school or not been taught right from wrong by my mum as I was growing up.

At the end of sixth form, while my friends were applying for university or jobs I applied to the West Midlands Police cadets for the September 1988 intake. Everything I'd done at school had been with only one goal in mind – to become a police officer. To be honest, school and sixth form were just something I did while I was waiting to become old enough to apply. I'd read a lot of literature about the police cadets and it seemed to be a great introduction to life as a police officer.

The first test for all police and police cadet applicants was the fitness test. Because of all the circuit training and running I was doing I was very fit and in the fitness test at the Tally Ho training centre I wiped the floor with everybody else who'd turned up. Although I was applying for the cadets, I ended up taking the fitness test with the people applying for the regular police. While people were struggling to do the required 20 press-ups in one minute, I knocked out 70. Gasps could be heard around the hall as the PT instructor called out my scores (he'd counted mine personally).

I was amazed when people who'd come to take the fitness test were failing the run or the press-ups and sit-ups. They must've known for months that they were coming, yet they were not prepared. I'd been running for months and trained every single day imagining myself passing with flying colours. I couldn't understand why a person would even bother to turn up when they hadn't prepared themselves properly. The Roman army's motto was 'train hard, fight easy', and I'd applied that throughout my months of physical training and it showed during the test.

A few weeks later after I'd completed maths and English tests I was called to police HQ at Lloyd House in Birmingham for a urine and height test. I took the train to central Birmingham and used a map to find Colmore Circus in the city centre. It was the most important event in my life to be applying to join the police, and every cell in my body wanted it so bad I tingled all over. I got into town two hours early to make sure I could find the place first. I then found a Burger King down the road and sat there reading a book until my appointment time arrived.

I've never taken drugs in my life and never drunk alcohol (I tried it once or twice but didn't like it) so I knew I was OK there. When I went into the medical room I was greeted by the training sergeant, Sgt. Valley, and one of the training constables. Sgt. Valley was a giant of a man at 6′ 5″ tall, had a badly combed mop of bright red hair and a thick bushy greying moustache. He stood there holding a measuring stick which had a moveable marker on top to gauge your height. He looked at the training constable and said, 'We're going to have problems here, Rod.' The training constable put his eyes above the newspaper he was reading and let out a giggle. Clearly, they both doubted that I'd be the required height to be a police officer.

I actually knew I was under-height, but I thought it was a silly rule. What difference does the height make as to whether you're going to be a good police officer? I measured exactly 5′ 7″ (170 cm) on the scale or just under 70 inches. I needed to be 172 cm (just under 5′ 8″) to be allowed in. At the time there were over 200,000 police officers working in the UK and not a single one of them was under 172 cm. The problem was that every single day for years and years I'd pictured myself as a police officer in vivid detail. I was already a policeman in my head and I wasn't going to let a silly rule about height get in my way.

The letter came to my home about two weeks later. They regretted to inform me that I did not reach the required standard of height so my application was refused. I was devastated but what could I do? It was a daft rule imposed by somebody for a reason that was never made clear, why 172 cm, why not 171 or 170 or 169? Everybody seemed to just lie back and accept that they couldn't be a police officer so either didn't apply or just accepted the rejection letter. Well, not me. I went to see my doctor and he very kindly wrote a letter to the head of recruitment and West Midlands Police Force surgeon explaining that I was only 18 and still growing and would likely reach their required height by the time I was about 20.

My stepdad John fitted a metal bar in the upstairs hallway in our house in Catherine Street and made me two rope hooks to put my feet in so I could dangle upside down to make me taller (don't laugh too hard, I was desperate). I also started to look at other careers such as insurance or banking since I had three 'A' levels, but I was gutted. I just couldn't imagine doing anything else apart from being a police officer. It just felt to me that I was supposed to be a policeman, it was as if it was my destiny. I'd built such a powerful image in my mind of my being a police officer that it was now part of who I was.

Another month later I was shocked and ecstatic to receive another letter from the West Midlands Police recruitment team. They'd read the letter from my GP and had decided to let my application continue on the proviso that I reached the required height by the time I finished my first year in the police cadets. There wasn't really much chance of that happening, but I wasn't going to tell them that. I wasn't the only one who this change saved. Six other police cadets had been rejected, but due to my letter they were all allowed to join the police cadets as well. I was absolutely overjoyed.

Many years later I went to a sales seminar where one of the world's top sales trainers said to all of us that when you're selling in business and somebody says 'no', it often means 'keep asking'. I'd kept asking after getting a 'no' from the police and it had paid dividends.

Soon after I was issued my appointment card to go to the police clothing stores in Bourneville Lane in Birmingham. It was sheer joy to be living the image I'd held in my mind for so many years. I didn't have a car then so I caught the train to Birmingham New Street and then a bus for about five miles to Bourneville Lane which was where the force clothing stores and force control room were (they take the 999 calls).

I was fitted out for my police cadet uniform. The tailors there made my trousers and tunic to fit me exactly and I was issued with my shirts and boots. As they took my measurements I just stood there smiling like an idiot, the tailors must've wondered to themselves why I was so happy. My family were delighted for me and I remember every time an aunt or distant relative came to visit, my mum would send me upstairs to put my uniform on to show them. I'd hear the gasps of excitement as I emerged from upstairs in my smart police clothes. I'd then parade 'round the living room showing off. I felt so happy.

The cadets didn't really turn out to be what I expected. I'd built up an image of fun, fitness and community service making a good grounding for life as a police officer, but it wasn't quite like that. It ended up consisting of running, running and more running. When we weren't running we were working in special schools and homes for people with mental handicaps doing community service. I actually enjoyed that immensely.

By late summer of 1990 our cadetship was coming to an end. Awards were handed out for the best runner, swimmer, hill walker and so on. I'd come top out of all the cadets in the academic tests at college, but there was no award for that. I felt very disappointed that the emphasis was just on physical ability. I hated running.

Before we were allowed to join the regular police a report was submitted by the sergeant in charge of the cadets to the superintendent in charge of recruitment. Not one of the seven of us had grown a jot and he wanted to know if we were to be dismissed from the police force or allowed to join as regular officers. The week we had to wait for his reply felt like a month; I couldn't bear the thought of not being a policeman.

As far as I was concerned it was that or nothing. Finally, we got the news back from the superintendent. Sanity had prevailed and on the report he said that he didn't see what difference it made to our ability to be police officers and that we should be allowed to join the force.

The height policy was finally repealed. It was later decided that it was racially biased against shorter races such as Chinese. I'd like to think that my efforts to get into the cadets played a major part in that happening. This had a knock-on effect on other forces up and down the UK which all finally amended their height policies.

ও গ

All police officers have to go to a national training centre for their initial 15 weeks' training and then additional modules are completed at their own force HQ. Our local training centre was Ryton, but it was full so we all had to go Bruche police training centre in Warrington near Manchester.

Bruche was a fantastic place to train and it was brilliant to mix the Mancunians and Liverpudlians who had loads of character. The place was run like an army camp and far stricter than Ryton, which by all accounts was like a holiday camp. At Bruch, we had to march everywhere and lights were out by 10:30 p.m. The halls were patrolled by sergeants who'd put you on report if your behaviour was 'unruly' or your room untidy. We had room inspections every other day and if things were out of place or messy we'd have to be on the parade ground at 7:30 a.m. the next day with our locker next to us.

It did sound very harsh, but there was a great atmosphere there and the social life in the bar was wonderful. We all had to attend the bar with a shirt, tie and jacket. The drill sergeant was always there to keep an eye on us. If you were first into the bar you'd be given a bollocking and the same if you were last out in the evening.

Lessons were split into theory and practicals. We had to do a huge amount of marching on the square for the passing-out parade. We also learned first aid, and, for some reason, lifesaving in the swimming pool. I don't know if it's still taught, but we all had to pass the police lifesaving badge. We had to pass a test at the end of the course where we jump into the water in pyjamas and rescue two people at the same time who're drowning. I couldn't help but think where on earth you were going to use that skill. Even if you came across somebody drowning in a canal, for instance, were you really going to jump in there after them, and where would you get a pair of pyjamas to put on?

Due to the identification of some issues with police training such as the Scarman Report it was decided that police officers needed more training in social skills and soft skills than legal training. I do remember the race riots in Brixton and Toxteth being all over the news. There was even rioting in Coventry, and I remember seeing petrol bombs being thrown across the road from my house when I was 11.

The riots and resulting investigation by Lord Scarman led to some very positive changes in society and the police force such as repealing the 'Sus Law' where the police could search people for no particular reason. He also recommended that racially discriminatory behaviour be a discipline offence in the police. All good things, but unfortunately a few people took this the wrong way and decided that police officers should be more like social workers, so a huge amount of legal training was swapped for people skills and equal opportunities awareness.

In any period of uncertainty in an organisation, strong enough characters can sway culture in a particular direction and it can often be in the wrong way. While I agree that the police should respect all races and religions, there's also a job to be done and we aren't here to talk about people's feelings with them when we go to a domestic. We swung away from knowledge of the law and now the force trainers became paranoid about not offending people due to age, sex, religion, or colour.

If a delegate in the classroom wanted to turn the heat down, we all had to take a vote in the class so nobody's feelings were hurt. Policewomen became 'police officers' and any differences between the sexes were to be ignored. The trainers were petrified of the word 'black' so the blackboard became the chalkboard and black coffee became coffee without milk. If you said the word 'black' the trainers would cringe or take you outside and give you a bollocking. I had to laugh because it completely missed the sentiment of helping police officers gain an appreciation of the different races and religions of the areas they police, and instead there was a general air of tension in case anybody was offended at all.

Fifteen weeks at national police training centre is followed up by force-level training and then training at your local station by the station training team. Every force and station does things differently, so you've to not only learn the law and how to deal with incidents, but how your force and station does things as well. It can get a bit confusing at times.

As part of the force training we learned how the force was made up. There's the chief constable and his team of assistant chief constables who are responsible for crime, traffic, operations and so on. There are some top civilians who look after finance and the admin side. Every police station covers a certain area and is run by a superintendent. Areas are called OCUs which stands for operational command units. There'll always be one main station in an OCU and often several smaller satellite stations that are closer to the area they cover. There are currently 21

OCUs in the West Midlands area.

It's up to the OCU superintendent how things are run and if he wants specialist teams such as drugs, car crime and plainclothes squads. There are always CID and traffic teams operating out of the main station, but it's upto the superintendent how he uses those specialist teams. He is given targets by the chief constable and if he doesn't perform, he's kicked off the OCU and replaced.

We all just played the game at training centre and did the group exercise and team events and filled in our personal development profiles (PDPs) so we could pass our two-year probationary period.

Happy Birthday to Me – 5 June 1971

I wake from a horrible nightmare. As soon as my eyes open, I feel an immediate sense of relief to find myself safe in my cot. I've kicked my blankets to the bottom.

I've had the same nightmare a few times now. In it, there's a monster chasing me through the house. I can't see what it looks like, but I can hear a terrible shriek as it comes closer and I feel the fear of it in the pit of my stomach. I run upstairs and block the door to my bedroom with a pillow trying to keep it out. I always wake up at that point with my heart beating out of my chest.

I'm in a dark room and feel a dreadful thirst. My mouth is so parched that my tongue has almost stuck to the roof. Every time I try to swallow, my throat feels rough and sore. I try to cry out but my voice has gone. All I can manage is a croak.

I've wet myself – I can feel the wetness pulling the heat from my body. It's so dark I can't see my hands in front of my eyes. I reach out and can feel wooden slats in front of me. I grab hold of one and manage to pull myself up slightly so I'm sitting upright.

All I can think about is my thirst, I don't think I've ever been this thirsty before. I'm all alone and I'm going to die. I begin to cry to myself. I've been abandoned. I'm going to die all alone. I'm very frightened.

I'm 1 year old.

Year 2 – The Smelly Finger

The life of a police officer means having to work shifts for the entire year in a revolving pattern, a constant cycle of nights, earlies and lates punctuated by two or three days off in between. You're gradually worn down as your body clock is continually thrown out of synch so after a few years you feel a lot older than you actually are. You can never really relax either, because one minute you could be checking over a corpse and the next being punched in the face by some drunken prisoner. Better than being punched in the face by a drunken corpse, though, I suppose.

You wolf down food whenever you can because you know you can be called out to a job any minute. Every situation you deal with has to be carefully assessed. Is it going to be peaceful or become violent? How far away is back-up, and can you rely on your partner to keep their cool or get stuck in if you end up fighting or are they afraid and unfit? Have you done all the paperwork right and called in what you're doing on the radio? Mistakes can lead to discipline proceedings and that's the last thing you need on your record or being thrown in your face at court by some smart-arsed lawyer.

The stress can become unbearable and the only place to go to unwind where people will understand is the police bar. You can't dump your problems on your wife or partner. If they knew what really happened when you go to work, they'd lie awake in bed every night worried if you were going to come back home alive.

Being a police officer is a lot like being a parent of naughty children. The children know the rules, but they break them anyway or push you to test you. When you enforce the rules, they throw a tantrum and run around screaming or become violent. It's so strange to deal with somebody who looks like an adult but when you stop them for speeding past a school they become irate and start shouting and screaming and go red in the face. I didn't ask them to speed, but now they've been naughty, the police have to step in and give them their punishment for being silly.

The naughtiest grown-up kids run off and tell their lawyer like boys run off and tell their dads. The lawyer comes in fighting for them saying that we made it all up or that the speed camera was faulty and must've been damaged by cosmic rays from the galaxy. Anything but be a grown-up and admit they actually were speeding and deserve the fine and points.

It's the same with domestics or fights in town – it takes a person back to playgroup where two children start to fight over a toy and end up rolling 'round the floor scrapping. You've to go over and split them up and sit them both on the naughty chair, but the grown-up equivalent is the police cells.

When I joined the police I'd no idea what I was getting myself into. All I knew was from the little I'd seen on TV and a couple of episodes of *Dixon of Dock Green*. I didn't know any policemen to ask what it was like. The chances are they'd never have told me. Who wants to put somebody off what they really want to do? Looking back, I'd recommend the police to anybody who wants to see a bit of life and have some excitement and variety – *for a while*. But I wouldn't do it for more than about three to five years, and then I'd be gone. The toll the job takes on your personal life and health is too much and there are far better-paying and less stressful jobs out there.

While my intake were undergoing our foundation training at Tally Ho training centre in Birmingham we were all told which stations we'd been allocated. Technically, we could be stationed anywhere in the West Midlands. We had to choose our top three stations and the operations team did their best to accommodate us. My first choice was Little Park Street police station which is in the city centre of Coventry. It's situated about a hundred yards from the Magistrates' and Crown Court and next to New Union Street where a large number of lawyers and estate agents are based.

Little Park Street covers the city centre and surrounding areas of Coventry so you've all the nightlife on the weekends and associated violence. It also covers many low-income areas such as Stoke Aldermoor, Hillfields and Stoke to name a few so you have the drugs, prostitution, car crime and theft to deal with.

The station is the headquarters for Coventry and so is very large because it has to accommodate a few hundred people from a small army of admin staff, typists, CID, traffic wardens, jailers' team, various squads, front office staff, and, of course, police officers. The station is a mix of the old station built in 1861 and the new site built in the 1990s.

The old station is a rabbit warren of old musty-smelling sterile corridors brightly illuminated by fluorescent lighting. It has cheap hard-wearing brown and grey floor tiles which have more hair on them than a camel's back. The corridors contain office after office of admin people and police supervisors ranking from inspector to superintendent. The station's cell block can also be found annexed to this building.

You've a choice of two views from the old building, into the rear yard of the station where you can see police cars coming in and out all day and see the roofs of the new part of the station or into the front yard which is used for private car parking. Your other view is of part of Little Park Street leading up to the Council House in Jordan Well. From there, you can see the Crown Court as well and the old BT exchange which used to be across the road from the police station.

The new part of the station was built across the other side of the internal car park. It is very modern-looking compared to the old station with half-decent carpet, wallpaper and ceiling tiles. While it's still pretty sterile-looking, it's at least easier on the eye when compared to the old part of the station. The new building contains the front office which is open 24 hours of the day every day of the year. Front office staff there deal with the public and take calls constantly.

At the back of the front office is the police parade room where briefings take place, the local intelligence office (LIO), CID office, and some offices for the sergeants and inspectors. Just a short walk up the corridor and behind the front office are the two most important parts of the station, the canteen, and the police bar which are both looked upon as places to socialise and relax out of the public eye.

I chose Little Park Street because it was one of the busiest stations to work at so I knew I'd always have something to do and because it was close to my home (big mistake). I was overjoyed when I found I'd been allocated to Red Watch at Little Park Street Police station. I was really chuffed because it was only a five-minute bike ride for me into work.

What I hadn't realised was that working in the same area you live in is not a great idea as a police officer. You tend to bump into the criminals you've arrested when you're off duty shopping or out for a drink.

Coventry is a great city to work in as a police officer. It really has everything you could want, including high amounts of drug use, high unemployment, a high crime rate, frequent large-scale public disorder, prostitution, regular violent crimes such as rape, robbery, etc. All of these issues are common in and around low-income areas.

No matter which of the three stations in the city you're posted to, you'll regularly come into contact with hardened criminals, organised gangs, prostitutes and a proliferation of offences. The news isn't so good if you live in Coventry though, because even the few decent areas are just a stone's throw from a local council estate. Here, many of the local inhabitants don't work and don't want to work.

They spend their days buying cars for £100 and spending £1,000 on them putting on wheel spacers, blacked-out windows, 'Turbo' and 'Max Power' stickers and devices to make the exhaust as noisy as possible. Soiled nappies are thrown into the front garden and left to rot next to the rottweiler, old engine blocks and part-worn car tyres. In the worst areas, 14-year-old mums push around crying babies in second-hand prams. The 5-year-olds are left to play in the street and babysit their younger siblings while mum chips off to the local bingo hall or off to prison to see their boyfriend. Don't believe me? Take a spin around the worst areas and see for yourself.

Now don't get me wrong, I was born and bred in Coventry and it's my home. I grew up in Coundon, Radford and then Hillfields which is notorious for drugs and prostitution. Hillfields was always known as the red light district and drug capital of Coventry but it's changed dramatically over the past few years. I love Coventry and spent the first 30 years of my life living there and many of my friends and family still live there.

I suppose there were two problems, though. First, statistically speaking, Coventry is one of the most violent cities in Europe to live in (yes, I know statistics are worse than useless). According to national crime statistics, Coventry has higher-than-average chances of you being robbed, burgled, raped, assaulted or your car stolen. Second, as a police officer, all you ever get to see is criminals and victims of crime. If this is all you see day after day, you tend to form a distorted opinion that crime is everywhere. If you actually live in Coventry, you probably won't see that much crime or violence unless you live in a really bad area.

Coventry used to be the industrial centre of Europe with famous car manufacturers such as Jaguar, Rolls Royce, Ford, and Peugeot based there. Over the years though, industry began to decline and unemployment began to rise. Low-income housing was built in Wood End, Willenhall, Hillfields and Stoke Aldermoor. Areas that were formerly just made up of working-class people were now mainly inhabited by the unemployed.

There's nothing wrong with being unemployed – I was briefly there once myself. There is, however, something wrong with being unemployed and *wanting to stay that way*, treating state benefits as entitlement and a replacement for making your own money. This sort of person is known as a chav, and we'll come back to discuss chavs later.

Little Park Street station and the other three stations in Coventry operated four units which are referred to as Watches: Red, Blue, Green and Yellow. There was always one watch on earlies, one on lates, one on nights, and one on leave. I was allocated to Red Watch. Red Watch were notorious in the areas of Coventry they covered and the local villains knew us well. Any burglar, car thief, robber or drug dealer knew that if they were caught when Red Watch were on duty they were in for a kicking.

I later found out that most of the local villains (also known as shits, scrotes, CROws which meant they had a record at the Criminal Records Office, scumshits, etc.) had worked out the shift pattern for Little Park Street and simply avoided going out when we were on duty. Especially on night shift when it was easy to drag some crackhead burglar down an entry and give them a beating.

One of the watch sergeants who was a devout Christian had coined the phrase, 'The laying on of hands' for this process. The theory behind the 'laying on of hands' was it prevented further offending and although somewhat draconian, it seemed to work rather well.

I remember my first day parading at the station and going into the briefing room. The briefing room was a tiny cramped little office, maybe about 15 feet by 12 but had to fit 20 PCs, three sergeants and one inspector. It had looked quite a respectable size when the training sergeant had taken us for a tour around the station but now, filled with people, it suddenly looked very small.

The room consisted of several old tables slotted together to make a rectangle with chairs all around. The tables were different sizes and heights so they didn't join together very well. There weren't enough chairs to go 'round so some constables had to stand in the corner. The only other furniture in the room were some shelves fixed to the walls which were the size of the slot in the front of a postbox. They were where we were all told to keep our paperwork.

It was night shift which ran from 10 p.m. to 6 a.m. and the tradition was to come in a bit early and have briefing 15 minutes before the hour so that the preceding watch could get off duty in good time. I was filled with nervous excitement at the prospect of actually going out on the beat and meeting real live criminals.

Half of the PCs in the briefing room were smoking so the room was thick from the ceiling down with smoke. The cheap metal-framed windows were closed tight and the smell of fresh cigarette smoke filled my nostrils. One police officer had climbed on top of the filing cabinets and was snoring loudly, another had covered his West Midlands Police logo on his jumper with the Tescos logo which he'd cut from a carrier bag. He later told me he had a sponsorship deal with them (yeah, right).

There was a loud cheer as I walked into the briefing room looking as worried as a new kid when he starts a brand new school. A new raw recruit to make the tea and give all of the shit jobs too. All 20 began to chant, 'Fresh meat, fresh meat!' I just stood in the corner of the room, so nervous I thought I was going to burst out crying in front of everybody.

It probably didn't help that I had a large bald patch on the side of my head covered with boot polish. I always shaved my own head with electric clippers down to a number three. I'd removed the plastic number three from the end just to tidy up the sides. I forgot it was off and went to touch up the side and shaved a large patch of it down to the skin. Everybody looked at me with my boot polish–covered patch and fell about laughing. It was funny I suppose, but I'd rather it not have been me who had it on their head.

I spotted a young PC sitting quietly at the table in the corner of the room, almost as fresh-faced as me. He managed a hint of a strained smile, and I guess he'd been the new guy on the watch until today. I could see him breathe a sigh of relief that his ordeal as the newest member of the watch was finally over. He motioned for me to come over and sit at an empty seat next to him. I shuffled past several people and sat quietly, not daring to say a word.

As I sat at the chair praying silently to myself to just get through the next 20 minutes I could see a sliding window at the end of the room. The window gave a view into the control room for Little Park Street. I could see the control desk with a huge old-fashioned monitor and a big radio-like something out of Z cars. Behind that was one of the watch sergeants, and next to him a civilian who did all the police computer checks on cars and people. She had bright red hair all the way down her back and was completely plastered in make-up. Her name was Ursula and she was the PNC operator as well as tea-maker.

After a few minutes the watch supervision walked in together, the inspector followed by two sergeants. Red Watch was led by an inspector called Peter Darry (not his real name). He was a giant of a man, only about 6 feet but stocky with hands as big as shovels. He was completely bald apart from a thin line of silver hair which ran from ear to ear. Darry had piercing green eyes which swept across the briefing room when he walked in. He looked at me but didn't acknowledge my presence.

Insp. Darry lived in the countryside somewhere outside Coventry and all the fresh air gave his cheeks a rosy red colour. He was an extremely intelligent individual and whenever he spoke to you it was like you were being interrogated. Every word you spoke to him had to be carefully thought out because you knew he'd be analysing it. He reminded me of Spike Milligan because he had an amazing mind but also bordered on madness. He lived on a different plane of existence from other people.

Insp. Darry had a huge scar 'round the circumference of his neck. I was told by one of the watch that he'd tried to hang himself many years earlier. The collar of his police shirt couldn't really hide the scar but nobody ever spoke about it openly. The senior management at Little Park Street police station had tried in the past to have Insp. Darry retired early due to mental health problems but he had a certificate from a psychiatrist showing he was sane so there was not much they could do. While he may have not been insane according to the traditional view, he certainly did exhibit some very strange values and behaviour during the time he worked with Red Watch.

Red Watch had four sergeants called Jed Leap, Malc, Bill and Ian. The sergeants' roles were broken up to custody sergeant, control room, station sergeant, and patrol sergeant. We'll come back to these characters later.

The room went quiet as the supervision sat down in their chairs and Insp. Darry began the briefing by reading out a few notices, the sergeant called Malc read out some vehicle registrations we needed to keep an eye out for because they were either stolen or being driven by disqualified drivers. Sgt. Leap read out the duties for the night, and I was put onto a patrol car with my tutor Alan.

We were put on a car with call sign Mike Mike 5 which covered an area of Coventry known as Cheylesmore and the Butts. There were three fast-response cars on the watch referred to as Zulus, and six Panda cars. The watch also had one PC who was on foot patrol and covered the city centre.

After briefing, Alan came up and shook my hand vigorously. 'Hi mate,' he said with a big grin on his face, 'I'm Alan, and I'm your tutor, for my sins.' He gave me a kind wink and I immediately felt relieved to be working with a nice bloke. Alan was about 6 feet and very slim bordering on lanky. He had mousy brown hair that seemed to be stuck flat to his head. He was married, with four boys aged from 2 to 10, and his wife was a social worker working for Coventry City Council.

Alan said, 'Lets go and meet the supervision.' I followed him out of the briefing room and along the corridor. We turned right into a pokey office where all the sergeants lived. It was only about 12 by 24 feet but had to house six desks and about eight lockers. The room smelled of old people, cheap coffee and stale biscuits. The walls were painted with a drab shade of tobacco-stained white but you couldn't see it for wall planners, A4 sheets of paper and remnants of blue tac.

The only sergeants in the room at the time were Jed Leap and Ian McDonald. Jed Leap was an older man, about 50, having greying hair held in place with Brylcreem. He wore a small pair of glasses with round rims which made him look like a schoolteacher. The rims were perched on the end of his small button nose. Jed's uniform was immaculately pressed and it was clear that he paid attention to every small detail. He later went on to bully me for the first four years of my service and generally make much of my time in the force a complete misery.

Ian was a new sergeant and had just joined the unit from the CID in Birmingham. He was young for a sergeant at about 25 and his fresh face gave away that fact. Ian was tall and well-built and had swept-back blonde hair but kept it short at the back to comply with police regulations. Ian gave a warm smile and said, 'Leave him with us for a few minutes, Alan.' Alan walked towards the office door and said 'No probs, Sarge.' Alan gave me a wink and walked out of the room closing the door behind him.

'Take a seat, Paul,' smiled Jed as he motioned to a seat opposite his desk, 'Welcome to Red Watch. Where are you from?' I took a breath and replied nervously, 'I live in Hillfields, Sarge.' 'Fucking hell,' he laughed, 'it's like the Bronx over there.' I joined in the laugh, 'It isn't that bad,

Sarge, once you get to know it.' Ian was sitting at a nearby desk smiling quietly to himself, watching and listening. I liked him immediately, he had a good energy about him and my first impression proved to be right.

Jed piped up, 'Well, there are a few things I want to say that were probably not covered at training school, Paul.' He now had a very serious look on his face. He pushed his spectacles further up his nose and said, 'We stick together on Red Watch and we back each other up. If somebody is in trouble, we are *all* in trouble. Do you understand?' I just nodded and replied, 'I think so, Sarge,' not really understanding at all. Jed could see I was a bit mystified so he clarified. 'Sometimes we have to do things to get the result we want, Paul. It can mean bending the rules a bit, but if it means we put the bad guys away, it's worth it, isn't it?'

I still wasn't clear but I was beginning to get the message. My mind drifted back to the briefing we received from the chief superintendent on our first day in Coventry. He'd come into the training room at Little Park Street and given us a lecture about telling the truth even if somebody else asks us not to. Now I understood what he was referring to.

The sound of Jed's voice brought me back into the room. 'We stick together in the police, Paul. We don't arrest our own or inform on each other. If complaints and discipline get involved, then speak to Alan or come and see us so we can get our story straight, OK?' Now I knew what he meant, 'OK, Sarge,' I said meekly, still not completely sure what would be required of me when the moment came. He was obviously implying that I was not to grass on other police officers, keep my mouth shut if I saw anything against police policy going on, and go and see the sergeants if I needed to have a cover story for something.

I left the sergeants' office and found Alan chatting to another member of the team nearby. 'Everything OK?' he chirped, 'Yes, all good,' I said. I was beginning to feel a bit sick from all the nerves in my stomach. I'd spent most of the day sitting on the toilet worrying about my first day and it was all becoming a bit too much for me already.

Alan took me to a pokey little room where the in trays for the paperwork were kept. Having a glass-fronted wooden cabinet attached to the wall, it looked like something off the antiques road show. The police radios were kept inside the cabinet and each radio was given a number. You had to sign your radio out in a small book so the sergeants could keep a track of who had which radio. Alan helped me sign my radio out and showed me which buttons to press. I had to be careful apparently because sometimes people accidentally pressed them while they were sitting in their cars slagging the watch supervision off and they'd get put on foot patrol for a month as punishment.

Alan showed me how to do a radio check with the sergeant in the control room so I didn't go out with a duff radio. He then nudged me with his elbow and said, 'C'mon Paul, let's say hello to the custody sergeant; his name's Bill, he's a good bloke.' We walked to the corner of an L-shaped corridor. To the right were the admin offices and the old front office. We went left which led to the rear yard and the main entrance to the cell block.

The cell block in Little Park Street is one of the largest in the West Midlands Police. It is designed to accommodate all the usual prisoners plus hold more prisoners pending transfer to the court cells. It's designed in the shape of a rectangle and along two of the longer sides from about a third of the way down you've rows of cells either side of the walls. Each row has 12 male cells so there are 24 in total. At the top left some distance away from the male cells you've four female cells, and near that you've two juvenile detention rooms.

Every cell is about 12 feet square. Inside, there's a wooden bench and a very tiny metal toilet annexed with no seat. Anybody looking through the hatch can see you having a shit, which isn't nice. There's a button above the toilet which you press to flush it. Every cell has graffiti scrawled all over it, there's the odd blood and shit stain over the walls that the cleaners miss.

The only way into and out of every cell is a two-inch-thick metal door which has a double-locking system. There's a small metal shutter two-thirds the way up every door which lets air into the cell which can be put up if the prisoner is noisy or starts throwing shit at you through it. If the hatch is up, there's a circular glass-covered viewing hole so you can peek into the cell.

Juveniles are not allowed to be banged up with adults for two reasons. First, the adults would be considered to be a bad influence; and second, they'd probably be shagged or at least abused if they got put in a cell with some of the adults. Juveniles don't go into cells – they have juvenile detention rooms which have wooden doors. Also in the cell block are three soundproof interview rooms, a fingerprinting and photograph room, and an admin room where all the paperwork is kept.

The block has changed slightly now but when I was first there you'd press a buzzer and the cell block PC (referred to as the striker) would unlock the door with a large key and let you into the holding area which then leads through another door into the booking-in area where the custody sergeant stands behind a raised podium where the booking-in desk is.

We were let in by Raj who was the striker PC. They made sure that the prisoners were all visited every hour (or half-hour if they were drunk) and they sorted out all the meals and phone calls to the police doctors or solicitors and helped make life easy for the custody sergeant. It was considered a nice cushy job by some because you didn't have to push a

Panda car or do any paperwork.

Raj was apparently the first Indian ever to work in the West Midlands Police. You could tell he'd been in for a long time because instead of having four numbers on his epaulettes on his shoulder he only had three. He was a very skinny man, but wore doc martin boots which looked far too big to be on the feet of such a slim man. He reminded me of the scene from the movie *Tommy* where Elton John has these massive boots on that you could fit a man into.

Raj was a very heavy smoker and must've got through a pack of 20 every shift. His teeth had turned brown due to years of smoking and he had permanent shakes which I put down to alcoholism. He wore a thick moustache and had Brylcreemed hair (as did a few of the watch by the looks of it) which was combed neatly back. He spoke with a thick Indian accent. He started most of his sentences with, 'I'll tell you one t'ing, mate.'

Raj was a very highly educated man who'd grown up in India and came over in the 1950s when his family moved to Coventry. When he'd joined the police, his family were not happy because where he came from, the job of a police officer was considered a very menial one which involved walking around with a big cane and beating up any thieves or suspected thieves (some things don't change).

Raj led us through to the booking-in area where Bill was standing checking over the custody sheets from the previous watch. Bill was about 50 years and ex–drugs squad. He'd seen more of life than most ever get to see. He was about 5' 10" and stood tall with his shoulders back which gave off the air of an ex-military man. Bill's hair was short at the back and sides but curly at the top and was always well-kempt because he was married to a hairdresser. He wore half-moon glasses so he could write on the custody sheet.

Bill was a smashing bloke and very much on the PCs' side. In the cell block the custody sergeant is God and back then he called the shots. You didn't want to upset Bill in any way, and you knew you'd gone too far when he took his specs off. I saw a couple of prisoners take the piss out of Bill by refusing to sign for their rights and throw the pen at him. He'd take his glasses off and walk over to them and the whole place would go quiet. He'd tell them that if they ever did that again he'd rip their head off and piss down the hole. They'd then apologise and quietly sign for their rights.

Bill shook my hand and welcomed me to the watch saying, 'Nice to meet you, Paul. You're in good hands with Alan.' He had very kind eyes and I knew I was going to get on well with him. Our introductions were interrupted by Raj. 'I'll tell you one t'ing, Paul,' said Raj, 'Go and see what the prisoner in cell 11 wants. He keep pressing the bloody blinking buzzer,' and before you say anything, he really did speak like that. I looked up at the prisoners' whiteboard behind the custody desk. It said that the prisoner in cell 11 was under arrest for being drunk and disorderly.

I walked off down the wrong corridor and eventually found cell 11. A man's weathered face was level with the hatch. I couldn't see his body but he looked about 60 years old and worse the wear for drink. The face was that of a man older than his years with deep cracks on his forehead and bags under his eyes. His huge bulbous nose was red and pitted, a telltale sign of years of alcohol abuse. He was wearing what used to be a white shirt but was now thousand-wash grey with curry, beer and vomit all down the front. Before he could even say a word I could smell the stench of alcohol coming from him.

'Boss,' he shouted, which is what all prisoners in the cells call police officers, 'my tea smells like shit.' I was a bit baffled by this statement so I asked, 'What are you on about, mate?' He clarified what he meant by saying, 'I got a cup of tea with my dinner and it smells like shit.' He held out his beige-coloured cup of maxpax tea through the hatch and motioned for me to smell it. I thought he might chuck it at me but I took the risk. I smelled it as he held it out and it was foul, it really did stink of fresh shit and I pulled my face away in disgust.

I took the cup off him and went back to see Bill, Alan and Raj with it in my hand. 'This prisoner's cup of tea smells like shit, Sarge,' I said. They were all laughing so hard tears were rolling down their cheeks, Bill doubled over laughing. I knew immediately I'd been the victim of some joke. 'Go on, then,' I said, resigning myself to the fact that I'd only been on the watch for 10 minutes and had my first practical joke played on me.

'That's Dirty Dean,' cried Raj between his laughter. 'Did he hold the cup under your nose, mate?' I just nodded helplessly. 'What he does is sticks his finger up his arse first and that's where the smell of shit comes from.' Dirty bastard. I went to the toilet to go and wash my face which had been right next to a tramp's shitty finger. I decided that if I saw Dirty Dean again I'd slap him into the middle of next week for doing that.

Alan and I went across the backyard and got into the Panda car which was an Austin Maestro. They were a great car to patrol in, only 1,300 cc engines but you could throw them around the roads and they were very easy to drive with a nice light steering and they stuck to the road really well. Just like all the other Pandas it had a red stripe down the side, the police logo on the front doors and a blue light on the top.

There's a myth that police cars are somehow 'souped up' by the police garage and have special performance-enhancing extras added. This is laughable – you're lucky if you get a car with an air freshener in. There are no extras, and they just go into the garage for the usual maintenance. They're on the road for 24 hours a day 365 days a year so they wear out after about two years.

Panda cars are just used for basic police patrol work and not intended for chasing cars or rushing to emergency jobs. Things have changed slightly now, but in order to even use the blue light you'd have to attend a five-week driving course. Otherwise you could only use the blue light when the car was stationary at the scene of a crash or something similar.

Alan checked over the Panda car for signs of damage because he had to sign the log book to say that it was in good condition. Very often the watch before you damaged the car but didn't own up to it. They hope you don't see the damage so you get in trouble for it and not them, which, of course, is a really bad thing to do to your colleagues.

We drove out of the backyard and into Little Park Street. It reminded me of the series *Hill Street Blues* when you see the patrol cars going out of the police garage onto their patch. We turned left out of the police car park and onto the traffic island which joined with the ring road. Just as we'd reached Coventry ring road Alan said to me, 'They're calling us on the radio, mate.' All I could hear on it was noise and crackling. Alan smiled at me and said 'Don't worry, it takes a bit of getting used to but you'll get there.'

Alan spoke into the radio and I heard some sort of conversation with the control room sergeant. 'Our first job of the night,' he said with a worried expression. 'What's it?' I asked anxiously, 'Is it a dead body?' Alan shook his head slowly as he turned the car around. 'No,' he said solemnly, 'it's worse than any dead body – it's Freddie the Fly.'

Frederick Linden Steele aka Freddie the Fly was a tramp – not just any tramp, mind you, but the tramps' tramp. I never knew his story, but he basically lived rough, sleeping wherever he could, begging for money and living off scraps he found in bins. He looked about 70-something but you couldn't tell because of the state he was in. His thick grey greasy black hair was infested with head lice and it grew in big clumps and sprouted out of his head like dreadlocks. His face was always crusted in matted hair, mud and dried blood from where he'd fallen over drunk. He was the scabbiest bastard you could ever find walking the streets.

The stink of Freddie the Fly was terrible, similar to rotting meat, decay and the worst body odour imaginable. Somehow, Freddie had lost his left eye. It was still in its socket but had caved in due to some sort of injury and so the fluid from it leaked out onto his chin and you could see into his eye socket. He was in a sorry state, no doubt about that.

Freddie had been found in the back of somebody's van. The owner had opened it to get a box out of the back and panicked when he saw

Freddie inside. He shut Freddie inside the van and called the police. Freddie was harmless enough as he just begged for money or food and bought cheap booze from any off-licence that'd let him in. I suppose the problem was that he looked offensive to anybody unfortunate enough to see him, or smell him for that matter.

Alan drove to Lower Ford Street in Hillfields and into a side street by an industrial unit. He was a very meticulous person and always parked the Panda car facing outwards for a 'quick exit'. He taught me that you never knew when you were going to have to speed off to another job so you should always back your car into a space so you could get out quickly. That lesson always stuck with me.

The van owner was a middle-aged man in his late 40s dressed in an Arthur Daley style like many men his age do. He was wearing navy blue tracksuit bottoms but with black loafer shoes on which looked terrible. He wore a thick gold necklace over a stained white tee shirt and a big thick sheepskin outfit finished the look off perfectly. He owned a storage unit outside which his van was always parked. The van was years old with four flat tyres and green mould all over the windows. It wasn't going anywhere fast.

The owner greeted us and began speaking to me. That also tended to happen when I went to a job with a WPC. The man would explain everything to me as if I was somehow in charge. I just stood there nodding at him not knowing what to do. I looked over at Alan who just smiled and winked back at me. 'Leave it with us, Sir,' said Alan to the van owner, 'we'll send him on his way.' Alan walked towards the van and stopped short. He beckoned me over and said, 'Freddie's harmless, Paul, but put your gloves on and don't touch or go near him. He's infested with fleas so we can't put him in the car or it'll have to be fumigated, and Bill will go ballistic if we take him to the cell block.'

Alan did a quick call on the radio and breathed a sigh of relief when he was told that there were no outstanding warrants for Freddie. He cautiously pulled up the concertina on the back of the van and shouted into the back which was in darkness, 'Come on out, Freddie, you'll have to move on, mate.'

There was a rustle from the back of the van and eventually Freddie emerged. He stank of alcohol and something that was dying, either him or something in his pockets. His clothes were in tatters and his grey trousers were held up by an old piece of string. I could see a wet patch where he'd recently pissed in his pants.

It reminded me of a boy in my class at St Mary's school where I went when I was 10. The poor kid was always pissing in his pants in class so the teacher would have to keep spare pants and trousers on standby. He always had nits in his thick greasy brown hair so nobody wanted to sit next to him. He had a squint and wore thick black-rimmed NHS glasses but they'd broken so his parents had put some plasters on the corner of the rim to hold the arm on.

His dad marched into school during class one afternoon. He was drunk and swearing and shouting loudly. Our teacher tried to calm him down but he was very aggressive. He dragged his son out of school. The poor boy could easily have turned out like Freddie the Fly.

Freddie climbed out of the van, stepped into the road, reached into the van and from the dirty wooden floor recovered two pieces of foul-smelling luncheon meat. He put one into his pocket and began to chew on the other as he walked off towards town.

There's not much you can do for people like Freddie. In Coventry, there's the Salvation Army hostel but it's usually overflowing and if the residents become a nuisance or are continually drunk they're asked to leave. Most of the bums I came across were suffering from mental health problems and so couldn't give a proper account of themselves or even ask for help. It was tragic to see.

I watched Freddie walk off into the distance. His image was eventually swallowed up by the darkness of the night. The last image I saw was Freddie shuffling along and holding his trousers up with his free hand. I was snapped out of my thoughts by Alan shouting to me, 'Paul, get in the car quick, Zulu 1 has asked for back-up.' I ran to the car and Alan turned on the blue light on the roof and we spun off towards the Zulu's location. I remember thinking that Zane and Rick worked Zulu 1 and that things must be bad if they needed help.

There are three levels of help you can call for on a police radio although it varies between forces. Calling for another car means you may need a bit of help or support. Calling for back-up means you're fighting or just about to arrest a violent prisoner and need urgent help. If you shout the word 'Assistance', it means you're in grave danger and need the support of several officers. If you do have to call for assistance all you need to do is shout the word 'Assistance' and your location and you know that everybody will bust a gut to get there.

It's all down to your judgement when you're at the scene, but calling for assistance is a last resort because you know that your colleagues are going to take calculated risks to get to you including speeding and jumping red lights. Police officers have even been known to throw prisoners out of their cars if they've been arrested for minor offences so they can attend an assistance call.

As we drove there I could hear Alan speaking into the police radio but I couldn't understand what he was saying because some of it was in police jargon and abbreviations that I didn't understand. Alan was a great driver and even though we were in a Panda car he got us there in about three minutes flat. It felt so exciting to be going through red lights on the way to an urgent job. We soon screeched to a halt at the scene of the shout.

Zane and Rick had been called to attend a domestic disturbance inside Unity House which is a 17-storeyed block of flats in Hillfields. I don't think the planners asked the fire service if that was too tall because their ladders only go up to the 13th floor so if there's a fire you've a long jump down to the ground.

The address was known to the police because a man called Paolo was often there harassing his ex-girlfriend. Paolo was a constant nuisance both to us and his girlfriend. He was from Spain and had lived with Shelly for a while until she kicked him out. Every other night he'd get drunk and go 'round to the block of flats where she lived. He'd ring every flat buzzer outside the flats until somebody buzzed him in, then repeatedly bang on Shelly's flat door begging to be let in. The neighbours would wake up and complain and he'd either be gone by the time we got there, or we'd catch and arrest him.

Paolo was not a big man at only 5' 7", he had wavy black hair, a swarthy complexion and deep blue eyes. He was very lean and muscular and spoke with a poor English accent with a strong Spanish tinge to it which must've sounded very romantic to some ladies. Paolo was a nice chap when he was sober, but he drank every night and then the demons inside would come out. He'd become rude and verbally abusive and eventually violent. When he raised his hand to her one night, Shelly threw him out and called the police. Paolo couldn't cope with it and when he got drunk he'd go back to the flat and try to beg his way back into her life.

I'm not sure what happened this night, because I wasn't there to begin with. Paulo was banging on Shelly's door as usual. Zane and Rick were dispatched to go and deal with the problem. It was usual practice to send two cars if violence was anticipated, but it had been a busy night already and Zane and Rick were big enough to look after themselves.

Zane and Rick went into the block of flats expecting Paolo to be gone as usual. He was still there when they arrived and a few minutes later there was a back-up call from them. We all rushed to get there but by the time we arrived the situation was under control. There'd been a fight of some sort and Paolo was inside under arrest.

Paulo was eventually dragged out of the front doors of the block of flats in handcuffs and thrown into the back of my police car. Alan told me to get into the back and sit next to him.

Paolo was a mess, his nose broken and pouring blood, his previously white tee shirt now soaked red. His right eye was so swollen he couldn't open it, his forehead was split open in the middle going into his hairline and covered with blood. The back of his head had a huge gash in it which obviously required stitches because I could see his skull through the gaping gap. He looked like he'd been gored by a mad bull.

They don't explain a lot of common sense stuff at police training centre, you've to find it out when you join your watch. Every prisoner who's put in the back of a police car should be handcuffed to the rear (hands behind the back), searched and sat behind the front passenger seat with a police officer next to them so they can't easily kick the driver when the car is in motion. That was why Alan had asked me to sit in the back of the car.

I saw Zane and Rick emerge from the block of flats, breathing heavily and their pegs (wooden truncheons) in their hands. The pegs were covered with blood and snot. They said Paulo had 'played up', which meant resisted arrest. How much he resisted I didn't know, but they never had a scratch on them and Paolo looked like shit. Like I said, I wasn't there so I can't judge because I may well have done the same to him if he'd tried to batter me.

I could see Alan chatting to Zane and Rick a few yards away from our car. I couldn't hear what they were saying but I guessed they were talking about what had happened. Their blue shirts were covered with blood (not their own). Paolo tried to speak to me and I could see space where his teeth had been not 10 minutes earlier. His English wasn't that good and he stank of booze which didn't help his speech much at all, well, that and his missing front teeth.

I presumed we'd take Paulo off to the hospital to have his head sewn back together. Alan drove us onto the ring road but instead of taking the exit for the hospital we continued on to the police station. I didn't ask any questions, just sitting quietly in the back of the car and watching what was happening.

The entrance to the cell block at Little Park Street station is situated in the far corner of the car park. You drive through a barrier, past about six rows of cars and turn left. About 20 yards in front of you is the entrance and exit (two separate doors).

As we approached the cell block entrance Zane and Rick were waiting for us. When you've a prisoner you usually back right up to the 12-foot-long corridor which has the cell block entrance and exit doors to the right. It means that you've just a short walk with your prisoner if they're aggressive. Alan drove forwards to the entrance and next to Rick who opened the rear passenger door.

Something told me that Paolo was in for a few slaps. It was the look on Zane and Rick's face that did it. Their faces were full of anger and hatred. Zane was wearing his short-sleeved shirt but also his black leather gloves which looked just terrible.

Zane reached into the back of the car and pulled a screaming Paulo out by his hair. I don't know who was more shocked, Paolo or me (probably him, come to think about it). He was handcuffed with his hands behind his back and so couldn't put his hands out to stop his fall so he landed onto the tarmac with a dull thud. Zane and Rick dragged him screaming and kicking across the tarmac car park and into the cell block. Raj was standing holding the cell block door open which is customary when you've a violent prisoner coming in.

As Paolo was being dragged into the cell block his eyes were bulging out of his head and he was screaming something in Spanish but I didn't know what (but I could guess). I'm not sure if he knew what was about to happen to him, but he knew whatever it was, wasn't going to be good. I followed the three of them in via the cell block entrance door and Paolo was dragged past the custody sergeant who was holding the internal door open. Paolo was pulled by his legs and arms into the rear holding area.

What followed is the worst beating I've ever seen dished out. Paolo was dragged past the custody desk and into the corridor where the first row of cells was. He was kicking out with his legs and screaming something incomprehensible. It was as if he was being taken to the electric chair or something, the screams and the look on his face were dreadful to see.

At this point he was lying on the floor with his hands cuffed behind his back looking up at the ceiling. Zane and Rick stood over him and proceeded to kick the living shit out of him. Paolo just did his best to curl up in a ball to protect himself. Zane worked the stomach and ribs by stamping down on it whilst Rick did the back, shoulders and kidneys.

The beating went on and on until both Zane and Rick were exhausted. Both being fat bastards, they stood over Paolo puffing and panting before gathering the energy to drag him off to his cell to begin the recovery process. I just stood there rooted to the spot. I don't know what Paolo had done to them exactly. I do know he resisted arrest and that they'd 'pegged' him several times causing the injuries to his head.

My thoughts drifted back to what they taught us what to do at police training college if we saw a fellow police officer commit a crime. We were to preserve the evidence, insist that the other police officers be examined by the police surgeon for evidence such as swollen knuckles, and to inform the watch inspector. I pondered on the situation very carefully and decided instead to go off to the canteen and eat my sandwiches since it was break time.

I never asked Alan about the incident, the custody sergeant didn't seem bothered, so I presumed this was all part of normal life in the police. And what about Paolo? Well, he never complained and the whole unpleasant situation was forgotten. He was later charged with a minor public order offence and fined in court.

This was one of a few beatings I saw dished out down the cells. I never saw one as severe, but then I wasn't always down there when violent prisoners were brought in. It wasn't exactly a regular activity, but happened often enough to become what I'd consider to be 'normal'. Maybe Paolo deserved it and maybe he didn't. Either way, I didn't really worry about the incident, to be honest. I just presumed that this was the sort of thing that happened if a prisoner had been very violent during arrest.

∿ ∿

The next night Alan wasn't at work. He had to give evidence in court on a two-day trial at Crown Court so I was crewed with an experienced WPC called Demi. Demi was a very keen volleyball player and competed for the West Midlands Police. She was about 5' 6" tall with bobbed black hair which she tied up in a mini-ponytail when she was working. She had a very fit and toned body as she trained every day. She could run faster than most of the blokes on the watch, in fact.

I liked Demi because she was a very thorough and professional police officer. She knew how to deal with almost every incident and was qualified for sergeant which meant she could apply for the next round of promotions when they were advertised. She was a very outspoken person as well, and with eight years' service, respected on the watch. I especially liked her because she used to give Zane some real shit before and at the end of the tour of duty. 'You lazy, useless turd,' she'd shout at him across the briefing room table, 'you've two years in and you're already a slacker. Pull your finger out of your arse and do some work.' Zane would sit there in silence, shrinking into his uniform. I didn't say a word but I loved it.

The only drawback to working with Demi was that when she was menstruating it was living hell. She'd have mood swings and bite your head off if you looked at her the wrong way. I was on the receiving end of her PMT more times than I care to remember. Often, we'd be out on patrol and she'd turn to me and say, 'We'd better go back to the nick, Paul, I need to change my rag.' Charming. When she was really bad, I just sat there next to her in the car saying nothing just in case I had my head ripped off again.

I'd been doing karate from age 11 to the current date and was 20 by this time. I'd passed my second dan black belt and had thousands of spars and entered competitions and once beaten the English karate champion. I thought I could actually look after myself in a scrape, but I was about to find out just how useless my karate was in a fight.

At about 11:30 p.m. Demi and I were called to attend a domestic dispute in Randle Street in Radford. A domestic could be anything from a couple arguing over what to watch on television to a husband beating his wife to death with a pool cue and the neighbours phoning to complain about the noise. You just never knew what you were walking into. Red Watch was pretty tight, so even though it was a discipline offence to leave your allotted patch, we'd always drift towards the location in case back-up was needed.

The first domestic dispute I ever attended was a strange one. A young couple who lived in a nice house in Coundon had been play-fighting in bed. They'd both been in the bath together and were in bed rolling around together naked. For a joke, the husband had held his wife's head down and farted on it. Unfortunately, the curried chicken he'd had for lunch hadn't agreed with him so some liquefied shit flew out of his arse spraying his wife on her cheek. She screamed in horror as the shit rolled into her freshly washed Timotei summer meadows–smelling hair and into her eyes. In her fury, she grabbed her husband's scrotum and pulled hard, tearing it open. One of his testicles came out of the tear, and, of course, he cried out in pain.

By the time we arrived it was all over. She was curled in the corner sobbing and her husband was being taken away by an ambulance. Although he didn't want to complain, there had been an assault so she was arrested and charged. Exactly who the victim was there I'm not sure.

We drove across Radford towards Randall Street. I'd lived in Coventry all my life but realised how little I knew about the city I lived in. I knew how to get to town and my mates' houses but that was about it. Once you work in an area for a while you get to know every street and landmark. To start with, you've to drive 'round with a map but as time goes on you build a map in your head. You get to know the main roads and then the smaller roads off them until you know every street on the patch.

We finally arrived at the address and parked the car up and knocked on the front door where the domestic was supposed to be taking place. I'd learned from Alan to give our call sign and the term 'TA' on the radio which tells the controller to note your time of arrival on the incident log. The controller also knows to keep an ear out to make sure you're OK. Demi was a professional so always put her police hat on when she was out of the car. I liked to wear my hat as well because it was part of my uniform and helped to identify me as a police officer and not a security guard.

Many police officers never wear their hats when they're out of the car which looks very scruffy to me. I think it's some sort of macho thing but

I never did get it. There have been cases where people have got away with assaulting police officers saying that they didn't realise they were police because they had no hat on.

The house was one of over a hundred terraced houses which ran either side of Randle Street. Radford was a typical working-class area of Coventry but wasn't a bad area at all when compared to some of the holes in Coventry. I lived just up the road from Randle Street, in fact. The front door of the house was ajar and there was silence from within the house. Demi knocked hard on the door and then shouted, 'It's the police. Is anybody in?' but there was no response.

Police officers have a power of entry to houses in order to prevent a breach of the peace. The power comes from the common law which is the law of the land from many years ago. We used this power when we pushed the door open and went into the house. The front door led to a small cramped hallway. The stairs were immediately in front of us, the hall to the left led towards the back room, and there was a door to our immediate left which led into the living room. The entire area was in darkness apart from a small table lamp which was on in the living room.

Demi looked at me but all I could do was shrug at her – I didn't know what to say or do. We turned left and entered the living room which was about 18 by 18 feet. It was your typical house for the area, very pokey, cheap stripy wallpaper on the walls, cheap ornaments from the market stall and Argos furniture. The chairs were all facing the corner of the room so everyone could get a good view of the TV. Well, they would've been facing the TV if the TV had been in the corner. It had been picked up and thrown onto a wall and was lying smashed on the floor; the sofa and chairs were also upside down. There'd obviously been a huge fight in the house; well, either that or there'd been a typhoon in there.

A very skinny man in his mid-20s slowly emerged from the kitchen which took Demi and I by surprise: we thought that the occupants had left the house before we got there. Even from across the room he absolutely stank of alcohol and looked very dishevelled. He was wearing denim jeans and a plain pink shirt which was torn by the shoulder and the buttons were missing all the way down to his stomach which was growing a small paunch which looked like it didn't belong on such a skinny man.

He slurred as he spoke, 'I've 'ad a barney with me misses but it's all sorted now.' Demi had seen all of this before. She said, 'Where is your wife now, Sir?' The man paused for a few seconds while his pickled brain pondered the question. 'Fuck knows,' came the reply, 'I fink she run next door maybe.' Clearly he was *non compos mentis* (look it up like I had to).

Looking at him and then about the room once more I simply could not see how this skinny man had managed to pick up such heavy objects and hurl them across the length of the room. You'll probably laugh at this, but looking back I realise I must've been pretty naive still because it'd never occurred to me that people sit at home taking drugs. In fact, as far as I knew when I was growing up I'd never seen anybody taking drugs and I'd never had a discussion with family or friends about the subject.

I know some of my friends regularly used cannabis at university but the concepts of heroin and crack addicts forming a significant part of the population of the UK never entered my head. Even the officers I worked with never said anything about it. They must've just presumed I knew, that's why the people we were dealing with were so fucked up.

It was clear to Demi and me that we couldn't let this guy stay at home as there was a danger he was going to hurt his wife seriously when she came back home from wherever she was. I'd learned at training centre that you've to tell somebody they're under arrest, what they're under arrest for, and then caution them. The caution is a set of words you've to repeat telling somebody their rights. The modern caution goes like this.

'You are under arrest for (insert offence here). You do not have to say anything but it may harm your defence if you fail to mention when questioned, something you later rely on in court. Anything you say may be given in evidence.'

Although every police notebook and statement says that they told the person this, it rarely happens. You're either too busy fighting with them and forget later, or you just can't be bothered to repeat all the words. In reality, you've to use your common sense. You usually do tell a person they're under arrest, but if you think that they're liable to 'blow up' on you and you don't want a fight on your hands you've to choose your words very carefully. Sometimes you've to be very vague about what's happening, and then when it's safer, formally tell them they're under arrest.

Alan always used to say, 'Let's nip down to the station and get this all squared up, mate,' which was a very good way to gain a person's compliance without the formality of telling them that they were under arrest. By the time we'd walked into the cell block and the door had closed behind them, it was then pretty safe to explain that they were going to be spending a night in the cells. They can blow up all they like in the cell block, but they can't go anywhere or cause problems for you.

I was with Demi now and not Alan, and I wasn't sure how she worked. She gave me the nod to arrest him, so I told the man he was under arrest to prevent a breach of the peace. Breach of the peace isn't actually a crime, but it does give a constable a power of arrest to prevent further behaviour which may result in violence to a person or damage to property.

The person is taken before the magistrate's at the next sitting and bound over to keep the peace. There are no fines and a person cannot go to prison for it. It is a bit naughty, but if a person was a real tosser or a well-known burglar, Red Watch would arrest them for a breach of the peace any time after 12 noon on Saturday. The magistrates had gone home by then and they'd have to sit in the police cells until Monday morning.

The custody sergeant hated it when we brought prisoners in for BOP on Saturday afternoons because they had to be checked and fed for the whole weekend. BOP was a favourite offence for Zane to use because he didn't have to complete any paperwork. As far as we were concerned on Red Watch, if we could keep bad people off the streets we were doing a good job. A career burglar can screw about 20 houses over a weekend, so consider it crime prevention.

My new friend didn't take too kindly to being told that he was under arrest. He began to shout and swear at us and became very agitated. 'Yuze can fuck off if you think yuze are arresting me, ya bastards.' I took this to mean that he didn't intend to come quietly. This had never happened to me in police training college where in all of the role plays the actors had all said words to the effect of 'It's a fair cop, guv.' I think for health and safety reasons they were not allowed to fight back at training centre.

I took hold of his arm to put the handcuffs on him (an arrest isn't lawful unless you touch the prisoner) and his eyes widened, he clenched his teeth tight together and then brought his hands up to my chest pushing me backwards towards the doorway. How dare he assault a member of Her Majesty's constabulary! I felt the rage grow in my body and I pushed him back and we fell onto a second sofa, luckily the only piece of furniture facing the right way.

Although I was a black belt in karate I was completely unprepared for this encounter. I couldn't wrestle to save my life and my armoury of fancy kicks and touch contact punches would not help. Demi ran over to help but the man kicked her hard in the stomach and sent her flying. She ended up in a crumpled heap on the opposite side of the room curled up in a ball, groaning and hugging her stomach. I began wishing that Rick and Zane were there. They may have been ultra-violent, but at times like that I think pegging somebody into the middle of next week is justified.

I couldn't shout for help because both my hands were busy trying to prevent getting punched in the face as he kept bringing his arms back to get some momentum to punch me. There was no way I was going to let this pissed-up knobber ruin my good looks. A couple of years later I learned a lot of grappling strangles and pins which would've easily incapacitated him, but at that time all I knew was karate and police self-defence.

As we were thrashing about on the sofa my mind wandered back to Bruche police training college where we learned basic self-defence techniques (it didn't really, but I love flashbacks in books). They were all based on aikido, which appeared to the police committee to be the most inoffensive looking way of restraining subjects. The 'Home Office approved' police self-defence system is a complete farce. The system was put together by a man who was something like a seventh dan in aikido and did a demonstration for the Home Office and Association of Chief Police Officers (ACPO). The man himself was very hard, but to get to his level took many years of training.

Police self-defence involves using friendly holds and locks that caused little pain to the prisoner but which looked very nice if members of the public were watching the arrest. ACPOs didn't want their police officers punching people in the face or doing leg sweeps on their prisoners. I feel that police officers are being badly let down in terms of self-defence training to this day. What they end up doing is panicking and bashing prisoners over the head with metal batons or gassing them with CS.

The truth is that realistic self-defence isn't pretty. It is quick, effective and devastating to the assailant. We'd been taught at national police training centre how to defend against attackers using rubber knives against us by plucking their hand out of the air and applying a wrist lock. It was at this point that I realised my arsenal of aikido techniques was completely useless against a violent aggressor whose methods are completely unorthodox.

So here we were, the man sitting on the sofa trying to punch the living shit out of me, me sitting on his lap trying not to get punched, and Demi lying on the floor across the room. In the absence of any useful self-defence techniques, I took my right thumb and shoved it as far into his eye socket as I could. I felt his eyeball squelch and squash as my thumb went in as far as the knuckle. My new friend didn't even seem to notice, he didn't wince or cry out. Bastard.

It was time for more drastic measures so I grabbed his testicles from the outside of his trousers and twisted them so hard that even my eyes began to water – but again, he didn't bat an eyelid. This was not good. I could've leaned behind him, grabbed his Tescos underpants and given him the wedgie from hell but I doubt it'd have worked.

Thank the Lord, Demi had recovered from the floor and managed to call for help and in what seemed like an age help arrived. Ten hairy-arsed police officers looked like the cavalry to me as they piled in through the front door. A back-up shout is cause for great excitement in the police because you get to drive like a lunatic and have a good scrap when you get there, and unless you're the arresting officer, you don't have any pesky paperwork to fill in when you leave.

As all the other officers surrounded us, I fell to the side of the sofa and they jumped on my prisoner. They pulled him to the floor and a barrage of punches and kicks eventually knocked him unconscious. I don't think he felt any pain at the time (more's the pity), but either way, the blows sparked him out so he could be handcuffed and dragged into the back of a police car. Served him right as well.

I was very fit but despite that, my jumper was dripping in sweat and I was physically exhausted. I could hardly get a word out, I was panting so hard. I just couldn't understand how the hell this little man could be so strong and also why on earth he'd not want to come quietly when we tried to arrest him.

Demi was a bit sore in her stomach but apart from that was OK. I drove us back to the police station and the man was left in the cell to sleep off the drink. I understand now that a mixture of drink and drugs is a very powerful stimulant and renders a person almost incapable of feeling pain for a while.

When he woke up the next morning he must've had a massive black eye and bollocks the size of a space hopper. He was charged with affray, assault on police, and a few weeks later in court he pleaded guilty and was given a two-year conditional discharge. That means that he had to be a good boy and not be found guilty of any other offences for two years.

When I heard the result I began to understand why some prisoners were 'punished' for assaulting us. Clearly, the magistrates didn't think assaulting a police officer was a serious matter, so what other way is there to let people know that this sort of behaviour is not acceptable? You may well disagree. To the outside observer it's easy to label something as right or wrong. It all depends upon your perspective.

∾ ∾

Early shifts began at 5:45 a.m. with a briefing which is a disgusting time of the day to be at work. I did have a paper round in Hillfields when I was 14 years old for two years and had to be up at 5:50 a.m. for that, but the shop was only across the road. For earlies in the police, I had to be up at about 4:30 a.m., have a bath (no showers in our house) and cycle or drive to work. As the new boy I had the responsibility of making the tea. I didn't mind that much since it was my only way of helping the rest of the team.

I'd only tried one cup of tea before in my life. I was about 12 and I hated it because it had sugar in it and tasted dreadful. On my first day of earlies I was shown where the kettle was and made the tea for the watch. We all used to walk into the canteen at about 6 a.m. after briefing and have a cup of tea. The teapot was massive, which was lucky because it had to cater for at least 20 cups. Most of Red Watch weren't fit for anything until they'd had at least two cups.

I thought that since I was making it I should give it a try. It was just an ordinary cup of PG tips, but I remember sitting there and taking my first sip of tea at age 20. At that time of the morning, it was like I was drinking the nectar of the gods. I was instantly hooked on the sweet taste trickling over the taste buds on my tongue and the warm feeling of it going down the back of my throat. I was hooked and have loved tea ever since. Simple really, but a wonderful pleasure.

I've heard a lot of stories of new joiners to the police who now refuse to make the tea at work. They've been told at training centre that they don't have to do it, which is technically correct, but it is a nice gesture and the rest of the watch are going to be helping you with your paperwork and teaching you how to do the job, so it's a very small price to pay. Refusing to make the tea for your colleagues is the sign of a very bad attitude.

My tutor period with Alan was supposed to last five weeks, but after four I'd picked up most of the basics. I knew how to work the radio, how to call in messages using all the police jargon, and how to fill in most of the paperwork. Alan was a very patient man and a great teacher to learn from. He was very quirky and prone to bouts of depression, so sometimes he'd be on a high and running 'round the station joking, and other times he'd be almost completely unresponsive.

When Alan was on a high his sense of humour was amazing. We'd be sitting in briefing and he'd burst out of cupboards in fancy dress halfway through causing the whole watch to burst into fits of laughter. Once at 3 a.m. we were chasing a burglar through the city centre on foot and Alan jumped out of his car in a full Batman outfit. He chased the thief and wrestled him to the ground. The thief just lay there in stunned silence looking up at Alan until the rest of us caught up. We'd stopped running because we were laughing so hard.

When Alan was down it was very bad. He'd sit in the corner of the room with his police jacket over his head and only answer his name when his number was called out on roll call. I didn't know much about depression back then. Clearly, Alan was a manic depressive, but the watch supervision never spoke to him about it or suggested he get any professional help. They just thought he was eccentric.

❧ ❧

I remember the very first time I was allowed out on independent patrol. The sergeants spoke with Alan and then me and agreed that it was time for me to go solo. It would start with me having a walk around the city centre on my own to see how I got on. I wanted to see what it was like to be on independent patrol. It's a bit like the first time you drive a car without an instructor: you're ecstatic, but also filled with dread at what could go wrong.

I walked out of the front entrance of Little Park Street police station towards High Street. It was only an hour before the end of the tour of duty, perhaps about 12:30 in the afternoon. My heart was beating out of my chest and I was praying inside that I didn't come across any incidents that I had to call in on the radio in case I froze. I must've been wearing the most painful look on my face as I walked along Little Park Street and into town. Part abject terror, and part desperation at not wanting to be asked anything by any members of the public.

It was a Saturday afternoon and the city centre was packed with shoppers and tourists. I walked through the city centre I knew so well because I'd lived there all my life. I knew the sergeants were expecting some work from me, so I was determined to come back with something for them. As I walked up Spon Street in the city centre I saw a car parked on double yellow lines. Putting a parking ticket on it was probably the only way I was going to do any sort of work before going back to the station.

I was very worried because although the car had no occupants, the driver could come back at any minute and start arguing with me. I filled in the ticket as fast as I could and stuck it on his windscreen. I walked away praying that he wouldn't come back to the car before I got out of view. I guess I was just nervous about being out on my own and wanted to avoid any confrontation.

I was supposed to take a slow leisurely pace when I was on foot patrol and look like a figure of authority, but I walked so fast that I covered the hour-long walk in about 25 minutes. Nobody even bothered to ask me for directions. When I got back to the station I was massively relieved that nothing had gone wrong while I was out and about.

❧ ❧

When I was out on my own with no tutor the bullying started. First from Sgt. Jed Leap and then another sergeant who was Jed's best mate, Sgt. Hiddle. I'd often find myself being dropped off in the middle of nowhere and left to guard scenes of crimes for hours on end, many times with no break. I didn't mind doing my fair share, of course, but there were other probationers who joined just before and after me who didn't seem to land such shit jobs.

One tour of duty I was posted to stand outside a house where there'd been a fire. I don't remember why I had to stand there, if there was an arson or just to prevent looters but it was a freezing winter day. It would've been just as easy to put police tape around the scene than to have a police officer standing there like a spare prick at a wedding.

I couldn't really go in the house because the fire had gutted it and it was ready to fall down. We don't really get any winter clothing or footwear in the police, and if you're out in the cold you've to keep walking to stay warm, which I couldn't do where I was. I just paced up and down outside the house for four hours. I was taken back for my refs break for an hour and then dropped back there again to re-freeze.

As I stood there shaking away I began to remember some of the shit jobs I'd worked in before I joined the police. I'd been a labourer at a building site for the summer when I was 16. My dad was working there and got me some work to earn some extra money. It was back-breaking. I spent the day mixing sand and cement with a shovel because there was no cement mixer. I had to slash the bags open and then shake out the mix into the right amounts of sand and cement with water and repeatedly mix it until it had the right consistency.

When I finished my 'O' levels my mum wanted me to go and get a job so I could bring money into the house. I wanted to do 'A' levels, but only because it was something to do before I was old enough to join the police. The only job I could've got was working in a factory with my stepdad.

During the next summer I did some more labouring with my cousins who had their own building firm. It was fun working with them in Dorset during the summer. We'd get home filthy every night from tearing down ceilings and knocking out walls. None of us wore any safety helmets or boots and it was a miracle we were never injured.

When I finished my 'A' levels I had to wait a few months before the intake for the cadets started. My mate's dad worked for a parcel company so got me a job working in a parcel warehouse at Digbeth in Birmingham near to the city centre. I'd have to walk four miles to get the train there in the early evening and take a packed lunch with me.

It was an awful job, 12-hour night shifts from 7 in the evening until 7 in the morning. There were eight of us who'd unload parcels from the back of articulated lorries and then load them onto trolleys and wheel them around a massive open warehouse into various bins which were numbered according to which part of the country they were going to. It wasn't like the posh modern warehouses you get now with nice floors and internal heating systems. It was dirty, grimy, dimly-lit and like being inside a freezer in the early hours. The toilets were absolutely rank and stank to high heaven.

It was very hard work. As soon as the first lorry arrived we'd run out of a portacabin we waited in and get a trolley. It was a sprint because out of eight trolleys five were OK, one was on its way out, and two had wonky wheels and were a right pain in the arse to push. If you ended up with the wonky one you were going to sweat your nuts off pushing it all night. There was a pecking order for the decent trolleys, but as far as I was concerned it was first come, first served.

We'd load them up and run from corner to corner for 12 hours throwing parcels into large containers and then back to the lorries. There were forklift trucks whizzing 'round the warehouse with a couple of manky old portacabins in the corner. It was amazing that nobody was run over by a forklift truck in there, none of us had reflective jackets and the forklifts went around at top speed. Everybody just wanted to get the job over and done with so they could go home.

It was freezing in the warehouse when the temperature dropped in the early hours of the morning and the only way to get any warmth was to stand behind the forklift by the exhaust that spewed out diesel smoke. It was smelly but warm. Forklift driving was considered a nice cushy job because you got to sit down for the whole shift rather than run up and down the warehouse like a blue-arsed fly. When I got home at about 8:30 a.m. I was exhausted and filthy. I'd blow my nose and black snot from the diesel fumes would come out all over the tissue and heaven knows what crap was in my lungs.

I couldn't drive at the time so I managed to scrounge a lift with one of the lorry drivers who used to drop me off on the A45 and then I'd have to run five miles home from there. One guy had been working in the warehouse for 20 years and had just got his son a job there. What a nightmare. Night after night of throwing parcels into bins with no hope of a break or promotion of any kind. I guess some people were contented to work and get paid and have no other worries or responsibilities.

Compared to that, I suppose standing in the cold for 10 quid an hour as a PC wasn't that bad.

❧ ❧

The Red Watch way of doing things took a bit of getting used to and I didn't like the work ethic of some of the constables. Being a keen fresh-faced probationary constable I was always keen to impress the sergeants.

One morning at about 5:30 a.m. I left the police station for a last walk around the city centre before finishing work at 6:45 a.m. The night shift had changed to a 7 a.m. finish, so when we were on earlies we could have an hour's lie-in and start at 7 a.m. instead of 6.

It was the start of a bright sunny morning as I walked out of the front car park at the end of Little Park Street. As soon as I was outside the station I could hear a banging noise coming from the end of the street by High Street. I looked towards the banks by High Street and saw a man with a big metal stick bashing it into the front of a cash point machine. Because he was so far away all I could make out was the jeans and black sweatshirt he was wearing and the fact that he was white.

I couldn't believe my luck and the man's stupidity. It was a very bright morning and he was about 200 yards away from the front of the busiest police station in the West Midlands. I knew that if I ran towards him and he saw me he'd have a 200-yard head start. There was no sneaky route to take to get to him because he was standing on the main road.

Luckily for me one of the Zulus emerged from the rear yard of the police station so I waved at them to come over. The driver was Ray. Ray was a fairly quiet man, he'd sit on briefing and answer questions if you asked him anything but didn't have much to say for himself. It was rare that you'd see him at jobs or in the cell block with a prisoner. On the unit back then, time in service counted for a lot so he was just left to do what he wanted to.

In short, Ray was an idle bugger and avoided work like the plague. He was a nice enough chap but clearly didn't want to be on the watch, but at the time he couldn't find a nice admin job so he was stuck. He was partnered with Kevin who'd started out very keen and enthusiastic. Kevin was a former army PT instructor and was super-fit. He was pretty short for a police officer, maybe the same height as me but with three years' service. He was short and stocky and the years of army training had helped him develop a great physique. Under Dave's careful tutelage Kevin had become bone idle as well.

Ray pulled the Zulu next to where I was standing and I leaned in through his window. I pointed down the road at the man bashing the front of the cash point in and gasped at Ray in excitement, 'Look, that bloke is screwing the cash machine, Ray.' Ray looked at the man and said, 'Jump in the back, Paul.' I got in the back of the Zulu. I was ecstatic that I was about to have a decent prisoner and that he was almost in my hands and caught red-handed.

Ray put his foot hard on the accelerator and sped off – in the opposite direction. He turned his head towards me and said very matter-of-factly, 'It's too late in the day for a prisoner, lad.' I sank back into the seat completely gutted. This would've been a nice little arrest. It's not often in the police that you catch somebody in the act. I could've arrested him and handed the paperwork over to the early shift so they could interview and process him. Ray wouldn't have even had to get out of the car, but even that wasn't enough for him to take action.

Ray drove around the block the long way. We met the man coming down High Street empty-handed. I arrested him and recovered a big metal pole from around the corner. The front of the cash point machine had been completely smashed in causing about 10,000 pounds worth of damage. The man protested his innocence as per usual. The whole thing came down to identification, and since I was some distance away and never caught him red-handed, the CPS (Crown Prosecution Service) wouldn't prosecute. I can't say I blame them.

I didn't bother to report this to the watch supervision. They already knew that Ray was a lazy git and hadn't bothered to take him off the fast-response car so what would grassing him up achieve? I don't know why people like Ray were so lazy. It actually took more effort to avoid work than do it as far as I could see. If you did have a prisoner you could be inside in the warm having a cup of tea while you dealt with him instead of dealing with shit jobs on the street.

One story I'd heard about Ray was when he was a Panda driver a few years earlier. He'd been sent to Coventry canal on the report of a dead body floating in the water. One side of the canal is covered by Little Park Street police station and the other by Stony Stanton.

Ray attended and found a dead body draped over the Little Park Street Side of the canal. Not wanting to deal with all the initial paperwork and stay at the scene, Ray got a big stick and pushed the body over to the Stony Stanton side. He radioed in that the body was on the other side of the water. There were no bridges for miles so Stony Stanton ended up sending somebody and Ray drove off back to the station to book off duty.

Ray later got a job in admin which I suppose suited him fine. To me, he seemed to serve no useful purpose as a police officer.

One of the other Zulu drivers was called Red but his real name was Kenneth. He'd served 20 years in the catering corps in the army before joining Red Watch. Red must've eaten most of the food he cooked in the army, because at just 5' 8" he was huge, borderline obese, in fact. His massive gut hung over his belt and was so big it was clear that it had been quite some time since he'd seen his dick (without the aid of a mirror on the end of a stick). Red struggled to get into and out of the Zulu and was incapable of running so foot chases were out of the question. He had balding cropped hair and a huge thick unkempt beard which was more grey than black. It helped to cover some of his chins.

I'd never bothered to ask him why he was called Red, partly because I wasn't interested, and partly because he had the most foul breath I've ever had the misfortune to smell. It was so bad he could knock a squirrel off a tree at 20 paces. He should've realised something was wrong when flowers wilted as he walked past them. OK, well maybe I made that bit up, but it stank something awful.

Red smoked about 20 fags during the eight-hour tour of duty and heaven only knows how many he smoked at home. He smoked in briefing, in the Zulu when he was driving, during his break, and in the debrief room we assembled in before knocking off duty. That accounted in some part for his halitosis problem. I can only guess that he ate rotting meat before he came to work, which is the only reason I can think for breath that bad. Red should've got the hint when whoever he worked with would come to work with extra-strong mints and offer him one every 10 minutes. Even in the coldest winter nights his partner would have the window open on the Zulu.

One of the funniest things about Red was watching him at breakfast at the police canteen. Eating was his favourite pastime and you could see the look of delight on his face as he walked up to the counter to order food to fill his face with. For breakfast, he'd order sausages, bacon, black pudding, fried bread, plumb tomatoes, mushrooms, hash browns and two slices of toast.

He'd have so much food that they had to dish it up on two plates for him. He'd waddle over to the table and tuck in. After a few minutes he'd pour himself a cup of tea, but the best of it was he refused to have sugar in it, producing a tiny box of sweeteners and dropping two into his cup. As if that was going to counteract the two thousand calories on his plate.

Red's other nickname was FLOB (fat, lazy, obnoxious bastard) due to his refusal to do any work or put pen to paper. He always preferred to work with junior members of the watch so he could get them to do the paperwork. Red ranked as one of the laziest police officers I've ever met, he rarely arrested anyone, rarely stopped vehicles or people for checks, and rarely did anything, in fact. It was staggering that the sergeants saw fit to put him on the Zulu. The problem was partly that the sergeants were useless, and that long service in the police counted for a lot back then so he was considered untouchable.

Red came into quite a bit of money when he won 20 grand on a scratch card. Rather than invest it in property or in a fund for his children's university tuition he wasted it on buying a second-hand mobile home. He had Sky TV installed back when it cost a bomb. He also spent about £500 per month in the police bar's fruit machine. He'd feed that machine for his entire refreshment break.

Six months later it had all gone. He had to sell the mobile home and ended up driving a second-hand Ford Granada which resembled a ship. The rear window kept dropping down to halfway so everybody on the watch used to throw their rubbish, empty pizza boxes and apple cores into his car when he was out and it drove him mad.

Nobody wanted to work with such a lazy git as Red. There was a silent joy amongst the watch when one day Red crashed the Zulu, injuring his back, causing him to take early retirement. He'd been driving the Zulu with a fag on and it had dropped from his big fat mouth between his legs. As he panicked trying to stop it from burning his bollocks, he crashed into a wall. Useless twat.

❧ ❧

Being young in service meant I had to spend a lot of time on foot patrol. The watches were very large then and there were enough officers to put out three fast-response cars and five or six Panda cars. This meant that there were a few walkers free to patrol various areas.

There was a permanent city centre walker on the watch called Gilbert. He was about 45 and had 20 years service. Gilbert was always drunk on duty, which explains why he was always put on foot patrol. As soon as he finished briefing he'd walk to one of the local pubs in the city centre and play pool all night and drink with the punters. At about 3 a.m. he'd go to the police box in the city centre and sleep until knocking off time when he'd stagger back to the station.

As improbable as all this sounds, it went on for some time. I'm not sure where Gilbert ended up. I think he eventually joined the local beat officer team. They were, generally speaking, a bunch of skiving gits who worked from a portacabin at the back of the police station. They had no sergeant so for them it was easy to pretty much do what they wanted all day long. You'd be lucky if you managed to get one of them to answer the radio, and I was told that they'd usually book on duty while still in bed in the morning. Right up Gilbert's street.

You had to earn a place in a Panda car in the police back then and I appeared to be a long way off that privilege. I certainly had no problem with this at all but it didn't seem to work out that way for all of us. The sergeants had a few favourites, who even though they'd joined one month before me always seemed to find themselves in cars or nice and warm inside the station helping out in the front office or cell block.

I'd absolutely no problem with walking on every shift, but I didn't like the fact that the walking rule wasn't applied to everybody equitably. It was one of my first lessons in a job, that things are rarely done fairly. There was one guy who joined the month before me and he never walked a day of his service. He was a very big chap and ex-army, so I think the sergeants felt safe when they were around him. He was even put as a passenger in the Zulu after a few months, which was practically unheard of.

To start with, nights were my favourite shift. It seemed so exciting to be up when most of the population of the city was tucked up asleep in bed. On nights, Jed made a point though of always sending me out on my own. While all the other watch members were double-crewed for safety, I'd walk around the city centre of Coventry on my own for a nine-hour tour of duty for a seven-day night shift. It did get very lonely, and coming into winter it became bitterly cold.

We didn't have the posh kit then, just a NATO acrylic pullover and a thin nylon black coat which was neither wind- nor rain-proof. If there was a very light shower you were OK, but if that wet rain came down (the kind that soaks you through) you were going to get very cold and wet. After about an hour I couldn't feel my fingers or toes. It was absolutely bitter some nights.

I was still very shy and too frightened to ring hotel bells and scrounge a cup of tea from the night porter. Thinking about it, he'd probably have been happy to have some company. There was no large shopping centre then with night security guards so the places to have a cup of tea and warm up at 3 a.m. were very limited. I was very eager to impress the sergeants and produce some prisoners but I found it very difficult on nights. I wasn't into winding people up, so as long as they behaved reasonably well it didn't bother me if they were loud and drunk.

During the week town would go dead at about midnight which left me walking about an empty city centre until 6 a.m. and then 7 a.m. when they changed nights to a nine-hour shift. As the months progressed I got to know the city centre like the back of my hand. I walked around the entire city centre many hundreds of times and I learned every street's name and shop's location.

I was very conscientious and knew that a couple of other walkers when they did nights used to hide their car in town and get into it in the early hours, put the radio and heater on and fall asleep. There was also a police box in the very centre of town where you could put the heater on and have a kip, but I never did. I just didn't seem to feel tired on night shift, at least for the first couple of years.

It can be frustrating walking the town on nights because unless it's the weekend, in the early hours it becomes like a graveyard. If you're keen to arrest people for crime, you're going to struggle a bit if no people are to be found. We did go through spates of burglaries in town and I'd always take it personally if a shop in town had been broken into while I was on duty. The entire watch felt the same way, actually. If you came on duty the next day and found out a house on your patch had been screwed (burgled) then you'd feel angry.

At around 3 one morning I was walking across the city centre car parks. You can cover most of the town without walking across the roads just by crossing the car parks which are linked together on the second storey. As I got to the car park which overlooks Coventry retail market I could hear a loud repetitive banging noise.

The noise continued as I walked across the upper car park levels towards Iceland in Corporation Street. My guess was that somebody was trying to break something judging by the number and frequency of bangs. The number of times a police officer will actually come across a burglary in progress is very small; in a 30-year career it may be only once or twice you actually catch somebody in the act. This is because we were always either walking around or driving around. The best chance one has is to catch somebody leaving the scene of a crime in a car and pull them over, or to catch them on the way to commit a crime carrying the tools of their trade.

The only crimes the police usually come across are fights in town on a Saturday night. To actually come across a car theft or burglary in progress is fairly rare. The best prisoner-takers I ever came across in the police were those who pulled over the most cars. It's all a numbers game, and the worse the shit-hole you work in, the more your chances of pulling over a car driven by a disqualified driver or somebody who's wanted for an offence.

As the banging continued, my heart began to thump heavily and my mouth went dry. If you panicked on the radio you'd look like an idiot in front of your colleagues and you didn't want that to happen. Walking around town in the dead of night was 90 per cent monotony. If this was to be an actual crime, I had to keep cool, call it in on the radio without being heard by the burglars, and direct other units into the scene to cut off the exit points.

I took my police helmet off and slowly peered over the wall of the car park. I was on the top floor so could see down into Rover Road which is a service road for several shops and Coventry Market. There were two men at the back of one of the shoe shops, the front of which is in a place known as The Birdcage. They were both white, aged about 20 and dressed all in black. One was hitting the padlock on the back door with a hammer while the other one acted as look-out. The adrenalin shot through my body but I managed to keep a grip on myself and call it in on the radio.

I turned the volume right down low and whispered into the radio. I had to cover the speaker on the radio because it was designed to be loud so you can hear it in the car. '7907, there are two men breaking into a shop in Rover Road. Is anybody free to make it, please?' Red Watch were for the most part superb; if there was a good job going on several cars would make their way there. This was my big chance, it may not sound like much to you but after months of walking about with only shoplifters to deal with I was really excited.

The control room sergeant asked me to direct units in so we could get all the exit points covered in case they tried to run away. We closed off exit points at Rover Road, the market's service road, and the alleyway at the top of The Birdcage. There was nowhere for them to go and they were still completely unaware of our presence. Perfect.

I ran down the car park steps and past Coventry Market to where they were so I could be much closer. I was worried that they'd both come 'round the corner but it was worth the risk because it would be far better to catch them in the act rather than a few minutes later when they'd left the scene.

Other officers went into their positions and we had them blocked in. The two burglars were so busy trying to get into the back doors that they'd no idea they were surrounded. It was then that I saw a wonderful sight for a police officer, the police dog man sauntering up Rover Road with his German Shepherd, Makk. Makk was whimpering, desperate to get to the job, but luckily he hadn't started to bark. Most watches have a police dog for tracking people from stolen cars and it can be used for some public order, but because they're so ferocious they often end up biting people.

Makk was a dreadful tracker. We used to laugh every time he came to the scene of a burglary or stolen car. He'd sniff around the outside of the car, jump inside and then smell his arse and piss up the car tyre. He couldn't track a fart in a jacuzzi. One thing Makk was brilliant at though, was biting prisoners. If he was set on one, he used to put his 42 teeth into their arse – a treat. When that happened we called it a 'Makk attack'.

As we had them blocked in, I got up from behind a skip I was hiding behind and ran towards the two offenders. Unfortunately for me, Makk had been let loose at the same time and was on target to eat one of the burglars. I ran straight into Makk's path and froze, my feet rooted to the spot. I was in grave danger of being eaten alive by Makk.

Police dogs don't understand the difference between a policeman and a burglar. Most of Red Watch were standing there and it looked like I was just about to spoil the highlight of my career so far because of a stupid mistake. I didn't know that Makk was going to be let off the leash, and technically, the dog man is supposed to issue a loud challenge before doing it.

I stood there motionless, praying that Makk didn't decide to bite me to pieces, and thank God, like a heat-seeking missile he'd already acquired his target. Makk took one of the men down by the arm and the other one stood there in terror. I arrested them both and put them into the police car. It was glorious. Two of the watch sergeants had turned up, there were about eight police constables and the police dog handler. It was exactly the thing we were there to do.

It turned out that if they'd managed to get through the door it actually led to a brick outhouse which contained two large bins full of rotting rubbish. Idiots. It would've been worth sitting there for an hour to see the looks on their faces when the doors flew open to reveal the bins. They were charged with attempted burglary and both received suspended sentences.

∾ ∾

The incident involving these two guys was one of many where people of very limited mental capacity to plan a crime were caught due to their own stupidity. I had a bit of respect for professional thieves who'd spend days surveying a bank and then work out the best location to drill a hole and find entry and exit points. The first you'd know about them being there was the bank manager finding the vault empty when he opened up in the morning. The jobs were usually pulled over a bank holiday, so the safe was full and the place was empty for at least three days.

Two pea-brains once decided to break into The Plough pub on London Road. They activated the silent alarm which goes through to an alarm company which then calls the police. The silent alarm gives the police enough time to be aware of the activation and make the scene before the audio alarm sounds.

When the job came through on the radio we all raced to The Plough and Alan and I were the first car there. As we pulled outside the pub we saw two men jumping out of the front window and running up London Road. Alan and I just drove after them as it's silly to get out of the car and chase somebody on foot when you can just drive behind them and let them get tired.

The two men were a right pair of fat bastards. Their huge tyres of fat and beer bellies just bounced up and down as they did their best to flee the scene of the crime. They were both wearing cheap jogging bottoms and had filled their pockets full of 50-pence pieces from the fruit machine in the pub.

As they ran their pockets flapped around their legs like elephants' ears and the money was falling all over the ground. It weighed so much that they were having real difficulty running because of the weight, and the fact that they were having to hold their jogging bottoms up by the waist because they kept falling down. You could see the crack of their hairy arses hanging out, it was a right sight. Alan and I sat in the car following them at about five miles per hour, he was laughing so hard I thought he was going to crash.

Both men finally came to a stop after about a hundred yards. One fell on the pavement in exhaustion and the other leaned onto a lamp post and just gasped away as if he was having an asthma attack. Too many beers, fags and curries, I'm afraid. Their pockets had burst open due to the sheer weight of all the 50-pence pieces. They had no money left and were drenched in their own sweat and snot from the amount of panting they'd been doing. We walked up to one of them and put him in our car after searching and handcuffing him. The other guy was taken away in another Panda car.

I sat in the back of my car with my prisoner while Alan and a few others went and looked at the pub and went to see if the licensee was awake. My prisoner was still panting and half slumped over trying to get his breath back. 'That was almost the perfect crime, mate,' I smiled at him, 'I bet it took a few months planning.' He looked at me and then just put his face on my arm and wiped the snot and sweat onto the sleeve of my shirt. Dirty bastard. I couldn't let him get away with that. I wanted to punch him in his fat face but I just gave him a hard slap instead, grimaced at him and said, 'Do that again, mate, and I'll put your fucking head through the window.'

They were both taken back to the cell block and later charged with burglary. They went to court and were given a conditional discharge.

Another time we were called to some back gardens where a burglar was hiding after breaking into somebody's house. Red Watch's new dog handler had come – this dog was called Billy and he was a brilliant police dog. He'd track for miles and almost always get you to the offender's house.

Billy was in one garden with his handler and we were in gardens either side. Billy kept putting his nose in the air and barking at the garden I was in. It was pitch black and we couldn't see a thing but the fact Billy kept barking made his handler think that there was someone else who'd either been in or was still in the garden I was searching.

I finally pulled back a big hedge to reveal a man lying in the mud underneath. He had his eyes closed and began to snore away pretending to be asleep. He must've thought I was insane, as if I was going to fall for the story that he was on the way home and had got tired and decided to have a kip under somebody's hedge in their back garden. Goodness grief.

≈ ∽

As time went on I got to know some of the characters on the other watches as well. Each watch had their own group identity which was moulded around the strongest characters.

Yellow Watch in particular worked hard and partied hard. For some reason, they'd spend their days off socialising together in the same shit-holes that the local villains and riff-raff frequented. For this reason they were always getting into fights off duty and spending their days off either in hospital or in the police stations writing statements for off-duty arrests.

About three times I came on duty to find lots of Yellow Watch officers at the station when they should've been off duty. It was because they'd all been at a club or pub together and been spotted by some of the people they'd arrested in the past. The villain would often phone his mates to come over and then pick a fight with them. After the fight the villains were arrested and thrown into the cells.

There's an old hunters' motto that you should never cook your food near to where you sleep when there are bears around. The bears will smell the food and come when you're asleep and possibly attack you. I made it a point to avoid socialising in the same area I worked. I did very occasionally go into Coventry city centre in the evening, but I was always very wary and kept my wits about me. Not drinking helped me do that.

Since they spent most of their working time and free time together it was no surprise that most of Yellow Watch were living with somebody else on the same shift. The PCs were shagging each other, the sergeants shagging the PCs, and the inspector was living with one of the PCs. This all led to very incestuous affairs and caused particular problems when one couple fell out, as all of their mates had to stop talking to the other party for fear of causing jealousy or offence. What a nightmare.

There was one strange character on Yellow Watch in particular. Darren was 26 and a bit of a loner, very overweight, had an unhealthy pallid complexion and always seemed to be a bit down on himself. He also smoked heavily and drank a lot, all signs of somebody who is down on themselves.

He was part of Yellow Watch but never seemed to get on in particular with anybody. Things changed for him when one day, during an arrest, his prisoner stuck him in the stomach with a knife. The wound was superficial (since he had a lot of fat to cut through) but Darren got a lot of attention from the whole watch and was recommended for a commendation for bravery.

A few weeks later Darren had another unfortunate incident. He was on patrol on his own when he was called to investigate somebody acting suspiciously in a wooded area. Darren called for assistance saying he was being attacked. When back-up arrived Darren was lying down and had a stab wound to his abdomen. He spent a couple of days in hospital and was released. During this event Darren again received a lot of sympathy and attention and again came back to Yellow Watch to a hero's parade (you can see what's coming can't you)?

The CID at Little Park Street launched a mini-manhunt for the offender. Everybody pulled out all the stops to find the piece of shit who'd done this to a colleague. We searched all of the homeless refuges, Salvation Army, YMCA looking for the assailant but he was never found.

Darren again had an even more unfortunate incident the next month when he was lying asleep on his sofa at home. He woke up to find an assailant in his house slashing him across the face. He was again taken into hospital. The cut on his face was superficial. The story he gave just seemed a bit strange. There were no signs of forced entry to his house and the knife was from his kitchen drawer and the sort of knife used to eat your chips with rather then cut things up. Either Darren was very unlucky, or something fishy was happening.

Eventually, after some good cop interviewing, Darren admitted he'd made the two incidents up. He was desperate for attention and having had a taste of it he wanted more. He was thrown out of the station in disgrace and sent to work in the jailers' department. The jailers all booked the prisoners who were appearing in Crown Court in and out. It was the elephants' graveyard, the place that all the old policemen went before they died or retired. I never saw Darren again.

≈ ∽

During my probation my plan was to learn as much as humanly possible. You can learn from everybody you meet, even the lazy people if you ask the right questions.

Red Watch's boss, Insp. Darry would never acknowledge the presence of a new recruit onto the watch until they'd had their first complaint made against them by a member of the public. He wouldn't speak to you and you weren't allowed into his office to ask questions. According to him, you were not doing your job properly unless you were having complaints made against you.

It took me a few years to realise that he was actually right. There was no way you could be out there arresting people, getting into fights with violent criminals and searching suspects for weapons and drugs without getting the odd complaint here and there.

Every probationary constable on Insp. Darry's watch soon came to dread Friday and Saturday of night watch. Because we were new to the job, we basically had to earn the right to sit inside a nice warm police car so we were sent out on foot patrol on our own into Coventry city centre. It was sink or swim because many of the car parks were black spots for our police radios and if somebody else was transmitting at the same time you were screaming for help as you were getting your head kicked in it was tough luck.

We didn't dread going out because of encounters with the public, but because of Insp. Darry. Every Friday and Saturday of night watch we'd quickly run out of the back door of the station and go out on foot patrol. We had to avoid Insp. Darry because he liked to go on patrol with the probationary constables – and he caused havoc every time. The guy was a one-man riot.

We'd be out on foot patrol and then the dreaded radio message from the control sergeant would come, 'PC Browning, can I have your location for the inspector, please?' If we happened to be walking with somebody else they'd say, 'You're on your own, mate,' and breathe a sigh of relief and walk off. Rather be on your own than out with the inspector.

We didn't dread the call because he was the inspector. Oh no, we dreaded it because we knew what was going to happen that night sure as eggs is eggs. Parts of Insp. Darry's modus operandi meant he was not so concerned with criminals or crime in general (I know this sounds far-fetched but bear with me). He was far more passionate about enforcing local by-laws and ancient common law principles such as obstructing Her Majesty's highway. What this actually meant we never knew, but woe betide anybody who stood on the same part of the pavement for too long when Insp. Darry was on patrol.

Coventry city centre was of course full every night of thousands of young people desperate to get as drunk as possible and then stagger off to the Parsons Nose chip shop for a bag of chips and curry sauce or Mr Porkys for a pork and stuffing batch (a Coventry term for bread roll).

Once you'd left the city centre it surely meant the weekend was at an end, so it was traditional to stand around exchanging drunken pleasantries with whoever would listen for as long as possible. This usually went on until around 3 a.m. when the last drunk fell into the last taxi or staggered off home with only their beer compass to guide them.

People standing around obstructing Her Majesty's highway was a major annoyance to Insp. Darry. They looked like they were just standing on the pavement to me, but obviously not to Darry. Whenever we came across somebody standing in the same spot for too long Insp. Darry took it upon himself to tell them to move along because they were obstructing the highway. He'd walk right up to them putting his face into theirs and speak to them as if they'd just burned the Union Jack or something equally dreadful. The victim of course would be completely baffled by this because they were just standing still on the pavement talking shite to a friend.

At about 11:30 p.m. one Saturday evening Insp. Darry met up with me in Broadgate in the city centre and we walked down Ironmonger Row together. We turned the corner from Tower Street and came to the entrance of the Pink Parrot night club. Several doormen stood at the entrance checking the punters for weapons, drugs and any signs of intelligence. If you had none, you were usually permitted entry unless you were so drunk you couldn't speak.

We walked past the usual crowd queuing up who whistled the Laurel and Hardy theme tune at us or shouted 'pigs' or 'filth' behind our backs. I'd always feel angry when people did that, not because it was at me personally, but they were slagging off what we represented, which as far as I was concerned was protecting the public from harm. It always amused me as I wondered who they'd call if some crackhead was trying to break into their house or rob them.

A well-dressed middle-aged man came towards us from the entrance and walked over with a beaming smile. At about 40, he was a lot older than the usual clientele and was dressed in a reasonably expensive suit which made him stand out even further. Add to that the fact that he'd been drinking orange juice all night because he was driving himself and his wife home and you had a truly rare individual. This man's name was Kenny and his opinion of the police was about to change forever.

'I'm sorry to bother you,' Kenny smiled at us, 'I am a paramedic. I came outside to get some fresh air and now the doormen won't let me back in because I don't have my ticket with me. My wife is inside on her own and my jacket is in the cloakroom with the ticket in the pocket.' Insp. Darry just stared down at Kenny who was a lot shorter than him. I began to feel the anxiety well up in my stomach. I desperately hoped that he was not going to make an example of Kenny.

Kenny filled the uncomfortable silence with some more explaining. 'I haven't had a drink tonight because I am driving us home. If you could help me out I'd appreciate it.' I was just about to have a chat with Kenny and offer to have a quick word with the doormen to see if they'd let him get the ticket from his pocket. I'm sure they were just busy and would help us out.

Insp. Darry saw this issue from a completely different perspective than both Kenny and I. 'Move along, you are causing an obstruction of the highway,' Darry barked into Kenny's face. Kenny just looked completely confused as if that comment didn't make sense to him at all. My heart sank. I knew what was coming. Unfortunately, Kenny had no idea.

The smile slipped from Kenny's face and he began to plead, 'But my wife is stuck inside the club on her own. Can you please help me out here?' Darry raised his huge hand and poked his finger into Kenny's chest causing him to fall backwards slightly, 'I am telling you to move on, you are obstructing Her Majesty's highway.' By now Kenny was completely bemused and my heart was beating like a bongo drum. This was a nice bloke with a very simple request. He was clearly in need of a bit of help and worried about his wife being on her own inside the club.

He began to restate the problem once again which was too much for Darry to bear.

Darry lost his patience and roughly grabbed Kenny's arm and twisted it behind his back. Darry was a giant of a man and Kenny quite small in stature. Kenny screamed 'Aarrgh' half in pain and half in shock. He'd probably never had treatment like this since he'd been bullied at school many years before. Darry shoved Kenny's face hard into the brick wall of the nightclub like he was some sort of violent and deranged crackhead, then brutally kicked his legs open into a wide stance. It was like something out of an American TV show where the SWAT team do a raid on a gang of arms dealers. I just stood there in dismay. I could see the bouncers watching from the nightclub entrance and they had confused looks on their faces.

Insp. Darry took his handcuffs out of their pouch and proceeded to cuff Kenny's hands behind his back. I'm sure Kenny was as confused as I was. In fact, Darry seemed to be the only person present including the bouncers and onlookers who knew what was actually happening. Darry called for the riot van to transport his prisoner to the police station. It promptly arrived and took a crying and very distressed Kenny away. I'll never forgot the look on his face as he was frog-marched into the van. I never got to find out what happened to Kenny's wife. I hope she had some money and the house keys on her. I still wonder what impression Kenny now has of the police and if he'd call us if he ever was in trouble again.

Insp. Darry's conduct often seemed to me to be disgraceful. Whatever possessed him to get upset about people standing on a pavement? One other time I was walking down Little Park Street with him. It was about 5:30 p.m. and the traffic on the road was horrendously busy. A young girl was riding towards us along the pavement on her bike. She must've been about 12 and was clearly not very confident on the bike. The pavement was very wide and the rush hour traffic heavy and dangerous.

Darry's face flushed bright red as he jumped out in front of this poor little girl and told her off for cycling on the pavement. He insisted she get onto the road and use that. The girl started crying as she put her bicycle onto the road and wobbled away next to the rush hour traffic. What an absolute disgrace.

This wasn't the only incident I got involved in with Darry. He seemed to cause complete havoc at any situation he was involved in and had a knack of making the simplest incident into a full-scale riot. It wasn't all bad though. On Red Watch, we could all rest happy in the knowledge that anyone who came into the police station to make a complaint against us would more than likely be arrested and dragged screaming into the cell block by Darry.

The whole watch used to love to hear a call go out from the control room requesting the inspector to attend the front office because there was a member of the public waiting there to make a complaint against one of us. I'd say that there was an official complaint made almost every night or at least every other night. The nature of the complaint was usually one of us being uncivil, rude or using too much force during arrest (how dare they).

We'd all drive back to the station as quickly as possible and run to the front office giggling like children. We'd hide behind the counter to watch the proceedings. It was always the same story. Darry would storm into the front office so angry that his face would be completely beetroot red. The member of the public would begin to state their case upon which Darry would scream at them at the top of his voice, 'Do you have any idea how hard it is for a police officer to carry out his duty?' The blood would be coursing through his body causing the veins in his temples to stick out like huge lines of spider web in his head.

He'd always poke the person in the chest, which would wind them up a treat. They'd then raise their voice or use the 'I pay your wages' or 'How dare you' response, upon which Darry would put them in an arm lock and drag them off to the cell block screaming and shouting.

I was always amazed how this could happen time and time again without any repercussions. Maybe the person was so relieved to get out of a rancid-smelling, piss-soaked cell full of the scum of the earth that they ran out of the station and never came back. Either way, the potential complaint had been nipped in the bud.

Insp. Darry's escapades didn't end there. One afternoon we were on patrol in the city centre covering a football match against Coventry. The matches during the 1990s were almost always followed by a full-scale riot with opposing teams running up and down Highfield Road kicking the shit out of each other for no other reason than that they supported another team.

While one such riot was in full swing, Darry was in charge of one of the public order vans. En route to the riot through the city centre he noticed that some vandal had walked through one of the flower displays outside the cathedral in Broadgate and pulled most of the flowers up. He screamed at the driver to stop, ran out of the van, and stood crying in the middle of the flower bed and for half an hour replanted each flower by hand until the display was once again complete. The police officers in the van just sat inside in stunned silence waiting for Darry to finish while the riot went on a few miles up the road.

Things came to a head when Darry went on foot patrol on his own in the town centre, this time during daylight hours. We knew it was only a matter of time before he'd be shouting for help on the radio and we'd all have to race to his aid. During my 12 years in the police I never heard another instance of a police inspector going out on foot patrol. Heaven only knows what was going on in Darry's mind. The inspector's role is to supervise the entire unit and be available for cell block reviews and urgent incidents, not to walk around town getting into fights.

Darry had been walking through Broadgate and come across yet another scumbag obstructing the highway. How dare they! In this instance the offender was actually a well-known thief and burglar so in our eyes was a fair target. While trying to arrest the man Darry ended up rolling around the ground trying to handcuff him. While he was on the ground the prisoner's friend came around and kicked Darry in the back. This was probably the single worst mistake the man had ever made in his life. If Darry was quite prepared to antagonise and eventually arrest seemingly decent members of the public, what was in store for this man?

The Zulu had transported the man who'd kicked Darry to the cell block and Malc was the custody sergeant that day because Bill was on holiday. Malc was a very tall Irishman with kind blue eyes, thick black hair, broad shoulders and rosy cheeks. He was a larger-than-life character whose two sisters were in the police and their father had been a police inspector for many years in Coventry. Malc smoked quite heavily, which must've affected his taste buds because he could easily eat a vindaloo every night and not bat an eyelid. He had a habit of eating raw garlic whilst at work peeling it with his penknife and chop the garlic bulb into small pieces and eat it. If he spoke to you, the smell would be so strong your eyes would water. It was worse than being sprayed with Mace.

Malc had passed the inspectors' exam himself but somehow couldn't seem to get promoted. Some people seem to go through the police with a black mark, and no matter what they apply for they get knocked back. But then again, he was a bit of a strange fish. One day he'd be really nice to you and help you out of a fix, and the next he'd be trying to catch you out by sneaking to a job you were at or trying to catch you making a mistake. He helped me out on one occasion when an interview I had with a prisoner went badly wrong. I was with another probationer and we messed up the introductions and forgot to explain to him his rights and we then got the interview questions all wrong.

We went out and told Malc what we'd done wrong. He took the tapes off us and threw them into the furnace in the basement. He told us to start again and make out that the first interview had never happened. That got us both out of a very embarrassing situation so I was grateful for that.

Malc was going through the booking-in procedure for the prisoner. You can only do so much without the arresting officer present, so he was taking down the prisoner's name and address and other details. Malc didn't like Insp. Darry, and Darry didn't like Malc. I don't know exactly why, but at a guess Malc didn't like the way Darry did his job, which I think we can all relate to. Darry had pissed Malc about; on many occasions they had several stand-up arguments throughout the time they worked together.

One time Darry had battered another innocent member of the public and brought the person before Malc in the custody office. After a heated argument about the fact the prisoner was not suitable to be detained and Darry insisting he was, Malc lost it and shouted at the inspector, 'Get the fuck out of my cell block, you prick.' Oh dear.

Darry had walked all the way through town back to the police station. The walk had not cooled Darry off because by the time he'd reached the cell block his face was supernova red. The cell block was full of police officers at the time, a few offenders were sitting on the benches waiting to be processed, and two solicitors were standing around chatting with each other waiting until they could speak to their clients.

Darry was let into the cell block by the striker, and he walked straight up to the counter where his prisoner was standing. His eyes were bulging out of their sockets and his teeth gritted so tightly they looked like they were about to crack. His prisoner was standing at the custody desk oblivious to what was about to happen. Darry lifted his right leg back and kicked the man so hard between the legs that he raised him off the floor by a good foot, even my testicles throbbed. Everyone present gasped including a wasp which had accidentally flown in through the window and was looking for a quick way back out. The gasp was partly because of what had happened, and partly in empathy for the man's knackers which were bound to be throbbing. The prisoner fell to the floor groaning and cupping his squashed testicles in his hands (as if that was going to help).

There was a stunned silence as all the onlookers stood there with their jaws open, you could've heard a mouse fart. Everyone was standing there waiting for somebody to do something but nobody knew quite what. Darry was just about to stamp on his head to finish the job off when three of the old-sweat policemen grabbed him and pushed him out of the cell block and into the car park. The door was locked to prevent him coming back in and killing the man, which was a distinct possibility due to Darry's size and strength.

This was a predicament: about 10 police officers, three prisoners and two solicitors witnessed a serious assault on a prisoner. Police standing orders dictate that all evidence should be preserved, the prisoner examined by a doctor, and then everyone record the incident in their pocket notebooks.

If anyone had a right to see Darry nailed to the wall by complaints and discipline it was Malc. But that was not the code. I was taught that we never ever informed on one of our own. Those who had were ostracised forever and were forced to work the rest of their career on their own as nobody else would work with them.

How everyone came to an agreement I'll never understand. The other prisoners never said a word. I think they just walked back to their cells and shut the door behind them. The solicitors finished what they were doing and quietly left. Malc put an entry on the custody record and every other officer present completed their pocket notebooks to the effect that the prisoner had launched an unprovoked and violent attack on the inspector and in self-defence he'd lashed out with his foot which came into contact with the prisoner's testicles.

The net effect of this story was that the prisoner had to be charged with the assault on the inspector in the cell block. I wonder what the case file said, maybe something like, 'The offender then assaulted the inspector by throwing his testicles onto his foot in a violent manner. This caused mild reddening to the inspector's foot.'

∽ ∾

There were many other occasions where police officers were assaulted. It's a natural consequence of the job because, depending upon where you work you'll be arresting people on a daily basis. The vast majority of the people you arrest will be committing crimes to pay for their drug habit. They know that if they're incarcerated they won't have access to drugs, and therefore will do anything within their power to prevent you arresting them. If this means head-butting, punching, kicking, stabbing or shooting you then so be it.

Assault on a police officer is considered a relatively minor offence and will usually result in no more than a fine or conditional discharge. Since this is no deterrent then one alternative is to kick the living shit out of the offending party to educate them that this is not a very wise thing to do. Let's leave judgement out of the equation at the moment, because until you've been spat at, puked on, head-butted, kicked, punched and so on, then you don't know what it feels like.

Every weekend in Coventry there's at least one riot van (called serial van) patrol which basically consists of uniformed officers patrolling a particular area in a large van. There's usually a sergeant, a driver and seven or eight constables sitting in the back.

The seat closest to the sliding door at the side of the van is known as the jump seat. The newest member of the watch was always nominated to sit in that seat and be first out. I'm not quite sure of the mentality behind that, either they wanted you to be in the thick of the action or the first one to get shot, stabbed or bottled if there was an angry crowd outside. It was a bit like being 'on point' in Vietnam. Since you were of least use to the patrol it didn't matter too much if you were taken out of action by the enemy.

Coventry city centre had to have a public order van or two out every Friday and Saturday night due to the fact that there were thousands of drunken people spilling out from clubs and pubs late evening and early morning. Every single Friday or Saturday night there was at least one fight and often several. Sometimes it would be just a scuffle, but often more of a battle involving several people and weapons.

The violence in Coventry came to a head every weekend where the week's pent-up aggressions, hate for the boss or spouse could be identified with anybody who dared to look at you the wrong way. From 10 p.m. to 3 a.m. every single weekend the riot van would speed from fight to fight. Officers would spring out of the van, smack the offending parties over the head with wooden truncheons and cart them off to the cell block to cool off. After a good night's kip and some maxpax instant coffee in the morning, what had been a completely violent animal resumed their meek and mild daytime persona.

When we were on late shift one evening and if we were on lates then Yellow Watch were always on nights for the weekend. Late shift finished at 10 p.m. but on Fridays and Saturday nights Red Watch manned the serial van and went out in the city centre from about 10:30 p.m. to 3 a.m. It was overtime, so tempting for anybody who wanted to make some extra money.

Everybody would pile into the bar at 10 p.m. and have a couple of beers. We weren't supposed to because we were on duty but a couple of the van sergeants would have a pint or two so that meant that the PCs did the same. Sometimes it would be easy money, just sitting sleeping in the back of the van but often you'd be rushing from fight to fight, throwing your prisoners in the cells and rushing back out again to another fight.

One of the watch sergeants had a mate who owned a pub in Wood End which is a very long drive from Coventry city centre, at least 10 minutes at full speed. I hated working the van when this sergeant was on duty. He'd have a couple of pints in the police bar, we'd then all pile into the van and drive 'round town for a couple of hours patrolling. The inside of the van stank of alcohol because everyone had been drinking. At about midnight we'd send the probationer (usually me) into the Raj curry house in Ironmonger Row to get 10 free curries and nan breads. We'd then drive to his mate's pub in Wood End where everyone would get pissed up for an hour (including the van driver).

I thought it was very dangerous because we'd all stink of beer (apart from me because I didn't drink) and we were miles away from town so if there was a shout it would take ages to get there. It actually happened once. We were all in the pub and a report came in that there was a massive fight outside the Parrot. We all ran to the van but it was a very foggy night. The driver could only manage about 50 kmph so it took a quarter of an hour to get there.

After a couple of times on the van with him I'd only put my name down for nights when he wasn't on the van. I just didn't like to be around him because I think he was taking big risks and it was all bound to go pear-shaped at some point and I didn't want to be there when it did. Some other PCs felt the same so the weekend van crews split into two factions: those who wanted to go on the piss, and those who preferred to be a bit more professional.

At about 11 p.m. one night in Corporation Street my watch were on van patrol and Yellow Watch were on lates as usual. Sometimes the van was a bit full so a couple of us would be let out to walk around the city centre and be picked up a bit later on. I was on foot patrol in the city centre with another probationary constable called Frank. Frank was ex-army and a good chap. He'd done 16 years in the infantry and was keen to get on in the police and have an enjoyable time in the service.

As we walked along Corporation Street we heard on the radio that a female officer from Yellow Watch was trying to arrest a drunken man with her male colleague but he was becoming very violent towards them. We hurried our pace because they were just around the corner and as we did so our serial van sped past us. When you're on foot patrol you rarely want to be seen running. It's something about the image of a calm cool and collected police officer. Running through the streets like a lunatic looks bad unless you're in a foot chase.

Our sole purpose on the van was to maintain an aggressive presence and meet violence with even more violence. Hopefully, onlookers would be put off wanting to fight knowing we were present. When we got to Corporation Street outside Kwik Save store the two Yellow Watch officers were struggling with their prisoner. Ten pints of beer and a few lines of coke had sent the man a bit loco and he'd lashed out and hit the female officer in the face. She was more upset than angry, but her male colleague was livid.

The very worst beatings were reserved for these people. Hitting a police officer is not allowed; hitting a female police officer is unforgivable. If you did that in the USA they'd probably shoot you dead. All the officers in the van saw the soon-to-be-sorry prisoner hit the WPC and they couldn't jump out of the van quick enough. Eight hairy-arsed policemen and one hairy-arsed WPC picked up the prisoner and dragged him kicking and screaming into the van. They literally picked him up and carried him to his fate inside.

I think at this point the assailant immediately sobered up and it began to dawn on him what was about to happen. Just like a man being carted off to the death chamber, there was nothing he could do about it but cry for forgiveness, 'I'm sorry, I'm sorry, I'm sorry….' Too late for that I'm afraid mate. He was dragged onto the floor of the van where I could see a mass of boots kicking him all over his body, the back of the van was very cramped so people usually had to wait their turn if they wanted to dish out some pain.

There was no room on board for me so the last image I saw before the door was slammed closed was several hairy-arsed policemen jumping up and down on the man like he was some sort of trampoline. The door slammed shut and the whole van rocked from side to side for about a minute. I could hear some muffled screams from the now-very-sorry man and then it went eerily quiet.

He was taken off to the police station for booking-in, or what was left of him anyway. I felt no pity for him as there was no need for him to assault the officers. I know he was drunk, but nobody asked him to drink too much and take coke. As far as I'm concerned he deserved what he got and if you bash a police officer you deserve 10 times back. Heaven knows, the courts won't do much about it.

At 2 a.m. the Pink Parrot nightclub shuts and around 200 drunken people spill out onto a pavement big enough to fit about 50. Almost every time people came out there was a fight. There were few exceptions to this rule. Somebody would knock somebody or look at their girlfriend the wrong way and they were fighting. We'd jump out of the van and arrest them. If anybody else got in the way or obstructed us we'd arrest them as well.

We'd race back to the cell block, throw our prisoners in the cells and rush back out again for the next fight. There was always a system for dealing with violent prisoners. Force was met with brutal force. It was a system of education that if you didn't come quietly you'd get battered. If you made us run after you, you'd get battered. If you beat up your wife or girlfriend, you'd get battered. The system seemed to work pretty well.

The van could be a dangerous place to work due to the fact that we'd often have to wade into crowds of people outside nightclubs. If you got separated from your team you were dangerously exposed and the idea of people respecting the uniform is a myth. Often, it makes you a target for angry people who see the uniform as a sign of authority and want to have a go at you.

We attended a fight outside the Parsons Nose one night. There was often a crowd as big as 200 or 300 out there late on Friday and Saturday night. They'd queue to get their chips and stay outside there chatting with their mates. Then they'd spill off the pavement out onto the road causing problems for the traffic and a danger to themselves.

There was always a strange atmosphere in this sort of situation. The air was usually highly charged with a massive mix of emotions in the air. Some people (the happy drunks) would be nice to us and tell us what a great job we were doing. Others would make snorting noises when they thought we weren't looking, and yet others would look at us like we were the SS marching out of a concentration camp.

With such a tightly-packed group of young drunken people who are there to release a week's worth of pent-up emotions there's bound to be trouble. Often, fights would erupt and we'd have to go into the crowd to arrest the offenders. During a fight one night we all waded in and one of the new guys on the watch called Duncan ended up rolling around on the floor with his prisoner. As he was doing that, some cowardly piece of shit kicked him in his back sending him flying onto the ground. I didn't see it, but I'd have given a month's pay to find out who it was and kick his teeth out.

We all fell back into the van fighting with the prisoners who were handcuffed by now. Duncan felt the back of his jumper and it was wet. He pulled his hand away and it was covered in blood. Some bastard had stuck him with a knife while he was fighting.

We were all so angry but there was no way of finding who'd done it. We had to take Duncan to hospital but it was only a flesh wound. At that time we were not given stab-resistant vests. It took another five years to get them because of the bureaucracy surrounding funding and police committees on uniform, health and safety, performance review and so on.

As the months went on I accepted violence on the watch as the norm. If somebody played up they were punished. Sometimes, even if they didn't play up they could still be punished if their crime mandated it. I never took part in any beatings. If I had to arrest a violent prisoner I did what I had to do to subdue them, but once they were handcuffed that was usually the end of it. I really couldn't see the point in hitting people once they were restrained, and I only hit people who were trying to hit me.

I'd heard at training school that it's always the same police officers who get assaulted, and it was because of their attitude. As I became more experienced in the police I found that this was generally the case. Although every constable is assaulted at some point in their career, there seemed to be the same ones on our watch getting into fights and being assaulted all the time.

One in particular was Larry. I'd put Larry in the top three or four of the most violent people on Red Watch. Rick was at the top followed by Zane then Insp. Darry then Kevin (the former army PT instructor), then funnily enough a female officer called Helen.

Larry was a blast, a real comedian. He had about six months' more service than me but acted like one of the old sweats. He was from Liverpool which immediately made him a constant target for jokes. When he'd speak to you, you'd just look confused and say to your mate next to you, 'What's he saying?' After a few 'What's he sayings' Larry would snap and tell you to fuck off, at which point, of course, you'd start to laugh.

Larry was about 5' 8" tall and had very pale skin which made him look like he'd just donated three pints of blood instead of one. He had a large beak-like nose with a black mole on the side which you couldn't help looking at as he spoke to you. His blonde hair was unmanageable and looked like a very cheap wig glued to his head.

Just like any working-class environment, if you exhibit any behaviour or trait that's out of the ordinary you'll be made the subject of jokes. If Larry was in the room we'd all speak in very lame Scouse accent and call everybody 'kidda'. Pathetic, I know.

Although Larry was a great guy, when he got out into the streets there was another side to him. He was capable of terribly violent behaviour which seemed very out of character to me. Larry had a pathological hatred of the villains who lived around our 'patch' and he also treated any prisoners who 'played up' with extreme violence. I didn't know what was going on in his mind, but there are many times I watched Larry dishing out some really brutal beatings.

One afternoon we were arresting a guy whom we'd chased from a stolen car. He must've been about 24 and what I'd call a typical car thief. On the dole, living in a council flat, never worked a day in his life and a string of previous offences. Larry had caught and handcuffed him and I opened the back door of our police car so he could put the prisoner in. As the prisoner was putting his head into the car Larry grabbed it and bashed it against the top of the door opening. The prisoner cried in pain as his head split open and blood came gushing out of the wound.

I just stood there and looked on – I could say in disbelief – but not much shocked me anymore. Larry just looked at the man who was now lying half in and half out of the car. He had an evil look in his eye and with a scowl on his face said, 'Serves you right you thieving cunt. Next time I catch you I'll break your fucking legs.'

Now I know what you're thinking. How could all these injuries be explained away? Surely, the custody sergeant would be asking questions of us, and if the prisoner made a complaint we'd be investigated. You'd think so, wouldn't you? Like some surreal dream the custody officer never batted an eyelid when the PIC (prisoner in custody) came in. He'd be seen by the police doctor if he needed it but most of the time they said nothing and never complained.

If a complaint looked likely, the officer who did the dirty deed would just swap his boots and clothes with somebody else so if complaints took his clothes there was never any blood on them anyway. This didn't happen all the time, by the way. Just often enough to seem ordinary to me. I just kept my mouth shut and nothing seemed to happen. I didn't condone it, but I did nothing to stop it either.

Larry always seemed to have a string of complaints lodged against him. The complaints form was called a WC666 and we had copies of the complaint served on us by the complaints department to give us notice that we were being investigated. Larry used to collect them and cellotape them to the front of his locker and display them like badges of honour. As soon as one was cleared, he'd have another to replace it. I think his record was seven open at the same time. We used to call him PC 666 because he had so many.

Complaints against police can range from everything including incivility to members of the public, assault or theft. Most never really went anywhere or the odd one ended up with a fine or black mark on your record. Like I said before, I had several lodged against me over my 12 years. Many of them had been lodged by disgruntled prisoners who wanted to get back at me somehow and this was the only way they could see of doing it.

Once I was with Larry in the back of the serial van. He had a prisoner lying on the floor who'd been fighting with another man outside the Parsons Nose and when Larry had arrested him he'd spat in his face, which was not a good idea. As the man was lying on the floor of the serial van Larry was punching him in the face and ribs educating him about what a filthy habit it is to spit in people's faces (especially his).

As he brought his fist down to chin the prisoner another time his hand caught part of the seat. Larry yelped in pain, he held his hand up and his wrist was flapping to the side in a most unnatural position. It was dislocated and in Larry's mind this was all his damn prisoner's fault – if his face had been there instead of the seat it wouldn't have happened. Larry reported to the custody sergeant that the prisoner had grabbed his hand during arrest and twisted it back, causing the injury. Larry got a few hundred pounds in criminal compensation and the prisoner got a six-month suspended sentence.

Although he was a great guy to work with, a good laugh and would always back you up Larry could also get you into a bit of trouble. I'd always dreaded being asked to falsely corroborate somebody's story because I felt it was the wrong thing to do, even to stitch up a criminal. I was about to find out how far I'd go.

I was sitting in the jump seat on the serial van at about 2:30 a.m. one Saturday when Larry shouted out that there was a knock (fight) behind the van. I don't know why we didn't just call it a fight. I leaped out of the jump seat and Larry ran past me towards a bend in the road. I was a few seconds behind him and when I turned the corner Larry was holding a pissed-up rowdy man by the arm and carting him off towards the riot van.

I helped Larry handcuff the man and we took him back towards the police station. As we were getting out of the van Larry turned to me and said in his Liverpudlian accent, 'Is it OK if ya rent for me our kid?' I was a bit baffled and just stood there with a confused look on my face. Larry said again, 'I need ya to rent for me, Paul,' and then the penny dropped. He needed me to corroborate the fact that the man had been fighting, since the magistrates needed two policemen to say the same thing in court to get a prosecution.

It seemed some police officers had been caught out lying in court before, so now it needed two of us to lie to get the conviction. Being a naive new(ish) recruit I truthfully told Larry I didn't actually see the fight take place so wouldn't really be able to help. Larry shouted to the van patrol sergeant and complained loudly in a mock crying voice, 'He won't rent for me, Sarge.'

The sergeant looked at me and scowled. He never said a word. I did what any other fresh face recruit just out of training would do: I caved in and agreed to say I'd seen the whole thing. Larry assured me that he'd admit the offence and probably get a police caution for the offence.

Two months later the papers arrived warning Larry and me for the upcoming court appearance. It seemed the man wanted to contest the offence and have his day in court. Now I was completely stuffed. If I withdrew my statement, it'd be clear it was false. If I went to court and said what I'd written down had actually happened, then that was perjury and if it was found out I never actually saw the fight I could end up in prison.

I began to have sleepless nights worrying. What if there'd been some CCTV footage found showing me coming 'round the corner after the fight had concluded? I began to imagine the defence solicitor producing a video showing just that in court which of course meant that I was committing perjury so was liable to serve five years in prison. If I changed my story at this late hour I was still guilty of perverting the course of justice so could still go prison.

The day of the court case finally arrived. Larry and I sat in the police room at Coventry Magistrates' Court. The procedure in the police room is to go over your statements and double-check your pocket books so you're both 'singing off the same hymn sheet' so to speak. I just sat there sweating, I felt like I was waiting to be executed.

When it's your turn to give evidence the court usher comes to the police room and calls you into court, you walk to the witness box and swear an oath to tell the truth. You're then interviewed by the prosecution solicitor from the CPS and then the defence who represents the defendant.

After about 45 minutes the court usher came into the room and called Larry and me in together. I didn't know what was going on. The CPS lawyer met us outside the court and said that the defendant had pleaded guilty and we could go back to work. I could've kissed him. I've never felt such relief in my life. As I walked out of the magistrates' court I swore to myself never to get into this situation again.

∞ ∞

Violence seemed to me to be part of normal life as a police officer. Nobody ever sat me down on the watch and explained why we hit prisoners or under what circumstances we hit back or even hit first. As the months progressed I got the general idea about who was more likely to be beaten up and under what circumstances.

First, if you 'played up', which meant became violent during arrest, you were liable for a beating. A beating could be a few digs or rabbit punches in the back of the head to a complete kicking involving broken noses, ribs, etc., but the latter was very rare.

Second, if you ran away and made one of us run after you you'd be given a few digs for making us run. I don't know if this really worked, because they'd be *more* likely to run away next time in the hope that they wouldn't be battered.

Third, if you were a well-known shit (criminal), you'd often get a few digs or some pain (bending your arm behind your back, punch in the ribs and so on). This was considered punishment for being a shit, and also for any other offence you may have got away with in the past.

A fourth category was wife-beaters. I learned this lesson early on in my service, in fact. One of the first domestics I went to was with my tutor Alan. Graham and Keith who were two other members of Red Watch had arrived well before us.

When Graham spoke he couldn't say his *r*'s properly which of course was a source of amusement for his Red Watch colleagues. When he was working in the control room he was responsible for checking the PNC for us when we wanted a vehicle check done over the radio. Of course, we'd look for any red vehicles to check, and better still, a red rover, because he had to say 'wed wover' on the air, which he hated.

It took us weeks but eventually we found a car for Graham to check. We did the check and he called back, 'You have a wed wover, owner is wodney woderwick who lives in wibble woad, over.' It was the funniest thing I'd ever heard on the radio.

The background to the domestic argument was the typical story we always saw. Boyfriend came home drunk from the pub after work, dinner was burned and so he got a mouthful of abuse from his girlfriend. After a few minutes of abuse he started to shout back and it erupted in violence. The prisoner had slapped his girlfriend in the face busting her lip open. The neighbours had called the police.

The girlfriend had gone to hospital to have her face looked at and we were left there to mop up the mess. It looked pretty much under control to us. Since the prisoner was now handcuffed and compliant I presumed he'd be taken to the police car outside and put in the cells to cool off. The prisoner was a scrawny slightly-built man, about 25, skull tattoos up his arms and of course still half pissed-up from spending an afternoon in the pub with his peers.

A few hours later he could be interviewed and charged with assault. If he was still a danger he'd be remanded into custody pending a trial or otherwise bailed to another address with conditions to stay away from his now ex-girlfriend.

As we went to walk out of the flat with Graham holding the man by the arm Graham quietly said, 'This isn't over yet,' and he grabbed hold of the man's ears like they were handles and then smashed it into the wall of the flat. I winced in shock and disgust and as I did so the man's legs buckled under him. Graham held him upright to stop him falling over and then continued to bash his head against the wall several more times until the man collapsed on the floor unconscious. I was relieved to hear the hollow thud as the head went into the wall which told me that it was a partition and not made of brick.

There was nothing to do or say. There was a 90 per cent chance that his girlfriend would either not complain or withdraw it completely once he'd phoned her begging for forgiveness saying he still loved her. The next time he thought about hitting her, even when he was drunk, he'd remember what happened to him the last time.

It was very frustrating to see the victim after the assault, take her statement and try to help her get the courage to take action against somebody who was supposed to love her as his wife or partner and mother of his children. Normally, the man would phone her or knock at the door shouting that they were sorry and they loved her. The pain of the incident would gradually go to the back of her mind and she'd come to the station to withdraw the complaint. If the assault was serious enough, the CPS would still prosecute. Many times though, the charges were dropped.

Giving the man a kicking was Red Watch's way of ensuring at least some justice. I realised that the officers knew what was going to happen a couple of weeks later and so were dishing out the punishment on the spot.

≈ ≈

I'd got on fairly well with all the sergeants while I was being tutored by Alan. Once I embarked upon independent patrol things changed for me though. Jed, who was the station sergeant, began to scrutinise everything I did.

I personally didn't rate Jed at all as a sergeant and neither did most of Red Watch judging by the comments they made about him. While I saw other watch sergeants go out on patrol so they could help out if needed or do what they were paid to do which was 'supervise', Jed never did. He'd spend the entire eight hours walking around the station chatting to people, filling in paperwork, drinking tea with the cell block sergeant or control room sergeant.

Jed's main project was the duties rota which is the sheet containing the listings of who's working on which car and who's on foot patrol. This was a major ongoing task for Jed and he used to pretend that it was a constant headache for him. He'd complain to whoever would listen saying, 'I have these damn duties to finish, there isn't enough time in the day.' The joke was that it was almost always the same people in the same cars, so apart from the odd holiday it was the same sheet every day. Silly twat. I did the duties when I was an acting sergeant and then a full sergeant and it must've taken me five minutes.

Jed had been promoted to a position of incompetence from a very quiet station out in the countryside somewhere. The problem with coming from a very quiet station is that you don't get the breadth of experience and when you get stationed at a busy area you can get lost on what to do and how to do it. Jed was well and truly lost. Give him any more than one task to do at a time and he'd stand there in complete confusion.

As with all bullies, Jed singled out one or two individuals for special attention. Since I was young, naive and inexperienced I seemed to fit the bill perfectly. Once I'd finished with Alan being tutored I was out on independent patrol and an easy target for Jed.

The bullying consisted of Jed picking to pieces any piece of paperwork I submitted. He'd pick the tiniest of faults and make sure there were other people in the sergeants' office to hear what he was saying. Jed would tear up the paperwork or put pen lines through it and make me do it all again from scratch, even for the tiniest mistakes. He'd also insist on giving me every crap job that came up. I watched to see if the other probationers were getting the same treatment but they were not. Jed did go on to target a couple of others later on who joined a few months after me.

I used to dread leaving the station on foot patrol after briefing because every time I got to the bottom of Little Park Street which was about five minutes' walk away Jed would call up on the radio asking for my presence in the sergeants' office. My heart would sink as I turned around and walked back in. When I got there he'd pick my paperwork apart and tell me to do it again.

I used to dread it. Why not leave me alone until I'd at least been on patrol for a while in town? There was just no need to keep calling me in constantly. Alan had seen what was happening and was furious but there wasn't much he could do. There was no grievance procedure then, and even if there was it wouldn't get me anywhere.

One example of Jed's bullying was during a particularly severe winter, of 1991. Thick snow grounded all the police cars, they couldn't drive in it because it was just less than three feet high all round Coventry. People were phoning for ambulances but there was no way to reach them. Eventually, the territorial army was deployed to act as ambulances. The problem was, by the time they'd got to the emergency which was about five hours later, the casualty was dead. We had to leave them where they were and go on to the next casualty.

For some reason, the powers that be had decided that the TA would need some sort of radio communication provided by the police. Rather than equip them with police radios it was decided that I'd have to sit in the back of the army lorry and relay any messages to them. If the truck got stuck, I was to get out of the back and dig out the snow so they could continue. Looking back now, I should've told them that I wasn't there to dig lorries out of the snow. Jed decided I was the man for that job. I spent the entire watch digging out snow and visiting corpse after corpse.

It never stopped there. The next day the snow had still not cleared. I was sent out by Jed into almost three-feet deep snow-drifts on foot patrol in the city centre. It was literally almost impossible to walk in it and all the shops were closed since people couldn't get to work. I only managed to make it to work because I lived a short distance away and could walk in.

I partnered up with Larry for safety and we walked around the city centre not seeing a soul. We were making fresh tracks in the snow wherever we went. We did have one moment of excitement when we found a butcher's shop in town had been broken into and somebody had stolen meat (of all things). The silly arse had left tracks in the snow leading all the way back to his house. The police dog led us right to his front door by following either the smell of the burglar, his footprints, or the smell of meat. He looked completely stunned when we knocked on his door. What a brainiac.

I'll come back to my point in a moment but another time the snow helped leave evidence at the scene of a crime. There'd been a stabbing outside a social club in Wood End and the offender had left bloody footprints at the scene. We called the scenes of crime officer (SOCO) who took some brilliant photos of the footprints with blood inside them.

Footprints are like fingerprints because we all wear out our shoes in a unique way which can be matched to the shoes when we recover them. The only problem was that when the sun came up the snow melted the evidence away. When the SOCO got back to the station he realised to his horror that he'd forgotten to load film into the camera. We never had a single photograph to use as evidence. CSI Miami or what!

So Larry and I finished our patrol 'round the city centre. When we got back for breakfast we were drenched through and freezing cold. I could hardly feel my fingers and my toes had gone numb. We stood there shivering in the canteen queuing up for a cup of tea to get us warm. Jed walked into the canteen. He was nice and toasty because he'd been sitting in the office all morning working on the duties like a real trooper. He was just wearing his shirt since the central heating in the station kept him warm.

He took Larry and me to one side and said, 'I don't want to see you both walking through town together after refs. You can cover more ground if you split up.' He walked off to get his sausage sandwich. Larry and I looked at each other in disbelief. If one of us should fall over we wouldn't be found until the snow thawed. What an absolute bastard.

We had our breakfast and walked out of the station in opposite directions. We met up around the corner and stayed together for the rest of the watch. There was no danger of Jed finding us in town since he never left the station.

I lost count how many times I'd come in for my break during night shift to find Jed and the other sergeants sitting in the office playing Trivial Pursuits. It wasn't just for an hour, because if you've ever played you'll know it can take about three or more hours to finish a game. Those lazy gits were sitting there getting paid good money to play games while the rest of the watch were being run ragged and I was freezing walking around town.

I almost snapped once when I was helping Jed out as a striker in the cell block. I heard one of the sergeants phone him to ask what numbers to put in my yearly performance review. In about 20 different areas you rate yourself from 1 to 5, with 1 being excellent and 5 being disgraceful. If you get 4 or below you've to undergo monthly reviews to get you up to scratch or they begin discipline proceedings against you.

Most people didn't want to look too bad or too good so they stuck to 3s with a few 2s here and there. I was a hard worker and by this time knew my job well for my level of service so I gave myself a few 1s, some 2s and maybe one or two 3s. I could hear Jed listening to the areas and giving me scores of a few 2s and 3s.

I was really angry. This was a man who never ever left the police station. He'd never seen me at an incident on the streets because he always spent his time at the station walking about doing his 'duties' and drinking tea. He was a disgrace, yet the one deciding how my personal record was going to look. My record was very important to me because it forms the basis of any applications for advancement or specialisation.

Things weren't always bad though, there were other probationers as well for people like Jed to persecute. There was also the odd non-conformist PC who the watch supervision would attack whenever possible. One such person was Steve Jaspal. Steve was part of a family of Coventry business people who were doing very well in several areas. They were all running successful companies and very nice people to boot.

Heaven knows why Steve joined the police. Maybe he just wanted to have a laugh or it was something he'd always wanted to do to see what it was like. Either way, the police was like a hobby to Steve and he never took it seriously. He was always running around the station telling funny stories, avoiding shit jobs or playing practical jokes on people or dropping stink bombs in the briefing room. He'd hide your kit if you left it lying around, or if your locker was left unlocked while you went on holiday Steve would deposit a large, smelly fish in there and cry laughing when you opened it a week later and retched at the smell.

Steve was a great laugh and we were paired together to be on foot patrol in Stoke Aldermoor for a while. Stoke Aldermoor is about an hour's walk from the police station. When we asked Jed if we could get a lift out there to spend more time patrolling, he laughed at us and said no way, we could raise our presence by being seen walking to the area by the public.

The thing was that the walk to the Aldermoor took an hour and it was up a busy main road which was only used by motorists on the way to work. It wouldn't have made a sod of difference to them at all. Also, a large number of the sort of people we'd be dealing with never got up before about 1 in the afternoon because they were on the dole. The only day they did get up was on a Thursday when the giro came and they could cash it in.

I was used to complying with instructions but Steve was what you could call more 'flexible' with his behaviour. He tended to do his own thing, much to the chagrin of the sergeants. I'm sure that being in the police was something Steve did to pass the time of day.

One early shift, Steve and I began to walk out towards Stoke Aldermoor. It seemed a waste of time to Steve and me. It was 6:20 a.m. and would take an hour to get there during which nobody would see us. Once we got there we'd have to turn around and walk back to work to get there in time for our allocated refreshment break (refs).

Steve had a better idea though. We began walking towards the Aldermoor but after about 10 minutes we were walking past a row of houses in Binley Road. We could smell the aroma of freshly-cooking bacon wafting out of the window of a large house. Our mouths were watering at the thought of eating a nice cooked breakfast. 'Fuck this,' said Steve nudging me in the ribs with his elbow, 'lets go and knock on the door.' I was horrified. We couldn't just bang on a stranger's door and demand that they made us a fry-up. I was also worried about getting caught by the sergeants. Silly really, because it would've taken a nuclear bomb to dislodge Jed from the station.

Steve had more cheek than an elephant's arse though, he banged on the door and a young woman answered it. 'Any chance of a cup of tea, love?' grinned Steve. I just stood there mortified. 'Of course, you can,' smiled the lady as if it was nothing out of the ordinary, 'c'mon in.' We walked in and it transpired to be an old people's home, what a bonus.

Steve and I sat in the living room. The old people were sitting there watching GMTV but most of them were completely out of it. I'm not sure if they had any sort of dementia but they just sat transfixed at the TV. I didn't think GMTV was that good myself. One man just sat there with his tongue poking in and out. Steve sat next to him poking his tongue in and out as well. It was a nasty thing to do but I laughed so hard a little bit of wee came out.

Steve and I sat there next to the warm fire drinking tea and grinning at each other. We drank two nice hot cups of tea and ate a slap-up breakfast. After about an hour we wandered back to the station laughing all the way. It was the first time I'd done something I shouldn't have in the police. You could say we were lazy but what on earth was the point of walking for an hour down the dual carriageway to get to Stoke Aldermoor in time to turn around and walk back again? I'd been given the Aldermoor to walk around as part of Jed's bullying process and so had Steve, so sod 'em.

Another time I was on patrol on late shift with Steve a few weeks later in the city centre. We were walking up Fairfax Street towards Jordan Well when a Panda car from another station passed us. We waved at the driver as he passed us but neither of us recognised him. As we got to the top of Fairfax Street we could see that he'd parked at the top outside a pub. 'Let's see if he's locked the car up,' said Steve and he hurried his pace up excited at the prospect of 'spinning' somebody from another station.

When we got there it was a bonus. He'd left his car unlocked which was a very silly thing to do in the city centre. Anybody could just walk up to your car and steal documents or equipment and you'd be in trouble. Steve got in and turned everything on, the wipers, fog lights, heater to max, twisted the back rest so the driver's seat was horizontal and put the car into reverse gear.

When the PC got back he'd see that it'd been sabotaged and when he turned the key the wipers, lights and blower would come on and when he turned the ignition the car would lurch backwards. It may sound juvenile and I'd have to agree but to us it was hilarious and the officer wouldn't be able to say anything because he was supposed to lock the car.

We ran down the road and hid behind a wall laughing like a pair of kids waiting for him to come out. A few minutes later he did – but it wasn't good news for us. 'Fuck sake,' gasped Steve, 'he's an inspector.' We'd sabotaged an inspector's car from Stony Stanton Road police station. Now we were in the shit.

We were no longer laughing; well OK, we were still laughing but not as hard. He stood there looking at his car scratching his head and then looked around but we were well hidden. He spent a few minutes fixing his car back to normal. He started the engine and the car lurched violently backwards which probably scared the shit out of him. He drove off and when we felt it was safe we emerged from the wall and resumed our foot patrol, ever eager to keep the streets safe from harm.

A few minutes later we clocked the same car coming down the road and we darted behind another wall. The inspector was on the prowl for us now. It was a hunt and we were the prey (sounds like the strap line from a bad movie, I know). We managed to dodge him for about half an hour but he finally caught us out in the open and pulled up to us. He opened his car window and called us over. 'There's no need to do that,' he said in a very serious tone. Steve and I stood there like two naughty schoolboys who'd been caught cheating on a test. He then drove off. Not much he could say to be honest because it was neglectful for him to leave his car unlocked when it was full of paperwork.

I dealt with a few other incidents with Steve which were always fun. Steve came from a large family which owned an IT company. Whenever we went to a job Steve would end up selling them a computer. Once, we went to a family domestic in a place referred to as Legoland which is a rabbit warren of houses in Hillfields. The bricks used to build the houses and dividing walls make it appear that they're made from Lego.

A father and his son (who lived next door) had polished off a few too many pints one Saturday afternoon. The son who was about 25 went back to his mum and dad's house and had a fight over something trivial. The dad had got out a knife and slashed his son's hand open. It may sound terrible to you, but this was an almost daily activity to us, dealing with dysfunctional families whose emotional issues are released after a few beers. All par for the course, as they say.

I went there with Steve. The son's hand was cut wide open and bleeding profusely. It looked like a couple of tendons had been severed. He needed to go to hospital and the father needed arresting for wounding, but that wasn't on Steve's agenda.

There's an unofficial process in the police known as batting jobs which is based upon cricket. The controller throws a shit job at you by sending you to an incident and you try to wriggle out of dealing with it by batting it away. The worse the job, the higher the score you get, and if it's a really shit job and you managed to bat it you score a six. People would listen to you get the job on the radio and if you later called in on the radio and reported that there were no complaints and no arrests, somebody would shout on the air, 'And it's over the border.'

I was very young in service so I just let Steve take over and watched. Steve calmed everybody down and talked the son into not complaining. After a few minutes everybody was hugging and crying. Steve then sat them all down and pointed out that all of this could've been prevented if they only had a PC at home. Steve sold them a nice one from his family's shop and somehow managed to get the job closed off as a family domestic dispute with no complaints! Steve had a reputation of being able to sell fridges to the Eskimos.

✤

Although I did see a lot of violence perpetrated against and by the police one has to remember that these were just more memorable because they were the moments of most excitement. The vast majority of Red Watch and the police officers I worked with were very peaceful and wonderful people. They did a very hard job the best they could under very difficult circumstances.

Some police officers were fighters, but there was the occasional poet and lover as well. One of the lovers was Callum. Callum had about two years' service and was just out of his probation. He was a Panda car driver who covered any car that was short but mostly worked in Hillfields on MM3.

Callum was a real pretty boy. His police uniform was carefully ironed and his shirts starched and pressed, his turnout always impeccable. He had his teeth whitened long before it was common to do so. He trained at the gym most days so he was muscular, with a slim waist. His hair was always gelled very neatly and he hated to wear his police hat because it created a ring around his hairline. Callum had a well-trimmed goatee, deep blue eyes, swarthy complexion and at 6′ and 22 years old he turned the ladies' heads. I wouldn't go as far as to say he loved himself, but he was very confident around the ladies and had already slept with several of the policewomen at training centre and at Little Park Street station.

I was posted to work with Callum on one set of lates (2 p.m. to 10 p.m.). The duty roster always generated a lot of interest in the police. You'd always want to know who you were working with for the following weeks. Like any team, there were some people who were your favourites to work with, and then some you didn't mind, and then at the bottom were the ones you fucking hated working with such as Zane and Red. If you saw that you were working with somebody you didn't like the next week it would ruin your mood in advance.

When one of the other watch members found out that I was working with Callum he came over to me and was already laughing. He said, 'I see you're working with cat pee this week.' I was a bit bemused by this comment. 'Why do you call him cat pee?' I asked, secretly not really wanting to know the answer. 'Because he'll shag anything,' he said, laughing even harder as he walked off.

I did like Callum as a person and a police officer. He was very keen to volunteer for jobs on the radio, very thorough and was a good teacher taking the time to explain why we did certain things and how to get the paperwork past the sergeants (which proved to be a big challenge to me). Best of all, he was a great laugh and had an easygoing attitude to the job.

At about 5 p.m. one day we were on patrol in Hillfields in the Panda car when Callum said, 'I have a special friend who lives just 'round the corner from here. Let's pay her a visit.' I didn't know what he meant by 'special friend' but I just replied, 'Sure, that sounds nice.' We pulled up to a house in a side street and knocked on the door. The door was answered by an attractive young lady who was about 19. 'Hi, Callum,' she said, 'who's your handsome friend?' I began to blush. Her name was Sam. She was a student at Coventry University and lived in a house with four other girls.

Sam was only about 5 feet, had long blonde hair, deep blue eyes, soft pale peachy skin and a fantastic figure. She was a stunner. She led us into the house through the hallway and into the lounge where four other girls were sitting watching *Blockbusters* on TV. They all turned around to look at who'd come in and shouted in unison, 'Hi, Callum!' They all looked pleased to see him there.

Callum turned and said to me, 'Grab a seat with the girls, Paul. Sam and I have to chat about something,' he gave me a wink and went upstairs with Sam. Two of the girls shuffled apart and I sat down between them while another got up and made me a cup of tea. Callum and Sam went upstairs which I thought was a bit strange.

There were a few polite questions about how long I'd been in the police but pretty soon everybody was engrossed in *Blockbusters* so we sat and watched it. I looked around and it was actually very tidy for a students' house. The carpet had been hoovered, the shelves were dust-free, the sofa and chairs nice and clean and there was a nice ambience to the house. You could tell that there were no men living there.

There was the faint smell of cannabis but since every student house I've ever been in had that smell I just ignored it. Besides, I don't think Callum would've taken kindly to me searching his special friend's house. They burned cannabis for us at police training centre so we recognised the smell if we ever came across it again. It's such a pungent smell that it's hard to mask it.

A few minutes into *Blockbusters* I began to hear a banging noise from upstairs. It was a rhythmic bang like a bed hitting the wall. I thought to myself, 'Dear God no, please don't let him be shagging upstairs.' I began to hear moans and groans and shortly afterwards I could hear Sam screaming like a monkey. Callum was up there shagging the arse off a student while I was sitting downstairs watching TV.

I looked at the girls' faces in the room and they never batted an eyelid. It was either that they couldn't hear her screaming (unlikely), or that this was such a common event that it seemed normal enough to ignore it. I sat there on the sofa dying, just hoping he'd finish up so we could leave. Unfortunately, Callum was a bit of a stud muffin so he was up there for about another 30 minutes.

'Do you want some more tea?' one of the girls asked politely. 'No thanks,' I smiled back. And I felt like saying, 'And if you could shout up to my mate to hurry up that would be lovely,' but I just sat there politely. I was just sitting there hoping that we weren't called to attend an urgent job.

Callum eventually emerged from upstairs. His face was flushed from 45 minutes of hard shagging. He chirped, 'Time we were off, Paul,' so I got up and said goodbye and left with him. By this time I wanted to stay a bit longer because the *Chuckle Brothers* had come on and I quite liked them.

We drove off up the road in silence and resumed our patrol of Hillfields as if nothing had happened. After about 10 minutes the silence was broken by Callum. 'Sam's a great girl, Paul. I pop over now and again. It's a no-strings thing.' I just smiled back, 'No problem,' I chuckled as I spoke. 'She's really flexible mate, I got her in the full nelson and she loved it.' I sat there wondering what the hell that meant. Callum could clearly see I didn't know but didn't offer any more information, just sat there grinning away at me waiting for the golden question. 'Go on, then' I laughed, 'the suspense is killing me.' By this time Callum was laughing out loud and I with him.

As we drove up past the blocks of flats in Victoria Street in Hillfields Callum explained, 'Well, when you're going at it, you reach your arm down and hook her leg up with your arm so it's bent. The joint in the middle of your arm catches the back of her knee. Then you grab her upper arm at the same side with your hand. Her calves aren't quite up on your shoulders but are almost that high. *That* is the half nelson.' I began to laugh harder. 'If that goes down well, you hook her other leg with your other arm so she's pinned to the bed with both her legs hooked under your arms so her feet are up by your shoulders. Then you go hammer and tongs for as long as you can last.'

I was laughing away as I pictured it. 'No, seriously, Paul,' Callum chuckled, 'they love it, women love to be pinned down during sex, it reminds them of years ago when the cavemen used to throw them onto the floor and have their way with them.' I looked over and said 'Sure thing, Callum,' making a mental note to try it when I had a girlfriend. I got the impression that Callum knew a lot about women and sex and I wanted to find out a bit more without looking as if I knew practically nothing.

Callum was enjoying the ego trip now so he continued, 'You know, when you give a woman such a tremendous orgasm that she just lies on the bed quivering, unable to speak for ages?' 'Yeah,' I lied, 'I love that.' I was 20 and painfully shy around women.

It wasn't until a couple of years later that I got a long-term girlfriend. After a while I got up the confidence to try the half nelson with her. As we were making love I hooked her first leg with my arm so it was almost over my shoulder and she began to cry out and moan with pleasure. I pulled her second leg over and she was almost screaming the roof down. I went hammer and tongs for as long as I could and eventually her whole body began to shake as she had a huge orgasm.

The fact that her legs were up in the air must've meant that she lost a bit of muscle control downstairs though, because as she came she let out the loudest and most ferocious fart I've ever heard a woman let rip. It almost blew my bollocks off, I could feel the hot wind rushing past them. It could've spoiled the moment, but I was the perfect gentleman and pretended not to hear it although it was loud enough to scare the neighbours. Afterwards, I had to reach down and check that my nuts were still there and there was no cac on them though.

Callum broke my thoughts by saying, 'I seem to be in demand because I give a guaranteed orgasm.' I thought he was just boasting now. 'How can you guarantee that?' I asked incredulously. 'Well, if I'm chatting a girl up I tell her that I guarantee she'll have an orgasm by the third time we sleep together, but usually sooner.' I was wondering if that came with a money back guarantee.

We were onto Callum's second-most favourite subject now – we'll come to his first favourite later. 'It's pretty easy, actually,' he insisted, 'I can tell you exactly what to do if you like.' I sat there nodding away, 'Well, first....' The police radio interrupted us, 'Mike Mike 3, can you please make a violent shoplifter at Marks and Spencers in town?' Bastard radio. We sped off into town and the conversation was to be continued. I never admitted my inexperience with women to Callum but spent a lot of the week grilling him about his methods and experiences and was secretly grateful for the long list of books about sex he recommended I read.

The sex education I received at school was pathetic. Our biology teacher went sick so a temp came in for the day. He drew pictures of sperms on the board and eggs and then played an old crackly 10-minute movie on the projector with kids sitting in the back of a bus joking about how one of them had 'done it' the other night. I was baffled. The nuns countered this by playing an abortion video where you saw the foetus having its arms and legs sucked off by a mini-hoover. We all sat there traumatised.

◈ ◈

It can be a very dehumanising experience to be a police officer at times and you can often find yourself having to do things that you never imagined you would. I'm not just talking about dealing with rotting corpses, but just how you've to interact with other people.

An example of this is strip-searching people. A police officer has a power to strip-search a person if they have reasonable cause to believe that they're carrying drugs or prohibited articles on their person. Prohibited articles include firearms and certain other weapons. Even if you're not under arrest, this power exists although most strip-searches are of people who're under arrest and who're known to hide drugs on their person or weapons.

Colin was a well-known Coventrian drug addict. He'd been on heroin for several years and I don't think he had many years left to live. When you inject heroin every day you've to use a needle which, of course, is obvious. What may not be so obvious is that if you do this repeatedly, your veins collapse (it's called thrombosis) so you can no longer inject into them. You've to start using the veins in your neck and then legs.

As they all collapse a drug addict will begin to inject into anywhere they can including their feet, between the toes, hands, armpits and in the later stages their eye socket and even their penis. I've seen it all. I can't tell you how many people I dealt with who were at this stage. All dignity is lost. As we used to walk our drug addict prisoners across the backyard and into the police cells many of them would kneel down on the tarmac and pick up dog-ends of cigarettes. They'd put them in their pocket and try to beg some rizla paper in the cells so that they could make a cigarette out of the spare bits of tobacco left in the dog-ends. Now that is somebody who's desperate for a fag.

Colin was a prolific shoplifter in Coventry. If you saw him you'd easily mistake him for a walking corpse. Although he was about 5' 10" he weighed about nine stone. His face was completely sunken in and he never shaved so he had a full beard but his cheekbones still stuck out as if he'd just come out of a prisoner of war camp.

Colin really did look like a walking corpse, his gums having receded to the point were his teeth had started to fall out because there was nothing left to hold them in place. He wore the same dirty brown trousers and green shirt for months on end. The trousers were held up with a thin red belt he'd found but because there was no buckle on it he had to tie a knot in it. Colin had no socks so he wore an oversized pair of black shoes he'd stolen from somebody in the hostel he slept at. Colin stank of something that had died a long time ago.

You can usually spot a drug addict just by the way they look. They're often very pale or the same colour as somebody with serious kidney problems, a sort of sickly light orange. They have sores on their face and around their mouths and their eyes bulge slightly. They have long since stopped caring about how they look so are usually unwashed and have been wearing the same set of clothes (including underwear) for several months. The classic druggie is usually alone because they've repeatedly stolen from their friends and family and are no longer welcome in their homes. They've sold everything they ever owned and so only have the clothes on their back and a mattress to sleep on left.

Colin pretty much fitted this description to a tee. His only way of generating income was to steal so he could sell what he'd stolen to buy drugs. That was Colin's only purpose in life now – to score. It was the first thing he thought about when he woke up in the morning as he put his clothes on and went out of the door. He fell asleep at night thinking about how he was going to score the next day.

What Colin needed to do was fulfil his part in the supply chain of criminal activity. He stole, he passed the goods to the handler (also known as a fence) and the handler then sold the goods to the buyer who is generally some member of the public who's usually knowingly buying stolen goods. You can usually tell they're stolen because of who's selling them to you (their background), the price (well under market value), or the location (the pub or at your front door).

If you want to know what one of the worst types of criminals in the UK is, it's the handler of stolen goods, that person many people go to or ask if they want a CD player or a nice laptop. The handler can get you almost anything you ask for but for some crazy reason his behaviour is condoned and even usually applauded. Arthur Daley type characters are criminals who make money from buying things stolen from your home, or at least the shops.

The handler is almost revered and his activities are laughed off as people call him or her 'a bit dodgy' or give him a cute name like 'Mick the Nick'. If you took the handler out of the equation then the burglars, car thieves and druggies would've nobody to go to. So the next time you get offered something by a bloke down the pub or somebody comes to your door offering you something cheap tell them to fuck off. That's unless you don't mind your car being broken into, your house being burgled or paying over the odds at the supermarket to cover the multimillion pounds worth of thefts they have to cover every year. It's all down to the laws of supply and demand. If people didn't want to buy stolen goods then the demand would dry up almost overnight. It may sound naive but it all starts with you.

I had Colin pointed out to me during one of my first weeks of patrol. By law you're not allowed to search a person because they have previous convictions, but this seems insane to me. That should be *the very reason* you use to search a person. If they're known to be an active thief and are walking past your house, would you rather the police drive past them and do nothing because they're powerless, or to grab them by the ankles and shake them upside down to see what falls out their pockets? Civil rights in the UK are very much weighted in favour of the active criminal at the moment, I'm afraid.

Of course, the police stop and search active criminals. We just have to say something like, 'They were acting furtively,' or 'As they saw us they tucked something into their pockets' which sounds better than 'He's a known thieving shit so I gave him a quick spin on the off-chance that he was carrying and I struck gold.'

Colin was usually either about to commit a crime, in the process of committing a crime, or wanted for committing a crime. He, like most other late-stage addicts was very overt. He didn't have time to 'case a joint' or draw up a plan. He'd walk into Dixons or any such place, grab something off the shelves and walk out with it. The staff weren't going to stop him for four pounds an hour, and who wants to touch an addict anyway?

I was out with Callum one fine sunny afternoon when we heard on the radio that Colin was spotted in town and was wanted for three thefts. A few minutes later we saw him walking down Ironmonger Row and we collared him. It was horrible going near Colin because he was HIV positive. He had shared needles at some point with the wrong person and now had the virus. We put Colin in handcuffs (very carefully) and took him to the cell block. The first thing we had to do was ask him to turn his pockets out. There are so many things they never teach you to do during police training and one of them is how to safely search a prisoner. It is learned by watching other police officers and through common sense.

You never ever put your hands into a druggie's pockets. Many police officers have done this and pricked themselves on hypodermic syringes. You get them to take whatever is in them out and then turn them inside out. You then have to get them to take their shoes and socks off and pull the insoles out. Druggies will almost always have some brown (heroin) tucked away in their shoes or up their arse in case they need to score in a police cell.

Callum said that we had to take Colin into the doctor's room for a strip-search. When I was young in service I didn't know what that actually meant apart from taking some clothing off. Colin obviously did. We went into the doctor's room and Colin took off his shirt. His ribcage looked like a xylophone, you could've taken two sticks and played a tune on his ribs they stuck out so much. As soon as his shirt was off the smell of body odour filled the room. He obviously hadn't washed for weeks and the smell of stale sweat was pungent. He pulled his trousers down and they were covered in stains and were ripped in several places.

Next, he pulled down his white Y-fronts. Well, I say 'white' but they'd long since turned into a sort of piss-stained dirty cream colour. As they dropped to the floor I looked at them and began to feel sick. He had either had a terminal case of dysentery or shit himself at some point. They were covered in dried shit from front to back and the gusset looked like a monkey's miscarriage.

Colin turned 'round, bent over and pulled his arse cheeks apart. He had piles like a bunch of grapes, his anus was caked in shit and heaven knows what else. Colin had been to prison several times and I'm not sure if his ring-piece had seen any action while he was there. Dried pieces of cac, tagnuts and winnets hung off his arse-hairs like conkers dangling on a string. The aroma of fresh shit began to tickle my nose and I felt myself gag. 'This isn't what I joined the police for,' I thought, 'to stand in a room staring at a tramp's ring-piece.'

We didn't find any drugs on or in Colin but I couldn't help but think about the whole situation. Colin had clearly lost all his self-respect and dignity quite some time ago. I was 20 years old and being paid to look at people's anuses.

I don't know what happened to Colin in the end. I heard he went to prison a few more times and eventually died alone in a squat somewhere. Nobody missed him.

❧ ❧

Areas covered by all police stations are divided up into beats. Every Panda car will have a number of beats it is designated to patrol and also its own call sign for the radio. At Little Park Street Mike Mike 1 (MM1) covered the city centre which is all contained inside the ring road. MM2 covered Radford and Coundon, MM3 covered Hillfields, MM4 covered Binley and Stoke Aldermoor, MM5 covered The Butts and Cheylesmore. MM6 was a floating car sometimes used for covering shortfalls or for tutoring. Each of the three Zulus covered two of the Panda areas.

One of the best and worst areas to work in was Stoke Aldermoor which is a very poor area of Coventry. Many years before it had been a lovely place to live and generally contained working families and elderly people. Coventry City Council designated it as an area to locate low-income housing for unemployed people. A few flats were built and cheap council houses. As the unemployed people moved in, the burglary rate went through the roof and the state of the neighbourhood went downhill.

MM4 was the Panda covering Stoke Aldermoor and it was probably the worst car to be on. Not because it was a rough area, but because of the sort of jobs you'd typically be sent to. It was often accusations of people stealing each others' dole cheques or cheap video players. Sons stealing from their mums or mates (to pay for drugs), serving warrants on people for non-payment of fines or people's dogs running around the streets biting people. Just real pain-in-the-arse jobs that took an age to deal with and never usually went anywhere.

When I was still being tutored, Alan and I were designated to work MM4 for a week just for a bit of a change from Cheylesmore. It's better to work in busier areas when you're training so you get more experience of different types of jobs. One afternoon we were driving past the Stag pub in the Aldermoor. We could see a group of five ne'r-do-wells standing outside drinking. It was about 2 p.m. on a weekday, so clearly they were not working for a living but instead, investing their hard-earned dole money in the pub. They'd spent the afternoon drinking and sniffing coke and were pretty much out of it. As we drove past, we got the usual hail of verbal abuse – but one of them threw a bottle at our car. It bounced off the bonnet of our Panda car and smashed onto the road.

The gang stood at the pub entrance laughing and joking. The beer and drugs had made them feel invincible, and with five of them standing together they felt very brave. They stood there making wanking gestures and spitting in our direction. They were all wearing jeans and Ben Sherman shirts which were all the rage then. Shirts used to be tucked in but the trend had changed to leaving them hanging out. It serves the purpose to hide men's beer guts and works to some extent.

Their moment of glory was to be short-lived. I didn't know what our reaction was going to be, but I sensed that Alan wasn't going to let this pass. He called the incident in on the radio and calmly explained the situation and asked for some help.

The thing about being a police officer is that you're representing the entire police force. If you let somebody take advantage of you, they'll think it's acceptable behaviour. Next time, instead of throwing a bottle it'll be a brick or they'll gob in your face. Where do you draw the line?

Alan didn't bat an eyelid. He just turned the car 'round and headed towards the crowd which was still standing outside swearing at us. Alan was not stupid and kept a safe distance, clenching his teeth together he said to me, 'Get yourself ready, Paul. We're going to be fighting in a bit.' Alan always gave me the nod when possible to let me know when we were going to be scrapping. He wasn't much of a fighter but would always get stuck in if there was a scrap. While he was talking to me I identified the three main protagonists who still stood outside the pub giving us the finger and throwing more bottles at us. They were clearly very drunk and thought they could take on the world.

There'd been some sporadic rioting in Coventry at the time and every community in the rough parts there thought they'd join in and throw their own petrol bombs. It was a way of bringing the community together, I think. Nothing like a bit of community spirit. High on the wave of the riots the three men egged each other on while their friends slipped back into the pub. They knew there could be only one way for this to end – and they clearly didn't fancy it for themselves.

The rest of Red Watch rushed to our location. It was very reassuring to see so many Pandas from the watch turn up with wheels spinning. Even two traffic cars attended, which was brilliant. Upon the arrival of 10 police cars, logic had finally filtered into the men's brains and they skulked back into the perceived safety of the pub. Alan and I had been watching them carefully because we knew we were going to be walking into the pub to fish them out shortly and we wanted to be sure we had the right men (it would be a shame to batter the wrong blokes).

The men's solace was short-lived. We all drove 50 yards to the pub car park. The Stag was a grotty place, but then the clientele was equally grotty. Red Watch calmly walked into the pub en masse. The bar was just a plain square room, chairs and tables around the sides, toilets and dart board in the corner. There was the familiar pub smell of stale beer and 20 years' worth of stale fag smoke penetrated our nostrils. There were about 30 men of all ages inside and the place was dead quiet apart from a tune playing on the juke box, I think it was 'And now, the end is near.' You find out who your mates are when you're in big trouble, and these guys seemed to have no mates left wanting to back them up.

We then identified the three offenders. They were sitting very meekly in a corner of the pub sipping their pints of beer quietly. They couldn't have looked more innocent if they'd tried. You'd never have known that they'd just been swearing and spitting at us and throwing bottles.

As the youngest in service there it was down to me to give them the bad news. Alan had told me to tell them that they were under arrest for violent disorder. We slowly and calmly moved the tables and chairs away from between them and us. We knew that we'd be needing more space to effect the arrest (and, of course, for the laying on of hands).

I looked down at the main protagonist sitting innocently looking up at me as if butter wouldn't melt in his mouth. When you go to arrest a person after the act they always manage to adopt this false look of surprise on their face. It's as if they think we're going to look at them and think, 'Oh no, this guy just looks so honest that he couldn't possibly have committed a crime.'

It seemed that the fight had gone out of them and they no longer wanted us to play with them. I told him and his mates sitting next to him that they were all under arrest for violent disorder and then we had the laying on of hands. We grabbed them and threw them to the ground. They were screaming that they hadn't done anything wrong. I'd have had more respect if they'd owned up or at least apologised.

These men who thought they could take on the entire West Midlands Police Force were now lying on the ground being unceremoniously handcuffed and manhandled by Red Watch. As we bundled the main offender into the back of our car he let out a loud fart which immediately became very wet and took on an altogether different sound. He was literally shitting into his pants in the back of our car.

There's nothing worse than having to sit in the back of a police car with a man who has shat in his pants. In fact, it happened a few times while I was in the police. We had to drive all the way to the police station with the windows open.

They were all interviewed the next day by the CID because violent disorder is a very serious offence and is indictable, which means you've to go to Crown Court to be tried for it. They were eventually charged with affray and were all given suspended sentences.

Happy Birthday to Me – 5 June 1972

My mum and Jeff have taken Cheryl and me to a country called Scotchland for a holiday. We drive a long way in the car and mum points out cows and sheep to me as we drive along the roads. We get to Scotchland very late at night, and our car can't get up the hill which leads to my aunty's house. It gets halfway up the hill and then rolls backwards; Jeff drives it up again and again but we can't get up the hill. Cheryl and I are laughing, it's so funny.

We are lying in my cousin's bed. He had a scary monster hand he puts on. It's green, has blood on it, and the fingers look like claws. When he hides 'round the corner and puts the scary hand 'round the door, Cheryl and I hide under the bedcovers. We shout at him to go away.

I'm rolling down a big, grassy hill; Jeff is holding me tight in his arms. I'm laughing all the way down, I want the hill to never stop. We're going very fast but I feel safe in Jeff's arms.

I'm 2 years old.

Year 3 – Find Your Own Tree

Dawn slowly opened her eyes, blinked a few times to focus and then could clearly see a clear, deep-blue sky. She immediately felt a warm sensation of happiness inside. Dawn always felt in a better mood when the weather was nice. It reminded her of summer holidays when she was young because there'd be no school and she had weeks and weeks to play with her friends.

There were some dreamily fluffy clouds drifting past at a very leisurely pace. The lumpy piles of cloud reminded her of her nana's mashed potato which always had lashings of butter and milk in and they tasted lovely. One cloud looked like Donald Duck, and another like the first teddy bear she'd ever owned. She felt as if she could lie there forever, in a dream-like state watching the clouds go by and letting her mind wander.

Dawn felt the cool grass tickling the palms of her hands which contrasted with the warm feeling of the sun shining on her face. What a perfect day to be lying down. She began to think about her nana again, she always seemed to be in her kitchen wearing an apron and covered in flour. Her nana was a wonderful cook and would always let her help when she was making cakes on a Sunday. She'd let her mix the eggs into the flour and after they'd spooned the mixture into the cake tray she was allowed to lick the bowl. Yummy.

Dawn began to taste something funny in the back of her mouth.

∾ ∾

As my second year in the police drew to a close so did my two-year probationary period. During this two years the police can decide to dispense with your services for any number of reasons. It's like working with the constant threat of dismissal hanging over your head. All of your performance has to be tracked and evidenced in something called a personal development profile or PDP. For many probationers the PDP becomes a huge weight over their shoulders. It can be used by supervisors to criticise you for mistakes or shortcomings and can often be the start of proceedings to dismiss you for poor performance.

I'd seen a few probationers leave the service during their first two years, but very rarely was it because they weren't up to scratch. It was almost always the fact that their face didn't fit and they became a target for bullying by the sergeants.

One such guy was Stu. Stu was Welsh, so of course everyone on the watch called him Taffy or Taff. He was a former social worker from Cardiff. I thought being a social worker would be a great background for somebody to join the police because of the people skills and empathy they often have. Stu had bright red hair and a thick beard and was a few years older than me at about 25. He was quite confident and would often voice his opinion, much to the annoyace of the sergeants.

I always got on well with Stu. He seemed easygoing enough but made a couple of mistakes during his tutor period with Katie and she started moaning about him to the sergeants on the watch. All of a sudden, nobody wanted to work with Stu for some reason, and everything he did came under scrutiny.

In the novel *Treasure Island* by Robert Louis Stevenson the pirate Billy Bones is handed a piece of paper with a black spot on it. The black spot pronounces a verdict of guilt or judgement. Billy Bones is so frightened when he's given the black spot that he has a heart attack and dies. It can be the same in the police, a person is marked for whatever reason and there's nothing they can do, they're going to be leaving the police whether they like it or not.

Admittedly, Stu had made the odd mistake but nothing that bad. For example, one day he was out on Panda patrol with Katie and he did a vehicle check over the radio. Unfortunately, he got some of the phonetics wrong. He said things like 'bread' instead of 'bravo' and 'kettle' instead of 'kilo' and this of course became a running joke amongst the watch. We all started doing vehicle checks but getting the phonetics wrong. 'Mike Mike 5, a vehicle check please, registration is mango, tampon, button, three, two, seven, barbeque, over.' I had to admit it was funny and a mistake I could've easily made when I was using the radio nervously.

Rather than find evidence of things he was doing wrong they just literally bullied Stu out of the job. The reason they didn't go about evidencing everything is because that takes effort, and of course evidence of which the sergeants didn't really have any apart from the odd rookie mistake. His paperwork was always sent back, he was given every shit job going, and every mistake he made resulted in a bollocking. He eventually cracked during one bollocking and resigned.

It was a shame because I'd seen him in action. He'd never have set the world alight, but he was fairly competent and certainly far more useful than a couple of watch members such as Red. At least he could take a statement and arrest people. As horrible as this sounds though, while the sergeants were going after Stu their attention was off me or at least the heat was off a bit.

I was probably regarded as a bit of a pain in the arse by some of my supervisors because I'd always question things. I wanted to know *why* things were done a certain way or *why* it was down to the police to carry out certain tasks. Take lost dogs, for example. We'd accept them at the police station and keep them in the kennels at the back for a couple of days and look after them and feed them. What on earth did that have to do with anything?

Why, when we did a court file did we have to photocopy form X three times and stick it in positions four, seven and nine in the case papers? Why, when a bank alarm went off did we all race to the scene and run into the bank? What if somebody was actually in there with a shotgun? Shouldn't we stay outside until the controller had phoned the bank to ask if it was all clear? I began to wonder if I was the only one thinking about these things. Everyone else seemed to crack on without asking any questions.

A few years after leaving the police I went on a business course and took a personality test. I came out as an entrepreneur, which means I hate to follow procedures, I question accepted ways of doing things, I don't like being told what to do, don't like to go into great details and don't like to do the same thing over and over. No wonder I wasn't happy in the police sometimes, which requires you do exactly all those things without question.

There weren't actually standard operating procedures (SOPs) for many of the police activities. Most of what you learned was by making mistakes and being shown by other people. Things like dealing with evidence from crimes, putting in court files, writing transcripts of interviews was all taught to you by somebody and you had to hope that they knew what they were doing.

The culture in the police is that if there's an accident, complaint or something else goes wrong the immediate reaction is to find somebody to blame. Did somebody forget to do something? Was there a lack of supervision? Did the controller forget to give you some important information? Rather than have a debrief, learn lessons and pass them into a central source of knowledge, the police usually find a scapegoat and discipline them.

For incidents like attending a burglary in progress, for example, you should do your best to make a silent approach so you don't tip off the burglar that you're on your way. We did that on Red Watch, but Yellow Watch used to drive there like lunatics with their sirens wailing. You could hear them miles off, so by the time they got there the offender had bolted.

Even learning basic things like how to search a prisoner and get them safely into the cell block was down to who showed you. Either that, or you got battered or kicked by your prisoner and worked it out the hard way. There was a force ops manual, but it was a right mess. Just a few notes about various subjects like what to do if you had to drive to another force in your Panda car or what forms you needed to put in for a forged note. In contrast, the army has SOPs for everything. It doesn't mean that they're always followed, but at least you know what you and your team are supposed to be doing in a given situation.

Another classic was attending an incident. If a lazy police officer such as Red went, he'd scribble down a few details on a crime report and submit it for the local beat officer to attend the next week to take a statement of witness from them. By that time the witness had forgotten a lot of the details, so their statement was next to useless. It should've been made part of the regulations that when you go to an incident you take as many statements as time allows.

When the letter came through telling me I was now confirmed as a police officer, the first thing I did was to burn my damn PDP in a big fire. It was full of ridiculous comments such as, 'I demonstrated the fact I am a team player by making the tea for the watch,' and 'I demonstrated awareness of paperwork when I submitted a court file for a shoplifter.' It used to drive me 'round the bend.

The second thing I did was to go on holiday. I was broke, but a couple of mates from the cadets fancied going away so we all decided to go to America for three weeks. It was a fantastic time for me. Nick, Bren and I flew to LA and we hired a car. We went to LA to visit a friend from Coventry who'd emigrated there. We also toured all over LA and then drove down to San Diego which was a bit of a hole. One of us then had the bright idea of going over the border to Mexico for one night to see what it was like.

We drove to a spaghetti restaurant for some food before driving over the border. We chatted with the waiter in the restaurant and when we told him that we were going to drive over the border to Mexico he looked a bit horrified. He strongly advised us to park on the US side and walk over and to take our watches and jewellery off as well before we went. 'Why, will some of the locals mug us?' I asked. He just laughed and said, 'No way man, the police over there will stop you and steal it if they see you wearing it.' I didn't know if he was joking, but I took my watch off anyway.

We parked next to the border and walked across a bridge where the army look after the point where you cross. The bridge went over a big river which had very little water flowing in it. It was full of bikes, cars and prams and looked more like an open sewer than a river; it absolutely stank.

I was expecting a nice little Mexican town on the other side but what we found was a shanty town. Hundreds of people were sleeping rough in the streets, children wearing rags were doing cartwheels and begging us for money. I was very ill at ease but Bren and Nick loved it. We went to a couple of bars which were literally derelict houses where somebody had put up a wooden board and was pouring tequila into glasses.

Mexican prostitutes who looked like your granny kept coming up to us offering, 'Fucky sucky five dollar.' It was absolutely dreadful and I didn't feel safe at all.

We went to a few more of these shit-hole bars and I finally persuaded Nick and Bren it was time to leave. As we headed back to the border Nick and Bren were desperate for a piss. There were no toilets where we were, people just pissed and shat on the ground. We found some shop fronts and Bren and Nick started to piss up a wall. After a few seconds I heard a click behind me and I turned around. There were six Mexican cops standing behind us. One had just cocked a machine pistol of some sort and the others were carrying shotguns and automatic pistols. They were all standing next to massive police patrol cars. We were in big trouble.

One of them spoke a little English. He said that he was going to throw us all into prison for a month. We were due to fly back to the UK in two days' time. If we were arrested I was pretty sure we'd lose our jobs, but even worse, I didn't think that Mexican prison would be like the UK. We'd probably have to eat cockroaches for breakfast before being made some big Mexican guys' bitches. No thanks.

Bren and Nick were drunk and so pretty useless as far as negotiations went. They started asking for the UK ambassador and the British Consulate but I just told them to shut up for God's sake. We had this agreement that if somebody was drunk and started to talk nonsense they'd take heed when the sober person told them to stop talking rubbish. We each wrote on a card, 'Shut up: you're drunk' and would hand the card to the person who was talking shit and they'd immediately cease and desist.

The policeman demanded 20 dollars each or we'd be arrested and thrown into prison. We had 30 dollars between us. I suppose I could've given him my 20 and 10 as a tip and told them that Nick and Bren would have to go to prison, but what sort of mate would do that? (Joke!)

I only had one card to play, and it was my police warrant card. I took it out and explained to the police officer that we were also police and that we look after police from other countries when they come to the UK. The police officer wasn't expecting this. He and his colleagues went into a huddle and began to have a heated discussion. It was either prison or them letting us go and I felt it was 50-50.

He came over to us and said we could go. We breathed a huge sigh of relief and walked out of Mexico across the border and never looked back. I promised myself never to go back to a country where the police try to mug you.

❧ ❦

There were four main night clubs in Coventry: Busters which had probably the toughest bouncers, Park Lane which was a bit posey (for Coventry, at least), The Pink Parrot, and Reflections, which was as rough as a bear's arse. What on earth possessed people to want to spend time in any of the clubs I'll never know. It cost a fortune to get in, and then you've to pay double price for drinks.

There were various crews who worked on the doors around town. Crews were hand-picked by a few leaders based upon fighting skills, rep(utation) and also which area you came from. There was some friction between different crews from areas such as Bell Green and Wood End. It was a bit like the friction between different football teams' supporters. The only reason you didn't like them was apparently because they lived in a different area than you.

In the early 1990s a brand new rave club opened in Coventry called The Edge. It was basically just a big empty building with a few different levels. It was a dreadful place, but people from all over the UK flocked there like bluebottles to a piece of dog shit. Raves were the big thing then and anyone who was anyone would go to a rave on the weekend, and if it was illegal then all the better. They only sold soft drinks there, but at a pound a can they must've been absolutely raking it in.

I didn't get it myself. Most of the raves were basically dance music being played in a farmer's old barn or an abandoned warehouse somewhere and you were charged 20 quid to get in so you could jump up and down and take E for eight hours.

A few weeks after The Edge had opened the CID began receiving information from an informant that another crew were going there en masse one night to beat up the door staff. At any given time there were about 10 doormen working there, but the posse which was going there to have a go was about 50 strong and would be armed with baseball bats.

The OSU had come over and our watch were on the vans that night. The OSU stands for operational support unit. It is basically the riot squad. Officers can work there for three years on attachment. The OSU are trained to a higher level than other officers for riot control and in searching areas. They also get involved in football matches or other operational duties such as large-scale searches or drug raids. We were all briefed by a senior CID officer that the offenders would be armed with baseball bats and other weapons. We had plainclothes spotters all around the area and we parked the vans out of sight.

All offenders were to be arrested by two police officers who'd then corroborate each other to the fact that they'd been arrested for violent disorder, which is a very serious offence under the Public Order Act.

The POA is a brilliant piece of legislation and lets the police deal with various levels of public disobedience. The lowest offence is Section 5 Threatening Behaviour; then Section 4 Intentional Harassment, Alarm or Distress; then Section 3 Affray; Section 2 is Violent Disorder; and Section 1 is Riot.

The Act lets you deal with most of the disorder that takes place over a weekend. Sections 5 and 4 usually result in a fine, Section 3 can often end with a conditional discharge, but Section 2 will usually go to Crown Court and you'll be sent to prison if found guilty. Section 1 Riot is never charged, because legally the Chief Constable is financially responsible for any damage caused during the riot.

Sure enough, at about midnight, 50 hairy-arsed Henley Green men were spotted walking down the road towards The Edge. They were carrying baseball bats, bricks and bottles so my guess was that they weren't going there for a dance. Just before they got to the front door the OSU tore around the corner from their hiding place and screamed to a halt in front of them with their van to stop them. The posse ground to a halt for a few seconds wondering what to do next, but they must've thought that this was the only van involved because they started to throw bricks and bottles at the van, which was very naughty indeed.

We suddenly emerged from behind them with our sirens wailing and tyres screeching which they weren't expecting. About 20 police officers jumped out of the vans in total. We all had round shields but just wooden pegs because Casco batons weren't used at the time. We started bashing anybody in arm's reach over the head with our pegs and the crowd ran away in all directions being chased by the police.

They were all big blokes, but I don't think they fancied being arrested for violent disorder. The police were more interested in staying together than grabbing prisoners, so after we bashed a few heads we got back into the vans. The mission was accomplished. There were about five or six arrests in total, plus a few caught by our video cameras.

Back at the station the incident room had been set up to ensure the evidence was solid and that there were at least two witnesses for every prisoner. That way we'd almost guarantee a conviction in court.

There were a few comebacks planned, but people on both sides knew detectives in the CID so we always knew what was going to happen before it happened. Clearly, the CID had a good-quality informant on the inside who had an interest in preventing any violence.

We were on lates the next week when we heard that a small crew with baseball bats was going to attack some of the Edge crew who were working that night at the Pink Parrot. Six men with baseball bats were spotted congregating in West Orchards Circulatory Road which is right next to a big shopping centre. A few Pandas and Zulus made their way there and I heard Steve Jaspal pipe up on the air asking for a lift there because he was out walking in the sticks with another PC called Ade. The controller said no for some silly reason which annoyed us all.

When we all arrived there we looked all around but couldn't see anybody. A PC called Kermit (you'll find out how he got his nickname later) was with us and had the good idea of walking up the car park a few levels to have a scope around. At the top of the car park he looked down and spotted seven men with baseball bats hiding on a balcony just above our heads.

They jumped down and ran towards us with the bats raised above their heads. The stupid bastards were going to have a go at us so apparently they didn't want to come quietly. We pulled out our pegs and got ready for a battle. Just before we clashed an ambulance came racing 'round the corner with sirens wailing and lights flashing.

The crew stopped and so did we. Nobody had been fighting yet, so who'd called an ambulance? Just then the ambulance skidded to a stop and the double back doors opened up. Steve Jaspal and Ade jumped out shouting 'Aarrgghhh' and waving their pegs in the air. They jumped into the crew who were just standing there in shock.

Steve had flagged down an ambulance and gone to the fight anyway, what a star. The men were all arrested and charged with public order offences.

❧ ❧

As my time in the force progressed I was still enjoying myself. Most jobs I went to I could deal with effectively enough and I felt a huge amount of pride because I was making a difference to people and I got a lot of satisfaction from arresting bad people and helping keep the general public safe. Things change though, and it only takes a new sergeant or inspector who's a bit of a prat to change things for the worse.

One such prat was a sergeant who was qualified to inspector. Dave Hiddle had joined the force from the British Transport Police. He'd constantly drone on about how things were 'better in the BTP' or how 'we did things in the BTP' which was a pain in the arse. We all began to wish he pissed off back to the BTP. Sgt. Hiddle had come to Red Watch as a sergeant and quickly become best mates with Sgt. Jed Leap. They were of the same ilk, meaning that they preferred to stay in the station all day long and drink tea.

There's a name in the police for people who never leave the confines of the station. We call them the 'station cat'. I think it must stem from years before when there were people who actually worked and lived at the station they were based at and actually kept pet cats there. We used to leave a saucer of milk on Sgt. Hiddle's desk and when he walked back into his office and found it he'd go ballistic. It was a pleasure to watch.

Sgt. Hiddle was 5' 10" tall with greying mousy brown hair; it was a bit of a mane of hair brushed high on his head so he looked like a mini-teddy boy. He wore a thick bushy goatee which was a mixture of several shades of grey with a couple of brown hairs here and there. He was about 40 and carrying quite a few extra pounds. He refused to admit that his weight was creeping up and to get shirts that would fit him so his fat would come over the collar forcing him to continually put his finger under it and twist his neck around to get some room to breathe. It became a bit of a twitch for him so we'd all walk around the station sticking fingers under our collars and twitching our necks around. Silly, I know.

Sgt. Hiddle got off to a bad start on the watch when he attended one job where Jack, my mate on the watch had to arrest a man from his car. The man started to play up and so Jack was rolling 'round the floor trying to arrest him and when he looked up to see where Sgt. Hiddle was he was nowhere near. Instead, he was running up the road trying to catch the prisoner's dog who'd got out of the car leaving Jack to struggle on his own.

My first of many negative encounters with Sgt. Hiddle was on early watch. I used to cycle to work through the city centre at about 5 a.m. It was a Sunday morning and there was no traffic about as you can imagine. At that time of the morning I used to cycle up to red lights and either mount the pavement or just make sure it was clear and cycle through. I know technically you're supposed to stop, but I was on a push bike and it was 5 in the morning.

I did it one morning when a car had stopped at the same lights I was at. I cycled through after checking it was safe. When I came out of briefing Sgt. Hiddle called me into the sergeants' office. He was furious. He was driving the car which was next to me when I cycled through the red light. He made sure there were other sergeants in the office so he could have plenty of people to impress. He sat at his desk poking his finger down his collar and screamed at me, 'If I ever see you do that again I'll report you for summons.' His face was bright red and as he shouted the spit flew out of his mouth. I couldn't believe it, how petty can you get. 'Fine, Sarge,' I responded calmly, 'and you've a faulty near side brake light, and if I ever see that again I'll report you for summons.'

He stood there aghast. I heard some of the other sergeants sniggering behind me but I just kept a straight face. Finally, the colour in his cheeks turned from red to purple and then back to pink. He realised that he'd committed a petty traffic offence as well and said, 'Just get out of my office.'

I know I should've kept my mouth shut, but that man was just ridiculous. He wanted to start off his time on the watch by bullying me in front of the other sergeants. From that time on though, he used to refer to me as 'the cocky little shit', which was fine by me. I quite liked it.

The job of a police officer is hard enough, but the very worst part of it for me wasn't the fucked-up crackheads, it was some of the supervision whose mission it was to make your job as hard as possible by bullying you, bouncing your paperwork, shouting at you in front of others and generally making your time at work a misery. If it wasn't them, it was superintendents continually changing your shift patterns or working conditions so you never knew if you were coming or going.

The incident with Sgt. Hiddle reminded me of my first day at Cardinal Wiseman School. The very first lesson was music and the teacher was Mr Radley. He was a very sickly-looking puny man with balding grey hair and a big bushy brown-and-grey beard. The brown was a huge nicotine stain from all the cigarettes he smoked. He had two yellowish-brown fingers on his right hand where he held his roll-ups. He had a nervous twitch and constantly grabbed the labels of his jacket and pushed them up whilst sticking his chin forward like a pigeon when it walks.

Mr Radley had massive bags under his eyes and his teeth were rotting brown lumps sticking out of his gums. We used to call him 'Nicotine' which was a cartoon character out of an anti-smoking TV ad which ran at the time where Superman fights a dirty cigarette-smoking enemy. He was married to a teacher who worked in the girls' school. I dread to think what it would be like kissing a foul-breathed bearded man. It must be like somebody throwing up in your mouth.

Our class consisted of thirty 11-year-old boys who'd been thrown together for the first time from various schools all over Coventry. We knew one or two from our primary school which gave us a little reassurance, but we were all very nervous. Mr Radley made us all stand up while he sat behind the piano. We were all wearing our school blazers and were only allowed to take them off with permission, and if one took it off, the entire class had to. Kids at school today have it easy.

Mr Radley began to play the piano to the tune of 'Jesse James'. As we sang, he pointed his hand and screamed at boys behind him whom he couldn't even see to 'Shout louder, boy' and 'Snap your shoulders back' and everyone complied immediately. He wanted to show that he had eyes in the back of his head.

At one point he jumped out of his seat and grabbed one boy called Wayne. He began to shake him violently by his shoulders 'Louder boy, louder' and Wayne began to cry. Now I realise what Mr Radley was doing. It was the same tactic many of the other teachers used. They wanted to put the fear of God into us so we'd jump into line for the rest of the year and not give him any trouble.

In other lessons that week many other teachers did the same thing or picked out a boy for some petty reason and gave him the cane in front of the others. It's called killing a chicken to train a monkey. In the olden days, zoo keepers would walk up to the monkey cage with a live chicken flapping about in his hands. As all the monkeys watched with interest, he'd get out a knife and hack the chicken's head off and let it run around the yard until it died. All the monkeys would be in a state of shock and panic but would never give the keeper any trouble from that day on in case they were next. I'm guessing that was what Sgt. Hiddle was trying to do, make me the chicken.

When we were short of an inspector Sgt. Hiddle was made acting inspector for a while. The entire watch was very upset but there was nothing anybody could do about it. The day it happened, morale on the watch plummeted. Jed being such a spineless sycophant immediately started to call Sgt. Hiddle 'Sir' all the time in front of us expecting us to do the same. No chance, you don't call an acting inspector sir.

He immediately started to make sweeping changes like splitting up crews who worked well together and taking double crews down to single crews, putting people in danger as far as we were all concerned. Although he was not particularly competent as a police officer or sergeant, Dave Hiddle wasn't stupid and could tell after a few weeks that morale on the watch had hit rock bottom. We all just sat silent during briefing. The heart had gone out of the watch, which was a tragedy. He decided to have some team-building exercises during nights. The entire watch drove to the railway goods yard at about 4 a.m. and we played rounders.

This may annoy you a bit because we were all supposed to be out on patrol, but what can I say? We were all told to go and at that time of the morning we were usually bored. We broke up into two teams and 23 uniformed police officers proceeded to play rounders for 40 minutes. It was actually a lot of fun, but didn't make us like Hiddle one bit more.

After the game of rounders we all played hide and seek in the city centre. The rules were that you had to stay in your car and hide in the city centre somewhere and the sergeants would come and find you. Car parks were out of bounds. My partner and I reversed down into a subway that the car barely fitted into. We were found right away. Zulu 2 did the best job, covering their car with cardboard boxes and wooden pallets so it was completely obscured from view.

It was just one night out of many hundreds of busy nights that we had a bit of a relaxed time. If it had been a regular occurrence, I suppose it would've been a bit out of order. The Zulus did have a bit more play time. They had a circuit in the city centre that was a timed event. They took turns tearing around the circuit like the Stig from Top Gear trying to beat each other's times.

꙰ ꙰

There were a few traits I hated about certain police officers. It's a working-class job and you can expect a good amount of banter about people's accents or things about them that make them stand out like being tall, short, skinny, etc. Even when I joined in the 1990s, people were still being called Taffy if they were Welsh, Paddy if they were Irish and Chalkie if they were black. Briefing was like a scene from Bernard Manning or Jim Davidson live on stage on some days. Not very 'PC' I know, but there was never any malice intended.

One thing I never found amusing was racist behaviour. Just like any other job, you're going to have a mix of different people from all sorts of backgrounds and some of these people are going to have racist opinions. They are of course entitled to have their own views, but most of us don't want to hear them. So long as they exercise impartiality in their duty as police officers I'm happy.

This often was not the case though. But before I tell the stories I want you to know that my witnessing racist comments or behaviour was actually fairly rare in the force, and when I did it was usually displayed by the same few bigots and out of ignorance. I know most of this book focuses on exciting and negative things but these are the things that stuck out in my mind after I left.

Actually, most of the job of policing involves routine and about 90 per cent boredom. I could've written about my seemingly endless number of witness statements, driving round and round the same areas in the dead of night with not a soul in sight but you'd be bored shitless reading it.

Anyway, my point is that things like racism, sexism, bullying, violence and corruption are far more interesting to read about. Most police officers are honest, reliable and decent people, but you just don't get to read about them in books or the news because there isn't anything sensational in it. The only newsworthy stuff about the police is when we do something wrong or one of us dies on duty.

Back to the racism.

Ian was a PC on Blue Watch at Little Park Street and a member of two minority groups. He was black and gay. He was open about being gay and I respected him for that, but mostly for the fact that he was a professional police officer who always did a thorough job. The problem for Ian was that certain people inside the force had a problem with black people, and some had a problem with gay people. He was a target for two types of discrimination for the price of one.

Strange things happened when Ian would apply for internal vacancies such as plainclothes and CID attachments. His applications would get lost in the internal mail and would then reappear again only to miss the cut-off date for applications. Ian went to see the chief inspector about what was happening but he just shrugged his shoulders. I had a suspect, but since paperwork went through the internal mail it could never be proved who did it.

Ian suffered from a run of bad luck for about two years. The strange thing about being in the police was that if you applied for more than one department at a time you got turned down from all of them. The bosses would say that you were like a kid in a sweet shop and just wanted to get off the watch so applying for more than one department at a time meant you weren't really committed. It was perverse logic, but that was the system.

There were two gay kids at school when I was 12. They were persecuted and ridiculed continually every day until the day they left aged 16. I don't know what it is about kids, but if anyone stands out from the crowd for any reason they're attacked. It must be part of the brainwashing process to prepare you for adult life so you're more willing to be a good docile employee.

The two gay lads were continually called 'gaylord' or 'bum chum' and many other derogatory terms. I had a lot of respect for them for being themselves and standing by what they believed in. There was the occasional non-uniform day at school where we'd all pay 10 pence and could go in jeans. We had one in 1985 and one of the hardest lads in school came in wearing make-up. He had some lippie and blusher on which really suited him. Nobody knew what to say when they saw him, they thought he was straight, but nobody dared asked him if he was gay.

It won't come as much of a surprise that probably one of the most vehement racists on the watch was Zane. He hated what he called Pakis, spear-chuckers and nig-nogs and said so on just about every occasion he could. He came out with racist terms I'd never heard of over the time I worked on the same watch as him. Since the entire watch consisted of white working-class people and only one Asian officer, he was never really picked up on his behaviour.

As equal ops gradually filtered into the police Zane was told to stop making his inappropriate comments. Instead of calling black people coons or gibbons he now called them 'stills' instead. When asked what stills meant he laughed, 'They're *still* coons.' But fate has a funny way of bringing events or people into our lives to teach us a lesson.

Zane was desperate to take his advanced police driving course. It's all changed now, but to be able to drive a Panda car (with the blue light on the top) you had to have a one-day assessment. When you passed this you were allowed to drive the Panda, but only turn the blue light on when stationary (say if you were at an accident). A standard car course lasted five weeks and meant you could turn the blue light bulb on (don't laugh) or drive the Zulu car (usually a 2-litre saloon) if an advanced driver was with you. The advanced course was two weeks of pursuit training after which, if you passed, you could drive the Zulu car or apply to traffic.

If Zane passed his advanced driving course it meant he could leave pushing a Panda car behind and join the ranks of the Zulu drivers. It was all a prestige thing really; I mean, who cares what sort of car you were driving around in? Well, quite a lot, apparently, because advanced driving courses were as rare as rocking horse-shit.

I didn't blame him for wanting to pass his advanced driving test because it meant less running, and running wasn't Zane's strong point. He ran like a middle-aged woman because his legs flew out to the side. It was hilarious to watch. The few times I was in a foot chase and saw Zane run I had to stop running because I was laughing so hard. At first I thought he was doing it as a joke, so when I told him to stop running like a girl because it made me laugh, he just shot me an evil glare.

The Zulu car was moderately higher-powered than the Panda car (2 litres instead of 1.3) but was equipped with two-tone sirens and a few more blue lights. More importantly, being in the Zulu meant little or no paperwork. The controller liked to keep the Zulu cars free from paperwork in case there was a pursuit or a job that needed a fast response. The Zulu would usually get to any job first, and then if there was any paperwork to be done, they'd leave it for the Panda driver to sort it out. This is where the phrase 'pushing a Panda' comes from, because it can often feel like an endless string of incidents and paperwork.

In the Zulu, you could spend the day zooming from job to job at high speed with the sirens wailing and take any glory that was to be had. The legwork was left to the poor sod in the Panda. This consisted of taking statements, filling out reports and making house-to-house enquiries. Why the Zulu had to be kept free at all times I never knew, but the net effect was that if you were an idle bastard who hated work the Zulu was the place to be. The Zulu drivers on Red Watch were a mix of really keen hard workers and lazy bastard work-shy shirkers (like Zane, Ray and Red).

Zane begged and begged for an advanced driving course and was eventually told he could have one, but he'd have to tutor a new recruit in order to earn his place on the course. Zane readily agreed. I felt sorry for the poor sod who'd be his protégé.

Zane was one of the few social chameleons I've ever met, a real master of rapport. He could blend into any group of people and immediately look as if he belonged there. He'd assume their way of talking, mannerisms and group culture, and of course everyone would like him because he was like them. Zane could easily imitate most people's accents and voices so he was often doing impressions of people and everybody would stand there laughing at him.

The characteristics he took on in the police were racism, violence, hatred of minority groups and the ultimate grail of the lazy bastard at work which is the art of looking busy whilst actually never doing anything constructive at all. I saw through him, but most of the rest of the watch and the supervision didn't. Zane had a motorbike so as far as the sergeants on the watch were concerned he was part of their club.

There was a new starter about to come from Ryton training centre the next week. His name was Win which sounded a bit of an odd name. All we knew was that he'd been in the Royal Navy from age 16 to 40 and had retired from there to join the police. Win had been in a special forces unit and worked all over the world and attained the rank of sergeant major.

When Win came on his first parade Zane's face dropped. Win, we found out was short for Winston and he was from Jamaica and as black as the ace of spades. To see Zane's face as white as a sheet was pure magic. Most of the watch sat there chuckling at the irony. Half of us on the watch thought that Zane was a pig-headed racist bastard who needed taking down a peg or two. Zane having to train a Jamaican was sweet poetry.

It must've been an agonising decision for Zane. If he didn't do it he'd have to miss out on the advanced driving course and have to push a Panda for another year. If he did he'd have to spend 10 weeks with a 'still'. Decisions, decisions. Zane – as you can probably guess – wasn't the ideal tutor constable. He always took shortcuts at jobs he went to and did the bare minimum, just enough so he never got into trouble. The irony was that tutoring a new joiner is a very important task and was always reserved for an experienced officer and one who volunteered to do it because they enjoyed it. There's no extra pay involved and it's often a repetitive and thankless task.

As Zane and Win worked together they immediately struck up a great friendship. You see, although Zane came out with all the racist remarks and seemed to take great joy in telling everyone how much he hated blacks, when it came to the crunch, deep down he was an OK-ish sort of bloke.

Win had spent a long time in the SBS and was fitter than a butcher's dog. He could drink and fight with the best of them, which suited Zane fine. If Win was in a fight, Zane was to be found standing next to him.

Some strange things began to happen as a result of this friendship. Zane continued to make his racist remarks in front of Win. Win would laugh at him and call him a 'honkey'.

The black population around Hillfields in Coventry didn't like seeing Win working there. They'd shout racist remarks at Win from the streets. They'd shout 'coconut' at him (brown on the outside but white on the inside). Win didn't give a shit. He'd seen active combat all over the world, jungle, city and desert. He'd fought in the Falklands and Iraq and killed men and seen men killed.

Racist remarks meant nothing to Win, especially since most of the people shouting at him were dole-scroungers anyway who were pissing their lives away in pubs or the bookies during the daytime. It was a bit strange, because when Zane used to say the word 'coon' now, he was obviously still a racist and took every opportunity to voice his opinions but he didn't seem to count Win as one for some reason.

Racism wasn't just restricted to the constables; I found that some of the sergeants held the same opinions as well, which I suppose is no surprise. We seemed to be in a continual state of reorganisation in the police. Our shift patterns were always being changed, and our working hours, terms and conditions, working areas and so on. It was very unsettling for everyone on the unit. Many changes are necessary, of course, because the police service matures and society changes but we often found senior police officers who were promoted wanted to make their mark by making sweeping changes that only upset morale and ruined any goodwill that existed.

One of my best friends was a firefighter in Coventry and it was the same there. Every few months the senior management would announce sweeping changes to the shift patterns there. It would cause upset and anxiety for all of the crews who of course hadn't been consulted at all. Once they'd all settled into the new unpopular shifts, they'd be changed again. It really was a disgrace the way they were being treated.

One such change in the police was a merger of watches. Decades of using a model that worked really well was changed when we merged with Red Watch at Fletchampstead Highway police station and the areas we covered increased dramatically. Without a say, our working hours changed so that some of our shifts went from eight to 12 hours. There was a lot of confusion because we struggled to work out what we were doing weeks in advance. People who'd booked holidays either side of days off had to rearrange the entire trip.

We quickly had some new constables and sergeants working with us at Little Park Street. One such sergeant was Kurt Green (again, not his real name). Kurt was a hard bastard, not that tall at about 5' 9" really and not particularly well-built, but he kept himself in shape so was fit and lean and just had that air of 'don't fuck with me' about him. He had tight curly fair hair and thick frown lines across his forehead. He had a deep scar along his forehead which I heard had been from a pub fight many years ago.

He'd been born and raised in Hillfields in Coventry which is known as a particularly rough area. Kurt had been in loads of fights over the years so fighting was as natural as going for a shit to him. I'll come to a couple of the fights I was involved in with Kurt later on. The only thing I didn't like about Kurt was his propensity to blurt out racist remarks regularly.

A couple of weeks after merging watches we were out on the riot van patrolling the city centre. It was late one night and Kurt was the van sergeant for the shift. We could see two black guys having an argument about 20 yards in front of us by a pub called the Town Crier. We couldn't hear what was being said, but clearly they were disagreeing about something. There was no violence between them, just finger-pointing and raised voices so there was no need for our involvement. Kurt watched from the front of the van with great interest but just sat there in silence. Eventually, he shouted out, 'Find your own tree,' which caused the rest of the van to break out in fits of laughter. I sat there wondering if I was the strange one for not finding that sort of comment funny.

Racism policy is a good thing and designed to protect people from being discriminated against due to the colour of their skin. I wholeheartedly agree with this. In an ideal world we'd all treat each other equally, but some members of the human race seem to have a problem with this so the lawmakers have had to step in.

Equal opportunities is a very hot potato in the police. Everyone was paranoid about offending somebody for something so the net result was the whole point of equal ops is missed altogether. I made an interesting observation when I saw the equal ops teams at HQ. First, that this type of role attracted a certain type of person, a person who was more of a social worker than a police officer, a person who was more liberal than most. Hard to put into words really, but they're more easily offended than most and more likely to take offence to casual harmless remarks. If they weren't in the police they'd have made good social workers.

Second, I never saw any ethnic minorities helping make policy decisions. When I went there, the equal ops team were all white. If this was the case, then how did they know that the policy decisions they were making were actually having the desired impact?

The core of the paranoia stemmed from police training college where all of the trainers seemed to me to be brainwashed. They never said the word 'black' in case it offended somebody, so it was 'coffee without milk' instead of 'black coffee', and the 'blackboard' became the 'chalkboard'. The same sort of lunacy led to the rhyme 'Ba ba black sheep' being banned from schools. It is idiocy such as this that makes a mockery of equal opportunities. Trainers never criticised but gave open and honest feedback. I often felt like I was being trained by social workers and not police officers. Even if you dropped a huge bollock you were never told so. You were just given 'feedback', which was just daft.

Due to the findings of the Scarman Report, it was deemed that police officers spent too much time learning about the law and not enough on communication skills. Exams were abolished for some reason and replaced with knowledge checks which didn't really form a part of your final course appraisal. Now you could scrape through police training without really knowing much law at all. Instead, we learned all about the Equal Opportunities Act and Sex Discrimination Act. It was a very strange atmosphere where we were told that the classroom was a place where we were free to express our views and opinions, but if we offended anybody we'd be nailed to the wall. Emphasis was taken away from the law and legal knowledge and put into conflict resolution and learning about the many religions of the world.

Any complaints of racial harassment or sexual harassment were dreaded at police stations or training centres. The person complained of would usually be taken off active duty and thoroughly investigated. Having equal ops is a very good thing and everyone should of course be treated equally. Things just never seemed to work this way, though.

One day at police training centre my mate held the door open for a female inspector. She was infuriated at this and called him into her office and was given a rocketing for being sexist. He tried to explain that he held the door open for everybody regardless of sex.

Equal ops rules can be used by people to gain an advantage as well though, which again is an abuse of the reason it was introduced. A great detective sergeant whom I worked with for six months had an Asian officer attached to his crew for three months. I knew the Asian officer for some time. His paperwork was always in shit order and late, he was devious and always dropping his colleagues in the shit, also his knowledge of the law was disgraceful. This was a fact and nothing to do with his race.

When he was deemed not suitable for appointment as a detective he put a complaint in against the detective sergeant saying he was a racist and had called him a 'Paki'. The DS was the kindest, nicest man I'd worked with and had played hockey for years with a team which consisted mostly of Indian men. He was always out socialising with them and who was what colour never made any difference to anyone in the team. Why would it? Playing the race card was always a sure way of getting into a department or getting a second chance.

This PC (we'll call him Jatinder, but that isn't his real name) was a nightmare. I'm glad he was on Green Watch and not mine. I'd taken over a few jobs from him and his standard of work was a disgrace. He cut corners whenever possible and was rude and aggressive to the public.

I'd been involved in one incident in particular in which Jatinder was involved and got himself and his partner into serious danger. It was when he was on patrol in Stoke Aldermoor one afternoon. He spotted one of the locals there riding a moped along the street. The guy was Jamaican and the moped looked just like one that had been reported stolen earlier that day.

Jatinder approached the man but unfortunately he (Jatinder) had very poor social skills and outright accused him of stealing the moped. The man was rightly upset. Jatinder tried to wrestle the moped from him but the man was having none of it. It was his and Jatinder had no right to take it away. Jatinder became irate and from my previous knowledge of him, he had a hair-trigger temper. When the man wouldn't let go of the moped Jatinder punched him hard in the face. The members of the local Jamaican population were watching from across the road and all of a sudden Jatinder and his partner were surrounded by a very angry mob wanting to tear them to pieces.

Jatinder's partner called for back-up and by the time we got there the two officers looked in real danger of being torn to pieces by the crowd. There were over 20 angry Jamaicans surrounding them both screaming for justice and to let go of the man with the moped who was lying on the floor wrapped around it still refusing to let go. Luckily, a very switched-on sergeant attended and took control.

He threw Jatinder into the nearest Panda car and he was whisked away to the station. The man with the moped had a huge black eye already which had a cut in the middle which looked like it needed stitches. The sergeant did what Jatinder should've done and asked about the moped's ownership. The man pointed to the motorbike shop across the road and said he'd bought it the day before. The bike-shop owner confirmed this. The man even still had the receipt in his pocket. No wonder Jatinder was turned down for the CID.

What a mess. The golden rule I was told when I joined the police is that if you ever have to give somebody a slap then you must arrest them. Even if they get released later without charge you're in deep trouble if you punch somebody but don't arrest them for something, even if it's petty.

Jatinder's police collar number was spray painted all over the flats and walls in Stoke Aldermoor, with comments like 'You're dead' which clearly meant he was a marked man. Word went out that there was a contract out on Jatinder's head and he was moved to another area so his face wouldn't be seen in the Aldermoor again. All because he didn't bother to ask a few simple questions of the man with the moped.

~ ~

There was other behaviour that I just found very odd in the police but which seemed to others to be the norm. One thing in particular was when people were promoted they immediately began to act as if they were better and more important than others. Newly-promoted sergeants started to shout at constables and give them punishment duties. Inspectors and above suddenly were entitled to a car parking space but those who did the work on the watch had to park in a local car park and walk into work.

Bullying by supervision is rife in the police and as I mentioned earlier, a new sergeant or inspector can make or break morale at a police station. A supervisor is there to encourage and support the team, to help motivate them and bring out the best in people. Alas, that sort of leader is a rare jewel in the police force. The promotion process really doesn't teach leadership. It covers the pragmatic things like discipline procedures and custody officer duties.

My memory of the many different sergeants and inspectors I worked with in the police were that quite a lot of supervisors had poor people skills and would shout, threaten and bully to achieve their ends. Some were horrible people who I was told were even hated by their kids, but some were very kind and supportive, and these were the people who you really wanted to work hard for and go the extra mile just because they saw you as somebody worthwhile and not just a number on a sheet.

I once had to dump my Panda car in a non-uniformed space at Little Park Street because the CID had put their cars into the uniformed space. I'd just arrested somebody and had to get to the cell block to book him in because he'd been transported in a different car from mine. I can't tell you how many times we were late attending urgent jobs such as burglaries and fights because inconsiderate people had blocked the Pandas and Zulus in at the rear yard.

When I got out of the car a man in a suit walked up to me. He looked about 50 and had grey hair and a grey beard. I'd seen him walking around the station before but I didn't know who he was or what he did. He was irate and started shouting that I wasn't supposed to park where I was. I just looked at him gone out. I shook my head and walked off leaving him standing there. He hadn't bothered to introduce himself to me so I had no idea if he was a civilian or a police officer.

It seemed to me that everybody felt that they were more important than the uniformed police officer who was at the bottom of the shit heap. We worked a 24/7 shift pattern and were the only thing stopping complete anarchy in the streets and yet we were often treated like second-class citizens.

When I got back into the parade room one of the sergeants came up to me. 'You've upset the DCI (detective chief inspector), Paul,' he said solemnly, 'you had better go up to his office.' I felt really angry. Who the hell did he think he was? I'd no choice but to go and see him in his office. I really wanted an attachment to the CID and he could block it with one sweep of his pen. I went up and listened to a half-hour lecture about how important it was not to park in CID spaces. I didn't argue, but was very angry inside because I felt that I was in the right.

I apologised and left his office. He'd been working at Little Park Street station for six months and never even had the courtesy to come and introduce himself to the people on the watches. That's how unimportant we were considered by some. I was just expected to know who he was and the fact he was a senior CID officer.

I think it's some sort of throwback from the army that first names are not used in the police. Everybody at Virgin calls Richard Branson 'Richard' but we have to call the sergeants 'Sarge' and anybody of inspector rank or above 'Sir' which I felt was ridiculous. Millions of companies all over the world manage to keep order and discipline and still call each other by their Christian names. It was just like at school where your surname is called out on the register and that's how the teachers address you and even the other students. I was called Browning by most of my schoolmates for years.

Not all ranking officers and sergeants had a superior attitude, but I'd say about half did. They'd forgotten that they were once a PC and each had their own set of rules that if you crossed they'd bollock you or do something to make your life difficult. I vowed that when I was a sergeant and higher I wouldn't shout and scream at PCs or bully them.

During yet another reorganisation of the force by one of the new chief constables he decided to get rid of chief inspector and chief superintendent ranks. It was realised that these people actually served no useful purpose whatsoever and that the force would be better off without them. I think that saved the West Midlands Police Force about one million pounds per year. It seemed strange to me then that if they were never needed in the first place, why had nobody noticed this a hundred years earlier, and what had they been doing all the time they were there? Yet another thing that was never questioned.

≈ ≈

About 18 months after I joined the police I was put on a one-day driving course so I could drive the Panda car. I was really delighted because I felt that I could contribute a bit more. I didn't like it when my partner in a car had to drive for the entire tour of duty. Police officers often accumulate crime reports that need to be investigated, so being able to drive a car about means you don't have to scrounge lifts from people. I wasn't allowed in a Panda car very often, even after my probationary period had ended. The watch had a lot of officers with more service than me who were higher up in the pecking order and also, Jed did the duty sheet, of course.

As time went on I did get to drive the Panda occasionally. I did really enjoy it, but was often put on my own by Jed. I started to bring a very small battery-operated radio into work with me. For some reason, when I pressed the transmit button on my police radio the volume on the personal radio would drop very low so the controller wouldn't know I was listening to music as I drove around in the car. For some reason that made me feel like I was getting one over on them and they weren't winning by putting me out on my own in the police car.

On one set of nights I was posted to work with Demi (with whom I'd been to my first domestic) a little later in my service. I have to admit, when you first get to drive a police car you can easily get a bit carried away and start to believe that you're indestructible. You can jump red lights, speed and wear no seat belt and nobody is going to pull you over because you are the police.

The police force in the UK uses an army of volunteer police officers called special constables. They work for free, are given some limited training and a uniform and are set loose on the streets. I never knew whether to respect them for what they did or look on them as very odd people. At least I was getting paid for being spat on, these guys and girls gave up their weekends and did it for free. Many had tried to enter the force as regular officers but didn't make the grade. They were often told to join the specials for a year and reapply. That was the biggest con I ever heard, but most of them seemed to fall for it.

Specials were always held in low regard, or at least viewed with some suspicion by regular officers due to the fact their lack of knowledge of law and procedures meant they were a liability. The general public could always identify them by markings on their uniform and so were always happy to shout out 'hobby bobby' as they walked passed.

There's very little training involved to become a special constable and yet they're deployed at potentially dangerous events such as football matches or sent out on patrol in busy cities and expected to deal with incidents as they arose. It seemed to me to be an accident waiting to happen.

I'd previously attended a call one night with Zane. Three specials were out on foot patrol together and had caught a drunk man trying to drive his car. When we got there they told us what had happened. Zane winked at me and whispered, 'Give them the breathalyser machine.' I handed the special the machine and he just looked back at me with a blank expression, he didn't know how it worked or what to do with it! They didn't bother to keep hold of the man, so just after that he bolted off down the road. I was pretty fast on my feet so he got about 30 yards away before I was on top of him and wrestled him to the ground. If they'd done what they were supposed to and kept hold of him I'd never have had to peg it down the road after him.

It used to drive me barmy. They didn't understand their powers of arrest, and if they did arrest somebody, they couldn't write a statement of arrest for toffee, so you had to take it from them which took an hour. You then had to interview the prisoner and do the court file because they didn't know how to do that either. It was a right pain in the arse.

You'd often find specials walking around in teams of three or more because there was a shortage of police radios. Once, I'd driven down Far Gosford Street and passed seven specials all walking down the road together. It was madness, but since they only had one radio between them they decided to go out en masse. I worked along with and attended incidents with quite a few special constables during my 12 years of service. There was a mix of really nice people who wanted to make a difference, and some right idiots who had a bad attitude and wanted to wear the uniform because it made them feel important.

At about midnight on the Saturday evening during the set of nights I was out with Demi in the Panda car and I was driving. It was one of those very rare occasions where a call came out on the radio and we were actually already at the scene. Only a police officer will appreciate how rare this actually is. A special constable had caught a burglar in the act breaking into a clothes shop in Corporation Street by the Belgrade theatre. I'm guessing that the offender had come into town with the wrong outfit on and wanted to get something decent to wear. The special was chasing him towards Upper Well Street – which was exactly where we were. Since I'd passed my one-day driving test I of course used every opportunity to use the blue light on the top of my Panda car and drive around at 70 mph.

The burglar ran out about 30 yards in front of us closely pursued on foot by the special. I put my foot on the accelerator and drove onto the pedestrianised part of Corporation Street in order to block his escape path. I was heading towards a fountain which is just outside the Belgrade theatre to cut off his escape route. Well, that was my plan, at least. Unfortunately for me (and him), it'd been raining that night and the pavement was made of red brick which was not designed for driving on. I hit the brakes but the car continued to move forward; it was skidding due to the fact that when rain hits a polluted area a film of grease forms on the surface of the street.

The burglar ran in front of my car. I was still skidding and he was right in front of the bonnet. He turned his head and looked right into my eyes and I could see the fear in them. Time slowed to a crawl, the front of the Panda car hit the burglar in his left leg sending him flying into the air. Up, up and away he flew doing a double twist with pike. Two people standing at the bus stop 20 yards away held up scores of 5.6 and 5.7 which I thought was a bit tight. The man landed in a crumpled heap on his back about three yards away.

It wasn't over yet, because hitting him had not really reduced my momentum. We skidded further and our progress was eventually halted when we hit a tree. I thought, 'Well, at least it can't get any worse than this,' at which point the tree we'd hit gave a loud crack and fell over onto the bonnet of the car. I looked over at Demi for a bit of moral support or a few words of consolation but she just looked back at me with an expression which very clearly said, 'You stupid prick.' I didn't feel so good anymore.

Worse was yet to come as the burglar stood up, looked up and down at himself surprised that he wasn't dead or at least had a broken bone or two. He couldn't believe his luck, but then the devil looks after his own, so he ran up Croft Road.

This was a very bad situation. Bashing a police car was OK so long as you got a prisoner out of it. Losing the prisoner and bashing the car was simply not an option.

Demi got out of the car and began to chase the burglar. She must've got about 20 yards when some absolute wanker standing in a crowd who was watching what was transpiring tripped her up sending her sprawling across the ground. I would've paid my month's wages to be able to go and kick the living shit out of that man. It would've been worth every penny to kick his teeth out of his mouth for tripping Demi up.

I backed the car off the tree and began to drive up Upper Well Street along the wrong side of the road. I was in enough trouble so some other motoring offences wouldn't make matters any worse. I knew if I could make it to the top end of Upper Well Street the burglar would emerge from the subway. His getting away was not an option anymore.

As I got to the top of Croft Road I pulled the steering wheel to the left to try to cross to the right side of the road. Unfortunately, the road surface was so slippery that I lost traction on the white chevron markings and even though I was steering right, my car was moving to the left. I then bashed my front wheel into a kerbstone. The wheel caved inwards with a loud clang as metal twisted and rubber tore open. It was like the scene from a movie when bad things keep happening to the hero and he's having the worst day imaginable.

But not to be deterred by all this, I slammed the gear lever into first and continued in my quest. The car limped on bouncing up and down due to the fact that my left front wheel now had a large flat section where it was once round. My car looked like something out of the circus, bouncing up and down as I tried to drive it on a flat tyre with a caved-in wheel. All I needed now was the clown suit.

Soon, sparks began to fly from the around the wheel and eventually the car ground to a halt in the middle of a traffic island at the top of Upper Well Street. I was about to get out my pen and draft my letter of resignation when, joy of joys, Demi shouted on the radio that she'd caught the burglar. The day was saved. Now the only problem was accounting for the fact that I'd run over a man, uprooted a tree, and then written off the police car. It was a pickle for sure, especially since the duty sergeant was Jed.

I knew that if Jed was called out I'd be nailed to the wall. I was looking at damage to police property and reckless driving at the very least. The only card in my favour was that Jed never ever left the confines of the police station unless it was to drive home at the end of the watch. Coming out to the scene of a pollac (police accident) was never on Jed's agenda. All was saved when I heard Jed ask my ex-tutor Alan to attend and deal with the accident as an acting sergeant.

Alan was crewed up with a guy called Simon on Mike Zulu 3. They were both old sweats and knew the score – there was more chance of the sky falling in than these two guys reporting me for any offences. When they came and met me at the scene Alan laughed at the state of the car. 'You wanker, Paul,' he said as he laughed out loud, 'I'm an advanced driver and I couldn't have done that if I'd had a hundred tries.' I felt so relieved that he was going to square this mess up.

We replanted the tree, and when Alan completed the accident report he moved the scene of the accident to a different location and squared all of the paperwork away. Job done. The prisoner admitted the burglary and never once mentioned being run over. I was so lucky that it all got sorted out without me being prosecuted for dangerous driving or damage to police property.

When I was in the job, police car crashes could often be dealt with quietly. It all depended upon who attended to deal with it. The philosophy was that we all did our best to get to jobs as quickly as we could to stop bad people hurting the good people (like you). Occasionally, we'd kerb the wheel of a car or spin and hit a lamp post.

We could usually write it off by saying that there was some diesel on the road or that a black dog ran out in front of us and we had to swerve to avoid it. During my time in the force that damn black dog must've caused about 50 police cars to crash all over the West Midlands. He sure had a lot to answer for!

A few weeks later I was on MM4 which covered Stoke Aldermoor. I was working with a great guy called Stephen who'd joined a few months after me. Stephen was 25, had a pale complexion and a thick mane of black hair brushed up in a teddy boy style. Everyone on the watch used to call him 'bouff' which is short for bouffant which, if you're up to sniff with your seventeenth-century history was a popular hair style back then involving the hair being piled high on ones head.

Stephen was a great guy but also very soft; he'd let people take advantage of him and didn't stand up for himself. Consequently, the sergeants would pick on him and give him lots of shit jobs. Stephen's surname was 'Larren', and when we were all sitting in the briefing room we'd hear the sergeants call for him from their office, 'Larreeeennnnn, there's two prisoners in the block and you're dealing.' It was the running joke on the watch that he'd always be asked to deal with the handover prisoners left by the previous watch.

Stephen and I were on lates and had driven over to my mum's house in Hillfields for a sneaky cup of tea. Technically, you could be disciplined for going off your beat without a good reason. That discipline offence is a throwback from when bobbies had no radios and were all allocated a foot beat and had to call back into the control room every hour via the police box to see if there were any jobs for them. We were drinking tea at my mum's when the controller shouted on the radio to us that there was a shoplifter playing up at the Kwik Save in Acorn Street in Stoke Aldermoor and we had to get there quick.

We ran out of my mum's house and sped off down Swan Lane. I was driving and put the blue light on. Technically, I shouldn't have, but we had to get there quickly and we were two miles away from where we should've been. We got to a red light at the junction of Swan Lane and Walsgrave Road, a coach to our right stopped to give way and as we passed by it a car drove into the back of it. As it did so we heard an almighty bang. It looked like nobody was hurt, but it'd cost a packet to get the back of the coach fixed. We were supposed to stop and call a sergeant, because technically we were involved in the crash because the coach had stopped to let us out. A sergeant is supposed to attend all police accidents. My heart sank and Stephen went white as a sheet. We were on the way to another job and if it was found out that we were off our beat we could be in trouble. Especially since we'd now caused a crash whilst using the blue light.

We drove on to the shoplifter. There was not much we could do at the scene of the crash because police are not required to attend damage, only accidents. The only issue was that, technically, we'd caused it by causing the traffic to stop.

We went back to the station expecting to be hauled into the sergeants' office for a bollocking. We guessed that the drivers would've come into the station to report what had happened and the sergeants would've worked out who was driving the Panda. Nothing was said that day, so Stephen and I agreed to say nothing and pray that we got away with it. If we were going to be caught it would be the next day. It was a very long night for me.

Stephen and I sat in briefing the next day at 2 p.m. and just looked at each other across the tables. We were sitting there waiting to be called into the sergeants' office after the duties were read out but we weren't. We heaved big sighs of relief and went back out on patrol. Obviously, the drivers had exchanged details and didn't report it to the police or come in to complain about us witnessing the crash and driving off.

This wasn't my only incident involving crashes and police cars. One of the best set of nights I worked in the police was with Bob F. Bob was an absolute hoot. He was always laughing and joking around and at the same time a really enthusiastic officer, a real pleasure to work with. Bob always did a thorough job, but also had fun while he was working. He had about three years' service in the police and had been bullied for most of it by two watch sergeants. I knew how he'd felt because it was happening to me now.

Bob and I were put on Mike Mike 3, the Hillfields car which suited me great. There's always something to do in Hillfields so I was happy as could be and grateful to be in a Panda car as opposed to walking on my own for eight hours.

It was about 1 a.m. and Bob and I were patrolling around Harnall Lane East into the Hillfields flats complex. I was driving and Bob was sharing one of his many funny stories with me. He was telling me one story of how Rick (Zane's partner) had grabbed a member of the public and put his head through a window in the front office.

As Bob came to the part where Rick pushed the man's head through the window his arms flew out and hit the inside of the car windscreen. Bob was wearing a ring, and as his hand hit the windscreen, made a loud bang and immediately caused it to crack. A huge star-like crack now went from the top to the bottom of the windscreen and about 4 in horizontally. We froze for a few seconds in disbelief and then burst into nervous laughter. 'Fucks sake,' said Bob in dismay, 'how are we going to cover this one?' I just sat there shaking my head.

Bob then came up with a brainwave. 'Let's drive into the flats,' he said with a look of excitement on his face, 'and put a brick through the window. We can pretend somebody threw it from the flats at us.' In the absence of a better plan I agreed. Why we just didn't go back to the station and admit what had happened I don't know. It was an accident after all. We could've even said it was a stone chip thrown up by a passing car.

We drove further into the flats to find a suitable spot. As we did so a shout came over the radio. One of the Zulus was pursuing a stolen car through the city centre. We had to abandon our plan for now and headed towards their location. A Panda car is technically not allowed to pursue because it is low-powered and the driver is not pursuit-trained. Back then we often did it anyway because everybody else did – it was just accepted. But if you did crash, you had some explaining to do and could end up being prosecuted for dangerous or careless driving. It was just a calculated risk.

We made towards London Road where the pursuit was now taking place. They were doing about 100 mph so there's no way Bob and I would've become involved. We were going that way (along with most of Red Watch) in case the offenders ditched the car and made off on foot.

To actually join London Road from the start you've to go around a traffic island controlled by lights. There's a sharp bend at the very start which is outside a large pub and a couple of restaurants. They've changed the layout now, but there used to be a car park outside the pub and to pull out was a bit dangerous because you had to join traffic where the bend was.

As we joined London Road and came out of the bend a car slowly emerged from the car park to our left. The driver had been stationary at the car park exit but pulled out in front of me without looking. It had been raining for a while so the road was wet and greasy (honest). I slammed on the brakes but it was useless. I'd have been better off throwing an anchor out of the window. We skidded right towards him and there was nothing I could do.

When you're in a crash or other traumatic incident time seems to get distorted and things appear to happen a lot slower than they actually do. As I skidded towards the car I began to think about all the paperwork we'd have to complete and the time we'd have to spend off the road. I aimed the front of my car towards the front of his offside so that I'd hit his engine and not where he was sitting. We hit him with a massive bang and sent his car spinning anti-clockwise into the opposite carriageway. Although I was only doing about 20 mph due to the bend in the road, it still felt like a huge crash.

Debris from the collision was lying all over the carriageway. There were bits of car bumper, indicator and headlamps all over the place.

Traffic cars sped past us through the debris throwing it up all over the place. They wanted to be in the pursuit so they didn't have time to stop and laugh at us.

We got out of our car and ran across to the one we'd hit. I looked in and could see the driver. He was in his seat, stunned, shaking visibly. I hadn't noticed before but he had a passenger in the car with him. It was his girlfriend and she was sitting in the front passenger seat. She was crying by now and also very shaken up. They had no injuries so we just called the incident in on the radio.

The driver got out of his car and began to light a cigarette. He was white, about 23 and wearing jeans and a pink Ben Sherman shirt. He was covered in gold sovereign rings and chains which gave him the look of a gippo although I don't think he was one because his car was taxed and his girlfriend wasn't related to him. 'I wouldn't smoke that, mate,' I told him, 'we both have to be breathalysed and it will affect your reading.' He just lit it anyway and began to puff away. His hands were shaking and he was clearly in shock at what had happened. Partly due to the crash, but partly I think due to the fact he knew he'd been drinking a skinfull that night.

I could smell alcohol on his breath so obviously he'd come out of the pub and just got straight into his car. I began to hope that he was over the limit because it would look far better for me. His girlfriend was sitting in the passenger seat crying. I made sure she wasn't injured and she was OK, just upset about what had happened.

Eventually, a very rare event took place. Jed came out in the car with the watch inspector. My first thought was that a major fire must've broken out at the station to force them out of the office. I don't think Jed had been out of the station since the Queen's Silver Jubilee in 1977. I'm surprised they could even find where we were because they surely couldn't have known their way around the patch having never left the station, and neither of them lived in Coventry.

The inspector came over to breathalyse me. There's a prescribed set of words you're supposed to say to a person before you breathalyse them but the inspector kept getting them wrong so he just said to me eventually, 'Blow into this Paul, usual requirements.' I was clear, but the driver failed, thank goodness. It went straight to red the second he blew into it which meant he was probably going to blow well over back at the station.

He was arrested for drink driving by Jed which must've been his first arrest in many years. His last arrest had been somebody for highway robbery and unlawful duelling. The driver's girlfriend was shouting at him and crying, 'I told you not to drink and drive, you stupid bastard.' She later attended the station and agreed to give Jed a statement about how much he'd been drinking at home and then in the pub that night.

She was very angry at him for putting them both in so much danger. The problem was that Jed didn't bother to finish taking the statement and decided to do the rest the next night.

When he went 'round to see her the next night she'd changed her story and said that I was driving like a lunatic and had caused the crash. Clearly, her boyfriend had wormed his way back in and asked her to rent for him. If that useless, lazy bastard Jed had done his job properly he'd have taken all of the statement that night and she would've signed it to say that it was her boyfriend's fault.

He was banned for 12 months and nothing happened to me.

Jed did his best to get me done for careless driving. He told me that I must've been speeding judging by all the debris on the road, but I said I wasn't. He said that I had my blue light on which I was not allowed to because I'd only been on the one-day driving course, but I said I hadn't. He even went as far as to have a word with Bob and try to get Bob to have a word with me as a mate and get me to say I had the blue light on and was speeding. I wish he'd put the same amount of effort into taking the statement of the girlfriend as he did trying to have me done.

That's one of the differences between a good and a bad supervisor. When you're in trouble or make an honest mistake a good one will do their best to help you out realising you're doing the best job you can and are only human. A wanker will actively look for ways to catch you out and search for any relevant discipline offence so they can report you to the superintendent for something. The best of it was that over the next few years I saw Jed drop two massive bollocks which could've cost him his stripes or his job – and he got clean away with it.

The one good thing that came out of all of this was that we didn't have to put a brick through the car windscreen. It was so smashed up by the crash that it was a write-off and the crack in the windscreen looked like it had been caused during the crash. Bonus.

I dealt with hundreds of drink drivers while I was in the police. I never really went out looking for them, but most evenings, if you had cause to stop a car for some reason you'd often smell alcohol on the driver's breath. It was always the same story. They'd say that they'd only had a couple, which of course means a skinfull. I just can't comprehend the mentality of somebody who drinks and then drives. It seems to me to be complete lunacy but of course we can never apply logic to the actions of a human being because we aren't logical creatures.

I personally would like to see instant prison sentences handed out for drink drivers. As soon as they blow over on the machine at the police station they should be carted off for a one-month stretch for the first offence. To be honest, I don't think that many people would be sent to prison before everyone else caught on and stopped drinking and driving.

A drink driver is basically saying 'fuck you' to the law and 'fuck you' to you or your family if they run you over because there's no way in a million years that they're going to stop and help you if they do run you over. Like true cowards they'll always flee the scene and leave you for dead. It's so easy to catch a taxi or scrounge a lift back home or kip on your mate's sofa if you're around their house.

People drink and drive because they think that it's worth the risk. The worst-case scenario is a ban which is obviously not a deterrent for the thousands of people who do drink and drive every night of the week. Knowing that you're going to go away for a month and probably lose your job and house may make people think twice. It seems to work well in countries like Singapore where you get a six-month stretch if you get caught drinking and driving. If you kill or injure somebody while you're drunk and driving you get up to six lashes of the birch on your arse in addition to prison. Funnily enough, they don't have much drinking and driving over there.

Drink drivers will usually do almost anything to avoid being caught. When I was early in service I was out on patrol one night at about 1 a.m. with Alan. As we drove past an Indian restaurant in The Butts we saw a couple of middle-aged men walk out of it and get into a newish Jag. The way they both looked at us indicated that they were a bit concerned at seeing us.

It's hard to put into words really, but a person gives a certain look or body language that betrays the fact they've done something wrong. It's just like when a child is telling a fib or is lying about brushing their teeth: you can see it on their face that they're feeling guilty. The fact that they were aged about 50 and had walked out of a curry house led us both to believe that they'd been to the pub and then had a few more beers while they were eating. You can also usually spot a drink driver driving because they follow the white lines on the road perfectly. They have to do that, or they'll weave across the road.

Alan drove past as if we hadn't noticed, and then quickly hid the car in a car park around the corner and turned the car lights off. I ran out and watched the Jag. The occupants just sat in it and were obviously waiting a few minutes to ensure the coast was clear before they drove away.

As soon as I saw that they were heading towards us I ran back to the Panda. As they drove past us we sped out of the car park we'd hidden in and began to follow them. The driver must've been aware of who was behind him because he turned his headlights off and tried to hide down a back entry.

We pulled behind him and got him to sit in the back of our car. You do that because if you breathalyse the driver outside their car and they blow over they can run off and you've to chase them. That happened to me once and I vowed it'd never happen again. The driver gave us the usual story saying he'd only had a pint but he stank of booze. He failed the roadside test so we arrested him and took him to the station to blow on the bigger evidential machine. He was three times over the limit and was later banned for two years at court. He'd only got his licence back the month before. What a prat. Can you see how a ban is almost no deterrent to most people?

☙ ❧

I'd mentioned one of the sergeants earlier – Kurt. Although I'd heard him make racist comments I think he'd been doing it as a bad attempt at humour rather than anything else. The reason is that one of the first fights I'd seen him in was with a skinhead.

One night at about 2:30 a.m. Kurt was driving down Tower Street past the Pink Parrot nightclub. The queue for the taxis outside the club was on the list of places to keep an eye on during nights because there was often a fight taking place there. The rank was full of the usual crowd of drunken men and pissed-up girls with their tits hanging out of their dresses (not that I'm complaining). Someone from the crowd shouted abuse at Kurt as he drove past. Most police officers would've ignored it and driven past, either because it wasn't worth the trouble, or because there isn't much you can do to find the cowardly culprit.

Kurt wasn't like this, if you offended him in any way you were given a smack in the teeth. Kurt got out of his car and walked along the crowd in the taxi rank who by now had fallen silent. You could smell it on him, Kurt wasn't a very big man but he was lean and could throw a good punch so by most people's standards was a force to be reckoned with.

The person who'd sworn at Kurt had by now blended into the queue at the taxi rank and couldn't be identified, which was a shame. At the same time a skinhead and his girlfriend were walking down the road. He was wearing the usual uniform of a traditional skinhead, skin-tight jeans rolled up to reveal 32-hole maroon doc martin boots. He had a white tee shirt on and a denim top. He was wearing a swastika badge and had 'skins oi oi' tattooed onto his neck. His girlfriend was dressed the same apart from a few tufts of hair she had growing at the back, which was again traditional for a female skinhead.

The two skinheads had been drinking all night long and were too drunk to know any better. The man was full of Dutch courage and wanted to impress his girlfriend. He started to make noises like a pig snorting in the direction of Kurt. His girlfriend walked behind him laughing at the hilarity of the situation. This would be the last time her boyfriend would be able to make the same noise through his soon-to-be-broken nose.

Everybody in the crowd was looking at this guy and his girlfriend with disgust, they might as well have been wearing 'Gary Glitter Rocks' tee shirts. Nobody likes a skinhead apart from other skinheads. Everyone is entitled to their opinions of course but it's the overt hatred they represent that seems to cause the most disgust in people.

Kurt walked up to the man and the crowd watched on with interest. Everyone but the skinhead knew what was coming up. Kurt said, 'What was that, mate?' to the skinhead. Kurt wasn't really interested in the reply. He wanted to get close enough to the guy to hit him and he wanted to have him thinking about something just before he punched him in the face.

By the time the words had filtered through to his brain and before his alcohol-numbed synapses could spark off an attempt at a witty retort, 'BANG'. Kurt hit him with a perfect left hook cracking him on the chin and sending him stumbling backwards onto the pavement. The crowd gasped, partly in surprise and partly in pleasure.

The blow hadn't knocked him out. The skinhead was lying on the ground on his back with his arms and legs flailing about like a turtle stuck on its back. As Kurt went in for the kill the skinhead's girlfriend screamed and ran towards Kurt. Kurt believed in women's lib: BANG, and he put her to sleep as well.

The crowd all cheered and clapped. Kurt's value system justified the event to him perfectly, and he was happy that what he'd done had been both lawful and necessary. The skinhead was still lying on the floor trying to get himself up but his legs wouldn't respond. He just kept falling over again and again.

Kurt called for the serial van to collect his prisoners. What happened next I don't know because I didn't see the rest. Sometime between the skinhead leaving the scene of the arrest in the van and him being found in the cell an hour later he sustained serious head injuries. He stopped breathing and had to be resuscitated at the police station by the paramedics. At some point somebody had put on their sombrero and done the Mexican hat dance on the guy's head.

Complaints and discipline got involved, of course. The skinhead couldn't remember anything due to alcohol and amnesia caused by the head injury. The crowd had all gone home and couldn't be traced. It was easy enough to borrow the cell keys back then and there was no CCTV in the cell block. Nobody had seen a PC going into the cell after the OSU had put him in there. On a Saturday night the cell block is a hive of activity and there's no way you can keep tabs of who is coming in and out. The end result was nobody was arrested or disciplined because nobody could be identified as having assaulted him.

Kurt was a good laugh and was good for morale on the watch. You'd always find him out on patrol and generally he had a 'I'm never going to get promoted again' attitude about him so he wasn't bothered about what the senior police officers thought about him. One thing I did find a bit unusual about Kurt was the fact that he had a pathological hatred of defence lawyers, the ones who all have offices near to police stations and make money solely representing criminals via legal aid. None of us liked the slimy bastards of course, but Kurt's hatred was on another level altogether.

I was in the cell block one afternoon with Kurt who was covering the custody sergeant's role. He was chatting about a prisoner's documenta-tion with one of the regular lawyers who attended the station to repre-sent criminals and then showed him out when he was ready to leave. He'd been smiling and laughing with the lawyer, but when he was gone it was a different story.

He came up to me and said, 'Defence lawyers are the fucking scum of the earth, Paul. Their purpose in life is to make money by defending burglars, rapists, child molesters and doing whatever they can to get them off with the offence.' I just stood there quietly listening to him. He continued, 'Defence lawyers are not born: when another one is needed the gates of hell open up and Satan's arse pokes out. He shits out a large steaming turd and in it he puts in a black lump of coal instead of a human heart. *That* is where lawyers come from.'

I thought he was being a bit over the top myself. Certainly I could never have done their job. You've to have a certain amount of moral flexibility to sit in a room with somebody who's glassed some innocent person in the face or been busy raping children. They have to put morals to one side and look at how they can best defend that person. If that means trying to have evidence thrown out on technicalities or calling the children the biggest slags on the face of the earth in the witness box, then so be it.

The most popular legal firms used by the criminals seemed to me not to be the best at what they did. They'd just be the ones to complain about us the loudest in front of their clients and stamp up and down in court calling the police liars and accusing us of making the whole story up.

I used to really enjoy giving evidence in court. We'd stand in the witness box and first the prosecution (CPS) would ask us questions and then the defence would have a go. They'd use all sorts of tactics to try to make our evidence look as if we'd made it up or at least that we weren't 100 per cent sure of what really happened. The good lawyers had prepared a defence and had looked for a few mistakes or omissions. The bad ones used to just stand there and accuse us of making it all up to which we would, of course, just stand there and say that we hadn't! Pathetic really, as if we were going to stand there and say, 'Yes, you are right: we made the whole thing up, your worship.'

Crown Court is a different matter altogether. There you have a judge, barristers, solicitors and a jury of 12 people staring at you. The barristers are usually as sharp as razors and can manipulate what you say so they can get the jury to believe something happened when it didn't. Their questions are very carefully worded and you're only supposed to answer what they ask and not elaborate. You've to count on the CPS barrister to stand up and clarify what you meant by asking you more questions.

I'd been told by Alan when he tutored me about 'dock asthma'. It's when you're in the dock for two hours being torn apart by a barrister, when he has you against the ropes and you're struggling to keep him off you, you can start panting and coughing and then pretend to faint in the dock. Alan had done this twice apparently and to great effect. He'd fall backwards and bang his head on the way down for dramatic effect. The jurors would gasp as he fell to the floor and the court usher would rush over with a glass of water.

Court would be called to recess, and by the time they'd reconvened the defence barrister had lost the edge and you'd got time to think of some answers to his tough questions.

It was hard not to take things personally when you were being called a liar or accused of fabricating evidence, but it was really all part of the game. In between the hearings or during recess the lawyers from opposite sides would be laughing and joking together like the best of mates. As soon as the judge was back in the room they'd be ripping into each other like sworn enemies. I couldn't understand it until I realised it was all part of the game to them. Just another case to fight before home time.

I personally would never have anything to do with somebody who is a defence lawyer. They have a job to do – but then so do people who club baby seals to death. It doesn't mean I want to hang around with them in my spare time. I just acted in a professional manner with them and did my job the best I could.

One guy I knew was dating a lawyer. Out of interest I asked him what she did and he said she was a defence barrister. I felt my stomach churn immediately, 'So she defends rapists and nonce then?' I asked. 'Yes, she does,' he replied nonchalantly, 'but she says she tries not to think about it.' I just walked away in disgust. That seemed to me to be like saying, 'I sell crack to kids during the day, but after I leave work I try not to think about it.' Like that somehow makes it OK to do it so long as you put it out of your mind.

One legal rep who often attended the station went a bit too far looking after her clients. Her name was Alice. She had bobbed peroxide blond hair, was skinny to the point of looking anorexic, was always plastered in make-up and wore see-through blouses so you could see her lacy bra underneath which I didn't think was very professional.

Alice worked for one of the most popular firms of defence lawyers in town which shall remain nameless. I was in the cell block one day copying some tapes of my interview when Kurt ran into the room. He was as excited as a kid on Christmas morning when they see their pile of presents. He grabbed my arm and said, 'Come quickly, Paul, you have to see this.' I thought that there was trouble and ran after him.

We ran up the corridor towards an interview room where three police constables where fighting to stand in front of the viewing hole. Each interview room has one exterior hardwood door for soundproofing and then an interior door three inches behind that for extra soundproofing. The first door opens out and the next one opens in. The second door has a small circular magnifying viewing hole in it which is the same as you get in many front doors. The viewing hole is to make sure that the room's empty before you go in and set it up for use. There's an 'Interview in progress' light outside the room as well but sometimes people forgot to turn it on.

Kurt pushed me in front of the others and put a finger to his lips indicating for me to be quiet. I peered through the hole and couldn't believe what I saw. Alice was in the room with one of her clients giving him a blow job. She was sucking his dick like her life depended on it. I'm not too sure, but I didn't think that was included in the bill of prisoners' rights. No wonder her firm was so popular with the punters! I fancied being arrested myself if that was part of the package they were offering.

We all ran away from the door after that, but Kurt couldn't help it. He hated lawyers, so burst in on them and pretended to be shocked at what he saw. He then reported Alice to the law society. She was never seen at the station again.

Shortly after that we heard that one of the most infamous defence lawyers in Coventry had been killed in a motorbike accident. For many years he was the first to be called by anybody who'd broken into your house or shoved a beer glass into your son's face. He had a great track record for giving the police a hard time and getting people off at court. Over his career he must've defended well over a thousand active criminals, many of whom he managed to get off with the offence. Just because somebody is found not guilty at court does not actually mean they're not guilty. There can be witnesses who are too scared to testify, an exhibit can be lost, or a jury can believe their lies and not be aware of the defendant's string of previous convictions.

I've seen many guilty people walk away. I was told by my tutor Alan not to take it personally, but I always did. My in-built justice value system hated to see a bad person leave unpunished.

When we heard that the lawyer had been killed nobody in the police cared. We didn't like him at all, he chose to use his skills and talent to defend some very evil people. His purpose in life was to build a reputation as the man who could get you off, and that's what he did. His nice car and house and private education for his children was built on the misery of over a thousand victims of his clients.

Kurt of course had an opinion on the matter. 'When he goes to the gates of heaven and is asked to give an account to Saint Peter of what good he did with his life, he's fucked,' said Kurt. 'The devil made him and the devil will want him back now his time on Earth is finished.' I personally didn't believe in hell, but I did feel that if there was one, he was going.

The only people to attend the funeral were a couple of colleagues and family. No police went, and of course none of the thousand or so clients he'd represented over the years. Why would they? There's always another lawyer out there to replace one if they aren't about.

At the end of the tour of duty the day Kurt burst into the interview room on the woman sucking her client off he handed me his handwritten list of the most evil people in the world. He'd spent many months compiling it and had obviously put a lot of thought into it. I opened the folded piece of paper and read down Kurt's 'Most Evil People List'.

Defence lawyers
Paedophiles
E-mail spammers
Paparazzi photographers
People who park in spaces for the disabled
People who let their dog shit in the street
Game show hosts
Car clampers
Queue jumpers
People who take up two car parking spaces

I read it and looked back at Kurt. I'm not sure if he'd written it as some sort of joke or it was his actual thoughts on degrees of evil.

Happy Birthday to Me – 5 June 1973

We're living in 222 Humber Road. We have mice in the house. Jeff chases them with his big platform boots and squashes them.

I wake up early one morning from a scary dream. I walk into mum and Jeff's room. The floors all have yellow flowery lino on them. I stand next to Jeff's bed but I can't wake him up – he smells of beer. My feet feel cold and wet. I look down and see I'm standing in Jeff's sick, made up of red wine and big, square chunks of potato.

I sneak downstairs and put a chair against the sink. I stand on the chair and reach over to a box where mummy keeps her tablets, they're orange. I suck them until the orange comes off and then put them back into the box. They taste nice.

My pet rabbit is dying. Mum lays it in front of the fireplace. It looks like it's sleeping to me. I reach out to stroke it but its head whips around and it bites me on the end of my finger. I cry out. I go outside to play with the dog next door. It jumps up and bites me on my lip. Blood is pouring from my mouth and onto my Action Man tee shirt. I cry as I walk back home.

I'm lying in bed playing with my Tonka Toy. There's a small lever in it. I put its end in my nostril and walk around the bedroom saying over and over, 'I am a dalek – I am a dalek.' I sniff and it goes up my nose. I start to bleed all over my pyjamas. My mum and Jeff's brother Ray take me to the hospital. The doctor is an Injian, he puts a big pair of tweezers up my nose and pulls the lever out.

I like Ray, he's funny. He has a brown mark on his back that looks just like a duck. He says he lay down on a duck once and squashed it. He has three fingers missing from his left hand. He makes me laugh.

I'm 3 years old.

Year 4 – 1001 Thieves

Coming into my fourth year on the watch I became tired of the never-ending loop of working earlies, lates and then nights. I'd had enough of the mentality of some of the people I was working with, in particular some of the Zulu drivers who behaved like a bunch of kids. They'd sit in the briefing room and throw things at each other and if anybody said something but made a mistake in their sentence they'd all fall about laughing. Everything was related to sex as well, so if you said something like, 'Have you come across Mary?' they'd piss themselves laughing.

The Zulu drivers then began pulling your chair from under you when you went to sit down. People started falling on the floor when they did that and one guy injured his back because he'd had an operation on it a few years before. I was close to snapping point. I felt that the watch supervision should've done something about how they were behaving because it was getting worse by the day.

The jobs you're usually sent to as a police officer can often be monotonous such as people's dogs biting somebody, kids causing a nuisance and investigating persistent children missing from the local authority. I like to learn new things and face new challenges and once I know what I'm doing I get bored. I'd become tired of pushing a Panda car 'round the same areas, having to ask permission to come in and eat my dinner and having only one weekend off per month ruined my social life. I always seemed to be missing birthdays or special events due to my shift pattern.

The supervision on the watch had changed a few times and we had a new inspector from Birmingham called Insp. Ranks. He was knocking on in service and had about four years to go before retirement. He was in his early 50s, overweight, and talked in a very high-pitched Birmingham accent that went right through you. Listening to him was like having a chicken clucking in your ear. He had little enthusiasm for anything. To be honest, he just turned up to work but you wouldn't know he was there most times. He came to work and went to the odd job, but apart from that just drank tea and took up valuable office space.

Insp. Ranks seemed to me to be a very ineffectual man. Of the very few ideas he had, they'd inevitably be bad ones. His first was to single-crew police cars on nights. This idea went down with the watch like a lead balloon. To leave people exposed on their own in some shit-hole at 3 in the morning seemed to us to be lunacy. There were a couple of radio black spots around Coventry where you simply could not be heard.

Another problem with it was that if you went to a job where you ended up fighting it could be a while until help arrived – *if* you were able to get to your radio to ask for help. The entire watch was very upset by this and felt let down but they went ahead anyway. What a terrible thing to do. The job is hard enough without your own kind shitting on you from within. The sergeants were weak then and didn't face up to Insp. Ranks, well apart from Bill in the block who told him his idea stank, but that was Bill for you.

I decided to apply to work in the shoplifting squad which worked from Little Park Street. The team seemed really happy and hard-working and it would provide a much-needed change of scenery for me. There were not many applications for the shoplifting squad because it was a very busy unit and involved a lot of hard work. For me, it'd be ideal because I wanted to improve my crime skills in readiness to apply for the CID in a year's time.

Shortly after I put my report in to join I was accepted and had to wait a month to get in because the next person to leave had served 11 of their 12-month posting. My leaving present from Jed was him trying to have me disciplined for losing the keys to the cell block. It was an accident waiting to happen as far as I was concerned because there are two sets of keys for the cell block and they were always being left lying around the block. The two sets are duplicate and they open the entrance and exit doors, the cell doors, the security doors at the end of each row of cells plus a few other doors down there.

The custody sergeant carries one set and the striker PC carries the other. The fundamental flaw was that people were coming in and out of the cells 24 hours a day seven days a week. They'd borrow the keys to get their prisoners out for interview, to get paperwork from the admin room or to open the doctor's room to let the doctor in.

When it got very busy people would forget who they gave the keys to or the PC would give them to another PC who needed them. They'd put them down somewhere and they'd go missing for a few minutes and be found again. It seemed to me to be a very dangerous situation. If those keys were lost it would cost thousands of pounds to change the locks to every door in the cell block and somebody would be in big trouble.

At about 2 one morning I brought a prisoner into the cell block for fighting in town. He was in and out in an hour and as per usual he was let out through the front office and walked home. The problem in the cell block is that the place can become terribly busy and it's easy to forget who's dealing with which prisoner, who's due to be fed or seen by the doctor and who's coming in and out of interview. You've to remain switched on for the entire watch or you can easily make a mistake. Not the best place for Jed to be working, actually.

It was shortly after my prisoner had left the station that Jed discovered that his set of keys to the cell block was missing. He started to panic and searched everywhere. All the watch supervision hurried down to the cell block to help in the search and eventually I was called back down to the custody area.

Jed started to question me asking if I'd been watching my prisoner all the time I'd been dealing with him and if he could've swiped the keys when I wasn't looking. I could see where this was going immediately. I wasn't an idiot and never let my prisoners go wandering around the cell block on their own. Anyway, they were Jed's set of keys and as far as I was concerned he was responsible for them. If he left them lying around and they were now missing then that was his responsibility. The fact he was trying to blame me now showed what a coward he was.

The sergeants decided to go to my prisoner's house and search it. The search was illegal because he was no longer under arrest and they never arrested him on suspicion of stealing the keys. The cell keys were not there and were never found. The superintendent flew into a rage the next day when he found out. Replacing the cell keys for the entire block came out of his budget and was an embarrassment for him because a telex had to go to the chief constable and around every other station. He said he was going to have Jed's stripes for this, but the devil looks after his own. The storm died down and nothing happened to Jed.

The whole thing just seemed like a sign to me that it was time to get off the watch. At the same time I made a mental note that when I was a sergeant working in the cell block I'd never ever let the keys off my person. It'd prove to be a very unpopular thing to do, but it'd ensure that they were never lost whilst I was down there.

∼ ∾

My sanity was eventually saved when I finally left the watch to work at the shoplifting squad. Coventry city centre alone has over 250 shops and stores and with tens of thousands of visitors every week it's a prime target for thieves. The squad consisted of one sergeant, five posted PCs and usually one PC on a three-month attachment. They worked from a pokey little office a few offices up from the briefing room.

As the name suggests, all we dealt with was shoplifters. One of the good things about the shoplifting squad was the fact we had every other weekend off and never worked Sundays. We worked more sociable hours such as 9 to 5 or 12 till 8 p.m. This basically meant we had most evenings free, which is a real luxury if you're in the police.

We also got to work with all of the other watches at Little Park Street which was great. We got on well with most of the other watches and supervision but there was of course the odd one who was a nightmare to work with. Blue Watch had a sergeant who was often obstructive.

He'd pester you on the phone all the time you had a prisoner in the block when he was the custody sergeant. You'd be busy taking statements and doing enquiries and he'd be on your back all the time threatening to let your prisoner go loose if you didn't hurry up. He also had a speech impediment which made it very difficult to understand him.

His name was John Laverdock but some very cruel people named him Sgt. Laverduck because when he spoke it sounded like a duck quacking. I'm not sure if he was born partially deaf but that's how he spoke. He could speak but the words were often not correctly formed so conversations would take a long time. He was in the cell block for a while and was a pain to work with because he was very slow. For some very strange reason he was then placed in the control room operating the radio. Literally nobody could understand what the man was saying so you'd have to keep coming into the station and checking on the computer to get information about the job he'd just sent you to.

Another day he was out on patrol and had arrested somebody. He came into the cell block with his prisoner when I was there dealing with a shoplifter. He went to the booking-in desk with his prisoner and explained the circumstances to the custody sergeant. The odd word made sense, and you had to try to fill in the rest just like if you knew a little French and were trying to work out what the person was talking about.

He explained, 'Oib arrebted dis mon becaube he baddad the dargent.' The custody officer just looked at him completely flabbergasted. 'You arrested this man because he battered the sergeant?' 'Dow,' replied Sgt. Laverdock shaking his head from side to side, 'he baddad the dargent.' The custody officer looked very perplexed now and replied, 'That's what I said, he battered the sergeant.' 'Dow,' gasped Sgt. Laverdock, 'he baddad the dargent,' he then hecked up in his mouth and pretended to spit. 'Oh, he spat at the sergeant,' said the custody officer relieved. 'Jes, thatd wad I daid' replied Sgt. Laverdock. It was too much for some people there who had to leave the block and laugh at the hilarity of the scenario.

The shoplifting team processed prisoners and arrested shoplifters all day long every day. It was a great foundation for anybody who wants promotion or wants to work in the CID – and I wanted both. Chrissie was the sergeant who ran the team. She was a great person to work with, very professional, enthusiastic, and was a great laugh. For the first time as well, I got to call a sergeant by their first name. I do think it's a bit dehumanising to have to call people by their rank.

There was no room for slackers on the squad because there was never a day when people weren't stealing from stores. We had a very good relationship with the store detectives from most of the big stores and we'd developed a system that worked very well. They'd catch the thief on camera, make an arrest and detain them. By the time we got there, they'd prepared a statement of arrest and completed the paperwork for the property. All we had to do was arrest, interview and charge the prisoner. It was like a well-oiled machine.

We also got to use a lot of the interview techniques we'd been taught at training school. One of the best courses I've ever been on in the police (but then again there weren't that many) was interview techniques. Some sort of psychologist had put together a package looking at every facet of the psychology surrounding interviews and how to read body language. Some top detectives helped to put the package together so we could use it to professionally question a person within the confines of the Police and Criminal Evidence Act. Before that, it was basically just ask them questions or try pathetic techniques like 'Good cop, bad cop', which was an old CID technique from back when you were allowed to beat your prisoners up (them were the days).

The strangest part of the course was getting us to establish rapport with your prisoner. Before you started asking questions about the crime you had to be matey-matey with them and chat about their favourite football team or where they'd been on holiday. I just laughed to myself. You arrest some bloke for rape or murder and have to sit there chatting about which team he supports before how he stuck somebody with a knife 10 times. A lot of the techniques were very good, though. The only problem was that once the owner of the company who'd devised the interview training package had trained all the police trainers and he wasn't needed anymore he went off and sold his package to lawyers, so now they knew the same techniques as us.

Some dozy git of a police commander who signed for the package should've got an exclusivity clause in there preventing them from teaching this outside the police without their express written permission. Even I knew that from the second year of my law degree. The whole package had to be changed at the cost of millions of pounds to the taxpayer. Oh well, I won't tell them if you won't.

Part of the remit of the shoplifting squad included dealing with thefts by employees. Most shops pay low wages and the staff usually handle cash all day long. Some would get tempted and start to help themselves. When they were caught, we'd have to make an example of them. They'd be arrested and frog-marched out of the store in front of all their work colleagues. They'd always be charged because they were considered to have abused a position of trust.

We always worked in pairs at the police station. We'd book the prisoner into the cells, do address checks to confirm where they lived, and often we'd search their house if it seemed that they were shoplifting regularly. We'd often search a house and find an Aladdin's cave full of all sorts of goodies. About half of these people were stealing to make money, but about half of the big finds were actually by mums or dads who were going through a life crisis and actually stealing as a form of crying out for help. They just stored things like cans of deodorant in their houses and sometimes weren't caught for months because they just didn't fit the usual profile.

Working in Coventry meant that dealing with shoplifters was a full-time job. There are hundreds of shops in Coventry city centre. Department stores, supermarkets and also many smaller stores selling everything imaginable. Outside town, there're the usual large retail parks, supermarkets, corner shops and specialist shops. Every store at some point will have somebody come in and steal property or at least try to.

I hadn't actually realised the scale of the problem until I'd been on the shoplifting squad for a week or so. It seemed to me after a few weeks in the squad that nobody paid for anything at all. I dealt with thief after thief and in 12 months had arrested around over 500 shoplifters of every age, colour and creed. Some days I was called to several stores and arrested five or more shoplifters during my eight-hour shift. The vast majority were petty thefts involving people taking pick and mix from the sweet counter at Woolworths but frequently we dealt with highly organised teams of criminals who travelled the country stealing select items.

These teams almost exclusively used single females to steal the goods which they handed to the ringleaders later in the day. If the woman was arrested, she'd take the rap. If she informed on her handlers, she'd have her legs broken or worse. The cowards who ran the teams struck fear into the hearts of the people who stole for them. I suppose it was a bit like having a job really. You did all the hard work all day long and they got all the rewards.

There were some serial shoplifters who appeared time after time. One such character was an 87-year-old former prizefighter. He was only about 5 feet tall due to his spine shrinking. His face bore the scars of many bare-knuckle fights. I bet he could've told a few stories. He was old and appeared very frail and could hardly speak due to his wheezing. Whenever the store detectives tried to arrest him though, he'd spring to life and knock them out or head-butt them left, right and centre.

We dealt with hundreds of children shoplifting every year as well. It was almost always small things they'd steal such as sweets or pens and pencils. I think that often, they wanted to get some attention from their parents and this was a way of getting it. The reaction of the parents would always be very interesting to me because it'd tell me a lot about how their son or daughter was going to turn out eventually. If the parent screamed and shouted then this would actually have a negative effect because it was giving them the attention they craved. Instead of scaring them so they didn't steal again, they'd often be out stealing again the next day. Often, the parents would just shrug their shoulders and carry on watching the telly. I felt like grabbing them by the hair and throwing them in prison instead of their kids. Clearly, they hadn't bothered to teach their own children right from wrong.

The most interesting ones were those who simply denied it'd happened. We'd take the child home after being caught red-handed and the parent would say something like, 'My Johnny would never do such a thing,' and even after I pointed out that they'd been caught outside the shop with the stolen item in their pocket and filmed on the store's CCTV they'd just refuse to believe it'd happened.

Out of the many hundreds of children I'd taken home or arrested and taken to the station there was only one parent I'd say acted in an appropriate way. His 12-year-old son had been a passenger in a stolen car which had been caught by the police. The parents of the driver refused to attend the police station so we had to get an appropriate adult to attend from a list of volunteers. The parents of the other passengers eventually came but just sat there passively. When the dad of our passenger attended and his son came out of the cells he tore strips off him in front of everybody. 'You think you're a big man stealing people's cars?' he shouted. 'People have worked hard day after day to afford that car only for you to steal it, I am so ashamed of what you've done.'

The boy had come out of the cell smiling as if he'd done something good but was crying now. Seven police officers just stood there in shock that a real parent had taken affirmative action. We saw the other children several times again at the station over the following months – but not the boy who'd been told off by his dad.

If you want to know where criminals come from, I can tell you with complete confidence that 99 per cent of them come from bad parenting. Not being brought up with boundaries from an early age and no respect for parents, other adults, the law – or even themselves. The worst parents would bring up their children to hate the police, so when we drove through the neighbourhood children as young as 4 would spit at our cars.

Bad parenting doesn't just involve leaving children to their own devices. I see it all the time when parents don't bother to cook their children a nutritious meal and instead feed them junk food and sugary drinks or cook them reprocessed crap day after day. They leave them to rot playing video games for hours or watching DVDs, and when they do go out, it's to so-called 'family pubs' where the sorry excuse for a parent gets pissed while their child plays with other neglected children on swings or in padded play parks.

I honestly believe that parents should be called to account for their children's behaviour just like if their dog runs wild in the street and bites somebody. If they were in court as a co-offender any time their child was in there, then things may be very different.

Probably the best way ever I saw to deter kids from offending was a couple of years later. Somehow, a probation officer had convinced a headmaster to permit an ex-convict to come and speak to a group of boys who'd all been arrested and looked as if they were about to embark on a life of crime.

They all fancied themselves as tough guys, took drugs, were all fathers at age 15, had tattoos, smoked and hung around in gangs. They really thought they were the dog's bollocks because they'd been arrested a few times. Now was the time that they were going to be given their last chance at making a different choice.

The ex-convict was called Vince. Vince was a former professional boxer, 6' tall, lean and very muscular. His arms were covered in tattoos and he had swallows tattooed on either side of his neck. He had a long goatee. His face was covered with scars from the many gang fights he had over the years involving razors and knives. Vince had served three sentences in prison by the time he was 25: one for wounding, one for robbery, and one for supplying drugs.

Something had snapped inside him during his third time in prison. Maybe it was missing the birth of his son or not being there while his dad was dying from cancer. Maybe it was the look on his sister's face when she sat opposite him sobbing her heart out during visiting hours once a week. When he left, he vowed it was the last time he'd ever be in prison again.

Vince left prison and got a job stacking shelves at Tescos during the day and cleaning offices in the evening. He saved every penny for two years and put himself on a plumbers' course. He had learning difficulties, but studied for hours every day and eventually became a qualified plumber. With his hard work ethic he quickly built up a large number of clients and the money started to pour in.

Now Vince had a lovely home for his girlfriend and son and had a second child on the way. In his spare time he worked with the probation service to help out boys who were entering a life of crime. His methods were unorthodox, to say the least.

On the day Vince was invited to speak to the boys I was asked to come along as a representative local police officer. We all met in an unused classroom. There were ten 15-year-old boys sitting there with smart-arse looks on their faces, they really did believe their own bullshit. The headmaster and teacher were present when the probation officer came in with Vince.

Vince looked as hard as nails, he was not a man to be fucked with. He slowly sat down on a chair in front of the boys and carefully looked them in the eyes one by one as if he was sizing them all up. The atmosphere in the room began to change. One of the boys who must've been the ringleader thought he'd be clever and said, 'What the fuck do you want you gay?' The others sniggered.

Vince lifted his arm and pointed at the youth saying, 'I've fucking stabbed men in the neck for looking at me the wrong way, you little cunt, you fucking show me some respect or I'll come over there and bite your nose off.' The room fell silent. The boys all sat up straight, this was not their geography teacher and they couldn't intimidate him.

Vince sat there in silence for a moment longer and then began. 'You all think you're hard men – you don't know the meaning of the word. You're all going to prison and when you're in there you're going to miss your children growing up. Your girlfriends are going to be fucked by other men who're doing something with their lives. It takes a real man to care of his misses and children, and at the moment all I can see here are little boys who think they're hard men. Little boys like you are just rent boys in prison. Men will be queuing up all day long to fuck you sideways, because let me tell you, a man's ring-piece feels just the same as a woman's.'

The colour began to drain from their cheeks and nobody thought they were clever anymore. You could almost see them squeezing their anuses tighter at the thought of being gang-banged by 20 cell-mates, all with dicks the size of a baby's arm holding an apple.

Vince stood up and looked at them once more one at a time. He said, 'Your choice.' He walked out of the classroom followed by the probation officer. In about five minutes Vince had done more than the boys' parents, the education system, the social workers and the justice system had done to impact the boys in the previous three years.

꒰ ꒱

The shoplifting squad got on very well usually. There was the occasional clash of personalities but on the whole they were all a really good bunch and a pleasure to work with. While I was there we often had officers from other watches come and work with us on attachment for anything from a few days to three months. They came for a look at what we did or to improve their paperwork skills.

One such lady was an absolute stunner from Green Watch called Rosy. There're only a few policewomen that I met who I'd say were real crackers, and she was one. She had a fantastic figure, a slim waste and perfect gravity-defying knockers – they looked like 32C to me. Her hair was blonde with a hint of colour in it, and off-duty she wore it down and it went past her waist. She had full rosy red lips and a perfect milky-white English rose complexion. Most of the men in the station would've paid good money to drink her bathwater, including me.

In the bar after work she'd often wear a black cat suit and the policemen would just sit there looking at her, drooling. There was only one teeny-weeny problem: she'd only sleep with married men. Seriously, she'd target men at the station who were married and begin an affair with them. They'd become hopelessly infatuated with her and after a few weeks or months would leave their wives and children to be with her. At this point, she'd dump them, leaving them stuck. They'd often beg their wives to take them back or have a nervous breakdown. To my knowledge, she did this four times at Little Park Street before being moved to another station to start the process all over again.

Although she was a stunner there was obviously some serious psychological problem there. She was for some reason punishing these men and engineering the situation to make sure they experienced maximum devastation and humiliation. At a guess, I'd say either her father had left her mum for another woman, or possibly she'd been dumped. I'd say it was probably the former, though.

∾ ∾

It was while I was in the shoplifting squad I met two people who were to later help change the course of my life forever. The first was a man called Bernard. Bernard was originally from Canada and had worked there as an engineer but in 1974 had moved over to a village on the outskirts of Coventry so his wife could be closer to her sisters and brothers who were all living in Coventry. A few months after they'd moved to Coventry, Bernard's wife developed cervical cancer and died shortly afterwards.

After that Bernard went into a deep depression and became an alcoholic. He'd drink a bottle of vodka every day to numb the pain he was feeling. He lost his house, his car and everything he owned because he could no longer face working. He ended up living in a shed at the back of a friend's house. This lasted for two years until one day he checked himself into the mental health hospital where he was treated for a nervous breakdown.

He slowly rebuilt his life and studied hard for two years and eventually became a fully qualified counselling psychotherapist so he could help other people who felt their lives were falling apart. His speciality was addictions, but he helped all sorts of people over the following years.

Bernard was in his middle to late 50s when I met him. Somebody had handed a wallet into the front office at Little Park Street while I was in there and the driver's licence was inside so I decided to drop it off to the owner who turned out to be Bernard. The address on the licence was a small village to the north of Coventry. It was a bit off the beaten track but close enough to drive to in about 20 minutes.

Bernard lived in a small cottage with a few acres of land attached where he had a small farm and grew his own vegetables and fruit. He didn't need to work, because after he checked out of the mental hospital he found a life insurance policy in his wife's name he didn't know about. It had enabled him to buy the cottage for cash so his outgoings were very low. Bernard worked because he loved being with and helping people. He loved to help them turn their lives around and because he had been rock bottom he was in a good position to talk from experience. They'd come to see him as complete mental wrecks, and a few weeks or months later be very happy and contented.

Bernard was about 6' 2" and very skinny. He had a full head of thick brown hair which joined into a very thick bushy beard. He wore a pair of small round metal-framed spectacles which made him look like what you imagine the perfect grandad to. Bernard wore a permanent warm smile on his face as if nothing ever bothered him.

When I gave Bernard his wallet back at his front door he was delighted. He invited me in and we walked through a small hallway with cream-painted walls which had several watercolour paintings of riverbanks and canal boats hanging on them. We walked through the hall and past his living room. The inside of the cottage was dead silent, no music or TV playing. Every room had a large lead-lined window which let the sun soak in, giving the cottage a wonderful energy. They all had soothing pastel shades of creams, yellows and burnt orange and you naturally started to feel relaxed just by looking around. On the walls of the living room there were black-and-white photos of people and places which I presumed were from Bernard's life in Canada.

We went into the kitchen which had large terracotta tiles all over the floor. The walls were all white, in the corner was a large wood-burning stove which had a pile of chopped wood next to it. The smell of the wood pile reminded me of walks around Coventry's Coombe Abbey park when I was a little boy. There were piles of fresh vegetables on the kitchen top which he'd collected from his garden earlier that day.

I sat at Bernard's kitchen table which appeared very weathered. The oak the table was made from appeared to be very old and bore evidence of thousands of dinner sittings, scrapes, spills and dents. It matched the energy of the cottage perfectly. Bernard stood at the far end of the kitchen humming to himself as he meticulously made us both a cup of freshly-brewed coffee. As he spooned the Colombian blend into the coffee pot the aroma wafted to my nose. It was heavenly. A far sight from the maxpax we had in the cell block.

It was a rare treat as a police officer to be given fresh coffee (partly because nobody had spat in it). Bernard sat down opposite me and we chatted about how he came to be in the UK and how he became a psychotherapist. He was such an interesting chap, and when you spoke to him you could see he had a passion for helping other people.

As you spoke to Bernard he'd listen intently to every word you said as if it was the most interesting thing he'd ever heard; he'd lean towards you and nod slowly, occasionally saying 'really' or some other such comment when you said something of particular interest. You naturally felt calmer and calmer as you were with him, it just felt that he gave off some sort of peaceful energy that you absorbed as you were with him. You'd have Bernard's undivided attention while you were chatting away, and you couldn't help but feel that you were the most important person in his world at that moment.

Bernard's wallet had been handed in with all the money and credit cards intact which was a big surprise to me. 'You're lucky to get your money back, Bernard,' I told him, 'most are never handed in, or if they are, the money and credit cards are gone.' Bernard smiled at me and said, 'Really?' He had a genuine look of surprise on his face, 'I knew that mine would come back to me with all the contents intact.'

I was intrigued at how he could be so confident about that. 'How could you know that would happen?' I asked half laughing and half surprised. Bernard stopped smiling and cleared his throat as if what he was going to say next was of great importance. 'We create our own reality, Paul. I put my focus on an honest person picking it up and it coming back to me with everything inside.' I just nodded but had a confused look on my face. I wanted to know more but was becoming lost already. 'The city's full of thieves, Bernard,' I exclaimed, trying to educate him about the harsh realities of the real world. 'Maybe in your universe, Paul, but in mine people are kind and honest and loving. I see evidence to support my view every day.'

I've heard a phrase that I now know to be 100 per cent true: 'When the student is ready, the teacher will appear.' I didn't really believe in all that fate stuff but I just had a feeling that the wallet came into the front office at the exact time I was in there for a reason, and that it had fallen out of Bernard's pocket in order to bring me to his kitchen table. 'I deal with thieves day in and day out, Bernard. Your wallet must've been picked up by the only honest person in the city centre that day,' I said, still trying in vain to educate him about the hard realities of life.

Bernard stood silently for a minute as if he was thinking hard about what to say next or maybe how to say it. 'We have very different perspectives on life, Paul,' he said as he poured more fresh coffee into our cups. 'If you like, I can share my version of the universe with you, but some people find what I share very uncomfortable because it leaves them with no excuses or mental safety nets. Are you OK with that?'

I just sat there and nodded. I've always wanted to discover more about life. I've often felt like I was living in some sort of dream where I was living out a meaningless existence of working, eating and sleeping with no hope of escaping, as if there was something far greater that I could be experiencing but didn't know where to even begin looking. I wanted to know what it was all about, and I didn't care if I was going to hear things that I didn't like.

Bernard began to stroke his beard slowly with his left hand, and I could see he was constructing in his head how to tell me what he was going to say in a way that would make sense to me. 'We create our own universe, Paul. Everything we experience is via our senses of taste, smell, hearing, sight and touch, but these only give us a very poor facsimile of what is really happening, a sort of fuzzy, limited picture. All these things from this limited picture are then processed by our brains which runs filter programmes. The filter programmes are made from natural human instinct, what we learned from our parents and the self-talk we have all day long. These programmes generate what we *perceive* to be reality.' I nodded slowly but intently. I can't say it was making perfect sense to me, but I didn't want to say anything to interrupt.

Bernard cleared his throat and continued, 'If we are running programmes in our minds, then the reality we perceive will continually produce results that comply with these programmes.' I'd never heard anybody speaking like this and wanted to know more. 'Can you give me some examples, please?' I asked. Bernard smiled and nodded slowly. 'Let's use your example of thieves being everywhere. In your reality, when a wallet is lost you expect it to never be returned, and lo and behold, that is what happens. When I lost mine, I expected it to be returned to me with my money inside, and that is what happened.'

I didn't think that was a great example, 'That was just a fluke,' I said. 'Exactly,' explained Bernard, 'anything that doesn't comply with your programme is either a fluke or ignored as if it never happened.' I understood what Bernard was saying, and at the same time I didn't. 'Can you give me some more examples then, please?'

'Sure,' grinned Bernard, 'let's say you have a poverty programme running in your head so you say to yourself in your mind over and over, "I will never be rich" or "I am always broke" then that will be your reality.' I piped up, 'I don't see how saying that stuff can actually make it happen, though.' I could see that Bernard was talking about his most passionate subject because his eyes opened wide and he began to sit up straighter in his seat. 'Have you ever bought a car and then driving down the road you see exactly the same model everywhere you go?' I'd experienced this phenomenon a few times I thought, 'Yes, of course I have,' I said. Bernard smiled and said, 'The cars were always there, but now they have been brought into your consciousness. Before that they simply did not exist in your reality, or more to the point, you never saw them even though they were right in front of you.'

I was starting to get it now. 'But what does that have to do with money?' I asked. Bernard began to chew his lower lip slowly as he thought. He then said, 'If you are playing the poverty programme over and over your reality will be that you are broke and everywhere you look you will see evidence such as late payment notices, the crappy car you drive and cheap meals you have to eat.'

This time I was topping up my own coffee cup. I'd never heard such stuff before and wanted to know more. 'So how else does this work?' I asked. 'There is the non-love programme as well,' said Bernard, 'if you feel that you are not the sort of person who will ever meet a truly loving partner, then that is what will happen. You will either go out with people who are nasty to you, or when you meet somebody really nice you will reject them. The reasons you give to reject them will seem perfectly OK to you, but they will be beyond logic.'

'Has this happened to you then, Bernard?' I asked. 'Of course,' he laughed, 'quite a few times, in fact. I dated a few women and we got on great, but when it became serious a crisis would form in their lives or they would want to "cool things off for a while". It could have been that they didn't fancy me, but often it is because at a deep unconscious level they feel that they don't deserve love and so will sabotage it when it comes.'

I left Bernard's house with my head spinning. I wanted to know more but that was enough for one day. I took his business card with me and he said I was welcome to come around for coffee and a chat so long as he didn't have a client round.

Bernard had an extensive library of books. He believed that books helped set your mind free and was a voracious reader. He lent me a copy of one of his books, *Psycho Cybernetics* by Maxwell Maltz which was amazing. He also lent me a very old set of books published in 1927 by Robert Collier called *The Secret of the Ages* both of which helped me start to think in a different way.

The other man I met who changed my life was called Rich B. I'll tell you about him later.

ñ &srquo;

Searching people's houses was a regular activity on the watch and an almost daily activity on the shoplifting squad. It's good practice to search a person's house if you've reason to believe they're stealing regularly. Many people think you need a search warrant to search a house but this isn't true most of the time. The Police and Criminal Evidence Act, 1984, gives an officer the power to search a prisoner's house if they've reason to believe there's stolen or crime-related property inside. I won't bore you with all the technical details, but they often have a power to search premises if you're at the station or have just come out of a house and have been arrested.

Police only need a warrant if they don't have a prisoner in custody and are not in hot pursuit of one, for example, if they think drugs are being dealt from a house or stolen property is being sold from there, they'll need to apply for a search warrant from a magistrate. PACE can also be used by police to enter to effect an arrest of a person or to enter to save life and limb in case of a fire.

A lot of lazy officers wouldn't bother to search their prisoners' houses because it was too much time and effort but we had some tremendous results on the squad as a result of taking an extra hour to go and search our prisoners' houses. We were usually very thorough on the squad and house searches would often lead to us finding drugs or stolen property.

One afternoon I was in the office when Debbie who worked on the team came back from a search of her prisoner's house. Debbie was just like one of the lads, had bobbed, dark brown hair, a lovely clear complexion and was fairly short at about 5' 1". She had no airs or graces and would always show you her tits if you asked her to. Good as gold.

Debbie walked into the office with a pained expression, but clearly trying her best to suppress a huge laugh as well. The office was full at the time because we had a two-hour crossover period between shifts. I had to ask her what had happened and she burst out laughing.

We all gathered 'round her desk to hear the story, just loving to hear anything funny. Debbie told us that she'd arrested a prisoner from Debenhams for stealing perfume, a massively obese girl of 18. She was a bit strange apparently, not only in her behaviour but cursed with an overactive secretion of testosterone in her body. This meant that she had a substantial beard which could be seen from some distance. Obviously, looking like this she struggled to get any male attention.

When Debbie and her colleague went to search her house the girl's mum answered the door. Her mum was even bigger than her and had a beard to be proud of as well. They only wanted to search her bedroom but the girl kept it locked with a padlock on the outside of the door which was a bit strange. Luckily, they'd taken her key with them from her property at the cell block.

As they both walked into the room with her mum their attention was drawn to the dresser table by her bed. On it was a jar of Vaseline and next to it was the biggest vibrator they'd ever seen. On the tip of the vibrator was a huge piece of cac. Debbie let out a half-laugh and scream in front of the mother who looked like she was about to faint. Her daughter had obviously been shoving that thing up her arse with such force that it had come out with shit on and she'd never bothered to clean it off with a wet wipe. Euggghh.

They did a quick search of her room but couldn't get out of there fast enough. We all fell about the office laughing. Priceless. I don't know how they could face her in interview without laughing out loud.

It was a very happy time for me working in the shoplifting squad. My crime investigation skills were improving dramatically and so was my confidence as a police officer. I knew I was building a strong foundation for detective and then sergeant.

For the most part, the team were a brilliant bunch to work with. There was the occasional fallout in the team, but it'll happen in any small unit of people. We gelled really well as a team. Chrissy who was the sergeant was a great lady to work for, very professional and really nice-looking which is a bonus. On Saturdays we all used to wear plainclothes and Chrissie would wear skin-tight leggings which went down a treat with the lads.

We had lots of freedom so long as we were there to deal with the prisoners and do a good job. We were there to ease the burden from the watches which'd be bogged down all day long with paperwork if they had to deal with the shoplifters themselves. Our unit dealt with over a thousand shoplifters per year, and each prisoner would take maybe five hours to deal with, so you can imagine the nightmare that would be to patrolling officers.

I made a couple of friends in the shoplifting squad. It was pretty rare for me to see people from work outside of work hours because I didn't really feel that I wanted to mix my work and my private lives. Some police officers seemed only to have police friends and only dated police officers, which I didn't want. One of my friends in the shoplifting squad was Nick. Nick was a smashing bloke who'd joined from Blue Watch. I didn't know him very well before that but he was always happy when I saw him in the station, always laughing and joking which was a great quality (and fairly rare in the job).

Nick was a bit taller than me at 5' 10" and had fair hair which he always shaved to the bone because he was going bald even though he was only 25. He struggled with his weight a bit carrying a few extra pounds, but his large frame managed to carry it well.

Nick was married and had three sons with his wife. They lived in a police house in Coundon and seemed very happy together although I know money was always very tight for them. I started to nip around Nick's for a cup of tea and a while later we used to go out for a curry or a movie once a month.

Nick and I were interviewing a female shoplifter one afternoon. There'd always be a lead officer in the case and in the interview. The lead officer asked most of the questions and dealt with the structure of the interview. The other officer would take notes and ask any questions if he felt that a point had been missed or needed clarifying.

The Mr Nice and Mr Nasty roles that people think the police use in interviews is a bit of a throwback to the 1970s. Detectives would use it I think to try to alternately intimidate prisoners, and win them over. With the Police and Criminal Evidence Act which came into effect in 1984 everything had to be done fairly and above board and also on tape so you couldn't get away with that even if you wanted to (well, I suppose you could, but it was a bit harder to get away with it).

Nick was going through some questions with the female prisoner. She'd stolen a bottle of wine from Marks and Spencers but was saying that she'd walked out of the store and just forgotten to pay which is a often-used excuse. The fact that she was a prolific shoplifter and had hidden it inside her jacket made us think otherwise. She had her solicitor present who was sitting quietly taking notes. Most solicitors were professional and fair, but there was the occasional one who was obstructive.

Nick got to the part where the plainclothes store detective apprehended her leaving the store. He hadn't thought of the wording of the question beforehand and so said to the woman on tape, 'So, when did the store detective expose himself to you?' As he finished the question he let out a yelp as if trying to suck the words back into his mouth and then began laughing uncontrollably. I was laughing so hard the snot flew out of my nose and landed on my chin, the lawyer's shoulders were bouncing up and down as he laughed and his spectacles fell off his nose. Even the prisoner was laughing. We'd lost all control and continued to laugh for a few minutes as the tape recorded everything. Eventually, we regained our composure and finished off the interview.

Unfortunately, the case went all the way to court and the defence lawyer there who hadn't heard the tape asked for it to be played. He'd just read the written summary of the interview which of course didn't include the part where we were laughing hysterically. The court contained two lawyers, me, some members of the public at the back including law students, three magistrates and the court clerk.

The tape came to the part where Nick asked when the store detective had exposed himself and where we laughed. I couldn't keep my composure and stood in the dock laughing. The magistrates couldn't contain themselves either, the lawyers were chuckling and even the clerk had to bury his face in his hands to suppress the tears of laughter. We managed to gain some order and finish the trial. It was so great that even something serious could be funny at the same time. She was found guilty of theft and received a fine.

ᘒ ᘔ

I always prided myself on being very level-headed and capable of making rational decisions and keeping my head in emergency situations, even when others around me were losing it. But we can all have a day off, can't we?

At about 8 p.m. one evening I was in the shoplifting squad office. I was working a late shift dealing with some shoplifters with a guy on attachment called Terry. Terry was a great guy to work with, a good laugh, pretty keen and always did his fair share of work, which is all you can ask really. Terry reminded me of an ex-public school boy because he was well-turned-out and had a very neat haircut. He was tall and slim and wore round metal-rimmed spectacles which made him look more like a history teacher than a policeman. He was a popular guy with all the watches and always had a polite smile on his face. He had about six years' service and had worked on Blue Watch which I rated as a good team. Terry was working on the shoplifting squad on a three-month attachment.

His inspector had sent him on attachment until some of his complaints had been resolved. Terry had seven complaints outstanding against him and the number was growing. He'd just broken the record for the most open complaints at Little Park Street but nobody was congratulating him. Most of the complaints were about unnecessary use of force on his prisoners. I was a bit surprised because Terry came across as a very gentle person. It goes to show that you can't judge a book by its cover.

One of Terry's outstanding complaints had been made by a prolific juvenile criminal called Nev. I'd arrested Nev when he was 11 for stealing a box of after-eight mints from a corner shop in Hillfields called Pommies supermarket. Pommies is still there now at the junction of Swan Lane and Harnall Lane. His mum never bothered to come to the police station so an appropriate adult came instead. 'Appropriate adults' are a group of volunteers from a list who come to represent children when they're arrested if their parents can't be bothered to attend.

Four years later aged 15 he was burgling houses, stealing cars and doing ram raids. He was a crack addict and ran his own team of prostitutes whom he regularly beat up if they didn't pull in enough money for him. He was a nasty piece of work, but because of his age he hadn't been sent to prison (you've got to be 21 to go to prison). He'd been to youth detention centre a few times but it hadn't put him off offending. If anything, coming out of prison or detention centre is worn like a badge of honour by most of the ex-inmates. You get extra street cred (credibility) once you've done your bird (prison time).

I'm not a social worker, but I can tell you why Nev was the way he was. He was born to a young mother and some anonymous father. Nev's mum was young and stupid and didn't like herself very much. She'd been abused as a girl and was in and out of foster homes and children's homes. She had a string of boyfriends who'd all be charming to start with, and then begin to beat her up if she didn't agree to be one of their prostitutes.

Nev grew up in this environment and sure enough, he was taken away from her by social workers when he was 3 years. Nev went through the same process of foster homes and children's homes and at an early age came to the conclusion that he was unlovable. Whatever poison Nev's mum had been given by her parents, she'd passed on to her son. It was a certainty that he'd pass it onto his children but fate had something else in store for Nev.

His mum saw him regularly, but Nev resented her and when I did see her at the police station where she had to attend when Nev was arrested due to his age the conversations were not pretty. Nev would look at his mum and the poison in him came pouring out, 'What the fuck do you want, you bitch – I don't need you.' Nev's mum would just stand there and say, 'Oh, don't be like that, Nev. I've bought you a new mobile phone, look.' Nev wouldn't be interested, 'I don't want your phone, you stupid slag, just get me out of this fucking place.' He talked to his mum like a piece of shit – but then why not, she thought of herself as a piece of shit as well.

Nev was a persistent offender and a very nasty piece of work. There was not a damn thing anyone could do to him. Supervision orders, conditional discharges, fines, probation orders, suspended sentences, detention centre and so on. Nev had no intention of stopping, in fact, he was getting worse and worse.

It isn't hard to see why a life of crime is so appealing to some persons. I've spoken to a lot of probation officers, social workers and youth detention officers. The young offender can make easy money stealing or selling drugs, you don't pay tax, you can spend your money on whatever you like. Your mates all think you're cool so you're popular and have social approval and lots of young girls want to be around you because you've prestige and cash. While you're doing all this you still get your dole money and a free house from the council. What possible incentive is there to go and get a job sweeping up somewhere for five pounds an hour? In fact, you'd probably have to be mad to get a job because you'd lose your benefits and have to pay rent.

Terry basically hated Nev and people like him. They caused misery for hundreds of people by robbing, burgling, molesting and beating them. If he wasn't doing it directly, he was hurting the local population by helping to turn their district into a haven for drugs and prostitution.

By 16 Nev was at the peak of his drug-taking and offending. He was running even more prostitutes and was set up to become a mini-crime lord. There was a rival crack dealer who was a bit older than Nev called Christian. Christian had once given Nev a few slaps in front of his crew and Nev had never forgotten it.

A few older and wiser drug dealers saw an opportunity to take some competition out so they took Nev under their wing. They spent hours feeding him up on crack and winding Nev up about the beating he'd taken from Christian. When Nev was sufficiently out of it and bursting with anger they gave him a revolver and drove him to where Christian was standing, at the front line in the middle of Hillfields. I don't know if that place got its name from the police or the locals but the front line was where all the drug dealing and prostitution took place in Hillfields and the people who did it were extremely overt. It was almost as if they thought they were untouchable.

Nev's new friends said they'd keep the engine running while Nev went over and shot Christian. They told him they'd arranged a flight to get him out of the country to Jamaica and he could come back when it was all clear.

Nev walked up to Christian in broad daylight and shot him three times in the chest. Christian was dead before he hit the floor. People who were standing next to Christian were running away screaming. When Nev turned 'round to run back to the car, it had driven away. He panicked and ran away and hid in a local flat's stairwell but was arrested by armed police about an hour later.

Nev was given a life sentence for murder to be served in youth detention and then prison when he was 21. Christian was dead, leaving the coast clear for his competition to raise their prices.

As sad and ironic as it sounds, Coventry was a safer place to live in after this incident, with two persistent offenders out of circulation. Nev's fate was sealed the moment he was born into this world kicking and screaming. Under different circumstances he could've been a doctor or even a policeman, instead he was a crack-dealing pimp. I'm not saying it wasn't his fault, he chose his life and his actions and he deserved to pay for what he did. I just feel that our future is very much shaped by where we are born and who we are born to.

Terry considered himself as a policeman-cum-judge and jury. He'd target the worst criminals and with his partner make up offences and arrest them. He'd pretend they kicked him or swore at him, arrest them and do his best to have them remanded into custody.

Perhaps you think this is disgraceful or perhaps you think it is justified. The people Terry would arrest were the worst of the worst. They were the scum that would sell your kids crack and think nothing of it or walk up to you and punch you in your face and take your wallet or mobile phone. Having these people in the police cells or prison meant that they weren't robbing people like you. I'm not justifying what Terry was doing, but I do understand why he and others did such things.

One day Terry was driving in Hillfields and spotted Nev standing alone in the street (before the shooting, of course). Nev had lost a few friends because the week before Terry had driven up to him when he was standing with his drug-dealer mates. Terry had leaned out of the window and handed him a 10-pound note saying, 'Thanks for the info last week Nev. We recovered a load of drugs and stolen property.' Nev stood there in shock and his posse looked at him in disgust. They were obviously too thick to see through Terry's little trick.

When Terry saw Nev another evening it was about 11 p.m. and Nev was standing at his usual place at the front line. Terry was in his Panda and his partner was driving. Terry called Nev over and told him that there was a warrant outstanding for his arrest. He sat Nev in the back of the car and got into the back with him. They didn't drive to the police station, though. They drove to an abandoned industrial unit and Terry produced a baseball bat from under his seat. He started to hit Nev on the legs and knees a few times. Nev was shouting and crying out but Terry wasn't bothered about that. Terry didn't hit him hard enough to break anything, but he did want to punish Nev for being a burgling, robbing, crack-dealing piece of shit.

After that they drove Nev to junction four of the M6 and threw him out of the car. It was a 20-mile walk back home for Nev. He couldn't use his mobile phone to call a taxi because Terry had thrown it over the bridge. The nice brisk walk probably did him good anyway.

Nev had later made a complaint but there was no evidence to back his complaint up. Terry and his partner denied all knowledge, and in fact were very hurt and offended at being accused of doing such a horrible thing. They said that Nev was always in fights so had probably injured his legs that way and was clearly trying to make them both look bad.

I believe that most offences are committed because there isn't a sufficient deterrent. You'd have to burgle a lot of houses to go to prison. Before you got there, you'd have to be caught, and the police would need to have enough evidence to charge you. You'd get a free lawyer and barrister at court. Even if you did go to prison it isn't too bad. You get to doss in a bed all day and be woken up for meals, no different from what you were doing on the outside anyway is it, really? Well, apart from the fact that you don't get your dole check when you're inside.

When you get out you're given your dole cheque and a free house once again. What incentive is there to go straight? I feel that if you're convicted of a crime, even if it is just shoplifting you should have your dole money taken away or reduced. Why should we pay people to thieve? You should lose your entitlement to free housing as well. If you want money you should be made to work for it. There are thousands of jobs all over the country, even crappy jobs like sweeping up pay enough money to feed and clothe yourself.

Back to the office anyway. Terry and I were sitting enjoying a cup of tea waiting for a solicitor to come to the station so we could interview our prisoner. We heard a shout on the radio that a stolen car with four men in it was being chased through Coventry and heading towards The Butts which was just down the road from the police station. We ran out to the backyard and got into our police car. We drove out towards The Butts hoping to be able to help out if they dumped the car and ran for it. Sure enough the shout on the radio came that they'd abandoned the car and had run into the flats complex in Spon End near to The Butts.

Terry and I arrived and saw several police cars in the area and I recognised a few friends from Red Watch there who were on duty at that time and had been pursuing the stolen car. We ran to the middle of the flats complex where the driver of the stolen car had last been seen. Most criminals know where to run or drive to so they have the best chances of getting away. There's no point running across an open field if you want to escape on foot. Spon End is a decent place to dump a stolen car because there are lots of blocks of flats and twists and turns so you've a better chance of escaping.

The driver of the stolen car had been pursued by Sean who was a Zulu driver and probably one of the best drivers I'd ever come across in my time in the police. When he got behind a stolen car he was like a heat-seeking missile, they just couldn't shake him off. He'd even drive right up to the driver's door as the driver was trying to escape and push his bumper against it to trap him between the half-open door and the door frame. That took some skill to do without bashing the car.

Sean shouted over to me, 'He's in the river mate, trying to get across.' There's a river that runs through Coventry called the River Sherbourne. It's more of a stream for most of the year actually, but can get a bit bigger if it's been raining heavily for a few days. I ran to the bank of the stream and saw the driver. It'd been raining on and off for a few days so the bank was very muddy and slippery.

I looked down and could see the driver of the stolen car. He was a young white guy, maybe 21 years, wearing blue denim jeans, a pale blue tee shirt which was by now covered in dirt and a Burberry baseball cap. He was lying down in the stream crawling across to the other side, keeping his head down so as not to be seen.

I was really chuffed with myself. I'd be able to walk up to him and have a nice easy arrest. None of the running around that usually happens with car thieves. I slid down the bank and then stepped into the water to grab hold of him. I expected the water to be a couple of inches deep but as my foot sank into it, it never found the bottom. I fell arse over tit into a deep river. The water went over my head and I was immediately swimming.

It had been raining for a few days, you see, and what looked like a shallow stream from the top had actually turned into a rather deep and fast-flowing river. I know what you're thinking before you say anything and yes, it was stupid but give me a break. It makes a funny story at least.

I realised by now that the thief wasn't actually crawling across the stream but desperately trying to swim to the other side without drowning. Nice one, Paul. I was wearing my full police uniform, heavy NATO pullover, doc martin boots and belt kit including radio, handcuffs, pocket notebook and other stuff.

I began to swim as well, the water was freezing and I was surrounded by old bikes, shopping trolleys, used condoms and old car tyres. I'd suddenly lost interest in the prisoner and was doing my best to get to the other side of the bank without drowning. During all my time practising lifesaving I'd been wearing pyjamas and was in a nice heated pool. Now I was flapping about in a freezing river wearing about 10 kilograms in kit around my waist. I couldn't swim back to where I'd come from because it was too muddy to climb back up.

It took about 30 seconds to swim back and I slowly crawled across the bank and dragged my sorry arse onto the side and collapsed into the mud gasping for air. I was soaked through to my skin. I fell onto my back and looked up: somebody else had arrested the thief just by standing on the bank and waiting for him to swim across.

I turned to look over to where I'd jumped in and Terry was still standing there. He looked at me like completely gone out. I think he was still in shock but he still managed to look at me as if I was the biggest idiot he'd ever seen. He just stood there shaking his head in disbelief and then cupped his hands around his mouth and shouted some words of support and encouragement over to me, 'You fucking twat, Paul.' I could hardly argue looking at the evidence, could I? It had been obvious to him and any idiot in fact that the river was too deep to stand in. I'd just been in too much of a hurry to get the glory of the arrest.

I've seen many other incidents of police officers taking risks to get an arrest or some glory. When I joined the force one guy on my intake had chased a burglar over some factory roofs and fell through landing on some machinery 20 yards below. He died instantly. Another bobby had jumped through a broken window chasing a burglar but severed his jugular on a shard of glass and bled to death. Both of them were married, with children.

I personally witnessed many accidents and injuries as a result of over-zealous police officers trying to catch bad guys. Once when I was in a police car as a passenger with a probationer we were making the scene of a car chase where armed robbers were escaping from a building society they'd just robbed. He said to me as we were driving, 'If we get in front of them shall we ram their car with our car?' I was horrified. He was actually considering ramming a car moving at high speed containing armed and dangerous criminals. I just told him that if he wanted to could he drop me off somewhere safe first.

I know it's a good thing to want to catch criminals, but I also think that you have to use your common sense and do your best to stay calm and collected when you're on duty. It's better to stay safe and keep your wits about you than take stupid risks. I'd learned an important lesson by jumping into that river. I made a couple of other silly mistakes over the next few years, but was generally far more careful from that day on.

Terry drove me back to the police station. The River Sherbourne is absolutely filthy with broken prams, dog shit, dirty nappies and heaven knows what else in it. I'd swallowed a fair bit of it while swimming across. Luckily, there were showers in the police station so I threw my soaked uniform into a carrier bag and washed the scum off my body.

Needless to say, I was the laughing stock of the office for several days afterwards. I was lucky not to get dysentery or tetanus from that river.

ॐ ॐ

The Gordon family was notorious around Coventry. The word was they were not to be messed around with because they'd come and pay you a visit and put you in hospital. They may have been hard in their day, but their day had long since passed and all that was left was a bunch of drug-taking, dole-scrounging chavs who got their reputation by shouting threats to whoever would listen.

Paul was one of the family heads. He was about 30 years old, 5' 8" tall and quite chubby. He had thinning jet black hair and a goatee. Paul had very pallid skin and always walked around with a scowl on his face which he thought made him look like a hard man. He'd never worked a day in his life, was an alcoholic and heroin addict who paid for his habit by stealing whatever he could.

One day Paul walked into a shoe shop in the Burgess in Coventry city centre, put on a new pair of trainers and walked out again, as bold as brass. I went to take the report of theft with a PC called Ben who was on attachment to the shoplifting squad from Red Watch. Ben was a really energetic guy of 22. He was always dashing around the station and arresting people on patrol and getting into scraps and foot chases. He was a great guy to be working with.

It was open and shut as far as I could see. The witness in the shop had known Paul from school, he was caught on CCTV and had left his sweaty old pair of trainers in the shop. The witness was willing to give a statement to us, which was brave considering Paul knew where he lived.

Paul lived in Gulson Road which is in an area of Coventry called Stoke. All of the Gordon family lived in the same street or just around the corner. It helped when they needed to form a posse to go and intimidate a witness. I've seen it a lot where gangs or criminals or families arrange to live next to each other because it helps them to live the life of crime and have their support crew on hand.

Ben and I went 'round to Paul's house to see if he was there. When we got there we were met by his sister who had a very warm greeting for us, 'What the fuck do you cunts want?' She was a real charmer, 35 years old but looked more like 50. She was covered in a chain of love bites around her neck, cheap gold jewellery and home-made tattoos all over her arms.

We could see Paul through the open doorway. He was pacing up and down in the back garden, and best of all, he was wearing the trainers he'd just stolen! We said we wanted a word with Paul (it would've been silly to say that we were there to arrest him) and we walked into the house. Paul's sister immediately tried to push the door shut in my face. She started screaming that we needed a warrant. She jumped on my back and shouted, 'Run!' to Paul who didn't have to be asked twice. By the time I'd thrown her off Paul had a good head start on us.

Ben and I ran after Paul and I shouted for help on the radio. Ben had got a head start on me (that's my excuse anyway). We had to jump over their six-foot fence to get out onto the street. I couldn't see Paul but I could see Ben as he ran and I presumed Ben had sight of Paul. As I turned the corner of the street and got into Acacia Avenue I could see Ben rolling around on the floor trying to handcuff Paul.

Paul's cousin Arnold had seen what was happening and decided to join in. Arnold was the same age as Paul but very lean and tall. He was cut from the same cloth as the entire family, on the dole but somehow managed to afford designer chav clothes and a rake of beer and fags every day. Arnold and Paul had committed many thefts, robberies and burglaries together over the years and also served time together in prison. For some reason, many people who have been to prison thinks that fact qualifies them as a hard man.

Arnold fancied a go with the police so we had to oblige. He stepped over the line when he grabbed hold of Ben's shirt and began to pull him away from Paul shouting, 'Get off him, you fucking pig!' I pulled Arnold off Ben and pushed him backwards shouting, 'Stay back!' I wanted to smack him but I had to help Ben tackle Paul, which was more important. Arnold made the mistake of coming back towards me. He must've mistaken me for somebody down the pub he could intimidate.

He came towards me with a fake hard man, screwed-up look on his face and was pointing his finger towards my face (it's called ballooning when you do that). It often worked for him with his victims or people who lived in the locality who were bothered by his reputation as a hard man. I didn't rate Arnold at all and could see through his act. He walked towards me still pointing his finger, pushed his shoulders out as if he was carrying invisible rolls of carpet under them and came closer to me shouting, 'You fucking slags!' I took this in the manner it was intended. BANG. I hit Arnold in the face with a straight right and his nose burst open like an overripe tomato. I hadn't lined the shot up properly so instead of knocking him out I'd just broken his nose. Bastard.

He stood there in shock for a few seconds while his brain worked out what to tell him to do next. I don't think anybody had faced up to him before and he was confused. The instruction came back from his brain to come towards me again – which I thought was bad advice, personally. He should've asked for a second opinion. He came back towards me to have another go. I didn't have time for this. Ben was struggling with Paul, and even though he was an alcoholic druggie was still strong and struggling away. A crowd of locals had started to gather around to watch and I knew a couple of them would come and have a go if they thought they could get away with it.

As Arnold came back towards me for round two, the cavalry arrived. Kurt came screeching around the corner in a Panda car. He aimed his car at Arnold and drove towards him staring over the steering wheel with a big cheesy grin. He hit him with the front of the police car with an almighty bang. Arnold bounced off the bonnet and landed on the ground in a crumpled heap leaving me free to help Ben handcuff Paul. That was him out of action for a bit.

I went over and handcuffed Arnold who by this time was sitting on the ground wondering what had hit him (it had been a diesel Peugeot 306). I grabbed him and threw him in the back of my police car. As I did so I heard Arnold let rip the loudest, wettest, most violent fart I'd ever heard and have ever heard since. Unfortunately for both of us, Arnold had lost control of his bowels and had shat in his pants. 'I want my mum!' he wailed. This local hard case realised he didn't want to be here any more. To be honest, due to the smell I didn't want to be there either, but life can be hard sometimes.

Back at the station we went through the same procedure I'd followed hundreds of times. Sit in the holding area waiting my turn with my prisoner. I gave the facts of the arrest to the custody sergeant. Because Arnold had shit himself there was a large space around him that people didn't want to enter.

Ben and I'd had about 10 minutes of excitement and now we were due for around six hours of interviews and paperwork to process the two prisoners. We knew that at the end of it they wouldn't go to prison. Probably some sort of fine or something similar. The reason for it is that for many years now there's simply been no room in the prisons. If you want to fit more in, you've to let some out on early release which is a dreadful idea. Don't even get me started on the prison system. Arnold immediately asked for one of the local firms of solicitors to represent him at the station.

Paul was found guilty of theft and got a suspended sentence even though he'd already been to prison several times. Arnold was found guilty of obstructing police and affray. He got a fine of £100 – which *you* had to pay for him because the only money he had was the dole money you gave him.

Happy Birthday to Me – 5 June 1974

Mum says that my dad is on his way to come and collect Cheryl and me. He's having us over for the weekend. I don't want to go, so I get on my bike and cycle to the top of the hill in Humber Road. I hide behind a railing and watch my dad's car come and go. When he's left I cycle back home. I want to stay with my mum.

Mum and Jeff are shouting at each other. I don't know what they're arguing about, and mum runs upstairs. I follow her. She's sitting in the toilet crying. I start to cry as well. I don't like it when my mum is upset.

The coal man has been. He's left a big bag of coal for our fire. Jeff shows me how to light the fire: we put small pieces of white firelighters in between the coals and screwed up bits of paper. When the fire is cracking I like to sit in front of it. I get some bread and put it on the end of a long fork and toast it in front of the fire.

I go to nursery with my mum, she works there. There's a toy car I want to sit in, but another boy has it and he won't share. I tell the teacher who tells him he has to share. He's very angry but he should've shared with me.

I'm 4 years old.

Year 5 – The Apprentice

As the clouds finally began to thin into tiny wisps in the sky which looked like strands of cotton wool, Dawn began to think back again to when she was a little girl. Her first memory was sitting on her grandmother's knee when she was 3 years old watching her knit. Dawn sat there in silent amazement watching the big thick needles click back and forth and the scarf she was knitting slowly appearing beneath them as if by magic.

Her nana was nice and cuddly and always had a sweetie for her in her pocket. She smelled of warm milk and ice cream. Dawn loved to see her nana. Nana eventually became ill and had to go into hospital. The last time she saw her she was lying asleep in the hospital bed. She had wires and tubes coming out of her. She gently kissed her on the forehead and whispered into her ear, 'I love you, Nana.'

At the funeral, Dawn's mum told her that her nana had gone to heaven but her body was going into the ground. She watched the coffin being lowered into the ground, her mum told her to throw some mud in and then they left.

Dawn's concentration came back to the sky again and then back to herself. What on earth was that funny taste in her mouth?

❧ ❧

As my time in the shoplifting squad came to an end I began to feel very dejected. I didn't want to go back to pushing a Panda car to job after job. I wasn't really interested in being a fast-response driver or in traffic. To me, a Zulu driver was just a glorified Panda driver, and if you do pass the advanced course you're expected to stay on the watch for at least two years so that they can get their money's worth out of you.

The two options for me were to become a detective in the CID or go for promotion. I thought I had what it took to be a detective and a sergeant as well. I was very thorough and had high standards, I loved to investigate crimes and catch bad people using my wits and intelligence rather than chasing them in cars. I liked to help my colleagues if they needed advice about policy, law or procedures as well. Most of all, I just wanted more out of life and pushing a Panda car for the next 25 years of my service was not an option.

Before I'd joined the shoplifting squad I'd enrolled for a part-time law degree at Coventry University. There were a few other police officers on it as well. We had to attend lectures two or three nights per week depending upon how many modules you were studying that year. Most of the police were doing a degree in criminal law but I specialised in business law because I wanted to do something a bit different. It meant that I had to do extra credits because my police service didn't count for business law but I did it anyway.

I think I'd always felt a bit intellectually inferior to my friends from school who'd gone on to do degrees when I chose to join the police cadets. I felt that they were somehow better than me and at a higher level. When I think back, that's complete nonsense. Those who finished their degrees almost always left university with massive debts. They ended up doing low-paying work that had nothing to do with their degree and most were unhappy. The promise of doing a degree and walking into a high-paying executive career seemed to all be a lie. Either way, rightly or wrongly, I wanted to have a degree as well.

It was very hard trying to fit the degree around working shifts in the police. I felt very annoyed when I had to take holiday time so I could attend lectures and every summer for five years I had to spend my summer holiday sitting at home reading books getting ready for end-of-year exams. Every summer I studied for my finals in property law, contract, tort and company law.

While I was studying for my business law degree I began to study for the sergeants' exam as well. Taking on the sergeants' exam was a big step for me. It involved reading four huge books and absorbing a lot of information. The books were on crime, general police duties, traffic, and evidence and procedure. It's like memorising four books each the size of this one jam-packed with facts and information. It wasn't just the sheer volume of information which made it hard but the way it was put together. Here's one extract.

Statutory Conspiracy. Criminal Law Act, 1977

Offence: Statutory Conspiracy. Criminal Law Act, 1977

Statutory conspiracy is defined by section 1 of the criminal law act 1977

Under section 1(1) if a person agrees with any other person or persons that a course of conduct shall be pursued which, if the agreement is carried out in accordance with their intentions, either –

(a) will necessarily amount to or involve the commission of any offence or offences by one or more of the parties to the agreement, or

(b) would do so but for the existence of facts which render the commission of the offence or any of the offences impossible,

He is guilty of conspiracy to commit the offence or offences in question.

Accordingly, it is an offence to agree to commit any criminal offence even one which is triable only summarily. However, by section 4 a conspiracy to commit a summary only offence can only be prosecuted by or with the consent of the director of public prosecutions.

Am I the only one that has to read it five times to make any sense of it at all? Now imagine four massive volumes of the above language.

I'd say that it was the equivalent of one or two years of a degree but condensed down into learning pure information. It was all about learning laws, statutes, powers of arrest, laws about heavy goods' vehicles, protection of children and a lot more. In order to take the exam and feel confident about passing I had to dedicate three hours per day for three months to study. This was on top of working shifts – and also studying for the law degree and doing lectures.

One month into studying for the sergeants' exam it was announced that anybody who wanted to join the CID could take the upcoming entrance test in four months' time. I did really want to be a detective, but that meant putting another two hours per day study in for that. There was a bit of crossover between the sergeants' and detectives' exams but most of it was new material.

It seemed an impossible task to fit in but I decided to try for it anyway. I put myself under a huge amount of pressure and my poor friends took a lot of flak from me while I was studying. I'd be in a bad mood most of the time. Back then I didn't understand stress and how it can affect how we're feeling and how we treat other people.

My routine was work for eight hours, go to my lecture for three hours, study at home for the sergeants' exams for three hours, and then two hours on the detective exams. I ran for 30 minutes three times a week to keep ticking over, but all I could do after all of that was sleep.

I used to come off a night shift at 7 a.m. and rush home for a shower because my lecture in contract law would be from 9 in the morning to 12 noon. I'd sit in the lecture theatre with the full-time students and all I could hear was moaning. They were all complaining that lectures started too early in the morning for them and they couldn't get up in time. They made a formal complaint and the university backed down and let them start at 10 a.m. I couldn't believe it. Moaning, whining bloody students, they didn't have a clue about real life. What about when they start a job and have to be there at 9 a.m., would they moan to their boss about it?

The worst thing was that the time had to be made up, so now the lecture was from 10 till 12 but we all had to go in another day for an hour's seminar which was twice as inconvenient now. I was so angry when that happened. I also used to get annoyed when people whine they have no time. What a load of rubbish. If you want something bad enough you *will* make time. Saying you've no time is just loser talk, it just means you don't put enough value on having or doing the thing you say you want.

There was one lady on the law degree programme who I admired tremendously. She was a foster mum to four children aged from 2 to 12 and she didn't have a husband or partner. She got up at 3 a.m. and did all her studying for the degree which she was doing part-time. She got the kids up at 7 a.m. and got them all off to school or nursery. She went to her part-time job, then to her lectures, and then collected the children.

She went to bed at the same time as the children which was 8 p.m. She got up at 3 a.m. again the next day and did the same thing. She never moaned about not having time or how hard things were. She just got on with her work and her life. She graduated with a first class degree and found work as a part-time lawyer.

Any person who is that dedicated deserves to be successful. While she was raising four children and getting up at 3 a.m. the full-time students were lying in bed and then moaning about how hard it was. Many of them failed their degree or just scraped by with a very low-class degree.

As I studied for the promotion exams my confidence in my job grew and grew. Often, police officers come across an incident and they're not sure of their powers of arrest. For some offences you have to catch people in the act to arrest, such as minor public order offences. Some have to be in a public place, and some can also be committed in private such as in your own home.

Powers of entry are also quite complicated. You've to be very careful about which circumstances you're permitted to force entry to a person's house because if you're there unlawfully and assaulted you've no comeback. Also, if you're there unlawfully any evidence you seize may not be admissible in court. I found as I learned more about the law and my powers I had to ask the sergeants less and less and more of my colleagues were coming to me for advice. I worked out the pass rate for the sergeants' exams and discovered that it was 17 per cent, which meant that most of those who for sat it were going to fail.

When the date for the sergeants' exam finally arrived I was very anxious but knew that I'd studied very hard and deserved to pass. I went to a university in Birmingham to take the exam. There were about 200 of us sitting in the hall. As I sat there I looked around and worked out that out of the five rows of us, four rows were going to fail. It was really important for me to pass, and there's only one exam sitting per year so I didn't want to waste a whole year of my life waiting for the next chance. The exam was three hours long and by the end I felt pretty confident, but you never know, do you?

The results are all marked by computer and take a few weeks to come out. The worst thing about the way the police do it is that results for any exams or posts are all sent out by fax to the front offices of the police stations. You usually hear if you've passed or failed something from the cleaner, who knows more than anybody else at the station, or somebody who happened to be in the front office when the fax came in.

About seven weeks later I was on duty in the station when I heard the sergeant in the control room on the radio announce that the results of the sergeants' written exams were in the front office for anybody who was interested. I ran to the office and looked on the wall where they'd already been stapled to the notice board. My heart was in my mouth as I looked down the list. I found my name and felt the rush of ecstasy surge through my body. I was walking on air for the rest of the day. Some of my friends on Red Watch came up to say well done, most of the sergeants were pleased for me and the inspector said well done as well.

There were no other constables on Red Watch qualified so it meant that I was eligible to be an acting sergeant. To actually become a sergeant you had to pass a paper sift where your experience is vetted by a panel of experienced senior officers. You then have a practical exam where you've to go through various situations with actors in them and deal with them. That was months away though, and for now I was just chuffed that I'd passed the written part of the exam.

Two months later I passed the detectives' exams, and that summer I also passed the fourth year of my part-time business law degree which meant there was one year left to go. It had been a hugely stressful time for me and I was doing an extraordinary amount of study but the results had been well worth it. I had to grin inwardly when I heard the students moan about their workload or other PCs whine about the fact they had to study an hour a day for the promotion exams. I just shook my head but said nothing.

It was the same a few years later when I left the police and was studying for some IT exams. I got up at 5:30 a.m. and went for a run, drove an hour to work and studied in a room for two hours. I studied during my lunch break and an hour after work and passed all the exams very quickly. When it came to pay review time I was escalated a few levels and everyone who'd been lying in bed or playing games on their PC at work moaned. All they could say was how lucky I was to get the money. Lucky!

Although I was back working on the watch it was a lot better than before I'd been on the shoplifting squad. My paperwork and investigation skills were at a very high standard and I knew more about crime files than the sergeants now. I'd passed my sergeants' written exams and was looked at in a different light by the watch supervision and my colleagues.

I was sent on a control room course so I could be the control room (acting) sergeant if needed and also a tutor constables' course. I'd tutored two new recruits before but I refused to tutor any more unless I'd been sent on the course. I felt that it was important that I'd been on the course for my promotion chances.

As soon as I got back from the control room course I was made acting sergeant working from the control room for a few weeks. I absolutely loved it. One of the old-sweat Zulu drivers was very upset because he usually worked up there which meant he could doss about for the entire shift. I replaced him because I was qualified to sergeant. On my first day in the control room he phoned me and told me I shouldn't be up there. He was clearly very jealous.

Being the controller is a very responsible task. You receive the incidents from the force control room which receives all the 999 calls. You're also sent jobs from the front office where members of the public phone in to report incidents or crimes in progress. You've to know the area you cover well and who the best person is to send to a particular job. You also need to have a lot of common sense and know when to send back-up or not to send people directly into danger. Knowing the police's legal powers well also helps.

I did my best to be fair and impartial while I was up there. The thing is though, that you're never going to please everyone. Eventually you're going to have to send one of your mates to a sudden death which they don't want to attend and they're going to resent you for it. That's why it's hard being an acting sergeant.

I also became a qualified police self-defence instructor, which included handcuff and baton training. It took quite some time but senior police and Home Office officials realised that police officers' protection equipment was inadequate for the job. The wooden truncheon (we called it a peg) was pathetic and the handcuffs with a chain in the middle were very dangerous as well. If you got only one cuff onto your prisoner they could swing the other end at your face and split your head open.

The first decent bit of kit we were issued was an extendable metal baton called a Casco. You just flick them with your wrist and they went from six inches to two feet long (sounds like a cue for a rude joke, I know). New kit being issued is a real highlight in the career of a police officer because it happens so rarely. When we got our Cascos we'd rack them open at any opportunity and chase each other around the station or rack them and use them to stir our tea. The crack it made whilst it was extending was great to hear. Very macho.

The baton training system made me laugh. We were all issued with a card with a picture of a man. Areas marked in red meant that you were not permitted to hit a person there and the head and groin were out of bounds. I wondered if the person who put the card together had ever seen an angry person in their lives.

The Home Office put these packs together and the top concern is to avoid any criticism. We were told that if we were attacked by a violent drugged-up offender that we were to hit them on the arms with flicking motions of the baton. We all practised with plastic batons hitting a thick pad. Of course, in reality when your back is against the wall and your life in danger you're going to smack them as hard as you can over the head and hope you knock them out.

Rigid handcuffs were issued later and they were a great tool. Once you could get one on then you had control of one of the prisoner's arms and could get him to the floor pretty quickly. A couple of years after that we were all issued with CS spray which has a similar effect to pepper spray. It's held in a small container and sprays out about three yards. It'd literally knock violent people over and they'd roll around on the floor clutching their eyes and screaming in a high-pitched voice, 'I'm melting, I'm melting.' The spray forces people to close their eyes tight and induces a lot of pain, though temporary.

As part of training we all had to have a dose. Even though it was a lower concentration than the live sprays it was still terribly painful and made your eyes water, snot dribble out of your nose and made you want to continually spit because it attacks the mucous membranes and any area on your body with moisture on.

There was some concern that the police would no longer try to reason with violent people, which was a valid point, but then again, when a person is drunk or drugged-up and violent there's little reasoning you can do with them. Better that they get a blast of CS than you hit them over the head with a metal baton.

There were a few instances of police officers making silly mistakes with the CS spray. One was chasing an offender down the road and got out his spray and tried to stop him by squirting it at his back. The policeman ran into his own jet of CS spray and hit the floor like a sack of spuds. Another time, a prisoner was fighting in the back of a police car and was sprayed with CS. The policeman driving the car was affected of course, and he crashed the car into a lamp post. Incidents like that just confirmed to me that police should never be routinely armed, it should be left to a specialist team.

❧ ❧

My doing well in my career didn't go down well with everybody on the watch. While I'd been away there'd been a few old sweats join Red Watch from other stations. During briefing they'd sit there laughing and making jokes at the most ridiculous comments. They'd formed a clique and if you didn't go along with their behaviour they didn't speak to you. It really was pathetic to watch, much like being back at school again. They'd throw things at each other and even had their own special noises they'd make and would fall about laughing when one of them made it.

I overheard Zane talking about me one day to a guy on one of the plainclothes squads. 'The power has gone to his head,' he moaned, which was just ridiculous. I had no real power. I know he was just a lazy bastard and hated to see other people getting on. He'd spent his entire service on the same watch doing the same thing, and all he wanted to do was drive around in his fast car with the lights on and the sirens wailing.

It wasn't just me though, anyone who stood out or who wanted to better themselves was made the target of ridicule by other watch members. You'd even be a target if you were a hard worker. One guy on the watch was the most proactive PC I've ever seen. From the moment he joined the watch he was arresting people every day, chasing cars and stopping and searching active criminals. His name was Roger Ledworth. The only thing he seemed to struggle with was catching people during a foot chase. They always seemed to get away so his nickname on the watch became 'Ledboots'.

Roger was 22 years, had curly fair hair and a swarthy complexion. He stood about 6 feet tall and was broad-shouldered. Roger was always laughing and joking and was well-liked by most of the unit. I did wonder how he got so many prisoners until I worked with him on one set of nights.

From the moment we left the station, Roger was stopping almost every car that moved. He'd do a PNC check on the car and the owner and if there was anything dodgy about either of them he'd do a search of the car and the driver. When I say search, he'd be all over the car as if he knew there were drugs in there somewhere. Most of the time nothing came of it, but very often he'd find drugs or weapons and have a prisoner.

In a very short space of time Roger knew most of the active criminals in Hillfields. He was the only PC on Red Watch who knew how to swear out warrants with the magistrates to do drug raids on people's houses and he even had his own informants, which was unheard of for PCs. These were all things that the CID usually did, and most of the sergeants didn't even know how to do that sort of stuff.

Roger was very self-motivated and it was lucky because he never had a single word of support or encouragement from the watch supervision. You'd have thought that he'd have been shown as the example the rest of us should be following, but no. Eventually, the sergeants decided to have their three-monthly reorganisation and they put Roger in a very quiet area where nothing happened. What a bunch of tossers.

Some of the members of the clique on Red Watch were happy about this because Roger was making them look bad. All they wanted to do was drive around the patch at high speed but not do anything particularly productive. On every briefing they'd take the piss out of Roger. They'd say they were joking, but behind their jokes was a lot of jealousy.

≈ ও

A few weeks after I started back at Red Watch I was asked to train a new probationer who was starting the next week. I didn't mind too much because when you're tutoring you can pick and choose a lot of the jobs you go to. It's also very satisfying to see a probationer's confidence grow. It always felt great to be passing on a lot of the things that Alan had taught me on to another person.

My new protégé was called Dale. Dale was the most unlikely candidate for the police force I'd ever come across. He was only 25 years but had already been a chartered accountant for a few years, had passed his degree, was highly educated and very well-presented and well-spoken. He'd use big words when we were chatting like 'gesticulating' and 'ephemeral' and I'd nod away and then look them up later in the dictionary to find out what they meant. He wasn't doing it to sound clever, I just think he was used to hanging around with more intellectual people than police officers. Dale looked out of place in a police uniform to me, I could see him in a nice expensive suit working in a business environment, not rolling around on the ground wrestling with shoplifters.

Dale was 5' 10" tall, had very neatly-groomed mousy brown hair which was centre-parted and slipped on to his forehead. He had a slightly tanned appearance which made him look perhaps half Italian although his parents and grandparents were all from the UK. He went to the gym four times a week and was pretty well-built. He was always immaculately turned out with clean hands and a very neatly ironed uniform. His wife was an absolute stunner as well. She reminded me of an English rose with her pale skin, deep blue eyes, rosy red lips and a great figure. She was a very intelligent woman as well.

The police force is basically a working-class or at best lower middle-class job. The pay is less than you get in a factory, you don't need any qualifications to join (any more). You're heavily supervised and all your actions and movements are controlled by policy and laws. Most of the officers I'd worked with were from working-class backgrounds and predominantly readers of the *Sun* or *The Mail* at best. I can understand why Dale left accountancy behind, but whatever possessed him to join the police I'd never understand. Perhaps he wanted to follow in his father's footsteps who'd been a police officer in the Met, and his grandfather before that.

It was a pleasure to tutor Dale. On the very first briefing he came to he came over and shook my hand and gave me a big smile. I thought, 'This guy's going to be great to tutor' – and he was. He had a great attitude, already had some life and work experience, and due to his previous occupation set very high professional standards, his paperwork was always impeccably neat. Dale was easily superintendent material or higher.

Being a police officer in Coventry was a real eye-opener for Dale. He was used to circulating with normal well-adjusted people with professional qualifications – and some of Red Watch were far from normal and well-adjusted. There were quite a few grown-up kids who laughed and giggled their way through briefing and ignored anybody who wasn't in their gang.

Dale was a threat to their intelligence and so didn't fit. That suited me fine, because I always felt that deep down I didn't belong in the police. I enjoyed the job but didn't feel that I really had anything in common with many of the people I worked with. I had very few friends inside the police, and those whom I did spend time with outside work hours were not your typical police officers. They were more rebellious and very seldom talked about the job when they were away from it.

Not only did Dale find some of Red Watch a little strange, but the small army of crack-dealing, wife-beating low lives we had to deal with on a daily basis were an entirely new group of society he had to adjust to. It was like an initiation by fire for Dale but he seemed to cope with it well.

Sometimes in the police you'll get a complaint made against you, and sometimes you can get a lot of complaints in a short space of time. This normally flags up a warning to the complaints department that you've become a liability and may need to be taken out of harm's way and put in an office job for a while to keep you out of trouble.

Dale and I managed to accumulate a complaint every week for six weeks. It was more bad luck than going around looking for trouble. I wasn't in the habit of carrying out the Red Watch practice of 'winding people up'. This is where you found a person walking down the street and made a concerted effort to piss them off so much that they flipped and attacked you and then they were arrested.

Wanting to be keen and teach Dale as much as possible, we volunteered for most of the jobs that came over the radio. Many of the incidents we went to ended up with us fighting with the prisoner and calling for help. A lot of the prisoners made complaints against us.

One such incident took place at about 3 p.m. one sunny afternoon when we were driving up Swan Lane in Hillfields. As we drove along the road, I could see just ahead of us, walking along the pavement, a guy called Marcus, one of the area's most prolific crack-dealing burglars. Marcus was a big strong man and at 6' 2" tall could be very intimidating. He was prone to extreme violence so you had to show no fear or hesitation when you were arresting him.

Marcus was about 25 years old and had been born and bred in Coventry. Before the persistent hard drug-taking had taken hold of his life he was a strapping handsome young man who'd turn the ladies' heads. Now, because he was covered with scars and had scabs all over his face, he turned their heads away instead. He'd started out on cannabis at school before graduating to heroin and then crack. He'd been to prison several times for drugs and burglary offences but was out again and screwing two or three houses a day.

Marcus looked up from the pavement as he walked and when he saw us he gave us a look of contempt which I always found baffling since *he* was the crackhead burglar and not I. As we got closer to him he coughed up a mouthful of phlegm and spat it at us. It hit the windscreen and exploded over it as if an eagle had just flown past and shat on it. There were members of the public walking nearby who were watching what had happened. I could take the odd insult or snorting noise, but gobbing on a police car in full daylight was not something I could let slip.

My philosophy was that if I let somebody get away with poking me in the chest, swearing in my face, or in this case spitting on my car, it'd mean that they and anybody who saw it happening would think they could get away with this sort of behaviour. What next? Slapping us in the face or giving us a quick dig? I don't think so.

I stopped the car and Dale and I got out. Dale had only been out of training school a couple of days so he just followed my lead. I knew that Marcus would be a handful if he played up. Even though he'd been abusing his body with heroin for a few years he was still tall, lean and powerful but I'd never back down from a confrontation. I also knew in the back of my mind that Dale wasn't a fighter; he wasn't afraid but wouldn't be a huge help if we ended up scrapping so if he played up I'd have to take Marcus out quickly and not end up wrestling if possible.

I called in on the radio that I was about to arrest Marcus. I didn't have to go into much detail because most of the watch knew who he was. I called in because if we ended up fighting I hoped that one or two other cars had already begun to make their way to our location in case we needed help.

I went up to Marcus and gave him the bad news, 'You are under arrest for affray,' I said with a deadpan look on my face. I didn't want to show any fear or signs of hesitation to him. I couldn't think of a more suitable offence to arrest him for really, as it isn't against the law to spit. Marcus dropped into a character that most criminals use when they're being arrested. He protested his innocence, rolling his eyes back in their sockets, throwing his hands into the air and shouting, 'I didn't do anything, for fucks sake.' In my earlier days I actually believed people when they lied to me. I even used to second-guess myself when I'd seen them commit a crime with my own eyes. It's a thief's instinct to lie, because by their very nature they're a dishonest person. They did it so often that they were very convincing.

But Dale and I'd seen him with our own eyes, plus the fact his greenie was still dribbling down our windscreen. I took hold of Marcus's arm and went to apply the handcuff to him. He wasn't having any of it, pulling his arm away. Marcus was a big bloke and very strong but I couldn't capitulate: he was going to be arrested even if it took half of Red Watch to do it. The police self-defence techniques are useless and only really work against a passive prisoner, which defeats the object of it then, really. As he began to struggle I had push him against my police car and then kick his legs from under him. He fell backwards against the roof of the car. I really wanted to punch him in his face to take the fight out of him but there were too many people around watching and he hadn't been violent enough yet.

Dale stood there in shock, he'd never been in a fight in his life and I don't think he could believe that people don't come quietly when they're being arrested. I got the handcuffs on one of Marcus's wrists. They were the new fixed type with a metal bar in the middle with a plastic housing. Once you got one on you can easily turn it and control your prisoner. Because I was a restraint trainer now I was very good at using the handcuffs.

Everyone has a point at which they will capitulate and Marcus had already reached his. He became more compliant after the second handcuff had been applied. We searched him for weapons and put him in the back of the car and Dale sat next to him. Marcus complained all the way back to the police station but we just ignored his pleas of innocence. He was charged with affray and made an official complaint against us for wrongful arrest. The incident went to court and somehow he managed to get a barrister to defend him at magistrates' court, which at the time was £150 per hour including preparation time, so let's call it an even three grand.

The barrister put up a very entertaining show, it was great. He got me in the witness box and told the magistrates how disgraceful my conduct had been. His poor innocent client had been walking down the road minding his own business. He had a terrible streaming cold and had to spit into the gutter. He didn't even know our car was passing but even so, his spittle missed our car by miles. Lawyers always pretend to be shocked in court and genuinely offended on behalf of their clients. I felt like clapping and throwing flowers at them after watching some of the shows they put on. What an Oscar winner.

I never took any lawyer's behaviour personally. They'd always call us liars saying we'd made it all up or that we had a vendetta against their client. They'd do anything to find a chink in our armour or a flaw in the case and expose it. It never washed with the magistrates. Marcus was given a suspended sentence (what a waste of time). The next week he was in court for burglary. The magistrates decided that he needed to go into rehab, so at a cost of 15 grand, the public (that would be you) paid for him to go.

A week after coming out of rehab and six more burglaries later he was found dead in his room in a hostel. He'd taken a bad fix of heroin and that was the end of him.

I doubt if anyone missed Marcus. His sole purpose was to take drugs, steal and burgle. That was what he did, it was his raison d'être. The winners out of his untimely death were the hundreds of people whose houses he didn't burgle, and the general public for not having to pay for his eventual incarceration in prison and his huge legal bills. The good news for us was that the complaint he'd made against Dale and me had to be dropped because he was dead. See, every cloud has a silver lining.

Another complaint Dale and I had against us was for assault. I did actually admit assaulting the prisoner, but I felt I did what I had to do. We'd been called to check an address in a block of flats to see if somebody who was wanted on warrant was there. Warrants are issued for many different reasons, but mostly for when people do not appear at court, don't pay their fine, or who skip bail. Warrants can be issued with or without a power of arrest (strange, I know), and yet other warrants you must have in your physical possession to arrest the person. What a pain in the neck.

We went to the address to check for the man and by some miracle he was at home. He seemed pretty passive as Dale told him he was under arrest under the power of the warrant. I believe that you should presume every prisoner is going to fight at some point even if they start out as very compliant. If they continue to behave themselves then great, if they play up then you're prepared.

I was very methodical when I did my job and taught others to be the same. Every prisoner was searched and handcuffed. The law actually says you have to fear that the prisoner will become violent towards you or injure themselves in order to be handcuffed. In reality, you should never trust a prisoner as far as you can spit them and *never ever* turn your back on them. The only people I didn't handcuff were old-age pensioners or children under 14.

One of the detectives I saw booking his prisoner in at the cell block made the mistake of turning his back on his prisoner once. He turned around to speak to somebody on the phone and the prisoner punched him so hard in the back of the head that he knocked him clean out. The prisoner had the living shit kicked out of him for that, but it was no consolation for the sparked-out detective. I made a mental note not to let that happen to me, no matter how nice the prisoner seemed to be.

Every single prisoner of mine was handcuffed and searched before they were put into the car. I can't tell you how many times I'd searched the back of my police car before I took it out and found blades and knives stuffed down the back seats by prisoners who'd been put in the back by the officers who had the car before me. Madness.

Dale had learned well and handcuffed our prisoner so his hands were behind his back. He searched him and I took hold of his arm to escort him out of the flat and to the car. The lifts in the block of flats were out of order. We only had to walk down three flights, which was easy enough. I kept hold of the prisoner's arm to make sure he didn't trip over or try to run away.

As we got a few steps down the second flight he suddenly flared up. He began shoving me with his shoulder and trying to head-butt me. I'd say that I couldn't believe it, but nothing surprised me anymore. I'm so glad that we'd handcuffed him to the rear and searched him. I could feel my feet slipping off the stairs, and they were so narrow that Dale couldn't get near enough to help me.

I knew that one of us was going to be falling down the steps and it was a toss-up between him and me. He lost. Just before I fell down about 30 concrete steps, I grabbed hold of the prisoner and pushed him down the stairs. He went arse over tit down every step smashing his face, ribs, head and shoulders. He landed at the bottom with blood all over his face and cuts and bruises everywhere. Oh dear.

We took him to hospital and the duty doctor looked at us like we were animals. I didn't bother to explain myself to him as it looked like he'd already made up his mind up about us. He stitched the man's face and head up and we took him to the cells. The warrant was only for non-payment of a fine for speeding, so I have no idea why he played up so much. The only explanation was that he'd had a few too many drinks and maybe taken some drugs.

He made an official complaint about Dale and me but upon booking him in to the cells, I clearly explained to the custody sergeant what had happened. I told him that I was in grave danger of being pushed down the stairs and injuring myself so I pushed him.

Over the years in the police I've seen so many police officers have to defend themselves and hit their prisoner. They then try to cover up what they did by denying it which seemed like madness to me. If you're so shit-scared that you've to punch or hit somebody with your baton why not come clean about it? Complaints and discipline came to interview Dale and me and we just told them what had happened. It was up to them to decide if I'd used excessive force, but after a few weeks they came back to me and told me there'd be no further action.

I'm proud to say that during my 12 years in the force I had many malicious complaints made against me by the people I arrested, but I was never once subject to disciplinary proceedings. Having complaints made against you is a regular part of life as a police officer. They're often made by the people you arrest (usually on advice from their lawyer) in an attempt to weaken the case against them. That never works though, because under sub judice rules, the complaint is never dealt with until after the court proceedings have finished.

The culture shock of police life was a lot for Dale to have to cope with. Although he was slightly older than the average recruit I found I had to be careful to point out things that would've been obvious to any kid brought up in a rough area. Hillfields was especially an eye-opener for Dale. When you got called to a job in one of the high-rise flats you had to approach it looking up in the air. If you didn't, you wouldn't be able to see if things had been thrown out at you. The usual things were rubbish and cups, but even the occasional radio or TV was thrown over the balcony at us.

Once Dale and I were walking towards Pioneer House. I was looking up and he'd forgotten to – I guess his mind was elsewhere. I just got under the lean-to at the bottom of the flats and Dale was a few yards behind me. I looked back towards him and saw something just miss his head and land on the ground about two yards away from him. It was a nappy full to the brim with runny baby shit. It exploded on the ground and the shit flew out and splatted up his trouser leg and onto his shirt. Dale just stood there looking at me totally gone out. I grabbed his arm and pulled him under the lean-to and told him he should've been looking up. If it had hit his head he would've been badly hurt or at least eating baby shit.

Another time we were parked in a side street not far from Unity House. We were what I thought was a safe distance away. As we sat there doing paperwork a mug bounced off the roof of our Panda car and broke into a few pieces. I nearly shat myself with the shock of it. It damaged the roof and I was very annoyed that some cowardly dole-scrounger had thrown something at my car. I'd have to complete an hour's worth of paperwork now.

I took the mug to the forensic team hoping that his fingerprints were on it. I would've paid a week's wages to get a print and then kick his door in at 5 a.m. one morning. I'd have stood over him in bed waving the mug under his nose saying, 'Hi, we came to bring you your mug back, mate.' It would've been worth it to see the look on his face. No such luck though: there was a partial print but not enough to be able to identify the person who threw it.

It was never a very pleasant experience going into the flats in Hillfields. The lifts always had large puddles of piss in there that you couldn't help but end up standing in. There were usually used condoms lying on the floor and used hypodermic syringes. These things were left in there by the very people who lived in the flats. I never understood the mentality of somebody who'd do that, but then, what's there to understand? It's beyond reason.

It's a particular trait of a certain element of society to sponge whatever money and accommodation they can but then proceed to ruin the very place they live in. It's known as shitting in your own nest or pissing on your chips. A case in point was a new housing development in Hillfields. Iden Road consisted of newly-built houses and some nice little flats. It looked really nice with manicured gardens and cosy little living rooms. The first half was sold to young couples or families, many of whom were new to Coventry. The estate agents always arranged to meet their clients at the office and then drove them to the estate along the least scabby route.

What they neglected to mention to the new occupants was that the other half of the estate was reserved for low-income families and unemployed people. In about three months the lovely new development went from spic and span to a war zone. Car engines appeared on the drives of the low-income houses. Dogs ran up and down the street shitting all over the place. Half-naked children played in the road and ran up and down past shitty nappies throwing stones through windows. New cars were scratched and repeatedly broken into and many of the gardens became overgrown so they looked like a jungle.

Nice walls were covered in graffiti and the people who'd moved in first never ventured outside their homes. When they were out at work, their neighbours were breaking into their houses and taking their possessions. When they got home they could see into their scumbag neighbours' living rooms and there they were, sitting down watching the TV they'd just stolen from them. They couldn't sell up either, because nobody wanted to move into something that looked like a war zone.

I don't really understand it, but some sections of society just prefer to live in complete squalor. I suppose it's a bit like hippos, really. When I went to the zoo one time I visited the hippo enclosure and it stank to high heaven. People had been complaining that the hippos were not being given clean water to live in and that it was cruel to keep them in such rancid filthy water.

The keeper eventually put up a sign for everyone to read which explained that the water the hippos live in was fresh and clean and replaced every week. The first thing the hippos do when it was cleaned was to continually shit in it for two days solid. They do it to mark their territory. The result is that the clean water looks and smells absolutely rancid in a few days' time. You see, some animals love to live in their own shit because it makes them feel right at home.

In about 1995 Coventry Council decided in their infinite wisdom to tidy up one of the roughest streets in Stoke Aldermoor. It was traditionally full of smashed windows on the houses, dog shit in the street, broken glass all over the place from car windows being broken and open bags of rotting rubbish.

About one quarter of a million pounds was used to give every council house in the street a new paint job, new double-glazed windows, hardwood doors and every front garden was landscaped. Half the money came from Coventry taxpayers and half from a European fund for tarting up chavvy estates. As the work was progressing several workmen went out of business because as soon as their back was turned their tools were being stolen and their vans being broken into.

The job was eventually finished, but no more than six months later the street was back to the way they wanted it. Shitty nappies and broken windows again. If people prefer to live in shit they'll ensure that their surroundings look like shit and you can tidy it up as much as you like but it'll always end up looking like shit again.

I heard the local beat officers talking about the street during breakfast one day. One was wondering how on earth it could've gone from looking so clean and tidy one week to like a war zone the next. The one who covered that street just turned around and said, 'You can't polish a turd.' I thought that said it all.

Dale was my star pupil and at the end of the tutor period I was happy to say that he'd make a fine but slightly out-of-place police officer. Unfortunately for Dale, Jed was still the station sergeant and Jed could see that Dale was very anxious to do well and so set to work on Dale as his new bullying project. While others with the same or less service than Dale were put on attachments to different departments and put on patrol in the police cars Dale was always left on his own to patrol Coventry city centre on foot.

Dale was put under constant pressure to bring in prisoners. It isn't that hard in Coventry, but walking around the city centre giving directions to tourists is the main function of any city centre patrol officer.

Policemen on foot patrol only serve to put the public's mind at ease. The chances of them coming across a crime in progress are minute.

There are only really two ways to get prisoners of any quality: wait until a member of the public reports a crime in progress and hope you get there in time, or go out in a police car to the roughest areas and stop as many cars as possible. If you stop enough in Coventry you'll come across somebody with weapons, drugs, wanted on warrant, disqualified for driving or committing some other offence. This is a fact.

Things would later get very bad for Dale before they got a lot worse.

∾ ᭡

I did continue to visit Bernard from time to time. He'd keep recommending books to me and we'd have a few nice chats. He was such a good listener I found myself telling him about my life and the people who figured in it. He'd just sit and listen and not really give any advice unless I asked for it.

Once I was complaining to Bernard about the way I was bullied by Jed and he made a comment that stopped me in my tracks. I was saying that Jed had made my probation a misery and was still picking on people on the watch. Bernard turned to me and said, 'We teach people how to treat us.' I stopped what I was saying and asked pointedly, 'What the hell does that mean?' I hoped he didn't mean that this was all my fault!

'Let me ask you another question,' said Bernard. 'You said that he only picks on a few people. How do you think he chooses whom to pick on?' I'd never thought of that. I thought for a few seconds and then said hesitantly, 'I guess he picks on those he thinks he can intimidate.' By this time I had an inkling where Bernard was going with this. Bernard nodded slowly, he was always gentle with the way he taught his lessons.

'And how does he know whom he can intimidate?' smiled Bernard. 'Well, I suppose we must give off some sort of signal that we won't stand up for ourselves,' I replied, inwardly starting to groan. 'That is it exactly,' said Bernard patiently, 'you are giving off a subconscious message that it is OK for people like him to bully you, and do you know why you are doing it?' I didn't have a clue; I just sat there and shook my head slowly from side to side silently wishing I'd never brought this up. I didn't want to go where I knew I had to.

I could feel a wave of sadness come from the pit of my stomach and up through my chest. I always suppressed my emotions and was as unemotional as I could possibly be. I guess it must've been to protect myself during the sudden deaths I went to and during the horrendous things I'd seen while in the police. Or maybe it went back even further than that, to when my stepdad walked out on us when I was very young.

I was devastated at the time and maybe I'd decided that I wasn't going to let anybody hurt me like that again.

My attention came back into the room and I gave Bernard my reply. 'I don't know, Bernard. Why would I give people the impression that it's OK to pick on me?' Bernard was like a gentle pit bull and wasn't going to let this one go. 'I know you don't know, Paul, but if you did know what would you say?' I began to feel very emotional, tears began to well up in my eyes and then quickly rolled down my cheeks. I can't remember the last time I'd cried. I'd usually feel embarrassed at crying in front of somebody else. When I was a little boy I'd always do my best not to cry because I wanted to give the impression I was strong. 'Is it because I don't like myself very much?' I whispered. As the words came out of my mouth I felt like a pair of curtains were being parted in my mind and behind them, the real me was being revealed, or at least an aspect of the real me.

Bernard stood up and patted me on my back saying, 'Brilliant, Paul. Most people go all the way through their lives not realising that.' He pulled a tissue out of a box and handed it to me. 'We will only let people treat us as badly as we treat ourselves. Only when they pass that limit will we say or do something to stop them.'

I felt that something was changing inside me, but it was not something I could put a name to. It was a big release of pent-up emotions and a feeling which went far beyond mere words. Bernard passed me a postcard-sized piece of blank paper and a pen. 'I want you to write something down and read it out aloud to yourself in front of a mirror three times a day,' he said, 'when you get up, at dinner, and before you go to bed.' I obediently picked up the pen.

Bernard dictated the following words to me which I was to write on the paper, then three times a day I was to look in the mirror and say to myself, 'I love you, you are a beautiful and worthy person.' Even as I wrote it I felt that I wasn't worth saying that to myself. Bernard said, 'If you want to transform your life forever, go over to that mirror and read it out aloud to yourself now.'

It took a huge effort to pull myself out of the chair and walk over to the mirror hanging over Bernard's open fire. Every step felt like I was wearing a pair of lead boots. I held the card up slowly and my hand began to shake. My voice croaked and quivered as I struggled to find the words as if something was trying to stop me, 'I love you,' I whispered, 'you are a beautiful and worthy person.' By this time I was sobbing uncontrollably. Bernard came over and did something that neither my father or any father-figure had ever done for me – he gave me a big hug. I felt more of whatever it was leaving my body as if poison was coming out of an old wound I'd lived with for many years.

As I stood there crying he softly whispered into my ear, 'Friends and women will come in and go out of your life, you can make money and lose it all ending up in the gutter, but if you truly love and accept yourself no matter what is going on in your life then you will always be OK.'

I left Bernard's house and went to work later that day. I had a huge knot in my stomach about speaking to Jed. I read in a book years later that when the pain becomes too much to bear people will usually take action, even if it involves doing something they're really afraid of. I'd reached my snapping point and although I was worried about the consequences I knew I had to confront him.

After briefing, I walked up to Jed and asked if I could speak to him in private. We walked to a quiet office and I told him how I felt. I asked him why I was the only one to be called back to the station day after day to have my paperwork pulled apart, why it always seemed to be me landing the shit jobs. I told him that I hated coming to work knowing he was there and even on my days off I worried about what was going to happen on the next tour of duty.

Jed just stood there listening to me. When I'd finished I was standing there shaking with worry. Jed remained silent for a few seconds and then put his hand out saying, 'I'm always hard on probationers, Paul. I didn't realise you were taking it that way. I'll bear what you said in mind from now on.' And it was over just like that. We shook hands and I never had another problem with Jed after that day. I could see him for what he really was, a sad insecure old man who was frustrated and scared inside.

Bernard had a motto he lived by: 'Fear no Man'. He never let anybody intimidate him. I sometimes wished it was that easy for me, but I seemed to worry when I was confronted by authority figures in my career from time to time. I'd worry about standing up to them and what would happen if I spoke to them about the way they were treating me and others.

∾ ∾

Just before I rejoined Red Watch from the shoplifting squad I'd begun to take private boxing lessons at the Flex Gym which is in Far Gosford Street in Coventry. I'd been doing weight training there for a while and was in pretty good shape. There was a boxing expert there called Glenn Smith. Glenn was about 30 years old but already had a full head of silver hair. He was about 6' tall and very lean and muscular. Glenn always had a bright smile on his face and a quiet wisdom beyond his years.

I always like to learn from authentic people, that is people who have

Me and my Tonka Toy 1975. I actually looked very fashionable back then.

Jeff Browning who named me after a bag of cement. Cheers Jeff!

The garages where the skin head threw the ladies handbag after he mugged her.

My brother John wearing my police hat. Me behind him.
I had to dress up in my police cadet uniform every time a relative came to visit.

My class at Bruches Police Training Centre. I'm centre row second in from the left.

The Pink Parrot Nightclub – Photo Courtesy of CWN

The alley where I first met Freddie the Fly

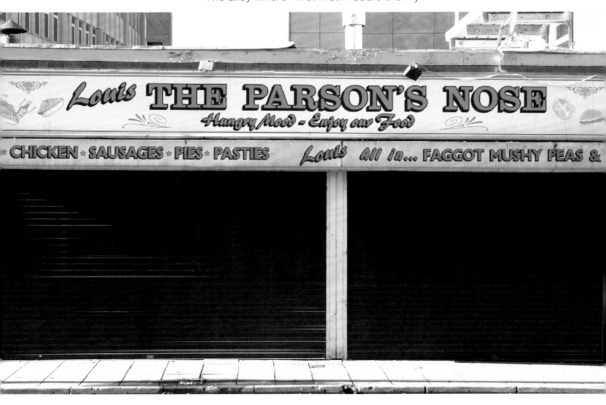

The Parsons Nose – Best Chips in Coventry (after a rake of beer)

Rover Road, where I caught two guys breaking into the back of a shop

Austin Maestro Panda Car – I crashed about 4 of these while I was in the police -
Photo Courtesy of Coventry library / Mirrorpix

Steve Jaspal PC 4373 – The Man the Myth

The site of one of my police car crashes.
Where I ran the burglar over.

Working hard in the shoplifting office.

The river I jumped into trying to catch the car thief.

The taxi rank and KFC – Where James was beaten up and lost his eye.

Glenn Smith (right) and Brian Collier – www.redcorner.co.uk – Coventry

Justin Gray (left) and Matty Evans.
European Vale Tudo Champions.
Photo Courtesy of Coventry library / Mirrorpix

The toilets where Dale was assaulted on duty -
Photo Courtesy of Coventry library / Mirrorpix

tested their skills in the real world. I found that I was in fights almost every day in the police and just didn't have the knowledge or skills to defend myself.

There are thousands of self-defence instructors out there but very few of them have tested their mettle for real. I don't mean that they've been out there picking fights with people, but they have been in real situations rather than the make-believe fights you have in sports like karate competitions or aikido. Glenn was in love with boxing and had been a feared competitor during the years he boxed in tournaments.

He'd been in the RAF for a few years and then began working as a scaffolder with his brother. His brother did him the biggest favour of his life when one day he told him that he had to go out and earn his own money. Glenn panicked and pleaded with his brother Steve to let him keep working with him. Steve was having none of it, so Glenn was forced to begin his own business. Soon, he was making twice what he did with Steve and running his own team.

Glenn eventually left and started teaching boxing at the Flex Gym and doing personal training. He quickly built up a big list of clients who came to him for private boxing lessons. In his spare time he studied for personal training qualifications as well.

After a few years Glenn took a brave decision to open his own gym in the Forum in Coventry called the Red Corner. (It can be found on the web at www.redcorner.co.uk.) But one of the things I really loved about Glenn's attitude was the fact that he was always pushing his comfort zone. He was not only a top boxing instructor but also attended grappling lessons with self-defence legend Geoff Thompson.

Geoff was a former doorman from Coventry and had over 200 fights on the doors. He was an expert in all forms of fighting including boxing, judo, ju jitsu, wrestling, kick boxing and also the psychological aspects that make up a street confrontation. You could only train with Geoff by invitation, and Glenn had been asked to come and train with Geoff and his small team. Glenn could only box, so for the first few months the grapplers would throw him all over the mat in the gym. As the months progressed Glenn's grappling skills improved so he could hold his own. It would've been easy for Glenn to stay at the top of his boxing tree but he humbled himself by starting as a beginner and I respected him enormously for that. Fate was kind and through the grappling and the friends we made our lives were to take some wonderful turns over the coming years.

I started having one private boxing lesson per week. It was very hard because I realised that my years of karate had built my muscle memory to pull my punches so I didn't cause injury when I sparred with people. This is obviously the opposite to boxing where the idea is to knock the other person out. It took many lessons for me to learn the basics but Glenn was a very patient and methodical instructor. As the months went on I became fitter than I'd ever been in my life. I also trained once a week at the boxing club as part of a group. I was running about 40 miles per week with a mixture of fast pace and endurance speeds. For anybody who wants to get fit, I highly recommend boxing training.

As my boxing improved I became interested in grappling as well. I found that the majority of the fights I was having in the police were more of a scuffle than a fist fight. Also, it looks very bad if members of the public are watching and you're busting people's noses and breaking their ribs. Grappling (or mixed martial arts) has so many advantages, but the main one for a police officer is that it looks very humane and usually only incapacitates the person on the receiving end without leaving them with injuries. Grappling uses elements from Thai boxing, judo, wrestling, Brazilian ju jitsu and other arts. It takes the best of all of them and adapts it for use in a realistic fight.

One of Glenn's best friends was a guy called Justin Gray. Justin was born and bred in Stoke Aldermoor, one of the roughest parts of Coventry. I don't know much about Justin's family background because he was a very quiet and private person. I heard that as he was growing up he had to look out for his younger brothers, so if they were bullied at school his mum used to send him on search-and-destroy missions to neutralise the offending person.

Justin had a lot of aggression inside him and channelled it through his Taekwondo. Somehow, he found out about Geoff Thompson's club and began to train with Geoff for many years learning about grappling and real self-defence.

Geoff took the best from many different martial arts and put it together into a system of self-defence that used hands, feet and grappling on the ground so the person had a complete range of techniques. Not only that, all his students had to use them in real fights that took place at the club. Apart from eye gouging, there were no rules. The only way out was to be knocked out or to tap the other person by way of submission. This was the first fighting system of this kind and woke a lot of the martial arts community up. It was originally called Vale Tudo but now is called cage fighting or mixed martial arts (MMA).

I began having weekly grappling lessons with Justin in his garage. The first lesson was horrendous. Justin was like Kato from the *Pink Panther* films. Every few seconds I was being attacked from every angle. Even though I was very fit I quickly became absolutely exhausted. By the end of my first lesson I had two black eyes and was drenched in sweat. Justin didn't have a bead of sweat on him and hadn't taken a single drink. 'I don't need a drink,' he said to me as I lay gasping on the floor,

'I haven't started sweating yet!'

I enjoyed the lessons with Justin and we got on really well. He was the real deal for sure. I saw Glenn the same week for a boxing lesson and told him how hard it'd been. 'That's Justin at one out of 10,' he said, 'he was going easy on you for the first lesson.' My heart sank. I consoled myself by thinking that if I got injured in any way I wouldn't be able to keep having lessons so he'd never injure me too badly. At least that was my logic.

I really enjoyed the grappling lessons. It used to take a lot of courage to pick up the phone and call Justin for the lesson. Over the next few days before the lesson I used to become very anxious for some reason and start losing sleep. I think it was just moving out of my comfort zone which caused the feelings of discomfort, but over the coming years I was grateful on more than one occasion that I'd learned how to fight.

I had it easy by all accounts. At Glenn's first lesson at Geoff's club he'd tried to punch Justin out but couldn't get close to him. He rushed Justin and pushed him against the wall but Justin grabbed Glenn's tee shirt and strangled him with it causing him to pass out. Glenn came to and rushed Justin again – and he did the very same thing. Glenn woke up looking up at the ceiling. As the months progressed Glenn and Justin became great friends and swapped a lot of knowledge about boxing and grappling.

Justin reminded me of a samurai warrior because he was a very decent person with an in-built code of honour and integrity. If anybody crossed him then they'd be quickly dealt with. Once, Justin went away to Cyprus for a few days with a friend of his who was a professional boxer. The boxer was going through a hard time and halfway through the holiday he started to abuse and insult Justin verbally while they were in their apartment. Justin ignored him, but when the guy tried to wade into him Justin took him to the ground and beat him so bad he was in hospital for weeks drinking through a straw. There was so much noise that the next-door neighbours ran in and found the boxer unconscious on the ground with blood splattered all up the walls. Oh well, you play with matches, you get burned.

Justin taught me two very valuable lessons in life. The first was visualisation, seeing what outcome you want in your mind before it happens. Justin was training for a grappling competition while I was having lessons with him. I chatted to him a few times about it. He'd already had the fight in his mind many times over and defeated the opponent easily. This is what Mohammed Ali used to do before a fight. He'd predict which round it would end in and with which type of punch. The second lesson was that pain is irrelevant (both physical and psychological). If your goal and will are strong enough you'll fight through the pain. During one lesson we got chatting about the upcoming fight and Justin turned to me with a deadpan look on his face and said, 'Even if he breaks my arm, I'm still going to win.' I then understood that pain is all in the mind. Justin was representing Geoff Thompson so the only outcome as far as he was concerned could be victory.

Beating one of Geoff's black belts would be a great outcome for whoever did it, so when it came to the fight, the organiser had changed the odds in his favour. Justin's opponent was over a foot taller than him and over a stone heavier. As they fought, every time Justin got him to the floor the referee would stop the match and get them to stand up again. This was because his opponent was a kicker and was no good on the ground.

Justin eventually beat the man despite the odds. He went up to the organiser's office to collect the winnings with Glenn and his mates, which was supposed to be 1,000 pounds as agreed beforehand. The promoter sat behind his desk smoking a big fat cigar and said, 'You can have 100 quid, take it or leave it.' Justin and Glenn were not amused. The guy was a cheat and a liar. The promoter had two minders with him but Justin, Glenn and their crew could've taken them on and beaten them, but that wouldn't have got them their money. They took the 100 pounds and walked out.

∾ ∾

Boxing lessons were very hard for me. No matter how fit you are, you always hit your own exhaustion level with boxing. I did dread sparring, but it's an important part of the learning process. Sparring with Glenn was a challenge both physically and mentally. His punches were laser-guided and always hit their mark. They stung even though he was holding back on the power. After several months' training I could last about five rounds with Glenn and maybe get about two punches in for every 10 of his. My philosophy of always going to the best to learn from paid off.

After months of training I reached a good level where I was one of his best students. I was no match for the competitive boxers, but at club level I was pretty good. With a combination of grappling and boxing I felt such a sense of inner peace and happiness, it was wonderful. The strange thing is that when you're sparring with someone, you're trying to punch their lights out, but at the same time you develop a deep respect for each other because you're both facing the same fears.

Some people used to ask me why I did the grappling and boxing. I told them that I knew one day I'd be on duty facing some huge monster of a man and I'd be on my own in a radio black spot. It would be just me and that person, and if he beat me, it'd probably be so badly that I'd be dead.

I trained hard every day and was physically and mentally prepared for the day somebody had a go at me, which was a regular event in the police. I ran six times a week, boxed every other day and grappled every week. I was a formidable opponent for the average person, not at the same level as bouncers or professional fighters, but I could take on 99 per cent of oncomers and dispatch them easily enough.

I'm not really a fighter and didn't consider myself a hard man. I just trained hard and learned from the best so I was confident that I could beat most of the people I was likely to come up against as a police officer who wanted to fight. I did meet some hard men while I was training. The funny thing is that the really hard men are very unassuming and often quite small. They don't need to shave their heads or show off armfulls of tattoos to prove anything. The best boxer in Glenn's club was also the smallest guy there.

As the years went on in the police I developed a set of 'rules'. If somebody breached them, I'd knock them out. First, if they pushed me or otherwise physically assaulted me or my colleagues. Second, if they approached me in a violent manner and appeared intent on harming me. Third, I'd also knock them out if I put my arm out to keep them away and they pushed against my hand twice in an attempt to invade my personal space.

If I felt that I was about to be fighting with somebody I'd do a mental calculation. I never really thought about it in great detail until after I left the police. I'd look at the size and strength of the assailant, work out if they'd been taking drugs or drinking, assessed if they were bluffing or if they were really hard. I'd then check to see if my partner was up for helping out or looked as if they were shitting themselves. I worked out how far away back-up was if I needed it. This was all done in a matter of seconds by which point I knew if I should call for help on the radio, try to calm the person down, or punch their head off their shoulders. Running away wasn't really an option while I was in uniform.

Knocking a person out is no big deal really. If you hit them hard enough in the jaw they'll be sparked out instantly. Personally, I'd rather never have to hit a person in my life but as a police officer you're facing some very violent and nasty people who have no regard for the uniform.

∽ ∾

One summer morning at about 8:30 I'd just finished a lesson with Justin and drove to my mum's house in Hillfields. She wasn't at home but I had my own key so I let myself in and made myself a cup of tea. After about five minutes I heard somebody knocking at her door but decided to ignore it since it wouldn't be for me.

My mum's house is hidden away from the road in an alleyway next to some private flats. It's nice and quiet but an easy target for burglars in that area because it's out of sight. She'd been broken into twice in the seven years she'd lived there. The person at the door kept knocking despite the fact that nobody was answering. I eventually got up and answered it.

When I answered it the guy knocking looked a bit surprised. The man standing in front of me was about 20 years old, had very pale skin which was covered in spots and sores around his mouth. His greasy brown hair poked out from under a black balaclava he was wearing. He was dressed in a black donkey jacket and carrying a black bin-liner over his shoulder. The only thing that was missing was a black-and-white striped jumper and the word SWAG on the side of the bin-liner.

The man stood out even more due to the fact that it was a sweltering day and he was dressed for winter. He stank of dirty clothes, body odour and bad breath. He came out with the classic line used by burglars when they knock at your door to see if anybody's in. The entire burglary has been rehearsed in their mind from start to finish including what to do if you answer the door.

'Is Bob in, mate?' he said looking a bit nervous. I wasn't sure if I knew this guy but I knew he was bad news. 'Bob who?' I growled, already feeling the rage building inside me. 'I brought him some stuff,' he said as he opened the bin-liner and showed me the contents. The bag was full of soiled dirty clothing and half-used jars of coffee, tea and Horlicks. The contents of the bag stank of stale piss and body odour. This didn't add up at all to me. He had a cover story but why would he be bringing around somebody some dirty clothing and smelly food?

I later found out that the contents of the bag came from a burglary he'd done 10 minutes earlier around the corner where he'd stolen a senile man's possessions. He turned his head and pointed towards the entry saying, 'I live just over there, I thought Bob lived here.' As he turned his head I could see a long scar on the side of his face. It went from his ear all the way across to the side of his mouth.

It finally dawned on me who this guy was. The man's name was Doyle and he was a notorious Coventry crack-smoking burglar, probably one of the most prolific burglars I'd ever known, in fact. I hadn't recognised him because he'd been in prison for two years and had grown up a bit. The last time I'd seen him was when he was a teenager.

Doyle had an identical twin called Len. From an early age they'd embarked on their criminal career terrorising the local population of Hillfields. From when they started to the present day they burgled on average two or three homes per day. The only time they stopped was when they were convicted and imprisoned.

They were part of a large family whose name at the time struck fear into the hearts of many of the residents of Hillfields because they were known to dish out some severe beatings. Doyle and Len managed to get away with many hundreds of burglaries and thefts due to the fact that when they were seen by a witness they'd blame the crime on the other brother. Identity parades were useless because they couldn't be told apart.

The second reason they got away with it for so long was that the victims were usually too frightened to call the police. You were considered a traitor if you called the police in the area of Coventry where they lived, even if you were the victim of a crime. There was some strange code that people lived by. Even if you didn't agree with the code, you were probably too frightened to have the police visit your house for fear of having a visit by the locals later.

One day karma struck. It was when Doyle burgled the wrong house. It belonged to a local drug dealer who found him in his living room squatting down shitting on his nice new axminster carpet. He didn't see the funny side of course, so he held Doyle down and pulled out a big knife and slashed his face, and from that day on the police could tell them apart. What a bonus.

Now this was a pickle for sure. He'd come to break into my mum's house and take what few possessions she owned. She'd have come home to find all her personal belongings stolen and her cupboard drawers all thrown on the floor. Anyone who has had their house broken into knows what I mean when I say they've been violated.

I was a police officer but I had no grounds to arrest him since all he'd done was knock on my mum's door and shown me a bag of old clothes. I felt helpless. I wanted to batter him really badly, and since I was off duty and he didn't know I was a police officer, now was a good as time as any. I knew I couldn't let him away with what he was about to do, so there was only once option left to me.

BANG. I hit him so hard in the face that his upper lip exploded and blood squirted all over my fist and his face. I hadn't lined the shot up properly (yet again) so it didn't knock him out. I thought, 'You stupid bastard, Paul, you should've lined him up with a question first.'

He staggered backwards in shock and then immediately tried to run but I pinned him up against a wall and went to work on him. I rained a barrage of punches to his head and ribs. He turned his back on me and tried to shield himself the best he could. I punched his head and all around his ribs and kidneys. BANG, BANG, BANG. I must've hit him all over his body with about 20 punches. As my knuckles hit his body I could feel the bones in my hand breaking but I didn't stop.

After what seemed like an age he made a break for it and managed somehow to scale a wall twice his height. He ran down the entry into the distance. I could've run after him and choked him out but then what? I'd have had an unconscious man lying on my mum's garden. I could've broken his neck but I had some small doubts whether my mum would've helped me dispose of the body.

Still think I was wrong to beat up Doyle? He and Len's modus operandi was to knock on your door while you were out at work or with your family somewhere. If nobody was at home, they'd force entry by one of a number of methods. Once inside, they'd find a suitcase and fill it with any of your valuables that they could sell to the local fence (stolen property handler).

They'd help themselves to any food in your fridge and then one or both of them would drop their trousers and shit in your bed. Probably as a mark of their strength and power. If you left a camera in your house they wouldn't steal it. Doyle would take a photo of Len sticking one your toothbrushes up his anus. You wouldn't know anything about it until they got the photos developed months later.

If you want to judge me then judge away. Next time you come home and all your children's Christmas presents are gone, there's shit in your bed and your toothbrush tastes funny, try calling a social worker or civil rights activist.

After I'd beaten up Doyle and the adrenalin began to subside I looked down at my hands. They were swollen, bruised and bloody. Punching somebody hard is nothing like the movies. It is bone hitting bone, the delicate bones in your hand break and your knuckles swell up and go purple and then black. It takes weeks to recover and your hands are never the same again. My hands still ache in the winter when the cold gets into the bones.

I went to my sister's house across the road and kept my hands in a bag of frozen peas for half an hour. I went to work that afternoon as if nothing had happened. Nothing to be gained by telling anybody.

My sister saw Doyle in town later that week. He had two black eyes, missing teeth, and walked hunched over due to his broken ribs. Ask me if I'm bothered. Believe me when I say that the world would be a better place if they were dead. They'll continue to burgle and do the same thing so long as there's a regular supply of crack and heroin for them to be addicted to. I've never ever come across somebody who steals to provide for their family or to give to the poor and needy. It's always to feed a drug habit.

✍ ✍

When I first joined the police I spent a week with a crime prevention officer called Reg. He was a detective with over 27 years' experience investigating burglaries. Reg was in his early 50s, had greying black hair which was shaved down to a number two. He walked with a straight back and had a military swagger about him. Reg had a slight limp which I heard was from when he was in the special forces but he never really spoke about it to anyone. He spoke with a very rough gritty voice which sounded like he had a permanent sore throat. Perhaps it was the years of smoking that had caused it.

Reg just had a couple more years left to serve and then he'd retire. When I was sitting in his office one day going through crime reports and the various modus operandi of career burglars he came and sat next to me. He put his cup of coffee down on his table and rolled up a cigarette and lit it (you were allowed to smoke in your office back then). He then gave me some advice I've never forgotten.

He said, 'If a burglar breaks into your house while you're there he knows he's taking a risk. This type of burglar is called a "creeper" because they have to creep around so you don't hear them.' In my 12 years' service I personally dealt with many such burglaries and the victims never had a sound night's sleep after the event.

Reg explained. 'The need to have a fix of heroin or crack is too strong to resist. If you hear something going on and see his face, the burglar knows that you'll be able to identify him later on. If he's identified later on he could go to prison where he'll no longer be able to get his crack. Logically then, you're standing in between the person and their crack and that's that. If you don't or can't defend yourself you're dead. There's no time to negotiate or reason, because if you hesitate, you're dead; if you capitulate, you're dead. You see, the burglar has come into your house with a plan he's executed many times before. He's chosen your house because you've no protection such as a burglar alarm or lights activated by movement and no noisy dog barking.'

I could see that Reg was giving me some important advice for my own safety as well as valuable advice to pass on to friends and members of the public if I thought they could handle the truth. Reg took a drag from his roll-up and inhaled deeply as if the nicotine rush was exactly what he needed. As he blew out the smoke he said, 'He's been trained by some of the best burglars in the UK in burglary school. Burglary school runs every day at 9 a.m. in your local prison.'

I could share some of their techniques with you – but I don't think I should. Just bear in mind that they know how to get in and out of your house without being detected or leaving evidence.

Reg had seen it all during his years as a detective and he'd dealt with over a thousand burglars. He knew how they worked and how they thought. He looked me in the eye and said something to me I've never forgotten. He said, 'Have a weapon in every room of your house and make the decision now that if somebody breaks into your house, to use it on them. Ignore any pleading or begging, because if you hesitate for even a second they'll stab you.'

Reg was only getting started. I knew from the way he was speaking that he'd seen this many times before. He continued, 'As you lie there bleeding to death you'll watch them slowly walk up your stairs. The last noise you'll hear is them smothering your children and then raping your wife eventually pumping her full of their diseased semen.'

I'm not sure if it was just me, but the room seemed to go very cold. I felt a shiver go down my spine but Reg was oblivious to it. He just went on with his cold advice very matter-of-factly saying, 'Your wife will lie there praying that the rape never ends, because she knows he is going to slit her throat when he's finished. All because you were too lazy and tight to buy a burglar alarm and set it, and too cowardly to wrap a baseball bat around an intruder's head.'

I could hardly speak when Reg had finished. After about a minute I asked him, 'What if you kill them though, Reg? Won't you go to prison?' Reg took a sip of his coffee and looked up towards the ceiling and pondered his reply. 'Fuck 'em, Paul,' he said, 'it's what it is. If you kill them in your house, just wait and see if the police come. If they don't come after half an hour, then chop the body up and feed it to the pigs. Make sure you pull their teeth out and chop their hands off and get rid of them so if the body is found it can't be identified.'

Reg casually took another sip of coffee and then said, 'If you think the police are going to come, then take a sharp knife out of your kitchen drawer and put it in their hands and give yourself a little stab in the stomach and say they were trying to kill you and you feared for your life. The worst-case scenario is you go to prison for a couple of years, but at least you and your family will be alive.'

That very day I went out and bought a burglar alarm for 50 quid and a spotlight for the back of my house which is activated by movement. It might not be very neighbourly, but the plan is to put the burglar off so they go to somebody else's house, somebody too lazy to get an alarm. I can't tell you how many burglaries I attended as a police officer, hundreds and then some. Out of all of those only one of the houses had a burglar alarm, and it went off just as they got into the house so they ran away without stealing anything.

I used to sit there in amazement when I took the details of a burglary and the homeowner was blaming the police for not being there. Listen, it's your bloody house, not the police's. There are about four officers on duty on any night shift covering a massive area. Half of them are probably stuck in the office filling in forms for five hours. The chances of them catching somebody burgling your house are minuscule.

I've dealt with thousands of victims of crime over the years. Don't be one of them.

৵ ৎ

Although I got on OK with most of Red Watch and could even have the occasional laugh with the juvenile Zulu drivers, there was one person on the unit who I worked with briefly and hated every minute of it. Jay had been a PC transferred to our watch from the criminal records liaison department. He was about 25 and ex-navy. He was a stockily-built Irishman with mousy brown hair cut in to a flat top. He had several tattoos on his arms which he'd collected during his travels around the world.

It was strange that he'd been in that department because they were a team of elderly police officers who were close to retirement. They filed paperwork and licked stamps all day long in between games of cards. It was basically a place you went to see out your last couple of years before retiring, so at age 24 it seemed unusual that Jay had ended up working there.

When he came onto the watch, Jay said that he'd upset his previous watch inspector and been sent from the station to work in the criminal records office. I felt really sorry for him, but not for long though. I later found out that the inspector had given him time off on many occasions because he was a keen cyclist and was part of a team that competed nationally. The inspector would let him have days off left, right and centre and often didn't take it off his leave allocation.

One day the inspector had asked him if he could cover for some sick leave for a few hours and Jay refused saying he was going out on the piss. The inspector was outraged, and one phone call to the superintendent later, Jay's transfer papers were signed and he was booted off the watch.

Jay was one of the most ignorant bastards I've ever had the misfortune to meet or work with. He was always in a mood, and on early shift he refused to speak to anybody; he'd literally ignore everybody, even when you said 'Good morning' or 'Hi, Jay' to him. We stuck a smiley face sticker on his paperwork box and wrote 'Cheer up, you miserable bastard' on it. Even that didn't seem to make him smile.

Strangely enough, the sergeants all liked him because he was a keen motorcyclist as well. If you rode a motorbike then the sergeants pretty much loved you because they were all at that age where men want to capture a bit of youth again and go out and buy a Kawasaki or whatever they're called and drive around at high speed on Sundays. They all used to chat on the watch about what tyres were best for cornering or where to go for custom exhausts.

I was partnered with Jay for a set of nights, nine hours in a Panda with a person who refused to speak to me. I'd actually quite liked him when he joined the watch but my opinion quickly changed. After ignoring me for the evening and morning at about 4:30 a.m. Jay would visit the newsagents and buy the *Times*. He'd park up in a remote spot and read it for an hour and then do the crossword.

I had to sit in the passenger seat and do nothing for two hours. After that it'd be time to go back to the station and go off duty. On the second night we were called to help the CID search a house. We pulled up to the house and I went over to the CID to find out what they wanted us to do. Jay drove off leaving me there on my jack.

I lasted three nights before I had to see the watch inspector. I asked to be crewed with somebody else because I couldn't bear it any more. I'd even have settled for Red, the lazy, smoking Zulu driver. He may have been an idle git with breath that could kill an elephant at 50 paces, but at least he could speak. I was pulled off the car and put with somebody else. I felt sorry for the poor soul who ended up with him. I did have to work in an office with Jay later in my service which is another nightmare I'll tell you about later.

≈ ≈

I do feel for the wives, partners or families of police officers. Having been out of the police for a few years now I've come to understand how the job can consume you. When I first joined the police I used to get home from work to my mum and sisters who were always keen to hear about how my day had gone. They wanted to hear exciting stories about the adventures I'd had during the day. I just used to say, 'Not much happened really – quiet day,' or 'Just the usual stuff, mum.'

What I really wanted to say was, 'Well, I chased a stolen car full of crackheads, we had a fight and one punched me in the head so I hit him so hard his teeth flew out of his mouth. Then I went to a cot death and had to carry somebody's beautiful dead baby to the mortuary. After that I got back to the station and my lazy bastard sergeant threatened to discipline me because my paperwork was a day late. Then I went to sit down to have some dinner, but got called out to a domestic. The man there spat in my face, so I lost my temper and kicked him in the bollocks and threw him in the cells to rot.'

The fact is that I don't think they could take the truth. If the families of police officers knew what really happened they'd lie awake in bed at night worrying and their children would wake up in the night crying. No, I just shrugged and said that not much happened. I swallowed all the badness and kept it inside. I'm convinced that if I'd stayed in the police I'd have eventually developed some sort of disease or gone insane.

I wish that there'd been regular counselling available to us all as a matter of routine. When we dealt with dead babies or were assaulted we were never offered any help. Even when we got back to the station, nobody ever asked if we were OK. There's very much a stiff upper lip mentality in the emergency services in the UK and the thought of seeing a counsellor for help is almost inconceivable. You just have to swallow hard and crack on.

Katie, who tutored me for a short time when I joined went to a cot death the day before I joined. I don't know what idiot sent a child-bearing woman to something like that. The mother was distraught and after quite some time wouldn't let go of her baby. Her baby had to go to the mortuary for a post mortem to find out the cause of death.

After a few hours, Katie had to wrestle the dead baby from her mother's arms and run up the road with him. The baby boy was wrapped in a pale blue blanket his mum had bought him, which she was going to put in a special baby box as a keepsake. I can't even begin to imagine how both Katie and the mother felt. Katie just had to suck it up and get on with the rest of her day at work when the incident had all been dealt with.

The only way I had of coping with the pressure was to go boxing and grappling. If I wasn't doing that, I don't know if I could've coped. I didn't drink or smoke, which is how many people secretly deal with their nerves.

I'm not looking for any sympathy when I tell you all this. I just want to try to help you see inside a police officer's world and perhaps help you understand why they can be the way they are, which is usually a bit of a closed book. When you're in the middle of it you can behave in strange ways and not even understand what you're doing or be able to control it.

My mum said that I was a very sensitive little boy as I was growing up. Being in the police changed me. I stopped caring about the violence and death I saw daily. The feelings were still there of course but I buried them deep down and changed as a person.

Years later they'd all come out again when I'd left the police and began seeing a counsellor. It all seems so clear to me now, but when I was in the thick of it, swallowing the feelings seemed to be the only thing I could do.

≈ ∽

I'd often take on the duty of acting sergeant at Red Watch which meant

I was covering the control room or was patrol sergeant. It was very difficult because you're supervising your own workmates. When you do get promoted you always move station, but whilst you're acting you usually do it on your own watch.

My first tour of duty as acting sergeant was on nights. I was so nervous I was shaking. As acting sergeant I wasn't really a sergeant, but I wasn't really a PC anymore either because I had the authority of the sergeant. It's a sort of limbo where you're neither. On my first night I had to read out the duties to the watch with another sergeant next to me and the watch inspector. It was a really strange experience because I was at the table at the top of the briefing room looking at all my colleagues, maybe 20 in total. Everyone was laughing and I later realised it was because the sergeant had stuck an 'L' plate to the back of my jumper without me knowing.

I was always as fair as possible, but at some point you're going to have to send one of your mates to a shit job and sometimes they resented me for it. There are some legendary shit jobs in the police that nobody wants to deal with. These include smelly sudden deaths, chavs stealing dole checks from each other and wanting to complain (they phone and say, 'My giro's been stolen and I know who's done it'), dog bites, dealing with the prisoners left in the cells by the last watch, babysitting suicidal prisoners in the cell block and standing outside a crime scene noting who goes in and out for eight hours. There're many more, but these are the most common 'shit jobs'.

One real pain job was dealing with missing persons. Not genuine mispers but children from local authority homes. A missing persons report is completed when a person is reported as missing and enquiries have to be made until that person is eventually found. You've to visit relatives, associates, places they're known to frequent as well as many other enquiries.

You may not know this but every city has a home for children whose parents don't want them. It's a bit like dog homes where dogs that are no longer wanted by their owners can drop them off and forget about them. Children's homes have children from about ages 10 to 17. There are three main ones in Coventry, and we were there all the time as police officers dealing with the kids doing a runner for a few days at a time.

The first time I went in it was like a chimps' tea party. The kids were running riot in there and the staff could do nothing. They were not allowed to touch them because it was classed as assault. The children, if they wanted to do a runner, just went out of the door and ran up the road and came back when they felt like it. Every time they did this it had to be reported as a missing person because they were in the vulnerable category.

It was really a terrible situation because the children were there because they'd been abused or their parents had died or simply didn't want them anymore. They were thrown into these terrible places and basically brought up with no parents. The staff did the best they could, but unloved children will usually rebel in some way. The boys would be out stealing cars as soon as their feet could reach the pedals. The girls would harm themselves by scratching their arms with scissors or knives until they bled. They're forms of attention seeking because really, deep down, they just want to love and feel loved but they've been deprived of it.

When the location of the childrens' homes was discovered by some of the local villains they'd be there trying to recruit them to go out and steal cars or car stereos to order. They'd also 'befriend' the girls from age 13 upwards. They'd buy them nice things and of course the girls loved it because it was the first bit of attention they'd ever received. Shortly afterwards, they were sleeping with the girls and either got them pregnant and then dumped them, or they'd get them hooked on heroin and force them onto 'the game' (become a prostitute).

It was really dreadful but what on earth could we do? These children were being let down very badly by society. Social worker management would just blame the government or policies. Once you look to 'the system' to blame somebody your complaint just disappears into a sea of grey suits.

If one of the mispers died there'd be 'calls for reviews' or somebody would say 'lessons have been learned' which is complete and total rubbish. Children are still there today and the cycle still happens. I felt helpless to do anything to change things. When we caught them we'd return them to the children's home and they'd run into the front door and then jump out of the back window and be off down the road again laughing.

I realised how lucky I was to have a mother who loved us all and wanted us even though she was broke and had five of us to clothe and feed. If she'd changed her mind, we'd have all ended up in homes and gone the same way as these mispers. Maybe that's one of the reasons why I joined the police. To stop it happening to others and make a difference.

I'd done my fair share of 'shit jobs' and more due to Jed allocating them to me whenever possible and I never asked anybody to do what I wasn't prepared to do myself. Also, I was regularly out on patrol unlike some of my own sergeants. It would take dynamite to get them out of the station, I swear.

✌ ✍

One Sunday at about 8 in the morning I was out on patrol with Red Watch's inspector, Insp. Lewis (not his real name). Lewis had been promoted from the CID in Wolverhampton. He was 6' 2" with thinning black hair which he cropped short and a goatee. He was very slim due to all the exercise he did, was an endurance athlete and often competed in triathlons.

Insp. Lewis was very much a hands-on manager and you'd often see him out on patrol and arriving at incidents. I respected him for that because I saw so many shift inspectors just spending the entire tour of duty bumming around the station. As far as they were concerned they were an inspector now and didn't need to get involved with incidents.

Coventry was one of the first cities in the UK to boast a rave club. It was a mystery to me why people from all over the UK queued for hours to go into a dark room where rave music was playing and pay a fortune for cans of Coke and bottles of water. When the club first opened it was called The Edge but since then has been through several incarnations. Last I heard it was owned by Coventry University.

There was always a problem with people wandering out of the club at 7 a.m. and into town. By this time many of them had taken a lot of drink and ecstasy and coke (cocaine) and would wander off towards McDonalds for some breakfast before driving back to Manchester or wherever they'd come from.

As Insp. Lewis and I drove along Fairfax Street towards the club we could see a young black guy standing in the street. I guessed he'd come from The Edge due to the fact he was wearing rave type clothing which at the time could be anything but in his case was three-quarter length jeans, a black-and-white chequered shirt and a red bandana over his head. He was about 100 yards from The Edge standing right next to the bus depot and people were walking past with their children off to the sports centre across the road.

I had to have a double take and Insp. Lewis asked me, 'Is he doing what I think he's doing?' I said, 'If you think he's having a wank then you're right.' He was pulling away on his pudding in broad daylight and people were walking past him with their children on the way to the swimming pool across the road. This, of course, is not acceptable behaviour.

We got out of the car and approached the man. I grabbed hold of his arm and told him he was under arrest. He was completely out of it and didn't even know where he was, his eyes were shooting off in different directions. As I grabbed his hand to put the handcuffs on I heard a loud squelch. He'd ejaculated into his hand and I'd just squashed it all in with the palm of my hand. Eeuuuughhhh! It makes me squirm just to write about it. Why oh why hadn't I put my gloves on first?

❧ ❧

The Red Watch I came back to from the shoplifting squad was very different from the one I'd left a year earlier. Insp. Lewis had seemed like a nice enough man when I was working on the shoplifting squad, but when I got to know him better I didn't like him very much at all.

When things didn't go his way or we didn't catch a criminal we were chasing he'd suddenly become angry. He'd start to grind his teeth and you could see the muscles by his temples sticking out as he bit hard on his back teeth. It looked as if he was changing into the Incredible Hulk. The whole of Red Watch were very wary of him because you never knew when he was going to snap at you next.

He was also a very religious person, a Christian who went to church every Sunday. I was brought up as a Roman Catholic and as far as I remember you were supposed to be kind towards other people. Insp. Lewis had some temper on him, and if you crossed him he'd rip your head off in front of other people on the watch and he swore like a trooper when he was angry. That's a sure sign of having 'lost it'.

On my first day on the watch after leaving the shoplifting squad I paraded on earlies but had completely forgotten to take my ear ring off. I wore one when I was off duty for a few years while I was in the police. I guess it made me feel less like a police officer when I was away from work. Equal ops had actually ruled that men could wear a stud because women could. I actually always left mine out on duty because I didn't want to catch it if I got into a fight with a prisoner.

After briefing I was in the radio room with a few colleagues booking out my radio. Insp. Lewis marched right up to me, his face bright red and the veins sticking out of his temple, he looked as if somebody had just spat in his wife's face. 'Get that fucking ear ring out of your ear,' he shouted at me with his face inches away from mine. If somebody had come up and spoken to me like that outside I'd have taken their head off their shoulders.

The other police officers stood there in silence just watching to see what happened next. 'Oh, right,' I said, 'I completely forgot it was in there, sorry.' He stood there looking at me and chewing his teeth.

What a disgrace. There's no need to treat people like that, all he had to do was ask. He later came up to me when I was having breakfast and said he was just in a bad mood because he was on earlies. I thought, 'I'm on earlies too but I don't take my bad moods out on people.' It transpired that he had temper tantrums many more times.

I have a particular dislike of people who blow hot and cold like that. They're particularly dangerous when they attain positions of power over others. The people whom they manage never know how to take them, or if they can relax and have a joke with them, or if they're going to be sacked or demoted for crossing them on the wrong day. From that day on I never liked Insp. Lewis and avoided contact with him which was a challenge because he was the watch inspector.

When I next went to visit Bernard I chatted with him about how religious people could act in such a way. 'I don't get it,' I protested, 'how can they go to church or whatever their place of worship is and then either be horrible to people or do bad things?' Bernard, as always, had his own perspective. He looked at me from over his cup of coffee and said, 'Nietzsche said, "God is dead", Paul.'

I didn't really know what he meant by that and I think he could see the look of confusion on my face. 'Is Nietzsche some bloke you know from down the pub?' I asked. Bernard spluttered as he laughed out loud and coffee flew out of his mouth onto his shirt. I didn't know what was funny about what I'd asked.

When he'd finished cleaning his shirt he said, 'If we could video record the lives of those who claim to follow some sort of organised religion and those who do not you would probably find a very similar level of good deeds and bad, violence and peace, honesty and dishonesty,' he said. 'How can God be dead if he is omnipotent?' I asked still looking a bit baffled. Bernard smiled, 'I think Nietzsche was saying that not to be controversial but as a metaphor. Really, we all can't help but lead a spiritual life although some people do say we worship a certain god or our god is better than your god.'

Bernard rested his chin on his hands and let out a big sigh saying, 'Just because somebody claims to be religious it does not mean that their behaviour will match your perception of how they should act. There are so-called evil people and criminals going to church or other religious places every day, and good people who have no particular religious beliefs. Your inspector thinks that going to church makes him a good person, but his behaviour betrays him as a very insecure bully.'

It started to make more sense to me. I left Bernard thinking that it was more important what sort of life you led rather than if you claim to be religious but then are incongruent with your actions and the way you live your life.

I remember having to go to confessions at church once a month as I was growing up. I think it was on Saturday evenings. My sisters and I would have to sit on the church pew in a line of other people and go into the confessional box and confess our sins to the priest. It really was daft because what on earth do children have to confess? We had to say silly things like, 'I pulled my sister's hair' or 'I broke a plate and hid it in the bin.' According to the severity of the 'sins' the priest would then give us a series of prayers to say. For me it was usually one 'Our Father' and three 'Hail Mary's' which I said as fast as humanly possible.

๛ ๑

Sgt. Jed Leap was still on the watch and still rarely left the station. It was slightly more difficult for him to stay in the station because Insp. Lewis was very proactive and always out and about unlike Insp. Ranks who rarely left the safety of the station. When Jed did have to perform some sort of operational role, it became clear why he avoided it. He'd cause havoc or put people in danger due to a complete lack of ability or simple common sense. He earned the nickname on the watch of 'Jelly Head' which was a character in *Viz* magazine. Jelly Head was born with lime jelly instead of a brain but used to get into all sorts of adventures nonetheless.

Once Jed was the control room sergeant and I was on my own in a Panda car. He sent me to a domestic on my own in a block of flats which you should never do. If it had kicked off it would've taken an age for help to come even if I could've reached my radio. The next week he sent me to the top of a car park where a group of youths were acting suspiciously. When I got to the top one of them pulled a machete on me and came towards me with it. I somehow managed to karate kick him in the head and send him flying.

Another time he was out on patrol and had to put out a description of an offender. You're supposed to give the details in stages and confirm that the controller has received it and then continue. He kept the button pressed in for a full five minutes reading everything out without stopping. If anybody else had been trying to get across the air in case of an emergency they wouldn't have been able to.

I'm not saying that he was all bad. Outside of work you couldn't hope to meet a nicer bloke, he was always smiling and very civil towards people. It was just when you put the uniform on him and put him under a bit of pressure he turned into a useless idiot. He'd have been perfect working in some rural area talking to farmers about poachers or badger-baiting, anything really apart from operational police work. I never know why he didn't apply for a nice cushy admin job where he could have weekends off and not do any harm.

Most of Red Watch including the sergeants were scared of Insp. Lewis. He was obsessed with numbers of prisoners arrested. He walked around the station with a red book under his arm which contained a tally of how many prisoners had been arrested by the watch. He'd compare our number of prisoners with the other three units and blow a gasket if they'd arrested more than us.

I think the red prisoner book was the first attempt by police management to measure performance. Unfortunately quality was not measured so some of Red Watch went around locking up anybody who looked the wrong way at them. It's so easy to stop some local toe rag, poke your finger in their chest and wind them up until they swear at you. You can then arrest them and throw them in the cells.

I never engaged in this pathetic ritual. Half of the time the prisoner was released without charge or even worse, custody refused by the custody sergeant because there was not even enough evidence to arrest, let alone detain and charge.

Unfortunately for us, the decision had been reached that we needed as many bodies as possible passing through the cells to keep his numbers high. If quality was not important nor if they were ever charged or not, how about arresting people for a minor offence and then giving them an instant caution at the station? That way our number of prisoners would be very high for very little effort. This of course had no positive impact whatsoever for the general public and was purely a numbers game. One of many I came across in my time in the police.

The watch supervision thought they'd struck gold when it was decided that every weekend we'd have a plainclothes operation staking out the local public toilets. The public toilets in Coventry were frequented by lots and lots of gay men. I had no objection about gay men doing whatever they wanted with each other in private. I find it offensive when they went to the public toilets and masturbated each other or fellated or buggered each other while members of the public including children were coming in and out of the toilets. I wouldn't want to find anybody of any sex having intercourse in a public place where children could walk in.

It was clear what was happening because the toilet floors were usually covered in semen and there was always a hole drilled between the chipboard in each cubicle wall which was about three inches in diameter. This was apparently known as the 'glory hole', and if you stuck your dick through it somebody the other side would give you a blow job or a quick wank. And so it was decided. Some of Red Watch would go out in plainclothes and observe this going on. We'd go into the toilets and if we were solicited to carry out these acts by another man we were to arrest them.

I had a couple of issues with this. I knew a lot about the law and powers of arrest because I'd passed the sergeants' exam and the offence of importuning for homosexual acts was not actually an arrestable offence, you could only report the offenders for summons but not arrest them. Second, you had to go into the toilets on your own otherwise the other person would be suspicious. This was extremely precarious from a safety point of view. Half of the time we were committing the offence ourselves by hanging around inside the toilets and looking at other men waiting for them to look back at us and make an offer.

It was dreadful. You'd be alone in the public toilets with a strange man. He'd nod at you and you'd nod back at him. You'd stand there nodding or winking at each other until he eventually dropped his trousers and started wanking.

The whole thing was an abortion, an accident waiting to happen. Being on your own in plainclothes in a toilet and out of sight of your colleagues was very dangerous. A lot of the men committing these offences we found were professionals who were married and had children. We caught accountants, chartered surveyors, teachers and many other professional people. When they were challenged they panicked, saw their professional and family life flash in front of them and went crazy trying to escape.

Because we were arresting them for a non-arrestable offence, technically any assault on us was not assault on police because we were not actually in the lawful execution of our duty. See the problem? The strange thing is that if you've an enigmatic leader, people will tend to follow them no matter how insane the plan they have. (Anyone remember Hitler?) I voiced my concerns on more than one occasion to the watch supervision but I was just stonewalled and told to shut up. They were obsessed with numbers of prisoners and they weren't going to let me get in their way.

I suppose I was perceived as being a pain in the arse to them. While others just went along with it or just wanted a quiet life I had to speak out when I felt something unjust or wrong was happening. The problem was that it happened quite a lot, which meant I had a reputation as a big-mouth to some people.

Sure enough, it went wrong and when it did, it went wrong for somebody close to me and the resulting aftermath left a black mark on the history of the West Midlands Police. Before the really bad incident happened, something which should've been a big warning occurred. A new sergeant on the watch tried to make an arrest as part of the importuning operation. He followed a man into the toilets and the man took off his coat to reveal a nice sexy basque, and when the sergeant told him he was under arrest all hell broke loose.

The guy was an accountant and screamed out in anguish at the prospect of being arrested and having his name in the papers. He thought that he'd be publicly humiliated and that his wife and children would be disgraced if he was caught. He kicked and punched the new sergeant while he was trying to arrest him. The sergeant ended up in hospital with a broken jaw and it took a long foot chase and violent struggle to detain the man.

He was later charged with several offences, but went home that night and hung himself. He couldn't bear to live with the humiliation of what he'd done, so he ended his life.

The operation was suspended for a short time. I felt that somebody in power should've been made accountable for permitting people to be put into danger, and I certainly felt that my opinion had been vindicated by this unfortunate event. But madness prevailed and it wasn't long before the operation was running again. The numbers of easy prisoners was just too good to pass up, the operation started up again a few months later when I was off the watch on an attachment. This time, a police officer would suffer far more serious injuries.

Happy Birthday to Me – 5 June 1975

Mum comes home with a baby. She says she's my sister. I'm angry. I take a bread knife and saw the legs off the dining table.

I'm in school. The teacher reads us all a story. It's nearly home time now. I need to go to the toilet but I can't ask the teacher as there are too many children in the way asking her questions. I'm desperate to go but I can't go without asking. Too late.

Cheryl goes to school every day. She has to wear a calliper on her leg. The bus that comes says 'Spastics' on the side, but I don't know what that means.

My friend Edward comes to stay over with his mum. We're jumping from the bunkbeds across the room onto the double bed. As I jump off the top bunk my foot catches in the sheets. I get halfway through the air and then fall crashing down onto the floor. I'm lying there and Edward's mum comes in and shouts at us to be quiet.

We go to visit my grandad, Balcarries. He's very old, his voice is very rough and croaky, and he sits on a chair watching telly all day. He eats winkles, he puts a pin into a shell and pulls them out and eats them – they look like slimy little worms. He keeps leaning over and spitting into a cup he keeps next to his chair.

He has a pet pig he keeps in the garden. I go and play on the railway track at the back of his garden. When we go to see him another week the pig has gone. I ask him where it is and he tells me to look in the fridge. I open the fridge and see the pig's head and lots of meat chopped up inside.

I'm 5 years old.

Year 6 – Bounce Baby Bounce

After another two years working there I gradually became desperate to get off Red Watch again. I'd sit in the same briefing room day after day and wonder what the hell I was doing there. I was going to the same jobs with the same people and there was rarely something new to learn.

At briefings when they called out your collar number and which car you'd be working on you were supposed to say 'Yes, sir' or 'Yes, Sarge,' but I just used to let rip a loud fart when they called my number out. It'd be '4335, you're on Mike Mike 3,' and 4335 would respond 'Sarge'; and '3318, you're on Mike Mike 4,' then 3318 would respond 'Sarge'; then '7907, you're on Mike Mike 5' and you'd hear me go 'quack' as I let one go. Everybody found it hilarious but it was just a way of me rebelling.

I'd completed a three-month CID attachment a couple of years into my service and was really keen to get back in. I'd passed the detectives' exams and when the interview boards were announced I jumped at the chance. I really fancied investigating serious crimes and using my brain and skills to catch criminals and put them behind bars. I could also see that detectives had a better quality of life with very few of the restrictions you have on the watch. They basically managed their own workload, didn't have to carry a radio around with them for the entire shift, and ate their meals when they were hungry, not when they were told they were allowed to.

I passed up the promotion boards for sergeant and decided that a stint in the CID would be time well spent. I flew through the CID interview board which were all graded from 'A' to 'D'. If you got an 'A' you went into the CID straightaway. If you got a 'B' you had to wait until all the 'A's' had been placed. A grade 'C' meant you didn't get in and a 'D' the same. I got an 'A' grade so started my CID posting after a couple of months.

I was overjoyed to be leaving Red Watch again. I could do the job standing on my head – there were no challenges left for me as a PC. It was just the never-ending cycle of shift work, drink drivers, shoplifters, domestics, and prisoner after prisoner. I was bored with it and sick of the attitude of some of the meat-head old-sweat PCs on the unit who acted more like 5-year-olds than grown men.

When you first join the CID you're known as a temporary detective constable or TDC. You have an assessment book and are graded on many different investigation and evidence-gathering skills. You've to refer to specific examples in your assessment book to prove you can cut the mustard and your detective sergeant does a three-month report on you. After the first three months you swap to another crew and do the same thing again. If you're up to scratch you're accepted as a detective.

Joining the CID was a revelation: for the first time in my police career I was treated like a grown-up. I didn't need to ask permission to take my lunch break or come into the station to have a shit. I was responsible for my own paperwork and making my own enquiries. So long as you were at work on time (or no more than an hour or so late) and did your share you were left to your own devices. Most of the Ds (detectives) tended to work in pairs and were very good friends spending a lot of time together outside of work as well.

I went into the CID determined to make the grade so my plan was to keep my mouth shut for my probationary period and work my brains out by volunteering for every job going, no matter how hard or crap it was. My rationale was that I did not fit the traditional CID profile of being a divorced, beer-swilling rugby player, so I'd better try to fit in by helping everyone else out as much as possible.

I was placed on DS Paul Kelly's team (not his real name). Kelly was a superb detective and it was a pleasure to learn from him. He was straight-talking and expected high standards from the whole crew. The crew were a great bunch as well and accepted me even though I was probably a bit out of the mould. The other guys all had some sort of bodily feature which made them stand out and they were referred to by that part of them. I worked with The Nose, The Ears and The Giraffe. I didn't qualify for a nickname, unfortunately (or not one I knew about anyway).

Little Park Street was a fantastic place to be a detective. When I used to come on duty in the morning I was filled with excitement to hear the news there was a rapist, armed robber or kidnapper in the cells to be dealt with. DS Kelly's crew had seen all this before though, and nothing fazed them. Everyone knew what had to be done and the whole team would go into action doing all the tasks and evidence-gathering.

Not a huge amount used to happen though, until we'd all enjoyed a nice, big breakfast at around 10 a.m. of course, and about four rounds of tea. Later in the day we'd all be unavailable for about an hour or two at lunch time since our crew used to all go for an five-mile run around the War Memorial Park. I thought I'd died and gone to heaven. I didn't have to walk everywhere with a radio turned on. I could be in charge of my own paperwork and go for a nice run for my lunch break instead of either missing lunch or having to rush out to jobs halfway through and getting indigestion.

It wasn't long before I was dealing with serious crimes myself. I dealt with many rapes, armed robberies, serious woundings and the like. These were almost daily occurrences in Coventry. You could almost guarantee that the morning after Friday or Saturday night there'd be some guy in the cells who'd either glassed or stabbed some bloke in a fight or drugged and raped some poor girl.

In the year I was in the CID there were 8,000 rapes reported to the police in the UK. By 2005 it had jumped to over 13,000. Many go unreported for any number of reasons. I had to investigate a number of rapes, and I really did feel terrible for the victims. There are lots of circumstances, including rape by husband or partner, date rape, and of course rape by strangers. Go to any city centre on the weekend and you'll see drunken young women lying in the street or shop doorways completely out of it. They're lying targets.

When they do report it, they have to hand all their clothes over to the police and then undergo a humiliating examination by a police doctor who's usually male. Then they have to be interviewed by a police officer who's almost always female and has been rape-trained. If the offender is caught and charged, they then have to stand in the dock and be torn apart by a barrister who'll make out they're a slag and were really begging for it. Not really a very pleasant experience.

There was another very common type of complaint that was reported to us and it really used to annoy me to have to investigate it. Almost every morning at the weekend there'd be some bloke wandering into the police station with the same story to tell. He'd bring along a friend to corroborate his story. It would usually go along the lines that he'd been standing in the pub or nightclub minding his own business when the bouncer had come up to him, punched him in the face for no reason and they'd then thrown him down the stairs and kicked him out of the door.

You wouldn't believe how common this is (unless you're a bouncer). As if any pub is going to employ doormen who randomly go and batter their customers. The pub wants people to come in and buy lots of beer and then fuck off home quietly at closing time. If the bouncers are battering the punters, there's nobody left to buy beer, and the other punters aren't going to want to go there anymore for fear that they'll be next.

Some of my friends from the karate club were doormen. They just wanted to make a bit of extra money and have a nice quiet night. They'd have a laugh and joke with the customers and if somebody got too rowdy they were asked politely to wind their necks in. If they continued to play up they'd be asked to leave. At this point the customer could leave quietly, argue and then leave, or have a fight. Your typical doorman would rather not punch anybody. What's the point? You get paid the same for a quiet night as a busy night.

I'd investigate the crime reported to me in a professional manner, but inside I'd be angry that I had to waste my time investigating a lie. I'm not saying that there hadn't been a fight, but nine times out of 10 the person complaining had been the one who'd started it. I'd point out before I took the person's statement that if they were making any of this up I'd arrest them for wasting police time and perverting the course of public justice. That was enough to stop a few false complaints, but some still insisted on complaining.

Almost every time the same thing happened. I'd spend days and days taking statements from witnesses, making enquiries and then I'd go and visit the doorman at work and have a quiet word with him. I'd tell him that they had to be interviewed and make an appointment for them to come to the station and bring their lawyer if they felt they needed one. Most of them were gutted to find out they were going to be arrested. They could often recall the incident – but it didn't happen the way the 'victim' was making out.

The CID were very civil that way. They nearly always made arrests by appointment. I'd arrest and interview the doorman and then at the end of the process the real story would reveal itself. The victim had usually got so drunk that he could hardly speak, he'd spent the night abusing other people, swearing at the men and groping the women. People would complain to the bouncer, who'd go over to ask him to behave. At this point the man would try to head-butt, punch or kick the bouncer and would be restrained. While this was happening the man's friend would come up behind the bouncer and punch, kick, bottle or stab him. Then all hell would break loose.

Bouncers in Coventry are a special breed, most of them are harder than the proverbial coffin nail. They've spent years conditioning themselves physically and mentally for a street fight. They've had years of verbal abuse, threats and fights and are battled-scarred and most of them battle-weary. Coventry nightclubs are often frequented by the local hard men whose personal lives are so devoid of meaning that the only significance they can achieve is to be a name fighter. Somebody who's feared because of their street-fighting prowess. These people usually gain their reputation by beating senseless anyone who looks at them the wrong way.

In the middle of this is the bouncer, a person who's often hated by the very punters they're there to protect. If he hits somebody, they're in the shit. They could seriously injure the assailant, be arrested and go to prison. Or the assailant could come back at a later time, even to the bouncer's home and exact his revenge with his mates. If he doesn't fight back, he's still in trouble. He'll be perceived to be a coward and every single bystander will think they can have a go as well. If that happens the bouncer might as well retire. Damned if you do and damned if you don't.

I could've started to work on the door after all my training at karate, boxing and grappling but I knew I couldn't do it. Not just because the pressure would've been terrible, but because I knew I had a temper and if somebody crossed the line I think I wouldn't know when to stop and I'd badly hurt them or worse and go to prison. A guy I knew from a karate club was on the door and had to defend himself when a guy tried to glass him. He broke the guy's arm and ended up doing three months inside. It was insane.

If you think I was on the side of the bouncer you'd be right. I did meet a few bad ones over the years but they were a rarity, to be honest. Most were great blokes and would do anything to help you out if you needed it and they'd do their level best to avoid a fight. Even when I came across a doorman hitting somebody I'd avoid arresting them or making any decisions until I'd obtained all the facts (or at least people's stories).

This approach worked well for me on a few occasions. One such occasion was when I saw a doorman I knew called Doug in the middle of a scrape. Doug was almost 6', very well-built and a handsome-looking man. I first got to know him when he worked at Park Lane nightclub which was at the bottom of Lower Precinct in Coventry city centre.

Doug's good looks had been marred somewhat by a long scar across his left cheek. He'd ejected a drunken fool from the club one night a year earlier and as he got him outside the man pulled out a razor and lashed out at Doug. Luckily, Doug had seen it coming so it missed his throat by a couple of inches and got his face instead. Depends upon what you class as lucky I suppose, but it was lucky compared to being dead.

Park Lane was a very large nightclub sprawling over three floors. Each floor played a different style of music, dance, acid and 1970s. It was a hard place to work at as a doorman due to the sheer size of it. I'd been there on one or two occasions as a customer but I always felt ill at ease socialising in Coventry city centre and avoided it for the most part.

I used to say hello and chat with Doug as I was on foot patrol in town. It was always a good idea to get to know the people who worked in town. Some of the doormen would refuse to speak to me when I walked up to them. I don't know why they were like that, maybe they'd been arrested at some point. They'd have been better off making an ally of the police than an enemy. One or two I used to see spit on the floor when they saw me walking past in uniform. Not close enough for me to bother doing anything about it, but I used to make a mental note of who they were. I wouldn't do them any favours if it came to it if that's what they thought of me.

I'd helped bouncers out a few times, or at least sided with them during an incident. This incident involving Doug was just one of them. At the time I was still on Red Watch just before I joined the CID. I was on patrol with one of the watch sergeants called Cole at around 1 a.m. Cole was 6' 4" and an international police Thai boxing champion. He was a handy guy to be out on patrol with in Coventry, but because I'm only 5' 8" we did look like an odd pair.

As we were walking along the Barracks Circulatory Road in the town centre we saw a fight at the back of the Dog and Trumpet pub. In the distance I could see two people fighting and a crowd gathered around them. I shouted to Cole that there was a fight and called it in on the radio.

As I got closer I could see Doug punching the shit out of some guy. Doug was twice the size of this man, who clearly couldn't fight to save his life. The guy was just covering up and trying to avoid getting knocked out. We got there just in time as the man was having seven bells of shit beaten out of him. My first reaction was to make an arrest. The police usually arrest the winner out of any fight and call him the offender, as we call the loser the victim of the crime. Probably not a very fair system, but there you go.

A large crowd had gathered around Doug and the man. Crowds of drunken people are a nightmare to deal with. Alcohol impairs brain functions and judgement, so trying to explain things or negotiating with them rarely works. Some of the crowd consisted of Doug's bouncer colleagues and the rest were screaming women and shouting men who were friends of the victim. Since I knew Doug to speak to I didn't make an arrest straightaway despite the screams of the witnesses who said the whole thing was unprovoked.

The 'victim's' face was covered with blood, his nose was broken and he had a black eye swelling up nicely. I took him to one side but his mates all followed to listen in. He'd been drinking heavily and stank of beer but explained that he was attacked for no reason, which immediately meant to me he was lying. As he spoke to me the blood splattered down his face and some of it began to spray onto my face.

I spoke to Doug who'd retreated back inside the pub. He told me that the guy had thrown a bottle across the dance floor and it had hit a girl on her head. She was inside the pub (the Bug and Black Bat) crying, but wasn't injured. I tended to believe Doug more than the victim. Either way, he should've been ejected or detained and the police called and not battered black and blue. Since we're living in a society governed by laws we're not allowed to take the law into our own hands without suffering the consequences.

Although I could've arrested Doug there and then from what I'd seen and heard, I decided to speak to the 'victim' and tell him to go to the hospital and come back in the morning if he wanted to make an official complaint. I knew he probably wouldn't bother to come back. The crowd which had gathered outside were not impressed, but I politely told them all to piss off as they'd not been assaulted. I'd investigate it the next day if he still wanted to complain, but if I found out that he'd assaulted anybody in the pub, I'd also arrest him.

I went back inside the back of the pub and told Doug and his fellow bouncers what was going to happen. They seemed to appreciate not being arrested or judged. Doug gave me a pint glass full of water to wash my face. The guy he'd hit had spat speckles of blood all over my face as he told me his version of events. We never saw or heard from the guy again.

I felt that my purpose as a police officer was similar to a bouncer's. We were charged with a duty to keep people safe and use violence if absolutely necessary. I suppose the only difference was that society gave us certain powers to do our job, and bouncers had only the power to use self-defence to protect themselves or others if they were making a citizen's arrest.

We all actually have a legal power to use force to defend ourselves or others and that force used has to be 'reasonable' in the circumstances. This is the same power used by armed police if they have to shoot somebody.

> s3(1) of the Criminal Law Act 1967 provides that:
> A person may use such force as is reasonable in the circumstances in the prevention of crime, or in effecting or assisting in the lawful arrest of offenders or suspected offenders or of persons unlawfully at large.

Of course, it helps to actually call the police if you've to batter somebody or it may not count as a citizen's arrest. As a police officer whenever I did have to give someone a slap I put the handcuffs on them afterwards and threw them in the cells. Even if they were subsequently released without charge it made the slap I'd given out appear more justified.

Somebody once said, 'Violence never solved anything,' but I didn't really subscribe to that philosophy. I found that violence solved quite a lot actually, and a punch in the face or choking out some violent prisoner often solved the problem very effectively indeed. You cannot reason or negotiate with some people, they're too drunk, drugged-up or just too irate.

While most of the bouncers were hard-working and nice people there was the odd bad one who got the others a bad reputation. They worked the door to get a bit of authority and a feeling of significance. I could usually recognise the bad ones because they shaved their heads, had their tattoos on full show, wore tee shirts three sizes too small to show off the fact that they did bodybuilding and took steroids. They didn't wear smart clothes or a dickie bow and would stand there with a scowl on their face chewing gum. They'd never greet the clients coming into the club and just tried to stare them out.

It's all to hide low self-esteem and they attack others because they themselves fear being attacked. Not good. They were in the job for completely the wrong reasons. I avoided places that used this type of doorman like the plague. I just knew that if there was any trouble they'd wade in with fists flying.

One doorman I dealt with when I was in the CID was Tel. Tel was about 20 and a giant of a man. He was 6' 5" tall and well-built. He had short spiky gelled dark hair and was always very well-presented. He spoke with a very quiet tone which made some people wrongly assume he was a big softie. Tel was a former boxer and he'd competed a few times but now the only time he boxed was when he was in a fight on the door. When you're off the door though, you're off duty and really, you should only use your skills to defend yourself or others.

Tel was in a wonderful situation. He had some learning difficulties at school and struggled with his reading and writing but he'd been accepted into the army. He was two months away from embarking upon a career in the Paras and it couldn't come quick enough for him. Tel felt very proud and rightly so. It was the first time in his life he'd achieved something significant and his mum and dad were really delighted for their son who'd always had low self-esteem. All of Tel's family were talking about how wonderful it was that he was joining the army, they'd tell anyone who'd listen, in fact.

Tel was off duty one night, had finished at a pub nearby and was standing talking to the bouncers working at McDonalds in Coventry city centre. It was about 12:30 a.m. and the town was heaving with the usual crowd of drunken people all trying to get some chips, a curry or just join the queue for the taxi home. There's a taxi rank just opposite McDonalds in Cross Cheaping about 20 yards up the hill. It's right next to a KFC and at that time of the night it's always very busy with people queuing up to get into a taxi.

As Tel was talking to his mates a bottle flew past his head narrowly missing him and it smashed against the wall behind him. Tel could see the guy across the road who'd thrown it. He was not impressed, but it had missed and nobody was hurt. Logically, Tel should've just left it but he made a decision to go and speak to the man he'd seen throw the bottle. A small decision that changed the entire course of both their lives.

Tel crossed the road and watched the guy walk into KFC with his friend. He was laughing and joking and clearly had had too much to drink (do you see a pattern forming here)? He walked into KFC and approached the man who'd thrown the bottle. The man who'd thrown it was called James. James was a student at Coventry University and was studying engineering. He was 19 years old, very short and slightly built. He walked with a slight limp due to the fact he was hit by a car when he was 7 years old and his right leg was now slightly shorter than his left. James stood inside KFC waiting in turn to get his chicken wings.

Tel went up to James and asked bluntly, 'Why did you throw that bottle at me?' James was drunk and full of bravado. He laughed at Tel saying, 'I never threw a bottle, mate' and he stood there grinning at Tel who felt even more insulted. Not only had this guy thrown a bottle and nearly hit him, but now he was laughing about it to his face.

BANG. Tel hit James so hard in the face that his eye socket fractured and James's eye burst open. James fell against the wall but it wasn't over yet. Tel hit James over and over again until he was unconscious. He then calmly stood up and walked away.

James's parents called the police the next day from hospital and my crew were on earlies on the Sunday morning. I drove to the hospital and went to see James. Half of his face was bandaged up. He was going to have to have an operation to put his cheekbone back together and the surgeons were not sure if they'd be able to save his eye.

I took a statement from James and explained that he must tell me the entire truth even if he did something to provoke the attack. It'd look bad if it turned out he'd lied in his statement even though he was still the victim. James said he hadn't done anything to provoke the attack. He was innocently walking into KFC when this stranger he'd never met hit him and that was the last he could remember.

James's friend told me the same story and I took a statement off him. I knew they were both lying because their story was exactly the same. It had obviously been rehearsed (badly) before I'd arrived. I believed the part about him being attacked, but since he described the offender as being dressed like a doorman I had a good idea that there was more to this than I was being told.

It took me a few weeks to track Tel down because the video in KFC was not working that day. I had to speak to a lot of people both officially and unofficially before I eventually found out where he worked. He was employed as a security guard during the day at a factory in Coventry. It was just a fill-in job while he waited three months for the next intake at the Paras to start. I phoned Tel at work and arranged for him to come and see me at the station for an interview.

Tel sat in the interview room with his solicitor crying his eyes out. He could hardly speak because he was so devastated. Tel could see his army career vanishing before his eyes and he had a good idea that he was in big trouble. His solicitor came out to see me before the interview. She was married to one of the PCs who worked in the station so was OK as far as lawyers go. She told me that he was going to admit hitting James and now really regretted it.

I interviewed Tel and he told me that he'd followed James into KFC but he'd only hit him once. He kept breaking down crying and I did feel bad for him, but I remembered looking at James's face as well. I asked Tel to explain how James could have such horrendous damage to his face from only one punch but he couldn't explain it.

I charged Tel with GBH section 18 (which is wounding or GBH with intent). For very serious offences you've to go to Crown Court because magistrates can only sentence to a maximum of three months. Tel got 18 months in prison and was not allowed to join the army. He's still working as a factory security guard 10 years later. James got a lifetime of seeing with one eye.

❧ ❧

I mentioned a man called Rich B. earlier. I met Rich B. while I was in the CID dealing with a spate of thefts of luxury cars in and around Coventry. Rich's Bentley had been stolen from a garage where it was being serviced and later found during a raid on a workshop. I had to go and take a statement of complaint from him.

It took me a while to find his house. It was in the countryside near Coventry and was before the day of sat navs – remember those days? To get to it, I had to drive up a winding country lane until I got to two imposing black metal gates. I pressed a buzzer and the gates opened slowly. I drove in and parked up just by the gates.

I saw a man walking down the drive who had a torn pair of denim jeans on, a white tee shirt and an old pair of trainers. I guessed it was somebody who swept up there or did the gardening but it turned out to be Rich B. who lived there and owned the land (and the Bentley). I expected Rich B. to be an older man for some reason, but when I met him I was surprised to find that he was the same age as me, 26. He was fresh-faced and clean-shaven. He had long wavy black hair and a very laid-back happy air about him.

We began to walk up the drive and eventually came to a very large building. It had massive hand-carved wooden doors at the bottom and huge windows at the top which were made of different shapes and sizes and arranged in a very decorative fashion. I was very impressed. 'Nice house,' I said to Rich. He looked back at me and seemed a bit confused, 'That isn't my house, mate, that's my garage. My house is just over here.' I felt like a right idiot, the massive building was his bloody garage, it even had office space on top.

We turned a corner and I saw Rich's house which was actually a mansion with 15 bedrooms surrounded by several acres of manicured land. He had indoor and outdoor swimming pools, a tennis court, gymnasium.... I couldn't help but be impressed. Rich led me to his front door which was built into an arch about six feet high. The door was made from hardwood with metal studs running up and down in vertical lines.

It was hard to imagine Rich actually living in this huge mansion because he just looked too young and out of place with his jeans and general working-class air. I expected his dad to come out of the house any minute and give him a clip 'round the ear.

As we walked towards the mansion I was looking forward to seeing what was inside. 'So,' beamed Rich, 'you managed to find me car then, did ya?' This didn't sound like a toffee-nosed guy to me. 'Er, yes,' I replied trying to hide my surprise, 'there was a raid on a car workshop where we found your car and quite a few others. I just need to take a few lines off you to make a formal complaint.'

As we walked through his house I could see several people walking in and out of various rooms. Apart from the odd suit they were all dressed casually but seemed to be there doing business of some sort because they were carrying files or speaking over diagrams and computers. I guessed that Rich ran his business from his house.

It was a sunny day so we went out of the back of his house and sat down on wrought iron summer chairs, then Rich B. went off to make some tea. The patio at the back gave a splendid view of several acres of lawn which dropped down a few levels in steps until it reached a woodland about 200 yards from the patio. Rich came back a few minutes later with two mugs. For some reason, I'd been expecting earl grey tea in a silver teapot and china cups.

I was intrigued so I asked Rich B., 'What is it you do exactly?' Rich pulled his chair closer to the table and said, putting his feet up on the chair next to him. 'I own an IT and a property company,' he explained as he poured some milk into his tea and continued, 'I was thrown out of school when I was 15 because I was going to make them look bad in the score tables. They said I was dyslexic and had something called attention deficit disorder.' He was laughing as he told me, 'They tried to explain it to me but I couldn't sit still long enough to find out.' I started to chuckle. I liked this guy already.

I was a bit confused, how could he have been running companies and not have been to university? 'I don't understand,' I said, 'did you do a degree or something or did your dad give you the companies to run for him?' Luckily Rich B. didn't take it as an insult. 'I never went to uni and my parents died in a car crash when I was a baby,' he said. 'Oh, I'm sorry to hear that,' I said, feeling embarrassed. 'No problems,' grinned Rich, 'it was hard to start with because I was in and out of foster homes and then eventually adopted.'

It made sense to me now. 'So you were adopted by a rich businessman like in that play *Annie*. It was him who handed you his companies when he retired then?' Rich laughed out loud and spat tea over some of his paperwork on the table. 'No way, man. The couple who adopted me were quite old already and didn't have much money. My adopted dad was a painter, but never sold many paintings and his wife was ill for many years and couldn't work. They both died when I was 18 and after that their house was repossessed and I moved into a council flat in Wood End in Coventry.'

I just sat there frowning. I didn't want to pry but I was a detective after all and wanted to find out how he ended up in the mansion. 'So how did you come to run two companies and have this big mansion then?' I asked inquisitively. 'I decided I wanted to be rich when I was about 16,' explained Rich as he dipped a chocolate hobnob into his tea. As he brought it up the wet bit fell off and plopped into his tea, 'Bastard!' he shouted, 'I hate it when that happens.' He got up and came back a few minutes later with a fresh mug of tea.

'Where was I?' said Rich. 'You were just about to tell me the secret to eternal wealth and riches,' I said. Rich spat yet more tea out of his mouth as he laughed. There was a hobnob crumb on his chin but I didn't want to interrupt to tell him, he could eat it later if he was peckish. He said, 'I knew that if I wanted to be wealthy I had to hang around wealthy people so I got a job in London at a gentleman's club. I bought a second-hand suit from the Oxfam shop and scrounged lifts into London from mates. I'd serve the rich businessmen at the tables and listen to what they were talking about.'

As Rich B. spoke to me he looked out onto his acres of land as if he was still taking stock of the fact he was living in such a beautiful location. 'I started to offer to do odd jobs for them like taking their suits to be dry-cleaned or get their cars valeted, and eventually they were inviting me to come along to their houses when they had barbecues. After a while they gave me their numbers and I used to phone them and ask advice about how to start my own business.'

It made sense now: he'd been coached by these guys so had been given exclusive access to all their secrets. 'Oh, right,' I exclaimed, 'so you started a company and made a fortune.' Rich looked at me and shook his head slowly from side to side. 'Not quite,' he looked a bit more serious now as he remembered some hard times, 'my first two companies went bust because I didn't understand what I was doing. I spent too much time listening to accountants and lawyers, who don't have a clue how to run a company. It was all good experience, though.'

He went on to explain how his third company was a success. 'I was advised by my mentors to go into property, so I began to find deals but had no money to buy them, so I'd pass them over for a commission to people who had money but no time to find deals of their own. When I'd done enough of those deals I could afford to put a deposit down on properties for my own business, and it has gone from strength to strength.' Rich dipped another hobnob in his mug and was successful this time in not dropping the wet bit off.

Rich took a bite of his biscuit and continued, 'Once I got the hang of it I started the IT company. I wrote a manual of operations and let the people with degrees and MBAs run the business for me while I kept an eye on it. I just apply the rules and principles I've learned and it all works great.' I wanted to know more but didn't want to push my luck. 'Which rules and principles?' I asked as casually as possible, forgetting about the reason I'd actually come to his house.

Rich put his mug down and looked at me. I think he was working out if I was really interested in finding out or a time waster. 'Do you really want to know, Paul, because people often get offended and defensive when I tell them?' I nodded slowly and purposefully. 'Well, you've to accept a few things first, otherwise the principles will just seem alien to you.' I was ready to listen, 'Hit me with it,' I said, 'I'm all ears.'

'OK,' said Rich. He took a deep breath and breathed out slowly saying, 'You've been brainwashed from the moment you were born by your parents, teachers, the media and society. They've brainwashed you to be a quiet little worker bee and to get a job and quietly pay your taxes.' Rich was looking far more serious now. 'Marketing teams design adverts to get you to buy things you neither want nor need, and loan companies advertise after that to help you pay for the things you can't afford. You cling to your job as if your life depended upon it because you need the money to pay for the things that you bought that you didn't need in the first place.'

It sounded harsh to me but rang a bell, 'Things like what?' I wanted to know more. 'People buy cars because they need to get to work, get mortgages for big houses because they feel they're supposed to, and take holidays they can't afford, to have a break from the job they don't like. It's like some sort of diabolic nightmare.' I could see that Rich was on a roll and didn't want to interrupt.

'When you suggest that they may want to consider leaving the job and do something they like or to get rid of the car they're struggling to pay for, they look at you as if you're the mad one.' Rich sighed, 'I've given up now. I've realised that most people are in such a deep trance that the things I say just sound ridiculous to them. I've drifted apart from a few friends who were just on a different wavelength to me. As soon as I started to make good money some of my mates resented it and started to tell me I was obsessed about money and that I'd changed.'

I knew what he meant, because some people at work had been funny with me when I passed my promotion exams. I also knew what he was talking about when he mentioned clinging to a job, but I was in dreadful debt and if my job came under threat I'd have gone into panic mode. I relied on my job to pay the mortgage, bills and the loans and credit card debt I seemed to have acquired.

Rich still hadn't finished. 'We're basically handed a script to act out by our parents and society. It's a poverty script which involves years of hard work and debt for most people, with no hope of escape.' I began to pull a long face saying, 'That sounds really depressing, Rich. Surely we all have a choice.' He shook his head. 'You'd think so,' he replied, 'but the vast majority of adults leave school or university with no understanding of how to manage their own finances. They spend what they earn and then some more which locks them into the job and a life of working the 9 to 5 grind.'

I thought it was time to come clean since it isn't every day you're sitting in front of a multimillionaire. 'I've gotten into debt and I'm having to work overtime to keep my head above water,' I admitted. Rich nodded back, 'I've been there, mate, I went bankrupt once before – but strangely enough it was the best thing that ever happened to me.'

'So what do I do now?' I asked inquisitively. 'It all depends upon what you want to achieve,' answered Rich, 'Do you want to be the next Richard Branson or just to live debt-free?' It was the first time I'd ever actually thought about where I wanted to be financially. 'First, I want to get out of debt,' I said, 'and then be rich enough to not have to work.'

Rich sat quietly for a few seconds and thought. He then said, 'Books will set you free, Paul. I'll write down a list of books for you to read. When you've finished, come back 'round.' Rich scribbled down a list of books for me to read: *Think and Grow Rich* by Napoleon Hill, *How to Slay the Financial Dragon* by William A. Stanmeyer and *The Richest Man in Babylon* by George S. Clason.

Rich was enjoying sharing his thoughts and I was hanging on his every word. 'Do you know what the root of the problem for 'most every adult in the Western world is Paul?' I shook my head solemnly. He took out some change from his pocket and put it into an empty glass on the table. I was a bit confused, 'What, they don't put money into glasses?' I asked innocently. Rich laughed out loud, as his head was in the air looking up some more bits of chocolate hobnob flew out of his mouth and landed on his forehead. I decided not to tell him.

'No, you funny git: they don't *save*, Paul, not one single penny. It's something they say they can't afford to do because of bills. It's this very thing that fills them with the fear of losing the job they hate so much – nothing to fall back on.' I'd been saving for a few years, but as I'd fallen into debt I'd taken all my savings out to make my monthly payments.

Rich went on, 'The curse of the working class is not saving, and hoping that the government will take care of them when they're old which of course they won't be able to.' I'd thought that was what was going to happen, 'What about the pensions?' I asked. Rich replied with a serious look on his face, 'The US and UK governments are close to meltdown, Paul. They've let too many people suck from their tit for too many years and there's no money left for the future generations' pensions. If you think they'll look after you when you grow old, you're deluded.'

'Well, what about those with a bit of money?' I asked. 'The curse of the middle class is having to continually upgrade their house and car so they have something to show off to their so-called friends,' replied Rich. 'They're living off their loans and credit cards, which forces them out to work every day. If the bank called their loan in or if they're made redundant they'll go bankrupt almost immediately. There's a big difference between *being rich* and *looking rich*.'

I thought about the one or two people I knew who I considered to have a bit of money. It was true, they were always upgrading their car which was paid for with a loan and they continually wanted to buy a bigger house or have it extended. My thoughts were interrupted by Rich saying, 'The song of the middle class is, "I owe, I owe, so it's off to work I go".'

It was then that I decided to be wealthy. I'd no idea how it was going to happen, but I knew I didn't want to work hard for the rest of my life and die broke or spend a life in debt having to work in a job I hated just so I could pay my bills and loans.

I took a statement from him and left Rich's house feeling very happy about the fact we'd met. He told me I was welcome to come back anytime I was in the area.

❧ ❧

After three months in the CID on Kelly's team I was getting the hang of things pretty well and still really enjoying myself. I appreciated being able to manage my own workload, and the fact that every day something different happened. I liked the CID crew at Little Park Street and it was a real pleasure to go into work because of the variety and good atmosphere in the office.

I was transferred for the second part of my six-month probation to a team run by a DS called Sean. Sean was about 40, very stocky and had curly fair hair. He was always clean-shaven and well-turned-out, even when he'd been on the pop all night long. Sean called everyone 'Bab' (even the superintendent) which made him all the more amiable. He'd say, 'Alright, Bab' to everyone who came into the office.

Sean was an old-school DS and a bit of a legend in the police in Coventry. He'd been a DS at least since I'd been in the job, which was seven years by then. He was a larger-than-life character who seemed to be a law unto himself. Sean would go on drinking binges and not come to work for weeks on end. He'd eventually get back on the wagon, come back to work and nothing was said to him about it. At least as far as I knew.

He was a great guy to work for. He never pestered any of the detectives on his team and let them crack on with the work they had. If you had a problem, you could go and ask him, but apart from that he left you alone. Perfect. Sean had been in a fair few scrapes over the years and he was known all over the three police stations in Coventry. It seemed that almost everybody had a story to tell about a job they'd been to with Sean during which something hilarious or outrageous happened. Sean gave no thought to equal opportunities or diversity. I don't think he even knew what they meant. He just cracked on with what he knew how to do – which was drink, and to be a detective.

By this stage of my CID career I was permitted to work as the night D (night shift duty detective) which was always fun. We tended to get together with the duty D from Fletchampstead Highway police station for a bit of company. I was eager to do that because it was my first set of nights as a detective and was very grateful to have another D there to help out if I got a bit stuck.

The night D had two roles. The first was to attend any serious incidents and give advice to the watch about preserving evidence or dealing with serious crimes. If there was an arrest for the type of offence the CID dealt with such as robbery or rape, we could make sure that the handover package for the earlies crew was up to scratch. Nights were great as a night D because unlike being on the watch, you didn't have to push the Panda endlessly around the same area. In fact nobody needed to know where you were so long as you were contactable on the air if you were needed.

The second and most important role was to drive any drunken detectives home from the police bar or any bars in town. You could get a call at any time and have to drive into town to pick up the lates crew who were bladdered after a night on the pop.

I was working with Gav who was the night D from the Fletch. He was more experienced than me so I was really glad to be working with him. We'd have to cover his patch as well but I didn't mind. Gav drove over to collect me at Little Park Street police station and we went out for a drive around the city centre at about 11 p.m. The CID use very basic-model cars that are usually the same cars the Panda drivers have but not striped up. We had navy or maroon Austin Maestros.

As we drove along Little Park Street Gav spotted another detective he worked with jogging down the street. It was a guy called Julian who I'd joined the job with, a great guy and a good police officer. Julian was an ideal detective because he was a keen rugby player and a heavy drinker, but also a good grafter. I'd been out with Julian before when we were at police training centre and the problem was he always became very paranoid when he had a couple of beers in him. He'd think that people were watching him or following him and he'd end up ruining the evening because you all had to leave and drag him out of the pub before he started a fight.

The time of night and location made it seem strange that Julian would be jogging down Little Park Street, but also the fact that he was wearing a suit and tie. We pulled over and stopped our car next to Julian. Gav wound the car window down, 'What on earth are you doing, Julian?' he asked. Julian leaned his head into the car and panted, 'I'm drinking in Yates with some of the crew (CID crew),' he then gasped, 'there's some bloke in there giving me the eye so I'm running the beer off in case we have a fight.'

'Listen, Julian,' said an exasperated Gav, 'just get in the car and we'll take you home, mate.' 'Nah, fuck that,' said Gav, 'I'm doing a few laps of the block and then if he's in there we're going to be fighting.' Gav and I knew that this was going to end in tears and maybe Julian being sacked. The trouble is – and I think I've mentioned this already – you can not negotiate with a drunk person because their brain has lost the ability to see reason.

After a few minutes we managed to get Julian in the car. He was a fit bloke and a keen rugby player and could've really caused somebody a problem. We drove Julian home which was in Cheylesmore and about four miles from town. As he got out of the car he said, 'Thanks, lads. I'm going to call a taxi and go back into town to see if he's still there.'

The dozy bastard ran off down the road to find a telephone kiosk to call a taxi. We drove off. Not much we could do really. It was so strange to see what can happen to a normally sane and rational person once they've had a couple of drinks: they often take on a completely different personality. This is why I avoided going drinking in town where you're known by most of the bouncers and some of the punters. If somebody picks a fight with you, the bouncers are just going to turn a blind eye as you get battered.

A classic example was Yates wine bar in the High Street. The bouncers who used to work there were not particularly pro-police. We had intelligence that one of them was regularly dealing drugs, he had a lot of previous convictions for possession of drugs, but this was before the days when door staff were checked for previous convictions. This was in the day when you could work on the door with a bit of 'previous' (convictions).

The CID were in Yates one Friday evening and two local hard men tried to pick a fight with them. The bouncers took no notice so they had to fend for themselves. I know you should be able to go out where you like, but the reality is if you're a police officer you can't play where you work. The way I saw it was, if you were a police officer covering the city centre, you were taking a huge risk going for a drink there.

                                       ❧ ❧

One thing I didn't like at all about being a detective was dealing with informants. It made me very uncomfortable in fact. Most detectives are expected to have a couple of informants on the go at any given time. You basically get them to inform when they're under arrest for some sort of offence. Your leverage is that you can make things a bit easier for them if they give you information.

There's a lot of cloak and dagger stuff involved in using informants. The paperwork is kept locked away in a secure area and every informant is given a code name and graded. If the info they give is for petty stuff then they have a low grade and they don't get much money or perks. If they're informing on organised criminals or large-scale drug trafficking then they'll be paid more and can have some favourable treatment if they ever get into trouble.

Informants are almost always active criminals. I did agree that they're a very good source of information, but there can be some very grey lines between what should and shouldn't happen. The best example is drug dealers. They'd be caught and give information to avoid getting a prison sentence. The information they'd give you would be about their competitors though, so not only would they avoid imprisonment but they'd also get rid of the competition.

The motives of the informant also had to be determined. They can be wanting to uphold justice (laughable), revenge, to avoid prosecution, financial gain and so on. I hated having to meet them in some seedy flat and act as if I was their mate. I hated having to take money with me and give them cash which I knew would be used to buy drugs.

Informants can be let out of the cells and then released without charge, be charged with lesser offences or get lighter sentences in court. There are the Home Office guidelines of course, and there's what really happens. Everybody knows what really goes on but the Home Office regulations make sure that the top people are protected if it ever gets out because they can point at them and say that they made it very clear what the procedures were.

It's all back-scratching, really. I can see why the system is in place and the importance of the information but I just didn't like associating with active criminals and being matey with them. I also felt that it left me exposed when I had to hand over sums of money. I saw time and time again informants getting away with things that they never should have. It was like they had a get-out-of-jail-free card. The informants' scheme was never intended to be used for this purpose.

One of my very first arrests was of the brother of a famous Coventrian sportsperson. I'd arrested him whilst on the serial van at 1 a.m. for drink driving. He stank of booze and had refused to provide me with a breath specimen at the roadside. He agreed to provide a sample back at the police station and blew just under the legal limit. He was still due to be charged with the offence of refusing to provide at the roadside, though.

I went off to do some PNC checks on him leaving him in the cell and about half an hour later I went back to the cell block. The duty detectives were talking with the custody sergeant. I saw that my prisoner's name was no longer on the board. I asked where my prisoner had gone and the custody sergeant told me he let him go because he'd blown under the limit. He knew full well that he was supposed to be charged with failing to provide at the roadside.

While I'd been out of the cells the prisoner had asked to speak to the duty detective who he usually gave information to. Ten minutes later he was driving home. I was really angry at the underhand way they'd gone about it and not even involved me. I was very young in service though, and there was nothing I could do about it. I know it sounds horrible but it would've served them right if he'd got drunk the next night and mowed their misses down.

It's really strange because the code of conduct between criminals is that you never 'grass' your mates up. Grassing is the lowest thing you can do, yet once they're in custody almost every prisoner would sing like a canary. They'll tell you everything they know to avoid being charged or especially remanded in custody.

Conversely, if a person is found out to have informed, he's punished by the person who he informed on. The usual punishment is to have your ear or at least a part of it bitten off outside the courthouse. I've seen this punishment handed out quite a few times. Obviously, if you're a criminal and have part of your ear missing it's a warning to others that you're an informant. Half of the time, the person doing the biting was an informant themselves! Mad or what?

Favourable treatment goes on all the time. As a custody sergeant the CID often asked me to give their prisoners bail after charge. These were violent drug-addicted burglars who could easily have murdered a person in their home if they found them in the act. If that had happened the detective would've just shrugged their shoulders and blamed me saying that I was the one who granted bail.

A favourite trick of the CID was to forget to mention the prisoner's previous convictions when they charged the prisoner. The custody sergeant needs to see those to decide if it's safe to the general public for this person to be free whilst on bail for an offence. I knew all the tricks so never let it past me but I know it still goes on to this day. No matter what information a person is giving, I don't think it's worth having dangerous criminals roaming the streets committing crimes.

ও ৎ

I did well during my six-month probation and was made a regular detective. I was really chuffed but still wanted more out of my career. Just after being made a regular detective I was sent on my detectives' course which was held at the police training centre called Tally Ho which is in Edgbaston in Birmingham.

It was a fantastic course and one of the highlights of my time in the police. It was a residential five-week course where we spent the entire time learning about how to investigate serious crimes. We learned how to preserve and gather evidence and how to deal with informants and suspects of serious crimes. Most of it was scenario-based where actual crimes had been documented to be used as training exercises.

We'd be given the details of the crime and start to make enquiries in teams and then as the enquiries went on we'd be fed more and more information. The exercise ended with the interview of the suspect which was captured on video and at the same time your team of eight fellow detectives would be watching you downstairs and taking notes to give you feedback later.

For every detective, the CID course is half about detective skills and half about getting pissed every night. Many of the people who go on the detectives' course get out a loan for about five grand before they go because this is how much they spend on beer over five weeks. I'm not a drinker as you know, but while I did go out a few nights, I do prefer my own company though. It was hard-core with most of the delegates drinking from about 7 in the evening and then out clubbing until about 3 in the morning. We'd wake them up at about 8:30 a.m. and they'd just have time for a shave and shower and then stagger into the classroom.

The rule was that you had to be able to function in the classroom the next day. If you showed signs of still being drunk or not being able to study for the day you were given a warning. The second time you'd be kicked off the course.

We all graduated after five weeks. I felt really proud because I'd worked very hard during the course and learned a tremendous amount about crime investigation that would help me for the rest of my career. I still wanted to be promoted as well, but had failed one attempt at the promotion boards and was determined to make the second try. The sergeants' boards consisted of an extended assessment which is a day-long battery of exams and group exercises. That's followed by an interview by some senior officers and a police federation representative.

The first time around I'd failed the interview board stage. The telex had arrived in the front office but I didn't know. As usual everybody else found out before me. I found out at the end of earlies when I went up to the bar. Jed was there having a pint leaning up against the bar, 'Sorry to hear you failed the promotion board,' he was smiling as he said it. I felt absolutely gutted. I desperately wanted to pass that so that when I felt ready I could apply for promotion.

I was devastated not just because I failed, but because of the reason for which I'd failed. I got the feedback from my interview: the police federation representative failed me because I appeared nervous and tapped my foot throughout the interview! I was so angry I could've gone around and punched his lights out. I could've put a grievance in against him but I really don't think it would've helped me. I felt very resentful about the reasons they gave for failing me.

It shouldn't have been a surprise though because the second time around while I was preparing I spoke to one of my old sergeants who was now an inspector and was part of the promotion board selection process for PCs applying for sergeants from stations outside Coventry. When I asked him for some tips for my interview the next time he gave me some very useful info, but then added that I should always wear black socks. I was a bit bemused because I thought we were all supposed to wear black socks.

He then went on to tell me that the first thing he checks for in the interview is the candidate's socks. If they're black but have a colour at the top such as rugby socks he always fails the candidates. What a bloody bigot. I have no idea how many people's careers he's blocked because they went into interviews wearing black rugby or football socks. I bet he didn't put that on their failure feedback form, though.

The second time 'round I really did my homework and felt really confident. I passed the board with an 'A' grade and was recommended for promotion. Even when you pass a board for any roles in the police you could still be waiting for months before you actually get your placement. I had to wait a while for a vacancy to come up, which suited me fine.

At the end of your six-month CID probation you're usually assigned to a department called the CJU for three months to polish up your court file skills. The CJU stands for the Criminal Justice Unit. The name sounds impressive, doesn't it? It makes you think of some no-nonsense sort of proactive task force which fights crime wherever it rears its ugly head. In reality it's the admin department. All the paperwork for traffic or criminal offences gets routed there. There's an army of admin ladies and men who stamp files, send out notices, lick stamps, tap things into computers and photocopy bits of paper all day long. Day after day, week after week and year after year. That sort of work would drive me insane, but obviously it suited some people down to the ground.

You'd think that the majority of staff working at police stations would be operational uniformed police but that simply isn't true. There are many more civilians who do various admin duties that are all ancillary to the job of policing. It's a bit bewildering because for the eight or so years I was at Little Park Street I never knew what most of them did. I just saw the same faces year in year out sitting behind their desks doing whatever they did for a living.

There are some police officers posted to the CJU whose job it is to go out and take statements and enquiries for court files and car accidents. It's really a job suitable for somebody in the last three years of their service or who can't go on the streets due to pregnancy because it's a nice desk job with weekends off. A lot of people who wanted to escape from shift work went there. I'd never have done that because after three years you're sent back out on the streets and are clueless. You haven't arrested anybody for ages and are completely out of touch with how things work.

Due to reorganisation of the force most of the specialist departments had been disbanded. There were not many rocks left to hide under, but the admin department meant plainclothes, regular hours and weekends off.

There's only one detective assigned to the CJU. They put all the committal files together. These are the files for Crown Court cases so it's rapes, serious woundings, armed robberies and the like. These files have to be watertight so you've to make sure all the statements are correct and the evidence chain is complete. If anything is missing you've to get it sorted before the court case.

I used to pull my hair out when I received some court files. The majority were of a very poor standard and nowhere near good enough to secure a conviction. We all basically had to run around taking statements and checking exhibits and lab results and covering up for bad police work. If you can't account for an exhibit from the time it's recovered to the time it's produced in court it won't be permitted as evidence. Everybody who's handled it has to submit a statement and sign the exhibit label.

One wounding I dealt with was where during a hockey match a man had hit another player on the mouth on purpose with his stick. He smashed most of his teeth out and tore his face open with the stick. There were about 30 people present including the players, referees and spectators. The lazy police officer who'd attended the incident had taken one statement only – and the one he took was dreadful. I wished I could've thrown it back in his face and told him to do it himself. It took weeks to get all the statements sorted out by which time a lot of important details had been forgotten.

If there are any enquiries the Crown Prosecution Service (CPS) want completing they send you a memo and you carry out the task. They'd review the court file and the evidence and then send a long memo pointing out where it was deficient and what needed to be done to secure a prosecution.

While I was in the CID and the CJU I developed a deep respect for the CPS. They're a team of overworked and underpaid lawyers who prosecute offenders and do their best to see that they're put behind bars so people like you and I are safe. They work under a huge amount of pressure and have to abide by many restrictive procedures and rules. They're basically fighting with one arm tied behind their backs. I got to know several CPS lawyers while we met to discuss certain cases. They were all highly professional, hard-working lawyers who could be earning a lot more money defending the scum they were prosecuting.

I didn't mind being on the CJU for a while. It would help my case-building skills for when I was a sergeant and give me some more free time to finish the finals for the last year of my law degree which were two months away. I was also glad to be out of the CID office for a bit.

There was only one drawback when I got to my CJU office and it was a big one. That gormless ignorant bastard Jay, who I worked with for two nights worked in the same office I was posted to. It got even worse though, because there was another guy in the office called Will. Will had been on Yellow Watch for years but went to the CJU because of his bad nerves. He had a nervous cough and tapped his foot all day long which would drive me 'round the bend.

I think Jay and Will were on friendly terms because for the three months I was in their office they refused to speak to me. The office was tiny and the only other person in the office was a female officer called Mary. They'd speak to Mary, but as soon as I'd walk in the room they'd shut up. I ended up working six months instead of three because I passed the promotion boards so the DI said he didn't see the point in me coming back to the CID office.

If you think women can be bitchy at work you've seen nothing. Men are far, far worse. The only noise to be heard in our office was Will's nervous cough which punctuated the silence every 30 seconds. I think Will had had a nervous breakdown at some point and was put into the CJU to recover. There were no 'Good mornings', 'See you tomorrow' or 'Do you want a cup of tea?' Even when my dad died and I came back to work after a week off I walked in and they never said a single word to me.

After three months with them I managed to convince one of the CJU sergeants to move me to the office across the corridor. It was heaven because the team in there were a great laugh. They all enjoyed what they did and got on well. There was a mix of part-time mum police officers and a couple of police sportspeople who needed weekends and evenings free because they played at a national level.

I really enjoyed my last three months with them. It seemed a long way off from pushing a Panda around some shit-hole and getting sent from job to job by the controller.

I studied really hard for my final business law degree exams. Every day I was doing about four hours revising advanced property law, data protection, environmental law and intellectual property. Each module was part course work and part exam. It was really hard going because I'd signed up for two extra modules so I could get the degree finished in five instead of six years.

My final exam was advanced property which was notoriously difficult. Most law students avoid it because there's a lot of Latin involved and a huge amount of case law. Getting high marks is very rare in this subject as well because it's so difficult. For some odd reason, I actually enjoyed the content, which was a bit strange. I like to break complicated material down into idiot-proof chunks so I can understand it and that's how I got through the property module.

The course was taught by a barrister who really knew her stuff. I went to lectures every Wednesday evening and most of the students were part-time and the average age was about 40. The problem was that the poor lecturer would stand there asking questions and everybody would sit there in silence because they hadn't done any preparation. It was almost always me answering or coming up to the board to answer problems she'd put there.

Ironically, some of the students started to bad-mouth her and started talking about putting a complaint in about her because she couldn't teach. I couldn't believe it. If they'd got off their lazy arses and read the books then they'd have been fine. I thought she was great myself.

When you sit the exams you've to sit in a big hall in Coventry University and sit on our mini-desks while the exam papers are handed out. I really did hate exams because you never knew what was coming. It was a three-hour exam but I'd written everything I could in about 90 minutes. I was gutted, but just got up and walked out. The other students shot me strange looks as if they knew I'd dried up.

I left the hall and immediately went to see the lecturer and told her I'd messed up the whole exam because I couldn't think what to write. She was great about it and told me to relax and wait for the marks to come out. The papers were marked by an outside agency and when the results came back I was gobsmacked: I'd got 70 per cent and come top of all the part-timers and full-timers. My lecturer said that the invigilator was really impressed with my paper. You could've knocked me down with a feather.

I passed my business law degree with exactly 60 per cent which got me an upper second class degree (2 : 1). I was now able to put the letters LLB (Hons) after my name. It might not sound like much, but at that time nobody in my family had been to university. We were not very well-off and all staunch working class so traditionally we left school at 15 or 16 and got a trade or went to work in a factory.

﹏ ﹏

I heard from a couple of friends on Red Watch while I was coming to the end of my attachment with the CJU that they'd resumed the operation to arrest people for importuning in the public toilets in the city centre. At the time the main locations where the offences took place were New Union Street (directly opposite the police station), The Quadrant and at the bottom of Hill Top which was in the city centre. The worst place was probably The Quadrant because you had to descend a steep set of concrete steps to get to the toilets.

I'd been down there a few times when I was part of the operation. The inside of the toilets was very cold, dark, wet and eerie and stank of stale piss and vomit. Going down the steps was like descending into a crypt. There was shit all up the walls and no locks left on the toilet doors due to the fact that they'd been kicked in so many times. The only way to wipe your arse in there was to take a newspaper with you.

It was ironic that all the offences were taking place opposite the police station and offices for most of the lawyers in Coventry. I really don't know why men would want to meet in such a place. You could easily have gone to a gay bar or met somebody through personal ads.

The whole operation stank as bad as the toilets did, but nobody on the watch had stood up and said that they had a problem with it. I guess they didn't want to have to face the consequences of what would happen if they did. I felt that the operation was made even more dangerous by the fact that it involved probationary constables as part of the spotting and arrest teams. This is a very bad idea, because they're young in service and you need a level head and experience for this type of work.

When you're working in plainclothes, you do not carry your protective equipment around your waist because it's a giveaway. Also, because you had no uniform on, the public would not know you were a police officer, so if you ended up fighting with somebody you couldn't count on getting any help from any passers-by.

The lessons that needed to be learned when the new sergeant had been attacked had not been. When I did speak up in these circumstances it made me a target for bullying or being passed over for courses, but I just couldn't sit back and say nothing when I saw the wrong thing being done. If we were actually making a difference at all then it may have been another story, but it was just a pathetic excuse to play a numbers game.

I eventually caught on to what some of the sergeants and inspectors would do to get promoted. They'd do their best to impress the station superintendent with spectacular operations or by submitting endless reports about various banal matters. One sergeant put in a report to the superintendent saying that police officers were scratching the serial numbers off the back of the police radios, which was criminal damage. A report came from the superintendent saying that anybody found doing this would be charged with criminal damage. It was then pointed out that the metal studs on the leather pouches were rubbing against the radios, which scratched the numbers off and it wasn't us doing it. Whichever bright spark at HQ who was sticking the brass number tags on the back of the radios hadn't bothered to check the pouches they were going in to see if anything was going to rub on them.

Another sergeant put a report in saying that police officers were driving the Pandas and deliberately forcing them into reverse gear when they were moving forward, breaking the gear box. The superintendent again said that anyone found doing this would be charged with criminal damage. It later transpired that there was a fault with the transmission on that model of car, so they had to be recalled.

It was an insult when these reports would be read out on briefing. It was as if we were looked at like a bunch of hooligans who liked to damage police property for no good reason. Why on earth would we want to damage our own equipment?

When I was working in the cell block at Stechford a female sergeant who was in line for inspector decided to make a name for herself. She put a report in to the superintendent complaining that the PCs were drinking the maxpax tea in the cell block and it was only supposed to be used for the prisoners. I could've slapped that stupid cow up and down the station. Having a three-pence plastic cup of tea or coffee down the cell block is a tiny perk and means a lot when you've been pushing a Panda up and down the streets for several hours and want a quick cuppa. The hypocrisy was that she'd been drinking it every day for years when she was a WPC and custody sergeant. She was just searching for something to use to get her name known by the superintendent. She later got promoted and last I heard is causing havoc at some other station.

On one Sunday my former protégé Dale had been put on the toilet squad in plainclothes along with some other inexperienced officers. I did speak to my mates on Red Watch regularly because I still worked in the same station. They weren't happy about doing the operation because it was being run with skeleton staff on Sundays when most people took days off so back-up was scarce if they got into trouble. About six members of the watch were put into plainclothes to do the operation and observations. There was one police officer in uniform patrolling nearby to transport prisoners.

The officers had been sent out on the operation with a short briefing but their powers of arrest had not been explained to any of them so some of them were unsure of their powers (but remember that there was *no* power of arrest).

The day had been going pretty well with the usual high number of arrests and instant cautions for every prisoner. Some of the plainclothes team were busy with prisoners. Jed had been having a go at Dale telling him he needed to get his numbers up (number of prisoners). It was then that a chain of events took place which was to alter Dale's life forever. It was also when the most scandalous cover-up I'd ever witnessed in my 12 years in the police took place.

The watch supervision were thin on the ground because Sunday was a popular day to have off. The sergeant who usually stood in for him was engaged on other duties which left the custody sergeant, who was of course working down the cell block. The observation team had come in for dinner and the other two plainclothes officers had gone into the police bar to watch football and left their radios in the front office.

There was now no back-up for anybody going into the toilets to make an arrest, but they didn't know it, and because the operation was using their own radio channel nobody else on duty that day would be able to hear back-up calls. Dale was eager to go out and get another prisoner to keep Jed off his back. He thought his team were there to back him up, but there was no supervision present ensuring his safety. Thirty minutes later Dale would be lying in hospital in a coma fighting for his life.

Throughout the entire operation there was supposed to be a police officer standing in the front office keeping a written log of what was happening outside in the toilets. Unfortunately the PC responsible was an alcoholic and had left his post to go for a drink in the bar. He left the log sheet he was supposed to be filling in as events occurred (the contemporaneous obs. record) lying on the window sill in the front office.

Dale went to one of the two public toilets within two minutes' walking distance from the station. He picked The Quadrant, which was a seemingly small decision, but with huge consequences. He slowly walked down the steps and into the rank-smelling piss-stained toilets. A man named Jeremy had gone down about two minutes before looking for another man to have sex with. Jeremy looked at Dale and thought it was his lucky day because Dale was a very handsome young man. Jeremy dropped his trousers and started to masturbate in front of Dale. Dale produced his warrant card and told Jeremy he was under arrest.

Jeremy was the manager of a large store in town and in charge of over 200 people. He was also married with children and had no intention of them finding out. He'd be humiliated at work and have to leave, and the chances were that his wife would divorce him and he'd never see his children again.

Jeremy's life flashed before his eyes and what was going to happen would be unbearable. He thought he was going to be charged and that his name and photo would be in the papers. If he'd known that he'd be cautioned and released about 30 minutes later, he probably wouldn't have done anything.

Dale was standing there on his own with no colleague to back him up. Dale called for transport for his prisoner, but the only person who could hear the radio channel in use for the operation was a very professional front office clerk called Laura. Laura could only hear it because Dale's back-up team had left it in the office while they went upstairs to watch football in the police bar. If she hadn't been listening, Dale would've surely been dead.

Jeremy tried to push Dale out of the way, but Dale was under pressure to get his man. He couldn't walk back to the station empty-handed and face more bullying from Sgt. Jed. Dale called up for help on his radio but there was no reply. Laura had heard and waited for Dale's colleagues to answer but the radio remained silent.

Jeremy grabbed Dale's head and smashed it off some metal railings in the toilet causing Dale's skull to fracture. Dale's back-up were shouting at the referee on the TV two minutes away, oblivious that their colleague was fighting for his life. Dale was no fighter and not in a position to put up much of a struggle. If I'd been there I'd have punched Jeremy through the wall.

The blow had stunned Dale but he was a tenacious chap; he tried to wrestle with Jeremy but his years of accountancy experience were of no use here. Dale kneed Jeremy in the stomach but this had no effect. Jeremy was running on pure adrenalin and only a knockout blow would've been enough to stop him.

Jeremy ran up the stairs followed by Dale who was by this time screaming for help on the radio. Laura was running around the station crying, trying to find somebody to tell so a shout could go out on the normal radio channel. Dale's colleagues were still sitting in the bar watching football and having a crafty pint.

Dale caught up with Jeremy 30 seconds later and tried to grab him. Jeremy turned around and punched Dale hard in the face which sent him falling to the ground. Dale was screaming for help on the radio and Laura was running around the station trying to find somebody to help Dale.

Meanwhile, Jeremy was stamping on Dale's head again and again and again bashing it into the concrete paving slabs. He then ran away into the distance. No help came while Dale lay there. He managed to get up and change his radio to the normal channel used by the watch. He screamed for help and than ran another 10 yards before collapsing onto the ground unconscious. He didn't wake up until a month later.

By the time the alarm was raised the only thing that could be done was call an ambulance. It was now panic stations. When there's been a major cock-up or mistake fear grips every police officer involved. They don't want to be the one to be disciplined for making a mistake, so many will do whatever they can to cover up their mistakes. This can, of course, include lying. When there's a big mistake in the police there's no culture of learning and working out ways to prevent things like this happening again. The management descends upon you and looks for somebody's bollocks to nail to the wall.

There was a quick meeting at the police station while Dale was being put on life support. The PC who should've been recording a written log was in serious trouble. Dale's back-up had gone into the station bar and had left their radios behind.

Have you heard of brainstorming? The police have something similar when there's a huge cock-up. It's called 'blame storming' and is where everybody looks around for somebody to blame and carry the can for the mistake. If there are too many people to blame, then a meeting takes place to agree on their version of events. The theory is that if enough people tell the same lie then that becomes what actually happened instead of the truth. Sometimes, the truth comes out because somebody cracks under pressure or somebody with integrity comes forward.

Everybody got their story straight and said they were on patrol or listening to their radios but never heard anything. The drunk PC who was supposed to be in the front office monitoring what happened and listening to the radio had staggered down the stairs from the police bar into the front office and then muttered to Laura that he was going to have to make the log up so he didn't get into trouble.

Laura went over to speak to Sgt. Jed Leap who was the radio controller that day. She liked him and wanted to tell him about what had happened. I'll always resent Jed for his spineless behaviour. Laura explained what had taken place to him. She said that Dale's back-up had left their radios in the front office and nobody had answered when he screamed for help. Jed was counting down to his pension and was also a man of little integrity. He turned around to Laura and said, 'Say and do nothing.'

Dale was in coma for a week while the damage to his brain was being assessed. The first part of the coma was induced by the injury, but the intensive care unit decided to keep him asleep while his body did its best to repair the damage. Dale's wife and his mum and dad stood by his side.

The day after Dale had gone into hospital the news of the incident was in the papers and on television. Jeremy had called in sick for the day. He'd lain in bed awake all night in a state of shock. Not only had he been exposed as a married gay man who had sex with strangers in public toilets, he had now put a police officer into a coma. He knew he was going to be caught and go to prison and lose everything in his life. The next morning after his wife had gone to work and his children had gone to school, Jeremy drove his car into his garage at home and killed himself with the exhaust fumes. He couldn't face what was going to come so he took the easy way out.

Dale never fully recovered from the damage to his brain. He was left with terrible migraines which no tablets could even touch. He had the occasional fit which meant he couldn't drive. He did come back to work, but for every two weeks he was able to work he had to have one off. Luckily for Dale, his memory of the event was perfect. He could remember every single detail.

Dale spoke to the police federation about what happened. They hired the services of a team of top lawyers and a barrister who looked at the facts. They agreed that he'd been placed in grave danger and that the chief constable had breached his duty of care towards Dale for several reasons.

You may not have heard of the phrase 'closing ranks'. It refers to the process of army or police grouping together to block an investigation into them by an internal or external investigating body. The constables involved had all got together and realised that they were all going to be in serious disciplinary trouble if the truth got out.

Dale approached me to give a statement when I was still in the CJU getting ready to leave for my new station as a sergeant. Dale knew that I objected to the whole operation and had voiced my concerns to the watch supervision several times and been told to shut up. Dale knew he was asking for a lot, because if you rock the boat in the police you can be a marked man for the rest of your career. A phone call is made and you find that you get a shit posting or turned down when you go for promotion or to work for a specialised unit. I didn't have to think twice.

My integrity means everything to me, so I gave a statement. Another member of Red Watch did the same, which was very brave of him.

The whole case hinged on Laura doing the same because she'd seen the two radios left in the front office by Dale's back-up team. It was even harder for her, because she was applying to the police to be accepted as a police officer and would be working with the very same officers she'd be giving evidence against.

I read a phrase a few years later by a man called James Allen which is so true. He said, 'Circumstances do not make a man, they reveal him.' When pressure is applied, people show their true colours. Some crumble under the pressure and have to live with the decision they make, and others rise up and show what they're made of. Laura showed great courage and integrity when she agreed to give a statement.

The whole event took about two years to go to court. By this time I was a sergeant working in Birmingham. Instead of agreeing that mistakes were made, the chief constable's legal team argued that he owed no duty of care to the constables who worked for him. They even argued that his going into the toilet on his own amounted to contributory negligence! I was gobsmacked. What a complete and total disgrace. I couldn't believe what I was hearing. He was washing his hands off any responsibility for our safety while we were on duty. It made me so angry to hear what his legal team were saying. I felt it was a very dark day for the police when their own chief constable says it's nothing to do with him if you're injured whilst carrying out your duty.

When I went to Birmingham County Court to give evidence the team that were supposed to be backing Dale up were there. They were all ushered into a private room by the police lawyers to make sure they'd got their story straight. The press was there and some of the family of the man whom Dale had tried to arrest in the toilets. I'm not sure, but I think they were suing the police as well.

I was called in to give evidence before the court. I explained to the judge that I'd complained from the start that the whole thing was unsafe but I was told to shut my mouth and get on with it. The police officers who were supposed to be backing Dale up just sat there together with grins on their faces. I'd seen this before when police officers all gave evidence against a criminal, but never when we had one of our own in court.

Dale and his young wife were left to sit outside the courtroom on their own during breaks in the case. Dale had since left the police on medical grounds. His dad had not spoken to him for two years because Dale was suing the police force. Dale's dad had been a police officer his whole life and believed that he should just keep quiet and not make a fuss about it. Talk about the sins of the father.

I sat in the back of the court with Steve Jaspal who'd come along to give Dale some moral support. Dale's lawyer had come over and told us that Dale didn't really want to speak to anybody in the police anymore, and it was nothing personal. I probably wouldn't have wanted to either if I were him. We did have a quick chat during one break. He was really grateful I'd come to give evidence. It was great to see him again, but clearly he was not the same man I'd known before.

The whole case hinged on Laura's evidence. She was now a police officer working in Coventry and I admired her so much for having the courage to stand up and tell the truth because it could've had serious repercussions on her future career. Testifying against your colleagues is what is known as a CLM (career limiting move).

Laura stood firm when the police barrister tried to tear her story to pieces. He accused her of lying and making it all up. He said that she'd made a mistake and told her to admit to the court that she never heard the calls for back-up. I don't know how that barrister could live with himself. Making money on other people's misery.

Laura was fantastic, the whole court fell silent when she began to sob as she recalled hearing Dale's cries for help on the radio. You could see in her mind that she was back at that very day, standing in the front office. 'I'll never forget the sound of his voice,' she said with tears rolling down her cheeks, 'he was screaming for help. I thought he was going to die and there was nobody answering him.' The chief constable's barrister knew he was screwed by this point, but a good barrister never lets his poker face change.

Laura told the court about Jed telling her to keep quiet. The chief constable's legal team knew their case was crumbling, but they kept a brave face on things. I felt really happy because the truth was coming out and it's very important to my peace of mind that justice is served.

At the end of the case the judge gave a summary of the facts and delivered his ruling. He decided that Dale's back-up team had lied on oath and were sitting in the police bar watching football while Dale was being beaten half to death. The supervision were never criticised for not being there to do what they're paid to do, supervise.

He said that Jed Leap had fabricated incident logs as the police radio controller. He clearly did this to cover up for the officers who'd abandoned their posts. The judge ruled that the chief constable did in fact owe his constables a duty of care and he could not wash his hands off us if we were injured on duty.

He also added that all the arrests made during the entire operation were in fact unlawful because the offence carried no power of arrest. He said that the briefings given by the sergeant in charge of the operation were wholly inadequate because they didn't explain the powers of arrest to the officers concerned and there was no safe way of keeping watch over the officers who were going into the toilets.

The police legal team appealed to the Court of Appeal, which meant that Dale and his wife had to wait another 12 months before hearing if they'd have to go through it all again. The Court of Appeal ruled in their favour. Dale won damages against the chief constable. It was the police insurance paying anyway, so it was no skin off his nose.

I'd guess that the taxpayer who had to fund the police legal team would've had a bill of well over 200 grand or more. To my knowledge, nobody was disciplined for neglect of duty on that day. Nobody was taken to task for lying in court on oath (it was a civil trial and not criminal).

∂ ∂

Plainclothes operations always sounded sexy to the participants. It smacks of Starsky and Hutch or glamorous TV programmes. They should always be carefully thought out and the risk assessed but in reality I never saw this happening. Somebody would just decide to do something in plainclothes and usually the probationary constables would volunteer because it sounded exciting.

About a year after Dale's case had finished I was duty sergeant in Alum Road police station in Birmingham. On the early shift (not my team, I hasten to add) there was one junior WPC crewed with an old-sweat PC out on plainclothes patrol. He'd been on traffic for years and was rusty when it came to anything that didn't involve vehicles. A rusty PC and a junior WPC young in service out in plainclothes. Whatever sergeant thought that up should've been busted back to PC.

The old-sweat PC went off on an enquiry and so the WPC went out on foot patrol on her own around a real shit-hole area which is just about the stupidest thing she could've done. As she was walking down the road in one of the rougher areas some young man wearing a 'hoodie' cycled up beside her and started chatting her up. She told him she wasn't interested but he kept at it. He didn't know she was a police officer since she was in her jeans and shirt. He chatted her up for a few minutes as she walked up the road on her own. Eventually, he got tired of talking and put his hand down her shirt and into her bra getting a quick feel of her tit. He cycled off and she stood there in shock. She radioed the incident in but the guy was never found.

She'd already been out when I got on duty, but as the duty sergeant she was my responsibility. I was fuming. First, her partner should never have left her alone; second, her sergeant should never have let her be in plainclothes; and third, she should never ever have gone out on her own. I was sometimes staggered at the lack of common sense of people who were supposed to be professional police officers, at all ranks.

I'd worked in plainclothes on Red Watch at Little Park Street quite a few times and also in the shoplifting squad. It's very exciting and a big bonus is that you don't have to wear the police uniform. It's a bit like non-uniform day at school.

At one point when I was on Red Watch as a PC we were having a lot of burglaries around the Stoke area of Coventry. We knew who was doing it, but the problem was catching them in the act. Burglars no longer wear stripy jumpers and carry a bag with SWAG written on the side. They usually have a clever routine they follow to reduce the chances of them being caught on the way to, during and after the burglary. When a burglar does steal things, he usually stashes the stolen goods in a safe location and goes to collect them later on rather than just carry them straight from the scene of the crime to the handler's address.

We also had an encampment of gypsies nearby and the burglary rate had shot through the roof. Perhaps I can set the record straight about gypsies. You get one half of people saying that they're thieves and the other half crying that they're honest Romany folk preserving their way of life and you should not call them 'gippos' or 'pikeys'.

All I can tell you is that when a new group of gypsies came to an area, they trespassed on land and the burglaries went up by over 500 per cent, old ladies had their pensions conned out of them for bogus repairs to their drives or roofs, and when they left the illegal site there was rubbish and shit left everywhere which the taxpayer had to pay to get cleaned up.

I did have several dealings with gypsies, and it was always when one had been caught stealing. Establishing their identity was a nightmare because they'd always give a false name and they had no fixed abode. If you did go to their caravan site, you were always stonewalled and lied to.

The facts speak for themselves. They have no income because they have no fixed address or job and yet all drive top-of-the-range four-wheel-drive vehicles and live in caravans which cost at least 30 grand. And of course they pay no tax whatsoever. It seems to me that their income is derived from tarmacing drives very badly, stealing things and burgling houses.

In Coventry the gypsy children used to go out all day knocking on people's doors. Although they were all illiterate they'd developed a series of signs which they drew outside people's houses on the pavement in chalk. The signs indicated if there was a dog in the house or an alarm, if the person was living alone, elderly or frail and an easy target. It was a nightmare because for a while we didn't know what the signs meant so we didn't know which houses to watch. We did our best to warn the people living in the area, but all we could do was knock on doors or drop leaflets which of course took an age to print.

I was working with Callum in plainclothes on one set of nights from Little Park Street. Callum was the guy who'd shagged the student upstairs while I sat downstairs with her housemates. Callum was still up to his usual tricks and had a string of about five or six ladies on his round in Coventry. His mobile phone would be going off all day long when he was off duty with requests for visits from his 'special friends'.

Callum hated gypsies. 'They're like a fucking plague of locusts,' he told me one night, 'they sweep into an area and leave when they've picked it dry.' All I can tell you is what I saw. I'm sure that not every band of gypsies are burgling thieves, but the ones I came across brought a mini-crime wave with them. Despite that, I never did and do not condone attacking them in any way. It isn't down to the general public to take matters into their own hands and attack gypsies but I did understand people's frustrations. I can't tell you how many frail old people I met who had their life savings swindled from them or their pension money taken.

Working with Callum was good fun. He was an off-the-wall character who loved to be out about sneaking around and catching bad guys. The one problem with plainclothes is that the non-uniformed police vehicles we usually had access to were very clearly still plainclothes police cars, diamond-White Maestros and then Peugeot 306s. The villains used to spot us a mile off. They were usually diesels as well so they could hear us coming long before we got there.

Another problem was that police officers for some reason look like police even when they're off duty. I don't know what it is, but the villains used to work it out straightaway. Mind you, the ex-army guys would always wear jeans and a camouflage ('cammy') jacket which was a dead giveaway. Still, without formal training we'd just do our best. I guess it was a fair trade because we could pick out a thieving chav from a crowd in four seconds flat, so it stands to reason they'd be able to spot us as well.

Callum and I used to park the car away in a side street and sneak around the alleys and entryways hoping to hear an odd sound or catch somebody in the act. Unfortunately, Callum would get really excited about being in plainclothes and catching prisoners in the act and would need to go for a shit about every two hours. One night, we were miles from the police station and we'd dumped the car about a mile away so we could sneak around on foot. Callum said to me, 'I'm desperate for a shit, mate; I need to find a garage.' I wasn't impressed, 'For fucks sake, mate, can't you hold it in?' I said. That wasn't an option for Callum, though. 'No way, mate', he said through clenched teeth, 'I'm locked and loaded.' He ducked off into an entry and shat in somebody's garage.

When he came out I asked, 'What did you wipe your arse on?' He grinned, 'I had some statement paper in my pocket so I used that.' I groaned and asked, 'But what about the police logo on the top?' I could imagine somebody finding that the next morning and calling the station. 'It will be obvious who left that shit there,' I was about to tell him to go and remove the evidence when he winked at me and said, 'Don't flap, mate, I tore the logo off first and ate it.' You couldn't make this stuff up if you tried.

The same thing happened every other night for the entire set of nights. Callum and I'd be walking about and he'd get stomach pains and have to run over to somebody's garage and have a shit in it. It was dreadful, I kept worrying that he was going to be caught and the owner would call the police and it would get into the papers. So if you lived in Stoke around 1993 and one day went into your garage to discover to your horror a big turd with a piece of lined paper next to it which said 'sign here' and 'witness here' on the bottom and was covered with shit, it was probably Callum.

Callum must've done about five shits a day and he had a name for every sort. 'The Sprinkler' would stray all up the side of the bogs; 'The Sweet Corn' was peppered in corn; 'The Teflon' was when you wiped your arse but there was no shit on the paper; and 'The Ghost' was when you heard it splash into the water but when you looked down there was nothing there. I'd always sit there laughing when Callum would come out of the toilet and announce to anybody who'd listen what sort of cable he'd just laid.

A few years later Callum met a lovely lady and they moved in together. He was around my house chatting to her on his mobile phone and then while he was chatting he went to use my toilet to go for a shit. While he was having a shit, he carried on chatting to her, straining away on the toilet.

When he came out I said, 'I can't believe you were speaking to your misses on the phone and having a shit at the same time.' Callum just looked at me gone out, 'That's nothing, mate. When either of us are having a shit at home, we sit in the bathroom chatting to each other.' I just stood there in shock. Some things are supposed to be private and having your misses there watching you pinch off a stinking loaf, wipe your arse and look at the tissue to see there's any shit on it is outrageous. But it was Callum we're talking about.

I did finally manage to ask him about his orgasm guarantee. I thought it was either just a trick to get ladies into bed or a boast, but then again, the girl who he shagged upstairs in the house was screaming the roof off. 'So what about the orgasm guarantee?' I asked casually as we walked down a dark road one night. 'Oh yeah, I forgot about that conversation,' grinned Callum. 'Every woman's different,' he said, 'some have G-spot orgasms, some are clitoral, and some are vaginal. You've to pay attention to the way their body moves, little moans, gasps or even the way they move their hips gives it away.'

I wanted a bit more information than that. By this time I knew what I was doing, but a lot of the time didn't know *how*, if you get what I mean. 'Can't they just tell you?' I said in exasperation. Callum laughed out loud, 'No mate, they expect you to be a mind-reader, I'm afraid. You can ask them "Is that nice?" but they're usually deep in concentration by the time you've been making love for a while.'

Callum could see the frown on my face. 'Listen, mate,' he said sympathetically, 'like I said, every woman's different. Some like you to make love slowly and tease and tickle them, some love you to pin their legs back and go hammer and tongs for half an hour before they come. It's just a case of watching and listening until you work it out.' I knew he was right due to my own experiences. I just didn't know why they don't come out and tell you about it up front so you could deliver the goods, but then again that would mean there was no mystery or adventure, I suppose.

We were out in the plain car one night during that week of nights. It was early in the morning and a message came over the radio that a white BMW 3 series had just been stolen in the Stoke area and they gave the registration. Literally seconds later it drove past us along Humber Road going in the opposite direction. My heart started to pound with excitement. It's important to give a clear commentary on the radio about what's happening, but at the same time you can often be in a bit of a state of panic and euphoria.

We began to follow it and because Callum was the passenger he called it into the controller. We followed the car as the Zulus rushed to the area desperate for a pursuit. There were two white men in the front but we couldn't make out much more. We were planning to follow it and then get out of the way of the Zulus when they came.

Unfortunately, the car pulled into the Peugeot factory gate as if it was going to turn around. It was about 4 a.m. and so if we'd stopped it'd have been obvious who we were. We had to think on our feet. We couldn't pursue it because our car was so slow, and we'd be in big trouble if I crashed while chasing a car (again).

We pulled up next to it and I wound my window down and motioned the driver of the stolen car to do the same. 'Alright, mate,' I said as casually as possible, 'we're a bit lost. Can you tell us the way to the city centre?' He was such a nice chap, he started to tell us the way and I acted as stupid as possible getting him to repeat it several times.

What seemed like an Ice Age later the whole place was surrounded by police cars and the two men looked completely shocked. They were about three streets away from where they'd stolen the car and had stopped to give us directions for about five minutes. They just sat in the car with their mouths open when they were surrounded and dragged out of the car, handcuffed and taken to the police cells.

Happy Birthday to Me – 5 June 1976

We move house and I have to go to a new school but I really don't want to move. My mum takes me to my new school which is called St Augustine's. We go in to see the new teacher but I won't let go of my mum's hand. I'm screaming and crying, the teacher is pulling one hand and I have hold of my mum's hand. My mum is trying to leave but I won't let go of her hand. The teacher pulls me into the class and my mum walks away leaving me behind. I sit there crying at the front of the class with the teacher. The other children are all staring at me.

At lunch time I walk around the playground with a nice lady who watches us while we play to keep us safe. I hold her hand as she walks around the playground. I don't want to let go. She wears brown mittens that keep my hand warm.

It's a hot summer. My mum takes me to Holbrook park and lets me ride there on my bike. I don't have a tee shirt on and the sun shines on my back all day long. Next day, I wake up and my back is very sore. When I go to school another boy pats me on my back and I cry out in pain.

My teacher at school is Miss Yakimovitch. I really like her because she makes us all laugh. Every Friday afternoon she tells jokes and asks us riddles until it's home time. She asks us a riddle. 'A man who was blind stole plums from a tree. He took one, he left one. Now how can that be?' We guess for ages before somebody gets the answer right.

I'm a good helper for my mum. I can change Gina's nappy all by myself. They're called Terrys nappies; you've to fold them in a certain way and be careful with the big safety pin.

Mum has a boyfriend called John. He watches **Star Trek** *every Friday and I watch it with him. I start to like it as well. John is clever, he's building a telescope in the garage. He lets me stay up one night and watch a scary film called* **Horror Express**. *There's a monster in it that kills people by looking at them with his red eyes. I can't sleep on my own for the next six weeks.*

I love Fridays. There's a programme on called **Monkey** *which is the best. There's a man in it with a stick which he keeps in his ear and when he spins it the stick grows. He can fly on clouds. It makes me laugh.*

I spent a lot of time watching TV with my auntie Gina. We watch a programme called **Sandokan**. *Sandokan is an Indian pirate who can kill a tiger with his bare hands. During the adverts we bet two pence on how many adverts there'll be before the programme starts again.*

Auntie Gina lets me light her cigarettes for her. She smokes Saint Moritz and they smell like polo mints.

One Sunday I'm walking to church with my mum. We go into a shop and I steal a white chocolate mousse. When we get outside I show it to my mum. She hits me over the head again and again and makes me take it back and say

sorry. It is wrong to steal, and when you do, you get punished.
I'm 6 years old.

Year 7 – Chavs

Dawn began to daydream about her first day at nursery school. Her mummy had bought her a pretty new dress, yellow with red tulips sewn into a pattern that went all around the bottom. She also had a pair of bright red shoes which had a shiny big buckle on the side. She practised for hours doing and undoing the buckle so she was really good at it.

On the first day at school she walked across the playground. She was holding tight to her mummy's hand. The playground had bright-coloured patterns painted on it, squiggly snakes, circles and hopscotch squares. The inside of the school had a funny smell, like chemicals.

When it was time for her mummy to leave she didn't want her to go, she stood there crying and crying until another little girl came up with a dolly for her to play with. They held hands and went to play on a tiny see-saw together and were instantly best friends.

Every dinnertime they both lay outside on the grass and looked up at the clouds in the sky just like she was doing now. They'd point up at the clouds and call out what they looked like. Balloon, pony, doggie, hedgehog, then they'd burst into fits of giggles.

Dawn began to giggle as well as she thought about it. Then she began to cough. That taste in her mouth was horrible. What on earth could it be?

ও ৎ

I bought my first house when I was 20. I didn't know anything about mortgages or property so I just found an agent who seemed to know his stuff. I didn't have a penny towards a deposit, so I had to borrow it. The house was in Somerset Road in Radford which is a working-class area of Coventry, about a mile from the city centre. It had belonged to a relative of mine who'd left it empty for a few years. It needed a bit of fixing up but was cheap enough. He'd obviously smoked because all the ceilings were brown from the cigarette tar.

I was like many other adults around the civilised world who had a steady income but didn't know the first thing about money or how to manage it. My family were all relatively poor and never had any savings. Holidays consisted of six of us piling into our stepdad's tiny Datsun 100 which was designed to carry four people in comfort. He had no driving licence or insurance at the time, but he was a good driver so had never been pulled over.

We'd drive all the way down to Dorset and sleep on mattresses on my aunty's floor and drive to the beach in the day and make sandcastles. It was heaven to us at the time and the concept of going abroad was not even considered. That was something rich people did.

As I grew up I just subconsciously took on my parents' values about money. No need to save, spend what you earn, and borrow the rest if you need it. We bought everything from the catalogue and we couldn't even manage our household bills. My mum paid a company called Secure Homes a weekly fee and they paid our bills for us.

I'm not blaming anybody for my financial situation at the time. Everybody does the best they can with what they know. They learned from their parents and so on. I got my first credit card when I was 19 when I was still a police cadet. I felt very important because for some crazy reason I managed to qualify for a gold one. I loved to show it off as I bought things with it.

My philosophy was to buy things with the credit card and pay the bill off at the end of the month with my salary. It just didn't work out that way. Something would break on my car or overtime would be cancelled and I'd tell myself that I'd pay it off the next month instead. The 'next month' never comes though, does it? Over the next few years I accumulated a few more credit cards and then a loan or two. I took a loan to pay off the smaller loans and 'consolidate them into one easy-to-manage monthly payment' just like the dancing telephone on the TV told me to.

I take full responsibility for my actions and the debt I got into. I think most of the money went into renovating my house, getting a new roof when mine wore out and getting double glazing and so on. I'd started a savings plan for every year I was in the police. The police have 10-year savings schemes which are wonderful. The problem is that you can borrow three times what you've saved at a great rate so the temptation became too great.

I had seven savings schemes built up over seven years. My debt slowly crawled up to 2,000 then 4,000 then 8,000 later 16,000 and finally reached 26,000 pounds. It'd have got higher but I became a credit leper. My bank wouldn't lend me any money and my credit cards (all six) were maxed out. Not even the 'we take any scumbag' companies at the back of the tabloid papers would touch me.

I'd get paid and then make the minimum payment on my credit cards. An hour after it cleared, I'd take that minimum payment out and use it to make the minimum payment on another card. I was in a huge mess and had buried my head in the sand for years. Looking back now I seemed to be in a trance, not accepting that I was in trouble and masking over the problem with more cards and loans.

Years later I was to read many books on financial intelligence and how to think like a wealthy person thinks. While I was in my 20s I'm afraid I was financially ignorant. I used to just pray for payday to come and thought that my yearly pay rise or some overtime would answer my problems.

Most of my colleagues in the police were the same, it was joy on pay day and two weeks later depression at the thought of waiting another two weeks to get paid. I had more month than money. The worst off were often those in police houses: they had no mortgage, but at the end of their service they had to move out and had no job to pay for a house.

The problem wasn't enough money, it was spending more than I made, and not learning how to delay gratification by saving for things. By the time I finally asked for help I'd cashed all of my savings plans in. I was up to almost 27,000 pounds in debt spread over three loans and six credit cards: 27,000 pounds was what I earned for a year in the police before tax.

For about three months I hadn't been able to afford shopping, so I just had porridge to eat for breakfast, dinner and tea. I used powdered milk to save money and went to see friends or family whenever I could and hoped that they'd offer me dinner. I never told anybody about my situation. I felt too humiliated that I had what seemed like such a good job and good income but was worse than broke.

I used to live in dread of anything breaking on my car because I simply couldn't afford to fix it. For years my budget for a car was 200 pounds. I told people that I wasn't really into cars that much and they were a waste of money. Really, I was too broke to afford a decent one. If I needed to buy a car I'd look in the *Coventry Evening Telegraph* newspaper. They had a car section broken down into price categories and I'd look in the under £299 section or the £300–399 at the most.

I drove a Ford Cortina for quite a while and I did love that car. There was a leak in the radiator but I couldn't afford the money to get it replaced, even with a second-hand one so I had to drive around with a watering can in the boot and continually refill the expansion tank. One evening I went out with a few mates and we ran out of water in the middle of the countryside. I had to get everyone to piss into the watering can so we'd have some water to put in the cooling system to get us to the garage.

My mortgage company were sending me letters asking why I hadn't paid them for six months and the loan companies were sending me red letters saying that they were going to send the debt collectors to my house. If you get into financial trouble in the police you can be sacked or at least disciplined. If you go bankrupt you can be sacked, and of course there's the social humiliation of having your name in the papers.

It's strange really, because when all this was happening I don't recall thinking, 'I'm in trouble here. I'd better work out a plan to get myself out of the shit.' I just carried on spending money and kidded myself that the way out was to earn more money doing overtime. The problem is that money was leaking out of my account faster than it was coming in. You can only last so long doing that before you've a serious problem.

The last straw was when I had to walk into town one day and open an account with a cash-a-cheque company. You write yourself a cheque from the salary you're going to get and they advance you some money on that and take a charge. Once again, this sort of company is just sucking the last bit of life out of somebody who's clearly in desperate financial trouble.

I had to sit in a bare front office and ring a bell. I felt humiliated at having got into this situation and very worried that a police officer was going to walk into the office to make some sort of enquiry there. Some spotty 18-year-old opened a door and called me into a private room. They stood behind a counter protected by safety glass. I had to fill in a form and get my photograph taken for ID. Hard to imagine a police officer being so skint that they have to resort to going to such a place so they can buy a bit of shopping to eat.

I went to see a police federation rep and he sorted me out an appointment with a debt management company. I look back now and regret ever using them. The companies that prey on people in debt can often be worse than the companies that lend you the money. People in debt are like a carcass rotting in the desert. Once the lions have come and ripped the meat off you, the vultures come and pick the meat off your bones. Then the ants come and bite off any pieces of ligament or sinew that may be left. It's like one big feast for the loan and debt management companies.

The company rep came and said it was either bankruptcy or an individual voluntary arrangement (IVA) which is one step away from bankruptcy. An IVA means all the creditors agree to take a monthly sum from you and you repay a percentage of the debt. It can be anything from about 10 per cent to the full 100 back, but they freeze the interest.

I owed £675 per month in interest payments alone and only had £600 per month left to pay them all with before I ate anything. I'm not looking for any sympathy here. I'm telling you this story because either you or somebody you know is here or will be here. At the time you feel that you're all alone and probably ashamed of yourself that it came to this.

The key is to realise that all the worry is generated by your mind playing a movie of an imaginary point in the future when you're living in the gutter and begging for scraps of food like a tramp. The reality of course is that this will never happen. Despite all their threats the bank can't do that much at all really. If your debts are secured on your home you can always renegotiate them. Just keep communicating with the debt companies and be steadfast and firm in what you can afford to pay them *after* you've bought food and other essentials.

There are many charitable organisations which'll bat your corner for you including Citizens Advice and the National Debt Line which are great. The banks deal with people like this day in and day out. Their existence is dependent upon you living a life of debt, because they can borrow several times more against the sum you owe them. Bastards.

I was desperate and agreed to sign the IVA. It appeared to be a good decision at the time. It got the creditors off my back and got court approval so they couldn't harass me. Looking back, they didn't get me much of a deal at all really. I still had to pay back the full amount – which is what I could've done myself.

About a year into it I was paying it off and I got a report back from the company which was managing the IVA. I'd paid about 5,000 pounds off and they'd taken away 2,000 of it to 'manage' the IVA. I was livid. It was going to take years extra to pay it off and they were creaming a huge chunk of the money away.

It took a while but I got the IVA set aside by refusing to pay the management company. It means that the debt companies could come after me, but I knew that they were all mouth and no trousers. Most of the banks sold their debts to scumbag companies which pick on broke people. They buy a five-grand debt for about 500 pounds and do their level best to get the full five grand off you. They hire university drop-outs and other losers who're paid to read scripts to bully and intimidate you into paying them everything you have or they'll 'take action' against you. I hope these people get cancer of the face and die a painful death.

I played hardball back, and after what seemed like a very long time I'd paid everybody off. Two banks had forgotten I existed altogether and had written off over seven grand worth of debt (bonus). A couple of others accepted 20 pounds per month interest-free. Another accepted a 500 payoff to settle a three-grand debt. The lesson I learned was that what you imagine will happen never usually does. Everything is negotiable, and for all their threats and letters saying debt collectors were coming, nobody ever did.

I was calm and persistent. I never got emotional and made firm offers to each company providing that they agreed to freeze the interest. I explained that my only other alternative was to go bankrupt and then nobody got anything, and they didn't want that to happen, did they?

∽ ∾

My date for promotion eventually came through. I'd chosen three stations I'd like to work at and Stechford was at the top of my list. It was a very busy station and not too far to drive to from Coventry, maybe 30 minutes from my house in Radford and up the A45.

Stechford police station was a very large building and even though it was not built as the headquarters for that section of Birmingham it was still a significant landmark in the area. Like most stations the front office was the focal point facing out onto Stechford Road. Directly at the back was the cell block and to the right a short corridor which housed the sergeants' and inspector's offices and just after that the canteen and police bar.

Upstairs in Stechford were another two floors which were very tight for space. Limited offices had to house the intelligence team, beat officers, police management, admin staff and CID. The building was always a hive of activity during the day, but usually by one minute past 5 it had pretty much emptied and you could find a spare desk to sit at to do some paperwork.

Getting promoted was one of the most painful experiences of my life. For longer than I could remember I'd strived for promotion. I knew I could do a better job than most of the supervisors I'd seen. There were only a few that stood out as great at Little Park Street and I vowed to emulate them. These sergeants I admired were true pros and a pleasure to work for. The rest were just people who'd somehow got promoted and drifted through their careers either keeping their heads down and avoiding trouble, or those who'd bully the PCs and cause havoc.

As the day for me to leave Little Park Street as a detective constable and start at Stechford as a sergeant approached I began to experience a huge amount of anxiety. I started to worry that I wasn't good enough to be a sergeant, and began to imagine that the watch were going to laugh at me if I made a mistake and I'd stand there crying in front of them.

I also began to have a recurring nightmare that I was a sergeant and had to go to an armed robbery in progress. I and the team all got there, but as we surrounded the bank the robbers came out and members of the public and my watch were shot dead because I made mistakes. I'd wake up every 30 minutes drenched in sweat. The nightmares were so realistic that it felt like it was really happening at the time I was having them.

Isn't it strange how we make ourselves sick with worry and stress by making mental images and movies of life falling apart for us? I did it for years imagining I was going to live alone for the rest of my life and never have a woman. That I'd go broke and end up as a wino pushing a shopping trolley around town. That I'd lose my job and end up cleaning the toilets in some factory.

I decided to go and see Bernard the psychotherapist to tell him what was happening. I was sure he'd understand and be able to say something to help me.

Bernard only worked three days per week and I was lucky enough to get him on one of the days he wasn't working. We sat in his back garden looking out onto miles of rolling hills and fields. Bernard had made us both a nice jug of fresh orange juice mixed with cranberry juice. As we sat with the sun on our faces, nothing seemed to matter anymore.

I told Bernard what was happening to me and that I was struggling to cope with the pressure. I said I was thinking of going to see the superintendent and telling him that I didn't want to be promoted anymore because I'd changed my mind.

Bernard nodded as I spoke and then looked out onto the fields. He pointed to a rabbit that was about a hundred yards from us on top of a mound of grass. 'Just watch the rabbit for a minute,' he said quietly. We sat there watching it. It hopped about and then stood still for about a minute chewing on a leaf. It casually looked around from time to time but otherwise just looked very chilled out. As I watched it, all my worries seemed to fade away and I gradually became lost in the moment. I felt like I was connected to the rabbit, and it was I standing on the mound with not a care in the world.

After what must've only been a couple of minutes Bernard spoke. 'The rabbit is happy because he is living in the moment; he isn't worrying about what is going to happen next week or feeling guilty about something he did last month.' He drew in a long breath and said, 'It is only human beings who can project themselves as some future image which if the image is negative then cause themselves stress based upon that future imagined scenario.'

I still felt a knot in my stomach and sighed, 'I just don't seem to be able to help myself,' I said helplessly, 'what do you think is wrong with me?' Bernard sat back in his chair and stroked his beard slowly as he thought. He seemed to become lost in his thoughts for a while. He then said, 'It sounds to me like you are dying, Paul.' This of course was not the response I was expecting. I looked over at Bernard who was still watching the rabbit, 'How can I be dying? Apart from the nightmares and anxiety I feel OK.'

He took another sip of his cool drink and looked directly at me giving me his full attention once more. 'Paul, the PC is dying, and that image of you is going through the pain of death. It is like when a snake sheds its skin and a new snake emerges leaving the old skin behind. What you are feeling is the pain of growth, but your ego is trying to stop you from growing.'

I could understand most of what Bernard was saying. Clearly, I wasn't really dying, but I did feel a massive amount of tension between where I was and where I was going. 'What do you mean by the ego?' I asked. 'That is a whole can of worms,' replied Bernard, 'but basically the ego is a false image of ourselves created to give us a reference point. It is the ego in us that wants us to have the biggest house in the street and a big car to impress people with. It is the ego that feels under attack when we lose our job or go for the promotion because it is an attack on itself. The ego hates change.'

'Why would I attack myself?' I asked in dismay. 'You aren't you,' sighed Bernard, I think he may have been beginning to regret taking me down this rabbit hole, 'you are carrying round a material image or blueprint of "you" which in your case is a 26-year-old detective constable, in debt, who drives an old banger of a car, and lives in what you call a "dog-shit street". Your current self-image can't accept that you are good enough to be a sergeant or, in fact, rich and living in a nice big mansion.'

I had to admit I could never see myself being rich or even well-off. Whenever I did look for a car it was always in the banger section of the newspaper. Bernard could see me engaged in deep thought, 'We create our own reality, Paul: the pain you are feeling is the ego not wanting you to change your current self-image. You will quickly adapt to your new self-image and probably seek a new challenge for yourself and then go through the same pain to move to that one.'

I sat there half understanding and half confused. I could see that Bernard was doing his best to explain something pretty complicated to me in a way I understood. 'Why would I attack myself though, Bernard? I should be happy for me.' 'It isn't really you, Paul,' replied Bernard, 'you have created an image or blueprint of who you are based upon your job, house, car, salary and your friends. You are made from pure energy, and as such have a connection to every other person or energy form in the universe. You were born knowing this but have simply forgotten.'

Bernard shifted in his seat and leaned towards me. 'Children realise this when they are very young, which is why they play together so happily. They do not fret about the past or future or worry about material things. As time goes on you forget who you truly are and assume a false identity.'

That all sounded very interesting I thought, but what about my nightmares? 'So what do I do about the anxiety I am experiencing now?' I asked, hoping for some sort of solution. 'That's easy enough,' answered Bernard, 'when the movie starts to play or you hear the voice in your head telling you that you are going to fail, just speak to it and say, "Thank you so much for wanting to keep me safe, but I know that everything will turn out just great." ' 'And that's all there is to it?' I exclaimed. 'Yes,' said Bernard, 'that mental movie you see is the ego trying to keep you safe from harm. It associates change with danger and wants to protect you from danger so really it is trying to help you out here.'

I thanked Bernard for his help and got up to leave for work. As I was going out of his front door he reached into his pocket and pulled out a piece of lined paper which had been folded four times into a perfect square. 'Read this later today,' grinned Bernard, 'It contains the secret mankind has been searching for since the time of Solomon.' I nodded and put it into my shirt pocket. As I walked out of his house towards my car Bernard shouted behind me, 'All change is painful, that is why people avoid it.'

Whenever I started to play the movie or heard a voice in my head telling me that it was going to be a disaster I'd just thank it and reassure it that everything was going to turn out great. The voice still came back to pester me, but the anxiety seemed to melt away.

ॐ ॐ

On my first day as a sergeant my alarm went off at 4:30 a.m. and I showered and changed, ready to drive to the cell block at Stechford in Birmingham where I was due to start as the custody officer. For the first time I was going to be wearing sergeant's stripes. It had been my dream for such a long time, but I felt ready for a new challenge in my life and career. I'd been posted to work in the cell block at Stechford for the first few months I was there.

Looking back now, I realise that the decision to put me into the cell block was a dreadful one. You're supposed to go on a training course to do that job because it's so easy to make mistakes resulting in prisoners getting off later at court. You only have to miss a meal or not visit them when you're supposed to and you can be disciplined or their court case can be thrown out. As far as I know, newly-promoted sergeants are no longer allowed to go straight into the cell block anymore and rightly so.

As I got into my car outside my house to drive to work I put the key in the ignition and began to cry. I wanted so badly to go back to being a PC where it was safe and where I could just be told what to do all the time. I wanted to drive to Little Park Street police station and tell the superintendent that I'd changed my mind and wanted to drive a Panda car again. I remembered what Bernard had told me about everything turning out OK so I started the car and drove to work.

I paraded at the cell block at Stechford police station at about 5:30 a.m. and introduced myself to the custody sergeant who was on nights. I recognised him as a sergeant I'd seen before when I was working in Coventry. He was a miserable bastard and was rude and obnoxious to every PC under him. Now I was the same rank he couldn't do that to me. It was the first benefit I felt as a sergeant, as only inspectors and above could give me shit now as I'd jumped a rank.

He briefed me on what was happening with the prisoners in the cells and who was dealing with them and off he went. I was left there on my own and was shitting myself. I'd never been on a custody sergeants' course to show me how to do the job. I honestly didn't have a clue what I was doing so I quickly had to read the custody sheets to see what the sergeant before me had written. I just copied that. I realised later that the sergeant I'd followed was next to useless at his job. I was very lucky because at the time there was a day shift custody sergeant who worked the 9 to 5 shift. He came in at 9 a.m. and I could've kissed him.

Malc was 50-something and had been in the admin department for quite some time. For some reason the station superintendent didn't like him at all so as punishment he threw him down the cell block to rot away. Malc was a lovely chap, very easygoing and always eager to help other people out. Spending his last few years working in the cells was not a great finish to his career but there was not much he could do about it.

I asked Malc if I could have a quick word with him in the doctor's room in the cell block. I explained that it was my first day down there and that if I'd made any mistakes could he let me know so I'd know not to make them the next time. He winked at me and said, 'No problem, Paul.'

I later discovered that Malc was not the most professional of custody sergeants. His knowledge of the law was very poor and he made quite a few mistakes while he was working in the cells. Mistakes can actually be made all the time: the only problem is when you get found out or a lawyer picks up on something you did wrong and uses it to get his client off at court.

The custody sergeant is one of the most dangerous roles in the police force. It's so easy to make a mistake and be hung out to dry for it. You're usually responsible for many prisoners who have to be visited at hourly intervals or more frequently when they're drunk, or even worse, suicidal. You have to know the law and the Police and Criminal Evidence Act in great detail and exactly what you can and cannot do. There are always lawyers who make demands and if you don't know where you stand legally you can be in trouble.

You need to know all the regulations about how juveniles are to be treated, when you can and when you cannot interview people without lawyers even when they demand one. You have to know all about taking samples from people and which rank must give authority and you must ensure that all custody records are kept upto date because they're stamped by computer. Nobody will believe you if you fed a prisoner but forgot to put it on the custody sheet. If it isn't on there, then it didn't happen.

When you hear the facts of an arrest from a police officer you've to determine if there are sufficient grounds to detain the person for questioning. Sometimes people have been arrested on a wing and a prayer and you've to have the moral fibre to refuse to authorise their detention. If you refuse you can really upset people and their inspectors who will make phone calls and try to bully you to do what they want instead. The bottom line is that you're the custody sergeant and the inspector or superintendent will deny any knowledge of pressurising you if it came to it because it isn't in writing.

Stechford cell block was a terrible place to work. It had no free-flowing air so was like a sweathouse in the summer and an igloo in the winter. When you walked in, the smell of rotting, stale socks wafted under your nose and you knew you were going to come out stinking eight hours later. There were only eight cells and you're supposed to only have one prisoner per cell but often three or four were piled into each. There was constant pressure from the inspectors to cram more and more prisoners in and if you didn't comply you'd be forced to work down there for even longer. All this will be denied of course, but it happened.

The Stechford area itself was a great place to work as a sergeant. The area is very much working-class with high unemployment but as a police officer working there you're dealing daily with hundreds of crack addicts, drug-pushers and dole-scroungers. These people, although in the minority, were the ones whose presence you were always aware of. I thought Coventry was a tough place to work, and it was but Stechford was in another league. At least Coventry had a city centre and some parks. Stechford didn't have a single place to go to escape for a while.

Working in the cell block it was a rarity to process a prisoner brought in from the local population who was employed. They were almost exclusively on the dole, mostly due to some mystery illness that, although it prevented them from working, did not prevent them from stealing cars and running away from the police.

Stechford, Glebe Farm, Alum Rock, Kitts Green, Shard End, it was a never-ending list of shit-hole areas. The population were mostly decent, hard-working people, but the only time I came into contact with them was when their house had been broken into by one of the local burglars. I saw a sick cycle in process where thick, useless, sorry excuses for parents would give birth and raise their offspring to be a carbon copy of themselves, the females getting shagged by the local shits as soon as they began puberty, and the males out stealing cars and taking drugs by the time they hit primary school.

This may come as a shock, but I was never very popular as a sergeant at Stechford, at least not with some people who worked there. Okay, it probably wasn't a shock then. I was very outspoken and had very high working standards. If anybody did anything to a standard I thought was not acceptable I told them so. Some of the CID at Stechford especially hated me because I didn't give them preferential treatment. I didn't let them jump the queue of people waiting to have their prisoners booked in, and whenever I caught them having a little word through the cell door hatch with their prisoners I'd give them a bollocking.

The process of having an informal chat with your prisoner before the formal interview on tape is known as verballing, and of course is illegal. The idea behind it is to establish whether they were going to admit the offence and they'd want to know what they'd be charged with if they admitted the offence, and more importantly, if they'd get bail because they had an appointment with their drug dealer that evening.

The best leverage against a prisoner is to arrest their girlfriend or wife at the same time they're arrested. An example is a raid on a drug dealer's house. You find a large quantity of drugs and drug-dealing paraphernalia such as bags, rolls of notes and weighing scales. If you just arrest the man he's going to ask for his lawyer, it can take hours interviewing him and of course he can claim that his lodger put it there and he knows nothing about it.

What's better is if you arrest his girlfriend as well. He's sweating away in the cell worrying if his misses is going to be charged and go to prison for possession with intent to supply. He'd be left to sweat in the cells for a while and then the officer would have a chat with him either sneakily when they went to take him a cup of tea or just before they turned the tape on and started the interview. You'd have to be quick, but you can always say that between the time you booked him out of the cell and into your custody and when you turned the tape on he asked for another cup of tea.

I know all of this is breaking the rules of conduct for treatment of prisoners, but look at it this way. This man is supplying heroin to drug addicts. These addicts are breaking into your house and stealing from you in order to buy drugs off the dealer. Isn't it in everybody's interests to get him put in prison? Short of fabricating evidence, risking my job or ill-treating prisoners I was up for doing what it took to make sure this man was taken off the streets. He'd almost always agree to admit possession with intent to supply so long as you let his girlfriend go and did your best to make sure he got bail after charge so long as he didn't pose a danger.

Verballing is strictly prohibited by the Police and Criminal Evidence Act. There should of course be no need to do this sort of thing, really. A professional police officer should gather the evidence and interview the suspect with the evidence in hand. Just sometimes you knew the whole case would be stronger with an admission and you knew the person was guilty.

The process of verballing established whether the prisoner was going to 'cough'. A cough meant an admission and this meant the officer felt that he didn't have to bother taking loads of statements since the offence was going to be admitted. That was a really bad idea on one level, because if they changed their plea in court there was little or no evidence to prosecute with. Verballing was an ancient process that took years to die out. It was handed down from detective to detective. When a uniformed officer went into the CID office to hand over a prisoner the first question they'd be asked is, 'Are they coughing it?'

If you're the custody sergeant and it's found out that prisoners had been verballed when you were on duty there it was *you* who'd be disciplined and not the person doing the verballing. Since I did not condone lazy ways of dealing with prisoners and since I made them do a thorough job I was seen as a pain in the arse.

I admit that in my first two years as a sergeant I was abrupt with other officers and needed to polish my people skills. All I can say in my defence was that the pressure of working in the cell block was extraordinary and doesn't bring out the best in people. It wasn't until two years later when I was in charge of my own team that I mellowed a lot.

‽ ‽

I was assigned to work with Red Watch at Stechford police station. They were on the whole a great bunch of people to work with and a very enthusiastic team. There were of course a small handful of wasters who needed to be watched all the time because they did less than the minimum they could get away with.

They did things a bit differently at Stechford. It's strange that we were all in the West Midlands Police but there just were a few subtle differences. When the sergeants and inspectors went to give a briefing they always went into the briefing room wearing their police caps and the constables stood to attention. I was shocked the first time I saw this because in Coventry everybody just sat there and you had to tell them to be quiet while you read out the briefing notes.

I always found that the tone of the watch or station came down to the management who led the attitude. We had a superb guy running Red Watch, Insp. Ross (not his real name). Insp. Ross was a superb leader who set very high standards for himself and expected the same from his watch. He was slim and tall and a very distinguished looking man and was always impeccably turned-out. His boots were polished to a high shine and his trousers well-pressed. He carried himself with an air of authority and when he spoke the whole team would stop and listen.

You'd always find Insp. Ross out on patrol, attending incidents and making sure everything was done right. He had just the right balance of checking up on you but leaving you to do your job. If you attended a job you were expected to take positive action, which is probably the single most important standard you can have as a police officer. Every domestic disturbance had to lead to an arrest. If things were so bad the police had to be called, then as far as Insp. Ross was concerned somebody should be taken to the cells to cool off.

The one thing that really set him apart from the other inspectors I'd worked for was that at the end of the tour of duty he'd get the watch together and thank us all for our hard work. I think perhaps only two or three sergeants and inspectors I worked for in the police over 12 years used to genuinely thank us at the end of a tour of duty. That one act meant more to us than anything else.

It was a breath of fresh air to be on Red Watch at Stechford compared to Red Watch at Little Park Street from a supervision point of view. The Red Watch sergeants at Stechford were rarely to be found skiving in the police station. We'd spend most of the shift on patrol turning up to jobs and doing what we were paid to do, which was supervise.

There was about 20 minutes' paperwork at the end of the tour of duty, but apart from that we attended jobs the PCs were sent on to make sure it all went smoothly. We visited the cell block to ensure our prisoners were charged with the right offences and that the PCs were expediting the investigation. It was just wonderful to be actually doing some proactive work. Some of the sergeants at Little Park Street for the most part spent almost the entire day inside the station and the ones on the watch who liked to get out and meet us at jobs were always highly respected by us.

The sergeants on Red Watch were Al, Mike and I. Al was a high-flyer in the police and I rated him very highly as a sergeant. He'd been on some sort of accelerated promotion scheme but by the time he'd got to Stechford it all seemed to stop for him. Al was 5' 9" and had a round slightly chubby fresh face. He had curly fair hair and a small button round nose. He was always laughing and smiling and usually had a joke to tell you.

Al was a well-educated former RAF (Royal Air Force) officer who had high hopes for a glittering career in the police force. Due to his special training he'd worked in many different departments in the four years he'd been in the job, but he was also a very effective person on the street as well. I rated him as one of the best sergeants I've ever worked with.

Mike was ex-Metropolitan Police and was very experienced as well. He was 5' 10", very bald and pretty tubby due to the fact he enjoyed a kebab or McDonalds every day. Mike didn't eat for most of the tour of duty, and then near to the end he'd be starving and stuff his face. I'd sit there wincing while the grease and chilly sauce dripped down his chin onto his jumper.

Mike had been a sergeant in the Metropolitan Police Force and had been married. He had to leave the Met a year earlier because his wife had died six weeks after being told she had cancer. She left him with three boys aged 2, 4 and 6 and no family nearby to help. His only relative was his sister who lived in Birmingham, so he had to move so he and his sons could be closer to her because it was the only help he had available.

I did admire Mike hugely, partly because he was good at his job and partly because he just got on with his life without any moaning or complaining. It wasn't until I'd been on Red Watch for about three months that I found out about his wife dying, and it was Al who told me. Mike hadn't even brought it up.

Mike had an interesting philosophy on people. As we worked together over the coming months we shared a lot about our lives with each other. If you work with somebody for a while you tend to get to know them well and often get to hear a lot about their lives, family and interests. We never met outside of work, but we could easily have become friends.

Mike and I were in the backyard at Stechford one day chatting and having a cup of tea when he turned around to me and said, 'There are two kinds of people in this job, Paul: alright people, and cunts.' I just stood there and listened to him neither agreeing nor disagreeing. He added a third category a few weeks later when he came up to me again and said, 'There are three kinds of people in this job, Paul: alright, cunts, and untested.' He walked off to go for a piss and I stood there laughing to myself.

I liked Mike because he was like me. (So he must be OK, right?) He dealt in absolutes so his opinions were very black or white, no grey at all. He either agreed with something or disagreed, no middle ground. I was very much on Mike's wavelength at the time so I enjoyed listening to him philosophise.

Mike would often wonder why some things happened, and more specifically, why people did what they did. He'd just look at me gone out and say, 'Am I the only one who thinks this is crazy?' That's the way I've lived most of my life. I look at people's behaviour or things that happen at work or even in the world and I think that either they're mad or I am. One example was the admin team at the police station. They'd send the internal mail down to us after checking the police officer's name against which watch they worked on. There was one letter for a PC Byron who'd never worked on Red Watch but due to a printing error had his name against our watch.

For weeks, the admin girl would keep sending the same letter down to us and Mike would write on the letter that he didn't work on Red Watch and never had. Mike would put it back into the admin post tray with the same note on. It came back every day for a month. The same woman just looked at the register, ignored the note from Mike and put it into our tray. It was like she was some sort of robot and couldn't comprehend the fact that he did not work on Red Watch. It drove Mike spare.

I'd developed a few opinions during my time in the police. It's hard not to become very judgemental when you're surrounded by shit all the time. Shit jobs, shit area, people who look at you and treat you like shit. Even your own bosses would often treat you like shit. You eventually begin to resent them and your own job.

One day Mike and I were driving down one of the rougher streets in an area called Shard End. The typical scene down there was broken-down cars, brown-stained nets on the windows (those that weren't boarded up), stray dogs and cats running around the street shitting everywhere. The thing that got to me the most was watching young children run about the street unsupervised. When I mean unsupervised, I mean that the parents were not even home. Children as young as 2 were running up and down the street half-naked playing. The lucky ones had a 5-year-old brother or sister there as well, but that was about it.

The first time I'd seen such a sight in Coventry I asked my partner if we should call social services. He just laughed at me. He said they'd need to come with a few coaches because there were hundreds of them about.

Mike and I drove along one road and we saw a little boy who looked about 3 playing in the street in his underpants. The poor little boy was covered in dirt and wasn't wearing any shoes. He looked a complete mess. Mike and I decided to knock on the front door of the house he was playing inside to ask his mum to put some clothes on him.

The front door was ajar but when we knocked nobody answered. A neighbour poked her head out of the window. She had a fag hanging off her bottom lip which wobbled up and down as she shouted, 'If you're looking for Sue, she's gone to prison to visit her boyfriend.' I looked at Mike who was frowning by now. 'So who's watching this boy then?' I asked. She just shrugged her shoulders and said, 'His sister should be about but she's probably 'round her boyfriend's.' 'How old is she?' I asked, and 'About firteen, I fink,' came the reply.

We went into the house and the little boy ran in behind us. I tried to speak to him and ask him where his mum was but he could only mumble, he didn't know any words which I thought was a bit strange. I tried to recall how old you usually are before you start to speak but I didn't know.

The house was a complete disgrace. There were no carpets so the two stained and torn sofas sat on the bare concrete floor. There was a stale smell all over the house, like damp clothing, smelly armpits, old stale cigarettes and going-off food. There were dirty plates on the floor with congealed food on and bluebottles crawling over them. They looked like they'd been sitting there for over a week. Worse than that was the dog shit all around the floor. You think I'm joking but no, they'd been left there so long that they were covered in green moss-like fur and some had gone white indicating that they used cheap dog food which had chalk as an ingredient.

The kitchen was filthy with flies all over the work tops and fridge. I looked at the cooker and a puddle of grease was floating all over the top. Old stains and pieces of food had been left to rot. The only thing to cook in was a dirty pot of some sort. I looked inside and it was just a chip pan with vegetable oil in it about three inches deep, one chip floating in it. This was clearly the only thing that was used to cook food.

As we were in the kitchen a dog emerged from behind the pantry door where he must've been kept in during the day. The dog looked like a cross between an Alsatian and a sheepdog and a few other breeds as well. It held its head down towards the floor and gave its tail a very limp wag. It acted as if it used to get beaten and didn't want to come too close.

As Mike and I watched it for a few seconds it walked into a corner of the kitchen, squatted and laid a big shit on the floor. As gross as it was we just kept on watching in disbelief. Never in a million years would I or anyone I knew let their dog shit in the house. The worst was yet to come though, because when it'd finished it turned around and began to eat its own shit. I cried out in disgust and Mick held his hand over his mouth and nose, half out of shock and half to stop himself puking. 'That's so wrong it ain't even right,' muttered Mike through the fingers over his mouth.

The dog lapped it up in about five mouthfuls, licked his lips and went back into the pantry. Now that was one hungry dog. Must've saved a fortune on dog food though, and no messy shit to clean up. I wouldn't want to be the next one through the front door to have my face licked by it. Nasty.

We climbed up a dirty and stained wooden staircase with gripper rods but no carpet. The upstairs was equally as repulsive. There were three bedrooms and the only thing to sleep on in them were filthy mattresses lying on the floor with no sheets on and quilts with no quilt covers on. They were all covered with stains of brown and various other colours. The piece de résistance was the toilet. There was no seat on it and inside were used tampons and six-week-old shit and piss stains which went right up to the edge. There was no toilet paper, just a magazine which was torn and used to wipe your arse with.

I looked at Mike. I couldn't hide the look of disgust on my face. That poor little boy was living in nothing more than a squat. His sorry excuse for a mum was away for the day seeing her boyfriend in prison and his sister had gone AWOL as well. If a nonce had seen him running about he'd have been an easy target.

We took the little boy into the police car screaming his head off. He was crying and kicking out and clearly thought that we were taking him away for good. We couldn't leave him on his own. We took him to the police station and gave him some food and one of the WPCs who was a mum and great with kids looked after him for a bit. Social services came over to the police station and took him back home.

The mum had eventually returned and called the police station to find out where her 'babby' was. The term 'babby' is used by chavs everywhere for their offspring. They don't usually refer to them by their names, just 'me babby'. I was always bemused to hear the cry of the chav mum or dad, 'I love me babby.' Maybe so, but not enough to actually look after them, cook them a decent meal, or not smoke in the car letting them choke on your passive fumes.

Some friends of mine had been desperate to have a child for years and had tried IVF five times and spent all their savings on it. If that little boy had been born to them instead he would've been loved and cherished. Strange how others can spit children out as if they're turds and treat them about the same.

You're probably thinking the same thing as me. The mother of that little boy should've been prosecuted for neglect of children and ordered to keep a clean house. Her boy was taken back to her and she had a couple more visits from social services but that was it. There were another 20 houses just like hers in that street alone.

I chatted to Mike afterwards. I said, 'I can't understand how people could live in such a shit-hole and leave their children alone in the street to play.' Mike looked at me and said something that has stayed with me ever since. He shrugged his shoulders nonchalantly and said, 'Don't judge other people by your standards. You see, what we think is disgusting is normal to them. Oh yes, just because we love our children and keep them safe and wipe their arses with quilted toilet paper doesn't mean everybody else has to.'

And what about the little boy? That scenario is played out to a greater or lesser degree in over a thousand houses covered by Stechford police station alone. If you multiply that by every other low-income area up and down the UK you're looking at tens of thousands of houses much the same. It's an almost impossible task to control.

That boy's mum was given a free house, income support and child benefit to make sure the house was clean and her family was clothed and fed. She chose to spend that money on bingo, beer, fags and train tickets to prison to see her boyfriend. It's enough to make you cry, I know, but there isn't a damn thing you can do to change it. People choose to live like this every day. I've seen many other low-income mums spend their money wisely and prioritise so that food and clothing are provided before fags and bingo money. It all comes down to how you're brought up and what your values are.

When I finished my shift that day I felt a bit low. I'm not sure if it helped or not, but Mike came over to me again and uttered another phrase that has always stuck with me. I was standing in the rear yard of the police station looking up into the sky and contemplating life. Mike had got changed to go home. He could see I was deep in thought about what had happened so came over to me. He patted me on the back, smiled and said, 'We didn't make this sewer, Paul, we just work in it.' He winked at me and went off home to his children.

Mike was right. We'd done nothing to make this place like it was. People's behaviours are much like the grooves in a record. They're cut deep when they're made and to expect a Beethoven record to play Tom Jones is madness. All we could do was do the best job possible and be the best person we could be. The little boy's mum would probably spend her entire life smoking, drinking and wiping her arse on magazine paper and there was nothing I could say or do to change that fact.

❧ ❧

The term 'chav' wasn't in common use back then but that's who we were all dealing with day in and day out. Our typical prisoner was a white male aged between 18 and 23. He was on income support and had never ever worked a day in his sorry life and never intended to either. He'd live in a council house somewhere provided for free. The house would have furniture from places that provide low monthly payments but extortionate interest.

The classic chav has very mixed priorities: they have very little food in the cupboards, but manage to afford a widescreen TV and a packet of 20 fags a day. They pride themselves on their huge collection of pirated DVDs. The chav will always be seen with the latest name brand of clothes which they got from the 'maaket' where it's nice and cheap.

There was a period in Stechford where bright orange trainers were the rage amongst all the chavs. All of a sudden almost every prisoner coming into Stechford cell block was wearing orange trainers. Mike and I'd drive around and stop and search any bloke wearing orange trainers because inevitably he'd be wanted on warrant or carrying drugs on him.

It was perfect, I think if all active criminals wore something like that it would make the police's job far easier.

The staple diet of the chav is greasy fast food which they live off, and the baby chav is quickly introduced to this rich source of nourishment from a very early age. Yes, Boyoncee, Kylie or Keanu is chowing down on thick shakes and chicken nuggets as soon as his or her first tooth shows through. Go to any McDonalds and you'll see chavvy mums spooning ice cream into her babby's mouth which of course will send its metabolism haywire as its pancreas desperately tries to release enough insulin to metabolise the 50 spoons of sugar it's just ingested.

The chav purpose in life is twofold. First, to sponge whatever benefits they can have from the government including disability benefits. The cleverest of chavs can even get free cars with servicing and insurance if they can make up a clever enough disability. The second purpose of the chav is to have as many children as possible. The point behind this is the more children you have the bigger the 'caansil aass' you can get. Chavs spread in a community quicker than salmonella in a gone-off chicken. A large council house is much prized in the chav community.

Although chavs seem to take on random behaviour there's actually a very strict set of rules and behaviours behind what they do. This is in order to identify themselves as a chav or chavette to others so that they don't mistakenly converse – or even worse – mate with a non-chav.

The male chav will usually sport jeans pulled low enough to expose their YSL boxers which you can get boxes of five for a quid from Bewise or the 'maaket', 150-quid Timberland or Rockport boots, a name brand jumper such as YSL or DKNY. They'll sport a few sovereign rings, fingernails chewed down to the bone and a nice large gold-plated belcher chain from Elizabeth Duke which hangs 'round their necks to draw attention to their love bites. The outfit is usually completed by a nice Burberry baseball cap. Not because it looks particularly nice, but because washing your hair is strictly forbidden in chav society.

The female chav ('chavette') will usually be found sporting a white or pink shell suit with lettering around their bums such as 'Sexy' or 'Babe'. They'll always wear white trainers with no socks because the male chav likes the scent of cheesy smelly feet in his face when he has the female's feet over his shoulders.

The chavette must always either be smoking or chewing gum and preferably both at the same time. If she's found not chewing gum when she has no fag on then she'll be badly beaten by other chavettes. For this reason they'll keep the gum in their mouths even during sexual intercourse. If you do get a blow job from a chavette make sure you check your bell end afterwards to see there isn't a piece of juicy fruit stuck to the tip.

The chavette uniform as well as including the shell suit must include the G-string from the 'maaket'. There are two signs of seniority in the chavette community. One is the high G-string, the higher it is the higher your place in the pecking order. It's preferably thinner than cheese wire so it cuts right into the crack of your arse. Also, large hoop earrings are essential. The leader of any particular chavette group gets to wear hooped earrings so big that their man's pit bull terrier could jump through them. Now that's class.

Any respectable chavette will be pregnant in her early teens. It's important to secure the biggest 'caansil aass' you can. The chavette will exclaim loudly to anyone who'll listen how much 'I love my babby' and yet will smoke heavily all through the pregnancy and drink alco pops as if they're going out of fashion.

As well as the traditional outfits, chavs identify each other through a complicated dialogue which sounds incomprehensible to outsiders. Chavs are all expert ventriloquists and are masters of speaking without moving their lips. The speech sounds very similar to somebody who's just suffered a stroke and is learning to speak again. Even world-class linguists would be hard pressed to understand what's being said.

Here's a brief conversation between two chav males (with translation in brackets).

Chav 1: Chap (Good day to you, sir).
Chav 2: Geez (And the same to you, good sir).
Chav 1: Jeet (Have you had breakfast yet)?.
Chav 2: Nahh. Jew (Not so far today. Have you eaten yet)?
Chav 1: Nahh (No, I haven't).
Chav 2: Got ya wages (Have you collected your benefit money yet)?
Chav 1: Yeah, sweet (Yes I have and I am very happy).
Chav 2: Bazza aat yet (Has your brother Barry been released from prison yet)?
Chav 1: Yeah, ees aat earning innit (Yes, in fact he is out breaking into somebody's house as we speak).
Chav 2: Sorted – two's up on a maccy dees (I am pleased, would you like to treat me to a spot of breakfast at the local McDonalds restaurant)?
Chav 1: Saand, giza blast (Of course I will, but may I enjoy some of your cannabis cigarette with you first)?
Chav 2: Bangin (Please do: what's mine is yours).
Chav 1: Let's chip off innit (Can we go now)?

Chavs live a very simple life of spending their state benefits and then complaining to each other when it won't stretch far enough to pay for their cannabis supply. They're often to be found in the local benefits office complaining loudly that they can't work but need more money. Common tactics include claiming that the benefit cheque never arrived or calling into the police station blaming their best mate for stealing it while they were over in their flat watching a pirated DVD.

The only way to stop an angry hoard of charging chavs is to throw your mobile phone at them. Chavs are mystified by mobile phones despite the fact that they've been around for years now. They'll often be found huddled around each others' mobiles making approving noises much like when the caveman discovered fire. The Excalibur of mobile phones to the chav is the one that plays the crazy frog noise. No matter how often they hear it they'll always fall about laughing at the hilarity of the tune.

The chav metabolism is very different from most people's. They're unable to digest water and so will never be seen drinking the stuff. They also avoid bathing in it in case some accidentally falls into their mouths. Chavs can only stomach high sugar-content drinks so you'll often see them walking down the road drinking cans of Iron Bru or Tango. Baby chavs are fed on a special diet of sunny D until they can progress to canned pops.

Drinking tea or coffee is acceptable in the chav community but it's only permitted if at least four sugars are put in there first. Any chav found drinking tea with less than four sugars is usually beaten to death by fellow chavs by bashing them over the head with bottles of Tango. Chavs often gather together at the local McDonalds restaurant to discuss issues of importance such as mobile phone ring tones, the latest *Hollyoaks* plot, who's due for release from prison next or what to call their latest babby.

All chavs must either be named after football stars or pop stars such as Kylie, Beyonce, Ronaldo and so on. Otherwise any name that can be shortened to end with the letter Z is fine: Baz, Daz, Kaz, Shaz, Dez, Suz(e), Gez and so on.

The Mecca for all chavs is the all-you-can-eat buffet. On very special occasions they all dress in their best tracksuits and go there en masse to give praise. The women wear their best hooped ear rings and the men wear their brightest belcher chains outside their jumper. It's one of the highlights of the chavs' year and the all-you-can-eat buffet is looked upon as a place of wonder and mystery.

For weeks before attending the buffet the chavs will tell anyone who'll listen about the fact that they're visiting the buffet. They'll announce in wonder that 'Ssallucaneat innit' and prod you with your elbow continually as if they've just discovered the eighth wonder of the world. The fact that they're paying four quid to eat slop that has been sitting under a 40-watt bulb for five hours growing salmonella doesn't even bother them.

They'll descend upon the buffet like piranhas on a carcass that had dropped into the river. The chavs are panic-stricken that the food will be taken away any minute so they sit there filling their faces and jealously watching other people go up and eat 'their' food. Rather than just eat until they're full, the chav will gorge him or herself until they're fit to burst. They'll then go around the buffet filling their pockets with food which they'll never actually eat. They just cannot bear the fact that there's food left on the table which hasn't been eaten yet.

You could laugh I suppose, but the dark side to all of this is that you and I are paying for the lifestyle of tens of thousand of such people. I've been unemployed myself once, but I was desperate to find a job and did within a few weeks. A chav will never ever work a day in their lives yet they'll be rewarded for their behaviour. What gets rewarded gets repeated, just like with children. The more children they have the more money and larger house they receive. It's reward for work as far as they're concerned, and they're *entitled* to it, why else would they be called 'benefits' or 'entitlements'?

I do resent the chav and at the same time who can blame them? They're getting paid to smoke fags, watch TV and breed. I booked over a thousand of these people into custody when I worked at Stechford cell block and arrested over a thousand when I worked as a police officer. A small percentage of the people I arrested did work for a living but the vast majority were on the dole. The instant they were charged with an offence their dole money should've been cut off. Looking after these people is not your or my responsibility. Let them find a job or beg in the streets for scraps. Why should we pay them to steal?

I had to search a flat in Hillfields once which one of the chavs I arrested lived in. As we were going through all the documents in his house looking for forgeries I found a letter he'd written to his girlfriend. It was an attempt at a love letter and was written by a 20-year-old man in handwriting which looked like a 7-year-old's. It went something like this.

'I love you. I love you when I slip my dick into your hot cunt. I love you when I pull my dick out and cum over your nice titties. I love you when you suck my dick and lick my balls. I love you when I tie you to the bed and fuck you hard....'

And there it was. It hit me like a brick over the head. This man – and I'm sure tens of thousands like him – were mistaking sex for love. This of course meant that he didn't actually know what love was. If sex wasn't love then what was? His girlfriend was probably suffering from the same condition as well. Why didn't he know what love was? Because the poor sod was never shown an ounce of love as he was growing up and the very people's behaviour he was modelling to show love were his parents who didn't know what it was either and were quite likely split up before he was 2 years old.

I sat complaining to Bernard one day about my hate for all things chav. I'd never actually heard Bernard say one bad thing about anybody before and I was just moaning away to him on autopilot. He listened to what I was saying and when I'd finished he said, 'When you judge others you don't define them, you define yourself.' He began to stroke his chin and continued, 'How we view others is a projection of how we see ourselves.' I didn't see myself a chav at all. 'What does that mean, Bernard?' I asked. 'If it wasn't in your mind, Paul, you wouldn't notice it. What we find annoying in other people is really part of us.' I still couldn't accept what he was saying, I began to feel that he was a bit off track with this one.

'Such as what, give me an example,' I asked. 'Sure,' he replied. He could see that I was a bit bemused by now. 'Everyone has character traits, agreed?' I nodded away. 'And many of those you don't notice at all. It is only the ones in your conscious awareness that you notice. If you're looking for signs of foul language you will notice it, if you swear yourself a lot or are used to it you will not notice it during a conversation.'

I got that part. 'So what does that have to do with me hating chavs, then?' Bernard had heard most of my life story over the previous couple of years. He said, 'You could easily have been there yourself if you had chosen different friends or your mum didn't care as much as she did as you were growing up.'

I sat there stunned. He was dead right: I'd always spot a chav a mile off and as soon as I did I'd complain to whoever I was with. Surely it must be because I was looking for them all the time because there were thousands of other people I passed every day and I never noticed the others unless they stood out for some particular reason. I could easily be the one wearing choker chains and have love bites all over my neck. Oh dear.

Bernard could see me in deep thought. I was snapped out of it when he said to me, 'You will only notice in others, what you don't like about yourself. At some level you feel you are better than them and you are judging them for the way they live. When you let go of your judging, life will become a lot easier and you will come closer to the peace you are looking for.'

The task felt a bit too hard for me to bear. 'I don't know how easy that is going to be, Bernard,' I admitted with a sigh, 'some part of me really resents them for the way they are.' Bernard gave me a warm smile, 'People are doing the best they can with what they know, Paul,' he shuffled his chair a bit closer to me and began to speak in a softer voice. 'It isn't for you or I to judge how people live their lives: the only person you can change is yourself, and when you get yourself right the rest of the world will be right.'

Bernard walked over to one of his bookshelves and came back with a very thick navy blue plain covered hardback book. The front cover had gold lettering which said *A Course in Miracles*. He flicked through the well-worn pages many of which were dog-eared and marked with pencil. When he found the section he was looking for he lay the book flat on the table and turned it around to face me while he pointed out a line. It said, 'What God created cannot be attacked, for there is nothing in the universe unlike itself.' I turned a few pages and found a passage which talked about making judgements about your fellow brother, 'He is the mirror of yourself, wherein you see the judgement you have laid on both of you.'

I felt very ashamed of myself for the harsh way I'd been judging other people, gippos, chavs, tramps, dole-scroungers and anybody else I didn't like the look of. Now I was beginning to realise that when I did that, it said more about *me* than it did about *them*.

When I left Bernard's house I knew that it was important to begin to work on myself. Not judging others and seeing God in all people would be one of the hardest tasks I'd ever set for myself and it's something I'm still working on to this day.

నా ఇ

Red Watch at Stechford were a great team to work with for the most part. There was a hard-core element of enthusiastic thief-takers, a sort of middle ground of police officers who did their job but not much more, and a small handful of slackers who had to be constantly monitored.

I loved Insp. Ross' monitoring system. He kept a book in which we recorded every arrest made by every officer and tallied them up at the end of the month. Every single month the same five or six PCs had arrested eight to 10 criminals. The less enthusiastic ones had arrested anything from four to six and the others about two at most. It wasn't just a case of arresting people for petty crimes. He looked at what type of offences people were arrested for and if they were charged, bailed or released.

It was the traffic officers on Red Watch who were the worst performers in terms of prisoners. Traffic officers working at Stechford had all been taken from their own department and allocated to the watch but for some strange reason some of them felt like they were only there to deal with traffic. So much so that they never got involved with crime unless the offender happened to be speeding in the car. Other traffic officers on the other units were great thief-takers and very proactive, just not ours.

We did have one traffic officer who was always going sick. He called in sick one morning on earlies and when I spoke to him his voice was so rough it sounded like a complete put on. I was expecting him to say that he had the flu or something hence the false sort throat but he said he'd put his back out. The prat thought he had to speak in a rough voice because he was calling in sick.

The system was very fair. Those who did the work were given the courses or good jobs and lots of slack if they ever needed time off. The slackers were rarely sent on courses, and if there was ever a suicidal prisoner who needed watching in the cells for eight hours it was always them who got called in. Equal ops people would've protested to this but who would you rather have out on the streets, a lazy git or somebody who's keen to arrest the local villains? No brainer, really.

For the first time I could actually see on paper who the producers on the watch were. It was such a simple system and it worked. A basic principle of success and productivity is 'what gets measured improves' and we measured how many bad people we were arresting and charging. By the end of the year, the most productive officers had arrested about 120 criminals each, many of whom had been to court and gone to prison. The less productive officers had arrested at the most 24 for mostly traffic offences or breach of the peace resulting in no bad people being put away.

I don't understand why some people would choose to do the minimum amount of work. You were there for eight hours anyway, and the day goes much quicker if you're busy with prisoners than driving up and down the same streets for hours on end. Dealing with poor performers became the bane of my life as a sergeant. Some officers had to be watched all the time because they'd always try to do the minimum. Everyone knew what was expected, but some just didn't want to do it for some reason.

An example is when a police officer is waiting for a solicitor to arrive for an interview. One solicitor had said he'd be at the station in two hours because he was with another client. The arresting officer went to the canteen and watched TV for two hours while he was waiting. When I caught him I was livid. For those two hours he could've been on patrol, done most of the court file, fingerprinted and photographed his prisoner, or done any number of constructive things.

I gave him a bollocking but he looked at me completely gone out. He had 10 years' service but thought it was OK to sit there doing nothing until the lawyer arrived for his prisoner. I sometimes used to wonder if

I was expecting too much for a police officer to use his time constructively while he had some free time.

᪣ ᪢

Shortly after I'd been promoted I started to see a wonderful lady called Molly. She was 29 and I was 26. I met Molly at a petrol station on the A45 which connects Birmingham and Coventry. I was off duty on my way home and I'd pulled in to get some fuel and spotted her at the side of the forecourt. She was struggling to change her flat tyre so I went over and offered to help out.

Molly stood up as I approached her. She was slightly shorter than me and very slim. She was wearing figure-hugging jeans and a white tee shirt. She had coffee-coloured skin so I presumed that either her mum or dad was Jamaican. Her long jet-black hair was tied up in a long ponytail high on her head.

I looked into her electric blue eyes and completely forgot what I was about to say. I just stood there with a stupid grin on my face. Molly laughed at me exposing her perfect white teeth. For some reason I heard a voice in my head saying, 'She's out of your league, Paul.' I did my best to ignore it and just began to change her tyre as we exchanged small talk.

Molly was a legal secretary for a commercial law firm in Birmingham city centre. She was just finishing off a part-time law degree so we had a lot to chat about. She was a very attractive and intelligent woman and I wanted to see her again. When I finished changing her tyre I casually said that it would be lovely to meet again for a coffee and she grinned back at me saying, 'I would love to.' We exchanged phone numbers and met the next week.

When we met again we were far more relaxed and got on really well. As the weeks progressed we went on a few more dates and each time found out a bit more about each other. We were very attracted to each other, also had a lot to talk about and a lot in common. We'd be laughing and joking all the time and I felt we were a really good match.

It's funny, but when you've strong feelings for somebody or are just beginning to fall in love you look for the good things and magnify them and ignore any things about them you don't like. As the initial euphoria of finding 'the perfect person' you've always been looking for wears off you start to notice the character traits that are not so desirable.

When you meet people they often tell you their story and part of the story can be unhappy childhoods and bad relationships. I learned in having counselling myself years later that these are indicators that the person has some things to get over themselves, and they're often looking for you to save them or to love them because the reality is they don't love themselves very much (ask me how I know).

After a couple of weeks of dating Molly and I began to sleep together. It is always really exciting to get to know somebody else and you're on your best behaviour for the first few weeks at least because you want to make a good impression. Molly was a very naturally sexual woman and had been on her own for about a year. She had no inhibitions at all, which was wonderful. Some women are very coy about sex and won't even touch your dick and won't suck it for all the tea in China, it's like they expect lava to shoot out of it or something. Others are down there like a whippet though, and that's much appreciated.

I don't know what the problem is. Some women make excuses not to give you head such as, 'I'm not very good at it' and I say 'all the more reason to practise, my love.' Some say, 'I have a jaw problem and can't physically do it,' some say 'I don't like to do it.' To me that's just selfish. It isn't that much fun to lick out a woman either, but you do it because it gives your partner a lot of pleasure.

Callum had once given me his definition of a perfect girlfriend. He must've spent a long time thinking about it because he had it down in great detail. She had to be good-looking, have a great sense of humour, up for sex all the time. When it was rags week she'd suck you off every night or at least give you a wank. She'd offer to massage you all the time.

She'd be a good friend and always up for having a laugh, be there for you when you were down but piss off out when you wanted to be on your own. She'd find it hilarious when you did a smelly fart and held her head under the bed covers to smell it (Dutch oven). She'd be fine with you going out with your mates and not grill you the next day about how many women you spoke to while you were out (or checking your mobile phone).

Not too much to ask for, I suppose. Bernard had once commented that people spend more time and planning when choosing a holiday than a life partner. They've given no thought to the sort of person they feel they'd like to be with and what sort of qualities they'd have. It's more a case of 'let's see what turns up' or 'I'll know when I meet them' which he felt was complete rubbish.

It's funny how when you first meet somebody you pull out all the stops. You wear your best underwear and make sure you smell great and your teeth are nice and clean for when you kiss them. You take an age in bed massaging and kissing them and being a considerate lover. A few weeks later you're holding their head down by your arse and farting on them (or is that just me)?

From the beginning Molly wanted to see me every night and it didn't seem strange to start off with because it was all new. She wanted me to come over and stay at her house in Solihull all the time. I agreed to start with because I was getting it every night and she was a brilliant cook as well. After about two weeks I told her on the phone one night that I fancied staying at my house for one evening. That went down like a lead balloon. She became a right bitch on the phone and ended up slamming it down on me. I was shocked. Could this really be the same woman who said the night before how much she loved me?

I was telling Mike, the sergeant I worked with, stuff about the relationship as we went on and he confirmed that a few things seemed a bit strange. After three weeks together Molly made a slip of the tongue. She said that she wanted to marry me which I thought was a bit strange since we'd only really just met. Later that night she was crying down the phone to me saying that she'd ruined the relationship by saying that. I reassured her that it was OK and it hadn't changed anything for me.

Molly used to do some strange things though, such as when I got home from being out somewhere she'd just happen to knock on my door two minutes after I'd got in saying she was just passing. She actually lived 15 miles away so clearly she'd been waiting just down the road from my house.

Molly became very obsessed with my ex-girlfriend whom I hadn't seen for quite some time. She'd say that I was still in love with her, which was ridiculous. She became obsessive about the fact there were women on my watch at work as well. It just seemed that she was doing her best to spoil things. I loved her very much but over the 18 months we went out we must've split up (for good) about six times. She'd bring my clothes around to my house and throw my house key at me. That night we'd be on the phone to each other saying sorry and getting back together. When I look back, it seems so pathetic now. If it was now, I'd drop her the first time she got pissy for not staying at hers.

There's a point to this story though, but I didn't understand it until years later and many hours of counselling for myself. When we first began to date, Molly told me her story. She'd grown up in a real rough area of London and her mum was still married to her dad at the time. One of her first memories was of her mum bundling her and her twin baby sisters into the back of a car and driving up the road watching through the rear windscreen as her dad ran behind them crying for her mum to come back home.

Bernard told me once that all of our childhood memories are linked to emotions and stored in our long-term memory and it usually takes a similar emotion to get them to pop out again. Being in a relationship or being bullied at work can trigger the same emotions that we first experienced as a child. If you suddenly explode or burst out crying or feel a very strong emotion at some event then there's a good chance that there's a link to an emotional memory you experienced as a child that's yet unresolved.

Molly's mum used to leave her on her own with her sisters in the house when she was about 7 years old. Her mum used to skip off to the local city centre with her mate for the entire weekend and get shagged by anybody who was available.

As she got older, her mum became a man-hater. She wouldn't even discuss the fact that men existed. She moved away to America to live and left Molly in London. By this time Molly was 21 years.

Years later, her whole story made perfect sense to me. Molly had a fear of abandonment which is why she latched onto me and didn't want to let go. She didn't have a clue about what a healthy relationship was so told me that if you love somebody you should be together all the time and never apart. Deep down she didn't think she was worth loving so she subconsciously did things to sabotage the relationship so either I'd finish with her or vice versa.

Bernard lent me a book called *Scripts People Live* by Claude Steiner. It was a truly amazing read and helped me to realise how our behaviour is a result of decisions we make as children. We're all born happy and complete and then learn to be sad, depressed or jealous. We spend the rest of our lives acting out the script that has been given to us by our parents and other influencing people.

I called Bernard a few days after receiving the book to thank him. A few minutes later I was ranting away about Molly and the whole mess the relationship had become. He listened quietly and let me finish my rant. He paused on the phone for a while and then said, 'You created all of this, Paul. The question is, for what purpose?' 'How on earth could I have made Molly such a jealous person?' I thought. 'I'm doing my best here, Bernard,' I said defensively, 'but she just seems to want to ruin it all.' I could hear Bernard take in a deep breath: another lesson was about to be imparted. 'You create your own life, and if this is the case can you tell me what lesson this is teaching you? Clearly, you have not learned it if you keep having the same thing happen.'

I sat back further on my sofa at home and thought about the question. I'd chosen to date Molly and had chosen to keep going back to her. Bernard waited patiently in the silence and said, 'I have a client coming shortly, Paul, but grab a pen and ponder over these three things. First, whatever is going on in your life, say to yourself "I made this." Second, ask yourself, "Why did I make this?" Lastly, ask yourself, "What do I want to make instead?" '

I sat and thought. If there was a lesson here, I was going to keep on having it sent to me until I got what I was supposed to be learning. Why else would I keep going back and having the same thing happen to me? I grabbed a pencil and paper and wrote his three questions down.

I made this. I realised that this was actually true. I'd *chosen* to date Molly and even though the early signs were there that she was a very insecure and jealous woman, I kept going back to her.

Why did I make this? I guessed that the lesson was that even if you truly love another person they're who they are and you cannot change them. They have to want to change for *themselves*, so love them as they are or leave them to move on to live their life with somebody who can accept them. Waiting for Molly to change into the type of woman I wanted would be like waiting for my cat to bark. If I'd wanted my pet to bark I should've got a dog.

What do I want to make instead? I wanted some time to myself and then to meet a loving woman who was secure and trusting and who'd let me have my own space when I needed it. I wanted a woman who was self-sufficient, had high self-worth and somebody who was fun and easygoing. I wrote down a long list of qualities that she'd have and the way our relationship would be. When I'd finished I looked at it and realised that Molly was not this person by a long shot.

I knew that it was time to finally finish things with Molly. The usual pattern was for one of us to say it was over and then the other one to phone up and talk their way back in. I had to be strong and not let her back into my heart. She was an attractive woman and had a good soul, but there was just too much damage there from her childhood and marriage.

I broke it off. Molly wrote letters, knocked on my door and continually phoned me for three weeks. She finally stopped calling. I know it was cold, but it was the only way I could do it and not weaken and get back together with her.

⨍ ⨍

You're probably wondering what happened to the piece of paper Bernard had given me the last time I met him (or did you forget about it?). Well, that day I finished my first tour of duty as a sergeant and drove home. As I was changing to get into the shower I put my hand into my pocket and pulled out the piece of paper he'd given me. I slowly unfolded it as if it was a delicate piece of ancient parchment. Written in black ink were the words, 'You will have the peace in your life you are seeking when you make it with yourself.'

Happy Birthday to Me – 5 June 1977

We have another sister now, called Louise. I'm very good at changing nappies now and I can help a lot.

We all drive to my Aunt Pat's house in Dorset. It takes a long time to drive there. We all sleep on the floor because there isn't much space there. There's an outside toilet and I don't like it because it's freezing cold. It's scary sleeping in the bedrooms because there are always daddy longlegs on the ceiling. I have a girlfriend in Dorset, Jenny. We sometimes hold hands.

I come home from my dad's house one Sunday evening. Mum and Aunt Gina are there. They tell me that Louise's dad John has gone away for a while. I lie on the sofa and cry…I can't stop crying. He has abandoned me. I curl into a ball and keep crying. Eventually, my mum carries me to bed.

John comes to see Louise a few weeks later. I sit and watch telly. He wants me to come and sit on his knee but I won't speak to him or go close. He's only going to leave me again.

I'm 7 years old.

Year 8 – Nonce

Nonce – (noun)
Not of normal criminal extraction:

a person who commits indecent crimes on or towards children, a person who is sexually attracted to children.
alt: paedo, kiddy fiddler, Rule 43.

≈ ≈

The police is always in a state of reorganisation. On the odd occasion I speak to a policeman now I hear the same things. The shifts and areas are all changing (again). Police management just can't help themselves. It's like they have some bloody personality defect that forces them to mess people about in the name of making things 'better' which of course is just hogwash.

All good things must come to an end and the new superintendent at Stechford felt it was his turn to reorganise us all, just to make everything work even better than before, you understand. They couldn't seem to go a few months before wanting to make a few tweaks here and there and if not that, a complete upheaval.

It was decided that I was to relocate to Alum Road police station. This was not good news because Alum Road police station appeared to me to be a complete lunatic asylum. I'd visited there a couple of times and was far from impressed at what I saw.

Examples of just how shoddy things were was that there were no briefings for the PCs. They just turned up to work and went out on patrol, if they felt like it. One of the sergeants insisted on having a copy of the shift rota on the wall and one in a folder on his table. The two were never the same so we were always wondering if people were supposed to be coming into work that day or not.

The teams we were supposed to directly supervise at the station worked a different shift pattern to us, so it wasn't that often we even got to see them anyway. It felt like madness to me. How could we be responsible for a team when we only got to see them one week out of four?

Alum Road was more like Billy Smarts Circus than a police station. Al worked there as well and we used to whistle the big top theme as we walked around the station. Whenever I had to parade there I just felt like crying out of sheer frustration. Many of the PCs took a dislike to me because I was actually making them do *work*. An example is one old-timer PC who did a 9 to 5 shift every day but was allowed to go out taking crime reports all day long and serving warrants. He'd been doing it for so long that he hadn't arrested a prisoner for over five years. His public order qualification had lapsed so he couldn't be put out on the riot van if there was a force mobilisation. It wasn't his fault, but Alum Road sergeants' and inspectors' faults. To let a PC become so de-skilled was a disgrace. I was very unpopular when I insisted that he be trained back to public order standards and asked to arrest a prisoner now and then.

When a prisoner was detained at the local Asda store for shoplifting I asked this PC to attend and deal with it. He just looked back at me with a look of panic on his face and said, 'I don't know how to arrest him, Sarge!' It wasn't his fault, I suppose. When the date for his public order course eventually came through he went sick with stress and ended up in an office somewhere.

He wasn't the only one though. There were a handful of very hard-to-manage PCs who'd blow up every time you asked them to do some work. They'd scream at you or burst out crying in the office and then go home. Another one refused to go on patrol with his handcuffs or baton, he insisting that if anyone gave him any trouble he'd punch them out instead! How things had degenerated to this level I'll never know. I could see that my high standards were not going to be very welcome at Alum Road, so I had a battle on my hands.

When I first arrived there I was in charge of my own team of PCs. As a sergeant you're responsible for the team, and responsible also if they get into disciplinary trouble due to your lack of supervision. I did an audit of the PCs' paperwork boxes soon after arriving and I nearly had a heart attack. Some of the reports were months out of date, and one guy's paperwork was two years old. He had crime reports since then involving assaults and thefts and had left them in his paperwork folder. The paperwork had gone yellow and started to curl up at the sides.

His previous lazy bastard sergeant had not kept tabs on him or his paperwork and now because I was his sergeant my neck was on the block. I had to sit him down and get it all sorted out so neither he nor I was disciplined.

Despite what some people thought I never sought to get anybody in trouble. I did whatever I could to help the officers I was responsible for. Sometimes they did things that left me no choice but to put a report in. Putting a police officer on report is known as being 'put on the sheet'. It basically means that a report is submitted to the superintendent for him to decide if they should be subject to a discipline charge. There are some things you can cover up – and some you can't.

It's funny really, because I used to live in constant fear of being sheeted when I was a PC. I didn't really know what it meant, though. All it was, was a general report that went to the superintendent. You'd really have to do something bad for a report to go in on you. Looking back at my time at Little Park Street I'd worry that everything I did would be scrutinised, or if I made a mistake and was found out that I'd be in trouble. It was an irrational fear.

One incident I couldn't cover up occurred at Alum Road police station. The sergeants' office was next door to the parade room and the wall was just a thin partition so you could hear what was going on in there quite clearly. I'd given a briefing to about six constables who were on duty for the afternoon shift. I went back into the sergeants' office and heard one of the WPCs scream out, 'How dare you smack my arse?' It didn't take detective skills to work out what'd happened. I sighed heavily and thought, 'Another day at the pleasure dome.' I had to go next door to identify the culprit.

The WPC who'd had her arse smacked was called Gail. As I walked into the room I could see that she looked very annoyed and had a red face. There were four other PCs in the room. I asked her what'd happened. Clearly, she didn't want to make a fuss about it. 'Oh nothing, Sarge,' Gail said, still with a bright red look on her face, 'we were just joking around.'

As far as I'm concerned there's joking and there is joking. Maybe a few years ago you could get away with that sort of behaviour but not anymore. The trouble is, if I'd left it and did nothing and it got out then I'd have been subject to a discipline charge of failing to supervise.

It sounds all a bit much to some but smacking a woman on the arse is an assault, i.e. the physical application of force to another person. I had to have a word with Gail in my office. I insisted she tell me what had just happened. She reluctantly told me that one of the old-sweat PCs called Derek had smacked her on her arse, but it was just a bit of joking around and he didn't mean anything by it. I told her that perhaps he didn't, but maybe he'd do it tomorrow and the next day or next time it'd be somebody else's backside who *did* mind. I told her to complete a duty report about what happened and put a note in her pocket book about it. She said she didn't want to, but I insisted.

I asked the other three PCs who'd been there to do the same. I then called Derek in the office. I'd had dealings with Derek before when he was on attachment to the CID. I found him to be an obstinate pig who didn't take kindly to being told what to do. I put my personal opinion aside and told him that it was not acceptable behaviour to slap female officers on their arse. He protested that they were just messing about and that he wasn't impressed, saying, 'You're making a mountain out of a molehill, Sarge.'

I did sympathise with him that it was probably messing about, but judging by the scream she let out she did not invite it. I asked him to complete a duty report and said that I'd have to put a report in to the inspector.

It was a bit of a mess and I could've just swept it under the carpet but the days of doing that had long since passed. Derek's behaviour had forced me into a position where I had to act as a sergeant. If I didn't I was taking a risk that if he did it again to somebody else and it came out that I'd been there then it was *me* who'd be busted down to PC and I didn't particularly fancy that.

I submitted the report and Derek just had to have a word with the superintendent but nothing went on his report. As much as I didn't like the bloke personally I didn't want to see anybody get into discipline trouble or have any permanent black marks on their personal records. You'd have had to have done something very serious for me to put you on the sheet and recommend disciplinary action.

You had to be very careful as a sergeant or any supervisory rank because even when you were off duty you had to act if you saw inappropriate behaviour. There was an inspector at the police bar having a drink one evening. He was off duty and there were a few other off-duty officers having a laugh and a drink. There was a young female officer in the crowd and one of her male colleagues reached to the back of her cat suit and pulled the zip down exposing the back of her bra.

Everybody (including her) laughed. Nothing was said but the next day she reported it to her watch inspector who was female. The report went to police HQ eventually and the off-duty inspector was pulled in front of the chief constable for failure to supervise. He was told that he'd witnessed an indecent assault and that he should've taken action against the offending PC. The next day he was busted down to PC and he was pushing a Panda car around some shit-hole.

The same thing could easily have happened to me. One evening I made a rare visit to the police bar at Stechford with three of my team. One guy was very much larger than life, you heard him before you saw him because he had a booming voice. Everyone called him Lech Walesa because he was always very loud. If you don't remember, Lech Walesa was Poland's first independent trade union leader and was a major pain in the arse to Poland's government for years until he was eventually elected president in 1990.

There was me, 'Walesa', Gaz and a policewoman called Judith all standing at the bar having a drink and a chat. Judith was a great police officer and I had a lot of time for her. She was about 40 but still in good nick, meaning you probably would have, given half the chance. She had the good sense to be going out with somebody who wasn't in the police.

We were all standing there having a laugh and Judith said something funny about Walesa which made us all giggle. He got her back by grabbing her nipple from outside her blouse and tweaking it. Judith gasped and whacked him on the face with her hand. 'What a slapper!' exclaimed Walesa, rubbing his hand on his freshly-slapped cheek.

My heart sank. What a stupid man, that was definitely grounds to be arrested and at least sacked. I looked at Judith to see how she'd taken it and she was laughing. Despite her finding it funny I really should've sheeted Walesa for what he did that day. Not just because he deserved it, but as a supervisor I'm under a duty to take action when I see things like this. If it got out then I could easily have been busted down to PC or sacked myself for failing to supervise. It was then that I remembered why I didn't socialise with the PCs.

Things are very politically correct (PC) in the police. Now you can even be offended on behalf of another person would you believe? I saw several people disciplined for making comments or jokes and the person they were made about was laughing. A police officer or civilian standing nearby would take umbrage to the joke and complain resulting in the joker being disciplined.

I'm not saying any of the above incidents were right or wrong. I'm merely pointing out that it's very easy to get into trouble as a police supervisor if you don't watch what you say or do. Even when you're off duty.

Technically, you're never off duty as a police officer even when you are. If you come across a crime in progress you're supposed to take action, even if it's only calling the police. They don't really expect you to tell people off for littering or not wearing their seat belts, but if something serious is going on you must do something affirmative. If you have your children with you, you can't really be rolling about on the floor with a person you've just arrested, but if the circumstances dictate and it is safe then you should effect an arrest and call the police.

I personally made three off-duty arrests while in the police and at the time, the circumstances were such that I felt I just had to take action.

The first was when I was walking from my house in Somerset Road to my friend's who lived in Newland Road in Hillfields. We were going to chill out and watch a video and eat pizza. I got about halfway there, it was broad daylight on a Saturday afternoon and I was just about to cross Foleshill Road which is one of the busiest roads in Coventry.

Police officers view the world with different eyes than most people. We have some sort of radar that picks up things that are out of the ordinary. They may seem normal to the casual observer, but it can be tiny things that just don't feel right. It could be a person's clothing, the way they're looking around, the car they're driving, or even the fact they're 'acting normally' which of course is an oxymoron (yes, I swallowed a dictionary).

I heard once that it's the part of the brain called the reticular formation which alerts us to possible danger before we're consciously aware of it. The RF can be trained by experience and this is what sends us some sort of alert when we see something we can relate to a past experience involving danger, or in the case of a police officer, activity which could be crime-related.

I looked across the road and near to the junction of George Elliot Road and I could see an Indian lad aged about 15 standing near the corner. He looked perfectly ordinary with his trainers, tee shirt and jeans, but it was the way he was looking up and down the road that caught my attention. Why would he be doing that?

It's hard to put into words but it wasn't the sort of look you'd have if you were looking to see if a friend you were meeting was coming. It was more of an 'I'm acting as a lookout' type of look if that makes sense which I'm sure it will if you're a police officer reading this. I heard some loud bangs behind him and there was another teenager about 10 yards behind him. He was mixed race and also wearing jeans and trainers. He had a brick in his hand and was bashing it against the driver's window of a nice new Porsche. I couldn't believe his cheek. Broad daylight on a busy street and this thieving little bastard was breaking into some guy's car.

I felt a surge of adrenalin rush from the pit of my stomach through to my arms and legs. I was on my own and didn't have a mobile phone or any way to get help. I didn't know if I'd be able to get close to the thief because of the lookout but I was wearing my scruffs so there was a decent enough chance. The two lads were not that big so I knew I'd be able to tackle one and the other would probably just run off. If he had a go at me I'd just spark him out and choke his mate out.

I carried on casually walking in their direction and got about 10 yards away from the thief who'd just managed to smash the window. He saw me coming and bolted off down the main road. His mate who was acting as a lookout just started to walk off casually. The guy with the brick was shorter than me but could run like the wind. He sprinted down Foleshill Road and then into George Elliot Road. I chased him down an alleyway and then up my mate's street which is Newland Road.

About halfway down he cut through an entryway which had a tall wooden gate at the front of it. I got to the gate but he was standing the other side pushing against it. I was breathing heavily from my sprint but I was pretty fit as well so knew I had plenty of puff left in me. He wasn't that big so I just pushed it and it began to give. As it opened about one foot wide his arm came round and swung towards me. I saw the flash of a knife and managed to dodge back in time for it to miss my chest. The little fucker was trying to stab me. Now I wanted to stamp on his head for that little stunt.

The entryway gate swung open and he started to walk backwards looking at me and waving the knife. I wanted to batter him so badly I could almost taste it. An Indian lady who lived in the house next to the entry came to the front door and started shouting at me in Urdu. I showed her my warrant card and shouted to her to call the police. She didn't speak a word of English though and just kept shouting at me in Urdu. We didn't understand each other.

The youth ran to the end of the entry and jumped over a very tall wooden fence. I could've continued to chase him but what was the point? He'd only try to stab me again. I went to my mate's house and a bit later a police car arrived. It was Red driving and he said to me, 'I'll have a look 'round the area for him,' which was code for 'I'm off to get a kebab and shove it down my useless fat face.'

I saw the youth a few days later when I was on duty. He was with a gang of lads and I considered arresting him but it would've been my word against his and identification evidence is an absolute nightmare so I let him walk. His time would come again.

In the cold light of day I considered my actions and realised that even though I was a police officer I'd put myself in a very dangerous situation. I was on my own and out of sight chasing a person for an offence which at the very worst would've earned him a supervision order but probably a caution or fine. No way in a million years will anybody go to prison for breaking into a car, so don't kid yourself.

If he'd stabbed me I could've died and nobody would've called the police or an ambulance. If I'd died, there was a very slim chance that he'd have been caught, and even if he had I don't think the manslaughter charge would've resulted in much of a prison sentence. Maybe eight years and out in three. Not worth my life anyway.

After that incident I heard about a few like it on the news where car owners have found some thieving shit breaking into their car and chased them down the road. The thief has turned 'round and stabbed them in the chest and they died.

If I may offer a piece of advice. Decide *now* what you're going to do if you come across somebody screwing your car. The insurance will pay for it and things can be replaced. Get a good look at them if you want and just call the police who'll probably know who he is anyway. If you run down the road and corner them, then what? You're on your own against the thief and his mates who're going to be carrying knives; I guarantee 100 per cent that they're going to be 'tooled up'. They decided a long time before they screwed your car that if you chase them they're going to 'stick' you.

When you're dead, who's going to love your partner and children? Is it really worth the risk? I don't think so. A burglar in your house is a different story altogether, because they have brought the fight to you. Wrap a baseball bat around their head and ignore any pleas for mercy because if you don't whack them they're going to stab you for sure. If they run away, don't chase them.

My second off-duty arrest was at exactly the same spot, believe it or not. I was minding my own business, listening to my walkman and walking to my mum's house to go and say hello. I was walking next to a car accessory shop by George Elliot Road and I saw a man approaching me. Even though I was miles away listening to music I was still aware of what was going on around me.

He was aged about 25 and 5' 8" tall. He had greasy long mousy brown hair and looked unwashed but not filthy. He was wearing scruffy clothes, a black tee shirt which looked like he'd been wearing it for weeks or wrestling in it because it was full of holes. His shoes were very worn out, I could see that he walked with a pronounced gait due to the wear on the soles (just call me Sherlock). If I had to guess I'd have said he was on the dole, probably a petty thief and definitely a drug user. Probably cannabis since he looked too poor to be able to afford cocaine.

He motioned for me to take my earphones out so I stopped walking and took them out of my ears. He produced a mobile phone from his pocket and said, 'Do you want to buy a mobile phone, mate?' I wondered if I looked like the sort of person who buys stolen phones off trampy looking skanky thieves in the street. I did usually dress like a scruff on my days off and never shaved so maybe I did to him.

'Where did you get it from?' I asked him politely. 'I found it lying on the road,' he replied. Wrong answer. Even if you find something lying in the street it does not belong to you. Obviously, if there's no chance of the owner being found then you can keep things such as 20-pound notes or pens but things that can easily be handed back like mobile phones should be given to the owner or the police.

I took out my warrant card and gave him the bad news. 'I'm a police officer,' I said, 'you are under arrest for theft.' Of course, I repeated the full police caution to him as mandated by the Home Office and took hold of his arm. He just stood there with the sort of look on his face you have when you're a kid and open your Christmas present to find clothes inside. His shoulders dropped and he just said, 'Shit.' I can imagine what he was thinking. Out of all the people he could've met walking down the road he had to meet an off-duty police officer.

We went into the car accessory shop and I showed my badge to the owner and asked to use the phone. I called 999 because I didn't know the number for the front office at Little Park Street. They never picked up the phone anyway so it was the fastest way. I very clearly explained that I'd made an off-duty arrest, that the prisoner was very calm and could I please have transport to the police station.

A full 20 minutes went past and then I heard the roar of several sirens and four cars screeched outside the shop. 'For goodness' sake,' I thought, they'd only just been told that I was there and they were told that I was fighting with a prisoner and needed help. How on earth my simple message got translated to that I'll never know.

I went to the cell block with him which was a right pain for me because I wanted to enjoy my day off. I booked him in and as I did so he gave me the code words that told me he was a police informant. 'Can I speak to DC Bates if he's here please?' I nodded and said I'd let him know he was in the cells.

I did my arrest statement and went to find DC Bates in the CID office. We had a quick chat and it turned out that my prisoner was giving some good info about local handlers (of stolen property) and drug dealers. The DC asked if I minded him being let off without a charge. I didn't mind so long as the phone got back to the owner. What did I care?

My third and last off-duty arrest was when I was in my favourite curry house in Holbrooks. I'd been a regular at Balti Delights since it'd first opened in 1993. I got on really well with Hussain, the owner, the food tasted great and Hussain never let people in who wanted another drink after the pub closed so it was all good. Over the years I'd introduced most of my friends to the place so he probably had over 100 customers personally introduced by me. I'd been there for birthdays, valentines and many special occasions.

I was there one evening at about 8 with my mate Eamonn who'd recently joined the police. My sister Louise was there, my brother John who was about 10 at the time, and Eamonn's girlfriend Lesley. Also my mate Ansa and his girlfriend Ruth.

We ordered our food and were chatting away when three Indian lads came in. I sensed trouble right away because they were all drunk and swearing. I immediately regretted sitting with my back to the door. It may sound a bit paranoid, but I always liked to have a good vantage point whenever I went out in case of trouble like this. The army call it shark watch. If you go out with your mates, one always stays sober and keeps an eye out for danger.

Hussain was in the kitchen and one of the young waiters showed them to a table. Hussain would never have let them in because they were rowdy but the waiter wasn't so experienced. As soon as he came out Hussain could see that they were trouble. He went over to the table and politely asked them to leave. I'd already anticipated trouble so I'd pulled my chair out slightly and shot Eamonn a knowing look that trouble was about to happen.

As Hussain asked them politely to leave they became irate. The fight sparked off immediately. One of the three stood up and punched Hussain in the face causing him to fall backwards. Eamonn and I were up on our feet immediately. The three of them were now rushing for the door to escape. I stood in the doorway with my arm stretched out in front of me. I didn't want them to get within punching distance.

They were partly angry due to being asked to leave but mostly full of fear at what they'd just done. They wanted to leave and run away but I was standing in their way. I took my warrant card out and had to put on my fearless policeman act. 'Police, you are all under arrest for affray,' I shouted at them. They stopped in their tracks and the bravest of the three came towards me with a hard man screwed-up look on his face. I'd seen that face all too often and there was rarely much going on behind it.

Men generally drop into learned behaviours under certain conditions and the hard man act is just one of them. It involves screwing your face up, puffing your chest out and pointing in a threatening manner. There's often pacing up and down involved and pointing their dick towards you as well. The objective is to psyche out your opponent. You'll often see animals doing it on nature programmes when it's mating time. I wasn't impressed so just stood my ground.

I kept my poker face and as he got close to me I pushed him away with my outstretched arm. If he'd pushed against it a second time I'd have chinned him. My friends and family just sat there in shock. They'd never seen me have to do this and I was angry that I'd been put in this situation by these drunken idiots. Now they'd assaulted my mate Hussain they were going to have to answer for it.

They backed off and started to plead with Hussain to let them away. Husain's eye was swollen and had a cut on the bottom. Eamonn had already called the police who were on their way. They continued to ask Hussain to let them off but as far as I was concerned they were too late, they'd interrupted my curry and they had to pay. 'You're wasting your breath,' I said sternly, 'you're all under arrest and are going to the police station.'

Two police cars came and I recognised the first two police officers who came in. I explained that the three were under arrest for affray. The police constable wasn't impressed. He thought he was going to have to arrest them and clearly didn't want to do any work. He started to ask me what my grounds for my arrest were which infuriated me. I felt like slapping him on his lazy face.

I politely explained that I was the arresting officer and I only needed transport for my prisoners. I could see the look of relief on his face when I told him that. The three prisoners were handcuffed and we all went to Stony Stratford police station.

I knew exactly what I was doing because I'd arrested and dealt with hundreds of prisoners by this time. I had to give Eamonn a hand because he'd recently joined the police and had never arrested anybody off duty.

The three men were charged with affray and eventually fined at court a few months later. A few weeks after that I was driving up Foleshill Road in Coventry at about 10 a.m. and saw the main protagonist. He was walking up the road drinking a can of super-strength lager. It was a sad sight.

❧ ❧

Brian lived in Stechford near to an area called Alum Rock which was also affectionately known as 'The Rock'. The claim to fame for Alum Rock was that you could get the cheapest heroin and crack for miles around. Brian was a short fat hairy grubby dirty man, in fact he looked more like a troll than a man. He was always unshaven and had dirty greasy dandruff-coated hair which he never seemed to brush. Whatever he'd eaten that week was usually smeared around his mouth; you could see bits of food and liquid stuck to the stubble round his face. He'd always wear dirty stained grey trousers and a brown pullover that had holes in and food stains down the front. He really looked the part.

Brian wore the thickest pair of spectacles I'd ever seen and the bottom half of the glass had an even stronger lens in them. He always had his face screwed up as if he was looking at very strong sunlight. Doing this exposed his brown tombstone-like teeth that looked like they hadn't been brushed for many years. You'd have needed a jet washer to get the crap off his teeth.

Clearly, Brian didn't like himself very much at all. He was once arrested for some minor offence and taken to Stechford cell block. He shouted the custody sergeant over and through the hatch popped out the glass from one of his spectacles and swallowed it. He had to go to hospital to have his guts cut open and have the glass removed. I personally would've sat there and watched him try to shit it out.

Why? Because Brian was a convicted paedophile or what's commonly referred to as a nonce. Brian (not his real name, of course) was a local resident of Stechford. He was always calling the police to inform on local petty villains and report suspicious goings-on in the neighbourhood. For this reason he was hated by the local population who knew he was a 'grass'. They'd have hated him more than they hated the police if they knew he was a convicted child molester.

I checked Brian's criminal record. He'd molested several children over the years and many years ago he'd raped a little boy for which he got 10 years (served five). He preferred little boys but girls would do equally well.

I had to speak to him a couple of times because he lived on the beat I covered in Stechford. Speaking to Brian made my stomach churn. While he'd sit there telling me who was spray painting graffiti in the locality I'd be nodding away to him but daydreaming that I was stamping on his head until he was dead and then feeding his body to the pigs.

There's something so inherently terrible about abusing innocent children that the very thought of it attracts universal disgust. Nonce need to have separate wings in prison because the inmates will tear them to pieces if they get to them. Being segregated from normal prisoners is known as being on Rule 43.

We'd processed a few nonce whilst I was custody sergeant. I had to be professional and impartial when I dealt with them and take extra care that they were fed properly and given their rights and entitlements. If I'd made any mistakes it could've made any admissions when they were interviewed inadmissible.

I don't know how their lawyers could sit in the interview rooms with them for hours working out ways to help them and going through case papers looking for mistakes or holes in them.

I dealt with several paedophiles whilst I was in the police, most of them during my attachment with the child protection unit. Also known as kiddie fiddlers, they carried out their sexual fantasies on children. When they weren't doing it they were trawling the Internet for child porn, swapping photos with other paedophiles or patrolling the streets looking for children. You'll find these people in every town. They walk or drive around looking for victims.

They've spent months or years planning how they'll trap their victims or lure them away from their guardians. They've also spent months planning and fantasising about what they'll do to them once they have them. Much like crack addicts, these people have a burning desire within them that has to be satiated. I personally don't believe that these people can be cured. Whether they were abused themselves is irrelevant. They present a clear and very real danger to society. Current laws prevent us from digging a big hole, throwing them in and filling it in again, but they should at least be castrated and then segregated from society.

It was stomach-churning finding out just how many active paedophiles there were in Coventry alone. Their tactics include befriending young single mums and offering to take the kids swimming or babysit for them while she goes out. One guy we knew had to sign on at the police station every day because he was on bail for molesting children pending a court appearance. He used to befriend some stupid young girl who'd had a young child and been abandoned by the dad. She was grateful for the attention because she thought that nobody else would want her now she was 'ruined'.

After a few weeks he'd kindly offer to babysit while she went out with her mates. When she was gone he'd take the child who was about 5 years old downstairs and blindfold her and play a game where she licked a banana. We couldn't prosecute on the testimony of the child because they hadn't seen anything, and we couldn't prove that it was his penis they were licking. The process of paedophiles worming their way into a family and gaining the trust of a child identified for the attack is known as grooming. It happens on the Internet a lot as well.

Every time this guy turned up to sign on at the police station he'd bring his new girlfriend with him and she'd always have her little girl with her. It was all I could do not to jump over the counter and stove his head in with a baseball bat.

While I was a custody sergeant at Stechford a school headmaster was brought in. For years he'd been getting his 6-year-old pupils to come up to his desk and stand there as he put his hands down their pants. After about five years of doing this one of the girls happened to be telling her dollies about this when her mum was in the next room.

When that man was brought into the cells he was devastated, crying his eyes out because of the humiliation and the fact that he'd be going to prison and would never be a teacher again. I ensured I had a PC outside his cell to keep a constant eye on him because I didn't want him killing himself while I was in charge down there. Not that I gave a shit about him, but topping yourself is the coward's way out and I wanted to see him rot in jail and live every day having to look over his shoulder.

The fact that a headmaster was doing this continually just goes to show that paedophiles cannot stop what they're doing. He knew one day he'd be caught resulting in him losing his job, his family, his house and serving time in prison. Even the threat of that wasn't enough to stop him abusing children.

Most of the time, the nonce had been so clever that we could never prove the crime. They'd dress up as Disney characters while they carried out their abuse or drug their victims. Although these people are desperate to abuse children, they're also very methodical. They form communities on the Internet or by other means and swap videos, photos or tactics and stories.

The HQ child protection unit had given us a talk in the lecture theatre while I was on my detectives' course for the CID. They said that child porn videos were sold for almost a thousand pounds each and are usually spliced into the middle of a high street movie where somewhere in the middle is a 10-minute slot of a child being abused and raped. When the movies were seized somebody had to watch hundreds of hours in the hope of finding one that had a clip in it.

The HQ child protection unit for some mad reason put together a video of the worst things they'd seized and played it for us. Heaven knows why they didn't just tell us. In the video there were children being raped, babies being abused, women being strangled, having their vaginas sewn up with no anaesthetic, and people shitting into each others' mouths. When I saw it I gagged and almost puked on the row of people in front of me.

I can't believe some of the things people watch to get their rocks off. I also thought that it can't help affect you as a police officer when you watch that kind of stuff day in day out. I wasn't shocked by much at all anymore, but watching that depravity and pretending that it's all in a day's work can't be good.

I later got chatting to a good friend of mine called Bri who joined the job a couple of years after me. He'd dated a WPC on the child protection team for a while. She'd joined on the same intake as a friend of mine. She was absolutely stunning with a fantastic figure and had a lovely personality. I was really attracted to her.

Bri told me that he went out with her for a few months but had to finish it. Bri was up for anything when it came to sex (so he said) but the only way that she could come was for him to tie her to the bed face down, put a golf ball in her mouth and tape it closed. He then had to shove a banana up her arse hole and mash it up there with his dick.

The odd bit of kinky sex is fine, but if this is the only way you can achieve an orgasm it's time to seek professional help. I kept that bit of info to myself because I didn't gossip and I did feel very bad for her that her mind was that twisted.

One classic technique is for nonce to attend naturist reserves alone. They go there in droves because families go there and spend the week doing the usual activities such as eating, swimming, football and so on, but all with no clothes on. How a holiday could be better because you have your tits hanging out or your dick flopping around is beyond me, but horses for courses as they say.

The highlight is the talent shows where all the children get up on a stage naked and do various things such as sing and dance. There's an army of photographers there (with their clothes on which should be a giveaway) snapping away. You can even buy naturist magazines which are cover to cover with photos of naked children from these naturist reserves. Hello! Am I the only person who thinks this is crazy? Why on earth would you want to look at that stuff in a magazine?

I'm not saying there's anything wrong with naturists or naturist holidays by the way. I'm just baffled why they'd parade young children naked on stages and let grown men photograph them. Who would want to look at those photos for recreation purposes?

I can't describe how difficult it is to deal with the victim and then arrest the offender and pretend you believe them. You really need to establish rapport so that they open up in the interview. Somehow you've to make them feel that what they did wasn't so bad so their embarrassment doesn't make them sit there in silence and hide behind their solicitor. I hated being near a nonce so to bring them tea and biscuits absolutely killed me.

Time after time after time we took a complaint from an abused child, arrested the offender knowing they were as guilty as sin. We'd interview them, submit the papers and were told that there was insufficient evidence to charge. It was enough to make you cry. The word of a small child against an adult, and often without any medical evidence to back it up.

The temptation was so strong to call some of the local villains or the local paper and get their name out. I never did it and don't know anyone who did, but when paedophiles were discovered they were usually beaten up, had their windows smashed and houses burned down.

We used to giggle during briefings when we were given an address of a local nonce and told that they were receiving death threats so we should make an effort to get there quickly if there were any incidents there. I laughed to myself and thought, 'Of course I'll rush there. Just as soon as I've finished my dinner and done a bit of paperwork and had a good shit. You can count on me.'

I don't condone firebombing their houses or murdering them but I do understand it of course. The problem is that half the time the attackers have got the wrong bloody person or attacked the wrong house. At least they could get their intelligence right before doing it.

The only solution I can think of is making them all live on an island somewhere where they can sew mailbags and make car registration plates and perform other tasks of service to the community. Just miles away from where they can do any harm. Convicted paedophiles are supposed to report their current address to the police station for life, but this scheme is almost impossible to administer.

The icing on the cake was when we had to go and visit nonce who were let out on licence from prison. They were put in approved flats or houses in the community and given the odd visit from the police or probation service. Can you guess where they were put to live? C'mon, you can do it. Where would you put a nonce to live when they're out on licence for molesting kids? Yes, that's right. Next to an infant or junior school. They'd have a great view of the playground.

It's just like putting a recovering alcoholic next door to the pub so he can smell the beer drifting out of the windows. For the love of everything holy! What next? Giving them jobs as lollypop men? Bloody brain-dead administrators and bureaucrats drive me mad, why did nobody bother to check the address physically before allocating it? You could even see on a street map that there was a school within 100 yards.

❧ ❧

There were a few moments of excitement while posted at Alum Road. The most serious incidents we'd ever attend weren't the fights or armed robberies. These were almost always over by the time we got to the scene. It was always the domestics that would turn into violent bloody battles, armed sieges or murders.

At about 3 p.m. one Saturday two officers from Alum Road had been called to a domestic dispute between a young couple in St Andrews Road, Bordesley which is just next to Birmingham City Football Club. The call came from a neighbour who'd heard shouting in the flat next door and then furniture being thrown around. After a couple of minutes at the flat the officers called for help because the male party was extremely aggressive and making threats to them.

I went to the scene with Mac, one of the other sergeants from Alum Road. Mac was a stocky man 5' 9" tall. His black hair was shaved very close so he looked like a skinhead. Mac always wore a bit of a scowl on his face which gave him the appearance of a real tough guy. One good thing about Mac was you could count on him in a scrape. I don't think he could actually box or fight much but when required he could throw a decent punch which was good enough for me. He had a bottle and if you were in a fight he'd be standing right next to you dishing out some slaps.

When we got to the scene of the domestic we were told by the officers there that they'd been called to the house because the man inside had punched his girlfriend in the face. Apparently, he'd been drinking all day long and taking coke which was par for the course, as they say.

Looking at the front of the flat I could see a problem straightaway. It wasn't a flat but a maisonette and the only way in and out was up a set of steep stairs. Effecting an arrest and getting a violent man down the stairs would be very difficult. We either had to go up and somehow get him downstairs without us getting injured, or coax him outside and then jump on him.

Although Mac and I never really discussed a game plan, the required action was obvious to us both, to get him outside and jump him. Second best was to go inside, which could be very dangerous to all concerned. As the sergeants we were in charge and never expected anyone to do something that we were not prepared to do ourselves. We also knew that it was very likely that we were going to sustain at least some minor injuries while we were struggling with the man.

There were about six police officers there excluding us. I took a look at them and worked out if they could be counted on if the man became violent. Every person is different, and some will just not be able to back you up if you're rolling around on the floor with some coked-up pisshead who's stronger than an ox.

A few of the man's neighbours had come out to watch the proceedings, and one had their video camera with them. Their right, I suppose, but tapes can be edited so that the public don't get to see the bit where he punches you in the face, just the bit where you kick him in the knackers (for no good reason, of course).

It was the same when the Rodney King beating was captured on video. King was on parole from jail for robbery, allegedly high on PCP. He was chased by the police in his car for some distance, for which, if you live in the USA, failing to stop for the police and comply is just about the silliest thing you could ever do. He resisted a lawful arrest and even the taser failed to work on him he was so high.

A few years later King was arrested for beating up his misses, failing to stop for police again, being high on PCP and indecent exposure. I'm not condoning the savage beating he received because that was barbaric. My point is that the public don't usually get to see the lead up to the event where the police officer has to use violence against the prisoner, so the entire incident is taken out of context.

Whenever I was arresting a violent person I'd always have to use force. And if they started to struggle I'd do what I had to do to protect myself including punching, kicking or spraying them with gas. I know this sounds horrible, and there was in fact a significant risk that they'd injure themselves or even die, but given the choice between them or me it didn't really take much thinking. There were so many police officers injured due to hesitation or due to not wanting to be seen to use any violence when arresting the prisoner. I also remember what had happened to Dale and the fact that the police force didn't want anything to do with him after he was injured on duty.

Many of my colleagues would often be worried that they'd be criticised for using excessive force. It wasn't until I'd been in the job for a few years that somebody explained to me that if you tell the custody sergeant that you were in fear for your personal safety so had to use force on the prisoner it looks far better than beating the shit out of them and then denying you did it.

At the domestic incident, Mac and I were in charge since we were the senior rank there. We could've stayed outside for a few hours and waited it out or gone charging in and hoped he wasn't armed. We would've waited, but the man's girlfriend was inside with him and we didn't know if she was badly injured.

As we stood outside the man came down the stairs to the doorway. He looked about 24 and at 6' 2" was a fairly big chap. He was only wearing a pair of jeans, had no top on so his upper body was exposed, and you could see an array of tattoos up his arms which were the usual skulls, 'Mum and Dad' and 'Liverpool FC' in case he forgot which team he supported. He was well-built but had the early signs of a paunch due to a regular diet of beer, chips and kebabs. His face was pale white and he had black rings around his eyes. He had the classic signs of a man who'd been taking drugs for some time.

He came to the door and clearly was not impressed at seeing several police officers standing there waiting to jump on him. The thing is though, when a person is high on drink or drugs there's nothing rational about their behaviour. They could curl up in a ball crying, or pull out a knife and stab you in the neck and you've no way of knowing which one it's going to be. Maybe they could do both.

He stood at the doorway and looked at us, hesitating for a few seconds. He was standing just inside the doorway and I didn't think we could get close enough to grab him without him shutting the door on us first. He shouted through clenched teeth, 'Fuck off, you slags.' He then wandered back up the stairs.

While I'm not remotely bothered about having a stand-up fight with a prisoner I don't go charging in either. What's the point? But I got the impression that this guy could not be negotiated with. Mac and I decided to have a quick peek up the stairs to see if we could see the lady inside.

In any violent situation, the first preference is always to try to talk with the person and calm them down. You at least want to have a go at that option before kicking the living shit out of them (joke). When the person has had a cocktail of drink and drugs this is impossible. The higher regions of their brain (if they ever had any) cease to function and the only instinct left is fight or flight. If they're cornered in their house, then fight it is. There are no considerations of the consequences of assaulting a police officer, no thought to possible prison sentence. Their only thought is inflicting as much physical damage as possible to anyone who gets in the way.

It was inevitable that some of us would be injured during the struggle but that came with the job. Our only weapons were metal extendable batons and pepper spray. We couldn't use the batons due to restricted space, and the pepper spray could incapacitate him but he'd probably quickly slam the door on us. There'd been so many burglaries in the area that the council made the doors so strong there was no way to kick them in.

After what seemed like an age, Mac and I walked tentatively inside. We couldn't stand there all day and we didn't know if his girlfriend was injured inside and in need of medical attention. I never asked anybody to do what I wasn't prepared to do, so Mac and I started to walk slowly up the stairway. I was in front and Mac literally one step behind me. As we almost got to the top the man emerged at the top of the stairwell holding an axe in his hand. My eyes nearly popped out of my head but I didn't get the chance to react. Mac grabbed my belt and practically dragged me down the stairs and out of the door. What a star.

There was no going back now, this man was going to be arrested and injured, no doubt, because he wasn't going to come quietly. At times like this I wished for some sort of stun gun like the police in America have. They always seemed to have such cool kit.

The man came to the door carrying the axe, swinging it in the air. I can't say I was particularly frightened, but I was obviously seriously concerned that he was going to kill one of us if he got close enough with the axe. I sprayed him with my CS spray. It was a gamble but this had been going on far too long. All of the neighbours were now watching and I didn't want this to turn into a debacle for 10 o'clock news where they'd be airing shocking films of some police brutality. Ten police officers jumping on one man should make the news for sure.

The gas had the required effect and as the man instinctively brought his hands up to his face I lurched forward and tackled him to the ground. The worst thing you can do in this situation is to try to handcuff the prisoner when he's standing up. He can punch, kick or head-butt you, at least on the ground you can avoid his head and feet. Less experienced officers would try to grab the prisoner's feet but often get kicked in the face. If you're up by the head you can give a few punches in the face which usually takes the fight out of most people. Whichever hand he throws at you, you can put the handcuff on and then put it behind his back to apply the second handcuff.

Due to the cocktail of drink and drugs he was as strong as an ox and it took five of us to restrain him. He was lashing out trying to punch us and swearing like a trooper. His girlfriend whom he'd recently punched was now standing there with a black eye screaming at us to leave him alone (again, a typical scenario).

The problem with using CS spray is that everybody in the vicinity gets a whiff of it as well. The particles bounce off the offender and as you struggle you get a good dose as well. It's hard to describe the effects, really. You can't see, there's terrible pain and discomfort in your eyes, nose and the back of your throat. You salivate so severely that you continuously have to spit and snot pours out of your nose. I know because I've suffered the effects several times. The only good thing is that if you've a stuffy nose it clears your sinuses a treat (and it goes nicely on your chips and pizza as well).

We eventually got the handcuffs on him behind his back so he couldn't struggle much. He was then bundled into the back of the police car. One of two things usually happen here (apart from them messing their underwear, which he did). They either calm down or get even worse. The man began to calm down somewhat and the trip back to the station was relatively quiet.

After several hours of paperwork and him being seen by the police doctor he was fed and left to sleep off the drink and drugs. Ten of us had to sit in the station doing statements and crime reports. The next day he was interviewed but he couldn't remember a thing. He was charged with affray and when he went to court he received a fine of £80.

The man was on the dole and had been for several years. He was young and fit and able but didn't feel like getting a job. And why should he bother? He got his wages every fortnight, which you kindly supplied from your taxes. He got disability benefits for his poorly back, which you paid for.

When he got back from his drug dealer with the coke (again, which you paid for) he went into his council flat which again you paid for. He watched his nice telly which you paid for as well. When he went to the police station he got a free lawyer which you paid for. He got represented at court by another lawyer which you paid for. You also paid for the court building, magistrates and clerks.

When the man was fined the £80 he was allowed to pay in instalments. He paid the fine over three months but he didn't have any money, of course, so really it was you who paid the fine. Wasn't that nice of you? In fact, I'd say that you're paying about 90 per cent of all the fines being enforced at the moment. Sick bag, anyone?

Happy Birthday to Me – 5 June 1978

We have some new neighbours moving in down the road – my dad says they're called darkies. One of the children is playing in the park behind our house. As she's on the swing my friend and I run over to her and shout, 'Cadburys make them and they cover them in chocolate.' We run away laughing, but as I look back she looks very sad; she's crying. I feel bad.

The next day we bang on the railings of the Brico factory which is behind our house. We bang and bang and then the security men come out with their dogs barking. We run into the house and hide behind the curtains. The security men bang on all the front doors in the street to find out who did it. We're told off.

It's Christmas time and I'm so excited. We have a real Christmas tree at home, but at school they keep making us sing carols and I hate it. I know where my mum hides the presents. I sneak into her room to take a look. I have a Star Wars light sabre, Six Million Dollar Man, Spiderman, walkie talkies and some picture books. I feel sad now because I know what I'm going to get.

I watch Kung Fu *on TV, it's my favourite programme after* Monkey. *My mum has a new boyfriend called John. He has red hair and a red beard. My sister Cheryl knows him because she speaks to him every day as he walks past our house on the way to work. John's brother Alan comes to stay a lot. He sleeps on the sofa downstairs with mum's friend Shirley. Shirley is a 'mod', but I don't know what that means.*

I'm 8 years old.

Year 9 – Alcohol, the Ruination of the Working Class

A big cloud came over the sun and the warmth on Dawn's face quickly subsided; she felt a cold shiver go up her spine. It wasn't so warm now the sun had decided to hide away.

The horrible taste was still in her mouth: what on earth could it be? It tasted familiar but it wasn't food, it had a sort of metallic taste to it. Oh yeah, it was blood. Dawn felt inside her mouth with her tongue, there were tender fleshy lumps where her front teeth were supposed to be.

She decided it was time to get up off the grass, but when she tried to move she felt a terrible stabbing pain at the bottom of her back; she screamed out in pain. It was like a hot poker had been thrust into her back. She felt a large pool of blood gathering in the back of her throat and immediately let out an involuntary cough.

Blood flew into the air and back down onto her face. Inside the blood was one of her front teeth which came to rest on her left cheek. She wanted to wipe it off but couldn't move her arms. As Dawn looked up again she could see a face looking down and smiling at her. The face was mine. 'Don't move, love' I said softly, 'an ambulance is on the way.'

As she lay there she began to wonder how on earth this had happened. Her memory of events began to return in small segments. She was 23 and lived in a block of flats in Stoke Aldermoor. She was a prostitute and had been so for a few years after going into care when at age 10 her mother died of cancer.

Her boyfriend had got her hooked on heroin and used it to control her. He'd watch her work her patch which was in Hillfields behind a local pub. She'd take her punter to the back pub and lie on a piss-soaked mattress as they slept with her: 10 pounds for a blow job, 15 for sex, 20 for sex without a condom or for arse sex.

Dawn had locked herself out of her flat by accident and was desperate to get in. She had a tiny amount of heroin hidden in a shoe in her wardrobe and really needed to score. She went to the back of the flats and began to climb up a drain pipe. She'd almost reached her balcony which she knew had an open window she could climb through. She lost her footing and fell about 20 feet onto the ground. As her head hit the ground her front teeth flew out of her mouth and one of them landed on the ground next to her.

I picked up Dawn's teeth and put them into a small bag, hoping in vain that they'd be able to put them back into her gums at hospital. I passed them to the ambulance crew who'd just arrived. They put Dawn into a stretcher and took her away.

She'd broken her back and was from then on paralysed from the waist down. Not much use anymore to her pimp though, so at least she was out of the prostitution game.

∽ ∾

I must've attended thousands of incidents during my time in the police. You can't help but develop a certain perspective on life and society during this time. I'd learned during the first year of my law degree about how laws are made. The legal system consists of the administration, the executive, and the judicature. The administration makes the laws. This is parliament, the House of Commons, and the House of Lords. The top lawyers from Cambridge and Oxford get picked to help draft the laws that we abide by (or at least most of us do) in the UK.

Next is the executive. These are the police officers, customs officers and the like who actually enforce the laws. We use the powers given to us by common law and statutes. We bring offenders in front of the judicature. The judicature are the magistrates and judges who actually interpret and apply the laws laid down by the administration.

Basically, I saw my job as a police officer was to protect the public from harm and to arrest bad people who'd broken the laws and put them in front of the courts. We also obviously have to do a lot more things like apply traffic laws such as no seat belt and local by-laws such as letting your dog shit outside schools. We also had a massive number of administrative tasks such as looking after lost dogs, checking up on firearms licence-holders and finding lost people.

We complied with our part of the deal and put people before the courts. That's where it often seemed to me to go wrong. Over 95 per cent of people charged go to magistrates' court. Most magistrates are lay magistrates. They have no legal qualifications and perform their role on a part-time basis for a small retainer plus their expenses. They need a clerk present who has passed some legal exams to advise them what their options are and the correct legal procedure.

I often found many of these magistrates spoke with a plumb in their mouths which indicated that they were upper-class, a long distance removed from the working or unemployed classes that they were dealing with. I'd see people I'd arrested walk out of court time and time again because they'd stand there and look plausible when they pleaded their innocence.

Even with a strong case there's no guarantee of a conviction. Many things can happen between a person being charged and their coming to court. They can decide to give information about active criminals to avoid prosecution (very common), or just admit one offence and ask a string of others to be taken into consideration (TICs).

It's rare for a person to be sent to prison from magistrates' court. They have very limited sentencing powers and the vast majority of the time they hand out fines, conditional discharges, probation orders and so on. If they feel a prison sentence is warranted they often refer the decision to a judge at Crown Court. When they find a person guilty, before they make a decision as to an appropriate punishment the magistrates will defer sentencing pending probation reports, interviews by social workers or any number of other pre-sentencing reports.

Crown Court is a different story altogether. I have a tremendous respect for the judges in County and Crown Court. Their command of the English language is second to none and every word they choose is precise so as to avoid any ambiguity. All judges were formerly lawyers who have now taken up a role in the Crown or County Court.

What can happen in Crown Court with a serious offence such as a rape is that the offender appears at court to answer for the offence. The witnesses are there, but severely traumatised because of the pressure of having to stand in the witness box and be torn to pieces by the defending barrister. The victim will have to relive the offence and suffer the humiliation of going through every detail in front of about 20 people or more including reporters and jurors, and of course her attacker.

Before the trial commences the defending barrister will often approach the CPS barrister and begin to negotiate. It's usually something like their client admitting to indecent assault instead of rape to spare the victim going through it all again. The barrister then calls over the officer in charge and asks for his or her comments.

It's all a balance between seeing justice served and sparing the witnesses from the ordeal of giving evidence. If we feel that the victim will crack under pressure and start changing their story or make mistakes, then it can shake the case and the offender can walk away scott free.

You see, the jury does not get to hear about the offender's previous convictions. So as far as they know, the guy is an honest, decent, upstanding member of society. He could be the biggest robbing, raping crack-dealing son of a bitch in the whole of the city but they wouldn't know it. The cards are firmly stacked in favour of the defendant every time.

The judge knows the score. The defendant can ask for the police to send the judge a letter telling him how much he cooperated. If the defendant has helped the police catch some serious criminals, then this will be taken into consideration. This is why you often see people found guilty of serious crimes getting very light sentences or even walking out of court with suspended sentences. Although there's a code between criminals not to inform on each other, behind closed doors the maxim 'There is no honour amongst thieves' applies. Most would shop their own mother to avoid going to prison.

I really don't think that prison is that much of a deterrent to be honest. You get fed well, get to watch TV, play pool, snooker and darts, you can work out in the gym, get any study courses you want for free, and get to lounge about all day doing nothing. I'm surprised more chavs don't want to go. The only drawbacks I suppose are that there's no beer and any sex you do have would be with another man.

Wouldn't it be nice to live in a country which was relatively crime-free? Where people didn't toss litter and chewing gum on the ground, where there wasn't dog shit everywhere you walk. Where you could walk down the street late at night and really relax and enjoy yourself without fear of being attacked by pissheads or robbers.

You may think that this is just a pipe dream but such a place exists. It's a country called Singapore. Singapore is one of the safest countries in the world to live in. Their legal system is considered brutal to some. If you litter you'll be fined heavily or given the birch. You can even go to prison for not flushing the toilet after you have a shit, how about that. A land free of floaters.

I gave evidence in Crown Court a few times, especially as a detective. The atmosphere is very different to magistrates' court. I encourage you to go to magistrates' court one morning, preferably somewhere busy like Coventry, Birmingham or another big city. Go at about 9:45 a.m. before the cases start. You're allowed to sit at the back as a member of the public. Ask the listings clerk what trials are on and go and have a nose. I guarantee you'll be amazed – and it's cheaper and better entertainment than daytime TV.

Magistrates' court is like an animal house with offenders all over the place. It's wall-to-wall chav where all you can see are shell suits, love bites, gold choker chains and people speaking some incomprehensible language that only they can understand. It's all a big joke to them because they know that they're not going to prison. Magistrates have sentencing rules to follow, and since we have almost no spare prison space in the UK how on earth can we send more people there? The only way is to let the current prisoners out, which happens, of course, much to the public's outrage.

Just as an aside, if a person gets sentenced to, say, 10 years, they'll never ever serve that 10 years. Prison sentences are always halved plus time off for good behaviour and being let out on licence. For a 10-year sentence you're looking at maybe three to four.

If the prisoner has been held on remand in prison before their sentence in court (because they're known to commit offences whilst on bail or skip bail) then this time counts as time plus one third. So three months on remand counts as four months. Often then, a person is sentenced but they've already served the requisite time so again they walk out of court. Madness.

Judges are not the sort of people you want to mess about or back-chat. I've seen them put people behind bars who were not even involved in the case. Once, I was in Crown Court looking after witnesses. There was some road work going on outside which was so loud the judge couldn't hear evidence being given. Since I was the only police officer there I was called in to see the judge. He'd cleared the court of the defendant and jury. He directed me to speak to the foreman outside and tell him to suspend work with the jackhammer for one hour until the court was in recess. I of course agreed and left the court.

I found the site foreman who was called Mick, a stout Irishman. Mick was about 50 years old and covered in mud from the hole he was digging. He had those thick beige boots with no laces in that workmen often wear, dirty brown trousers and no top apart from a reflective vest and hard hat on. He had tattoos all over his arms dating back to when he'd been a teddy boy many years before. Mick stank of body odour so I had to move from down- to upwind as I spoke to him.

I asked him to down tools for an hour so the judge could finish up the trial. He laughed and said, 'Tell the judge oim here to dig and fill this hole. Oil stop digging when oim finished – and that's that.' I could see Mick's six workmates had stopped work, were smiling at me as if I didn't have a leg to stand on and would have to walk away in shame. Mick wanted to look important in front of his crew. I smiled politely and said, 'Tell him yourself, mate.'

Mick had made it clear he was in charge here and by now didn't want to lose face by backing down. I took him with me into court and told the clerk that the man wanted to speak to the judge himself because he was refusing to stop digging. Mick was used to being the big 'I am' on site and he wasn't about to let some wig-wearing judge tell him what he could and couldn't do. The judge very politely told Mick that he was in contempt of court and was to desist digging the road for one hour.

'Oim not stopping for anyone, oim in charge of the soyte and oive a job to finish.' The judge asked, 'Is that your last word?' 'That's me last word,' replied Mick.

Bang. Down came the judge's wooden hammer. 'One day for contempt of court. Take him away, bailiff.' 'You can't do that!' exclaimed Mick.

Bang. 'Two days for contempt of court.' 'That isn't legal!' said Mick lamely (though how he came to this conclusion I'll never know).

Bang. 'Three days for contempt of court.' Mick was not taking the hint. 'I know me rights….'

Bang. 'Four days for contempt of court.' Mick fell silent. He'd got the message. The bailiff led a very subdued Mick down to the court cells and the trial continued.

A very subdued and repentive Mick came back before the judge later that day. He apologised profusely and the judge let him go free.

If a judge had ever asked me to do anything I'd just say, 'Yes Sir.'

≈ ∾

Alcohol was a constant issue in the police as well. It can be a very stressful job and at the time almost every station had a bar built somewhere inside. It was so easy to go there after a set of earlies or lates and have a few bevvies with the watch to wind down. When I was on the watch at Little Park Street I used to go on the last day of earlies or at the end of the last day of lates at about 10 p.m. I never did drink so it was easy enough for me to have a glass of orange and then drive home but I usually cycled anyway.

Almost everyone on the watch did drink and it was common for some of them to have three or four pints and then drive home. It's obviously very hypocritical for police to drink and drive because part of their duty is to stop that sort of thing. I did work with a few police officers who'd been done for drink driving and luckily managed to keep their jobs. I think that many police officers felt that they had some sort of immunity from being bagged (breathalysed) because of the fact that they were in the job.

At the time I joined it was practically forbidden to breathalyse police officers. The ones that seemed to get done were the ones who had to drive through another county to get home, usually Warwickshire.

There was a traffic officer who worked at Little Park Street police station. He was pointed out to me my very first day there because nobody ever worked with him. He was always posted on his own. I was told that he'd breathalysed a police officer once and now was ostracised by everybody else.

I later got all the facts. The police officer he'd breathalysed was a persistent drink driver who'd been given several gypsies warnings to stop doing it but continued anyway. He was at some point going to run somebody over while drink driving. If he was too lazy to call a taxi home then as far as I was concerned he was fair game.

He was breathalysed by the traffic officer one night and later lost his job. He became a runner for a local firm of lawyers. The traffic officer spent the rest of his service working alone. I did spend a week with him when I was sent to work with traffic as part of my probationer training. I thought he was a nice chap myself.

One of my first incidents in the police was dealing with a drink driving police officer. I was on nights with Alan and at about 1 a.m. a call came over the radio that a car had been spotted crashed into a tree near to the

War Memorial Park in Quinten Road.

We drove along there and about halfway down we saw a car that had mounted the pavement, driven across the grass and came to rest in a hedge. As we got out of our car we were joined by one of the Zulus. We walked over to the car and were shocked to see the driver slumped over the steering wheel. Alan pulled him back and it was one of the sergeants from the late shift. He stank of booze and was clearly as pissed as a fart.

I just thought, 'This guy's career is over.' We'd have to call the inspector and he'd be breathalysed and probably get the sack. The off-duty sergeant wasn't hurt and was half awake, mumbling incoherently to himself. Alan called me over to help him out of the car. We half walked and half carried him over to the Zulu and lay him down in the back. I stayed with him while Alan spoke to the Zulu crew. Alan came over and told me that the Zulu driver was going to drive him back home, the other PC would drive the sergeant's car back to his house and park it.

I never argued, what could I say? Apparently, we didn't do police officers on our watch. I saw the sergeant on duty the next day. He looked a bit rough but was back at work as if nothing had happened.

I've seen alcohol ruin many lives and many careers of police officers. I'm not sure whether the pressures of life in the police turn a person to drink or whether they'd have been a pisshead whatever job they were in.

Paddy was an old-sweat PC who joined us at Bordesley Green but not on my unit (thankfully). He'd been in the CID for several years. It must be very hard going from the freedom of being a detective to the very restrictive life of a uniformed police officer. Paddy was a nice chap and very knowledgeable but a few weeks after joining the unit people began to notice that he started to come to work smelling of alcohol. Paddy was also stopping by the police bar at the end of every late shift and visiting the bar every day off earlies which is a bad sign (afternoon drinking).

Paddy was given a gypsies warning by his sergeant and by a couple of traffic officers who saw him leaving the police bar and getting into his car to drive home. I've seen this happen time after time. Once a person starts coming to work half drunk then you know that they've lost control of it. It was only a matter of time until Paddy had an accident or a member of the public noticed the smell on his breath and reported him.

Paddy was separated from his wife because she couldn't put up with his drinking any more. He went to the police bar one night after lates and had a few pints. He drove to her house down the road and had a big argument with her and then drove off. Hell hath no fury as a woman scorned. She called 999 and reported the fact that her ex-husband had driven off from her house and was drunk. Paddy's fate was now sealed.

When Paddy got home the traffic car and duty sergeant were waiting for him. Paddy was breathalysed at the roadside and failed. When this happens, you're arrested and taken to the police station to blow twice on the evidential machine. This machine's readout is used for evidence in court and the lower reading of the two is the one that's used against you. The threshold for charging is 35 and some lucky people have blown 35 and then 34 which means their level is going down and they're not charged. Paddy blew 97 which is getting towards three times over the limit.

The decision on whether to sack an officer lies with the chief constable. I'm not sure what criteria he uses because I've seen some officers being prosecuted for drink driving but somehow keep their jobs. No such luck for Paddy. He was prosecuted for drink driving and the next day went to see the chief constable and was dismissed from duty. As the chief told him he was sacked, Paddy stood there crying his eyes out.

The days when a policeman could get drunk and drive and get away with it have now gone. Now there's no stigma attached to arresting a fellow police officer. For the record, I think whoever you are if you drink and drive you should pay the consequences. It's a calculated risk, but not only that you're risking killing another person out of the sheer laziness of not calling a taxi or kipping in a cheap hotel. I just don't get it.

When I was on independent patrol I never did have to deal with an off-duty police officer drink driving, thankfully. I don't honestly know what I'd have done. If you got caught letting one off then you'd be sacked yourself and possibly go to prison yourself for perverting the course of justice so my philosophy was rather them than me. As a sergeant I had to bag a couple of off-duty officers but they never failed the roadside test so I didn't have to arrest them.

Mike, the sergeant I worked with at Stechford had a very interesting perspective on alcohol and I had to agree with him based upon what I witnessed. We were out on patrol together just leaving the scene of another violent domestic where a man had punched the mother of his three children for turning the telly off when he was watching it.

The man had done the same thing he'd done every other Saturday for years now and his father had done before him. He got up and went to the local club to play cards, watch sports on TV and drink with his 'mates'. He drank a few pints of wife-beater (a famous brand of beer which will go unnamed) and staggered off home looking for food at about 3 in the afternoon.

His wife had been doing her best to contend with three demanding children all day and had spent the week working to make some extra money in the local supermarket. When her man came home there was dinner in the oven but it was burned. She asked for help with the children but he just sank into the sofa and turned the TV on to watch another match. She started to shout and cry out of sheer frustration and went over and turned the TV off.

Anger surged through him. He wasn't angry at her, of course, but at the hopelessness of his own life. He was angry at himself for putting up with a bullying foreman at the factory and not having the guts to stand up to him. He was angry because his dad had been an alcoholic and had beaten his mum. He was angry because he couldn't afford a holiday for his family this year (because he'd spent all the money on beer and fags). He just didn't realise it.

He punched the mother of his children in the side of her head sending her flying across the room and onto the sofa. He then fell to the floor and curled up into a ball and began to cry. His son and daughters began to cry as well. They were all learning how to act when they were grown-ups.

Mike and I got there along with a couple of officers from the watch. He was carted away for assault and thrown into the cells to sleep it off. He'd be released the next day when the booze had worn off. She'd withdraw the complaint after he came home crying and begging for forgiveness, only for the whole scenario to be repeated like groundhog day next weekend.

As we pulled away from the house Mike turned to me and uttered the immortal worlds, 'Alcohol is the ruination of the working class.' I pondered on his words and reflected back on every damn domestic and fight I'd been to. Mike was right, and at the same time I knew that there was not a thing I could do to change anything. Dealing with the aftermath of alcohol in the police was like the game in the fairgrounds where you've a hammer and you hit the little heads as they pop up out of the holes in the machine. Eventually so many pop up that you can't keep up with them all. All I could do was whack the heads as they popped up and hope I didn't get tired.

We have a strange attitude to drink in the UK. It's worshipped as a ritual and more is better. You can walk into almost any local pub on any day of the week and there'll be people in there drinking away. Teenagers can't wait until they're old enough to sneak into pubs or nightclubs so they can start. Adverts on TV brainwash us into thinking that we're trendy if we drink their product and we'll be irresistible to the opposite sex.

I wish I had an answer to the problem. Fines for disorder don't help. Now the police can issue on-the-spot fines for city centre disorder which seems to me to be completely pointless. Giving some drunken idiot a ticket won't stop anything. It's how alcohol is perceived that's the issue, the thing that millions of grown-ups in the UK turn to every night and every weekend as part of what they consider to be 'normal' life.

It's considered normal to have several pints and get drunk; it's even considered by friends as a laudable activity. Pubs are now child-friendly or so-called 'family pubs' so now sorry excuses for parents can have a few pints while their children run about climbing on frames or swinging off ropes for a few hours. The adults now were the children of parents who'd leave their kids in the pub car park with a bag of crisps and a bottle of pop while they got pissed inside. It's as if they think that taking their child to the pub while they piss their life away drinking counts as quality time.

I'm doing my best not to sound judgemental because people can do what they like in their own free time and it has no bearing whatsoever on me. Watching children being taken to pubs reminds me of when I was growing up. We'd be taken to the pub or club by my dad and be left to our own devices while the grown-ups would drink the night away. On Sunday my dad would take me and my sister to church and he'd go to the club 'round the back.

When my sister and I had come out of mass we'd go to the club where my dad was. We'd sit there bored out of our minds while he'd play dominoes for hours with his mates almost all of whom were divorced, broke and miserable. Strange really, because he only got to see us once a fortnight so you'd have thought he'd savour every moment he had with us.

Once when I was visiting Bernard I asked him about alcohol. He'd helped many people with addictions and so had a lot of experience in that area. Bernard once said to me, 'All forms of addictions are a symptom of another problem.' He'd been there himself so he had first-hand experience. He told me that, 'Basically, everybody wants to feel good and the addiction helps them stop feeling bad for the time they are indulging in it.' I'd personally dealt with alcoholics and drug addicts and until then I thought that was the only sort of addiction really.

'An addiction is anything you can't stop doing,' said Bernard. 'It can be alcohol, drugs, food, sex, TV, spending money, masturbation or many other things.' I started to wish I hadn't asked. I'd wank myself into a coma every night and never thought there was a problem with that. I made a promise to myself to cut down to once or twice a day.

Bernard said, 'We can even be addicted to other people's dramas. We all know people who thrive on learning about other people's marriage problems or when misfortune befalls another person or family. Every day millions of people tune into soap operas which are another form of addiction. The only way the viewer can find meaning in their own life is to watch an endless series of dramas happening in other people's lives.'

I remember having to sit through hours of *Crossroads, Emmerdale, Prisoner Cell Block H* and the like as I was growing up. Bernard cleared his throat and continued. 'They watch it because they look at the characters and secretly think, "I hate my life but at least it isn't as bad as theirs." They then go to work the next day and live them out again by chatting to their work colleagues about what they watched on TV the night before. The problem is that they need higher and higher levels of drama to maintain the same feelings of euphoria so the soap operas now have their characters engaging in hateful and spiteful behaviour, rapes, drug and alcohol addictions and even murder.'

It's actually very difficult to deal with people who've been drinking. Like I mentioned, alcohol impairs brain functions so when we were called to sort out domestics or situations that could flare up it was like speaking to somebody from another planet.

We'd do our best to explain why it was a good idea that they went home or that a drunken husband should go and stay at a mate's house but we might as well have been speaking Swahili.

Insp. Ross was very proactive with domestics. The rule for the watch was that if you were sent to a domestic you had to effect an arrest.

It may sound harsh but if there's violence in a home severe enough for the police to have to attend then affirmative action is required. It's a personal disgrace for a police officer to be called back to attend the same domestic a second time. On Red Watch at Stechford, if there was trouble at home flaring up then we'd arrest the violent party, which was always the husband. He'd just be bound over to keep the peace the next day so he never had a criminal record afterwards and the bonus was that the beer had worn off by then.

The standard method of police going to domestics was to calm people down and then give advice but it wasn't until I worked with Insp. Ross that I realised what a waste of time that really was. We're not social workers and you simply can't negotiate with drunk people and there's a real risk that once you leave the wife is going to be slapped about by her husband. If that or worse happens then it's very much the fault of the police for doing nothing.

We're not paid to provide marriage counselling or to 'give advice' to fighting couples and every domestic is a wounding or potential murder. Don't believe me? Then it's time for another story. Get yourself a cup of tea and listen to this.

Stephen and Julie were a married couple. They lived in a fairly nice part of Stechford but then that's a bit like saying it has the least amount of dog shit and active burglars there compared to most of the other streets in the neighbourhood. Stephen was a businessman who ran his own international trade company. It sounded pretty posh I suppose but it wasn't making much money. It was actually losing it but that's quite normal for a company to do during its lifetime.

Stephen was originally from Greece but had grown up in Birmingham after his parents moved over in the 1960s. He was very well-educated with a degree and an MBA and had dreams of being a high-flying businessman but a few bad decisions and lack of real-world experience was letting him down.

Julie was a trainee nurse and on a very low income. She'd run away from home when she was about 14 because her dad kept abusing her. He'd wait until her mum was asleep and then get into her bed and have sex with her. When he did he threatened her that her mum would have a nervous breakdown if she found out so it was best if she never said anything.

Julie was a very quiet person and didn't think much of herself at all. It was very easy for her to be bullied because she wouldn't stand up for herself. When she first met Stephen it was at a mutual friend's house and she was flattered when he took an interest in her. She'd always thought that no man would really want her. Stephen was looking for an attractive woman to have on his arm but one who'd never argue with him and always be impressed at the fact he was a businessman. And so a dysfunctional relationship was born.

As money got tighter Stephen began to drink heavily. He became very aggressive towards Julie and although he never hit her he'd grab her by her arms and shake her until she cried. Julie was a very petite woman and easily intimidated. Stephen began to resent Julie because she wasn't bringing much money home. He went back on his promise to support her through her nurse training and to provide for her.

One evening at about 10:30 p.m. Stephen came home drunk. His latest business deal had just fallen apart and he was on the verge of bankruptcy. He was in a foul mood. Julie offered to make him some dinner but Stephen just flew into a rage. He started to shout at Julie blaming her for not making any money.

As the shouting went on the next-door neighbours became concerned and called the police. If Red Watch had attended he'd have been arrested but it was two less enthusiastic old sweats from another unit who attended. Julie said that everything was OK, although to anybody with half a brain it was obvious that she was shaking like a leaf.

Stephen was advised that the next time the police were called he'd be arrested and the police officers left. The next time they called was an hour later and Stephen was arrested for murdering Julie.

The disgrace of having the police in his house was too much for Stephen. In his drunken rage he dragged Julie into the kitchen and threw her to the floor. He grabbed a kitchen knife and cut her throat open. It took her about three minutes of agonising terror to pass out and a few more minutes before she died.

The point was that in my humble opinion Julie would not have died that night if the police had taken positive action. I'm not saying that it may never have happened at some future point, but nobody can say. Maybe she'd have passed her exams and met a decent man and left Stephen. She never had that chance, though.

Happy Birthday to Me – 5 June 1979

I don't like my teacher at school. His name is George Alan Parker but we all call him GAP behind his back. He has thick glasses and a big black bushy moustache. His hair is falling out and there isn't much left. If you don't listen to him he throws chalk at you across the classroom.

I get caught talking during dinner one day by the deputy headmaster. He hits you with a ruler on the fingers if you're naughty or talk too much. Six of us stand in a dark room in front of him and he stands there in silence. We're all shaking with fear and praying to ourselves, hoping that he doesn't hit us with the ruler. He eventually lets us out of the room without hitting us.

My friend tells me a joke at the dinner table the next day. I laugh so hard that a massive amount of snot flies out of my nose onto my green school jumper. I have nothing to wipe it away with so I have to use my sleeve.

I have a girlfriend who lives across the road from me. Her name is Anne. I write love letters to her and meet her in the entry sometimes but I don't know what to say to her. I give her a present, a bottle of my mum's perfume. My mum is angry and shouts at me because it was her favourite perfume.

I'm 9 years old.

Year 10 – Death

I saw my first dead body when I was about 12 years old. We were living in Catherine Street in Hillfields and there was an old lady who lived across the road from us who owned a sweet shop. She knocked on our door one evening asking for help saying that she couldn't wake her husband up. He was about 75 I think and spent the whole day sitting at the back of the shop in his wheelchair watching the telly. He'd died sitting in his wheelchair. He looked like he was sleeping to me; I couldn't see the difference.

When I joined the police, part of the induction process was to watch a post mortem at Coventry and Warwickshire Hospital's mortuary. I went there with the six other recruits I'd joined with. We'd all known each other from the police cadets, apart from two other guys with us who hadn't been in the cadets but I'd got to know them well because we'd shared cars driving up and down to Bruche police training centre together.

We were all taken to the mortuary by the old-sweat training PC responsible for Coventry. He introduced us to the lab assistant who was in charge of getting the bodies out of the fridge and putting them onto the slab for the doctor. I can't even imagine who'd want that sort of job. Putting dead bodies onto slabs all day long and then going home to have your dinner and talk about your day with your misses. I can imagine the conversation as he sits down, 'I'm bloody knackered, love, been pulling corpses out of the fridge all day long. What's for dinner tonight?'

Post mortems are horrible affairs: the body's placed on a bare slab naked. The top of the skull is cut around with a circular saw and the skull lifted off. The brain is scooped out, dissected and weighed. The ribs are cut out and all the your vital organs are cut up and weighed. The whole lot including the brain are then thrown back into the abdomen and sewn up ready for chucking in a coffin.

I don't know why we were taken to watch the post mortems but the theory may be the more bodies you see the more inured you get. We were told that if we didn't like it we could walk out at any point. It was very morbid, but I was also very interested in how the human body is put together. All I'd ever seen was the odd diagram in our biology books at school.

I sat through three post mortems as the doctor explained what the bits he was pulling out were for. The first body was of a young man who'd been in a motorbike accident and had broken his neck. The other two had died from old age. One was a smoker whose lungs looked like two brown sponges. Yeuch. The other person was very old and had suffered a massive stroke. The doctor cut up his brain and found a big blood clot in there which he determined was the cause of death.

There was always a morbid fascination with dead bodies in the police. I went to so many sudden deaths where colleagues stood over the body making jokes and laughing. I was never sure if it was just bravado or whether they just didn't give a shit. The very worst were the elderly, who sometimes were not noticed for a while after they died. Most of them lived alone with no friends or family to visit. Sometimes weeks went by and people were only alerted by the fact that several of the free weekly papers were hanging out of the letterbox and there was a foul smell emanating from the flat.

A sergeant is supposed to attend all deaths that police officers attend but in reality most don't bother. They're called 'sudden deaths' in the police for some reason. You could've been dying of cancer for months but even so, once you pop your clogs it's referred to as a sudden death.

When I was duty sergeant at Alum Road I attended a sudden death that one of the watch had been called out to. The other PC attending was called Daz. A neighbour hadn't seen the old boy next door for a few weeks and there was a bad smell coming from the his flat. When we got there, there was no reply at the door. Daz forced entry. The smell was so rank that we had to breathe through our mouths to stop ourselves puking. The worst part of attending a sudden death is walking 'round the house. You know you're going to find a dead body at any minute, but you just don't know which room it is going to be in or what state of decay. It's a bit like hide and seek, but when you find them they don't get up.

Three small dogs ran up to us as soon as we entered and one jumped up onto Daz so pleased to see a human being. The dog was still licking Daz's face as we went into the living room.

They old boy must've been dead for a couple of weeks. The dogs had run out of food and so in their desperation had started to eat him. They'd eaten most of his intestines out and also his penis. Daz had to run outside and vomit before washing his face. Not good.

This was all in a day's work. By this point of my service I'd already seen people with their heads blown off, hanged, drowned, murdered, burned to death or hit by trains. It actually becomes normal when you see enough of it. It was probably one of the worst parts of the job, I suppose. Not actually seeing the body, but acting as if it doesn't bother you one little bit when of course it probably does, quite possibly because it reminds us of our own mortality.

I'd arrested one guy for harassing his ex-wife by continually calling 'round her house all hours of the day and night. When he was charged and bailed to keep away from her he went to the end of his street and phoned her. He told her that he was going to set fire to himself and it was all her fault.

He poured a can of petrol over himself and lit a match. He must've taken a while to die. I was called to the incident to identify him but simply couldn't. He was completely cooked and looked like a pork scratching. The only way I knew it was the guy I'd dealt with earlier was because there was a copy of the charge sheet in his pocket.

It was his last sad attempt at making his ex-wife feel guilty. As he'd lit the match he must've been thinking, 'This will teach that bitch a lesson. She'll feel like shit after this.'

I actually thought I'd seen a police officer kill a person once or twice. There had been the odd death in police custody at various stations. It was usually when the police were fighting. You all end up wrestling with the prisoner and the pathetic police self-defence system is useless.

You just end up rolling around the floor trying to restrain them the best you can. Often, a police officer can panic and put an arm around the prisoner's neck trying to hold them down. If you grab too tight and for too long they stop breathing, but because there's so much fear and adrenalin you won't notice until they go blue. By then it may be too late to bring them back unless you're skilled at resuscitation.

One night in Little Park Street one of the Pandas brought what they thought was a drunk in. A man was found collapsed near to a pub. He was incomprehensible and unable to stand up. I was always very worried about such prisoners (drunk and incapable) because they could easily choke on their own vomit in the cell and you wouldn't know until you'd visited them maybe 30 minutes later.

This guy who was brought in was completely out of it. He was mumbling and couldn't stand. Everybody in the cell block was standing about joking about it and laughing. He'd pissed in his pants and the arresting officers couldn't wait to throw him into the cell. Luckily for that man, Bill was the custody sergeant. Bill felt that something wasn't quite right. He seemed drunk, but he didn't really smell of booze. Bill came from behind the desk and checked his pockets and then around his neck. He found a pendant which said he was a diabetic.

The man was going into a diabetic coma, and if he'd gone into the cell could easily have died. We called an ambulance and gave him some hot chocolate which brought him 'round a bit. His life was saved that night by Bill – not that he got any thanks, but then being in the police is usually a thankless task.

The second time I thought I'd seen a death will not surprise you to hear was at the hands of two people on my unit at Little Park Street. Connor and Jon were two old-sweat Zulu drivers who'd come over during a reorganisation. They were prone to giving their prisoners a few slaps and would often be out winding people up so they could have an easy arrest.

I was working with Duncan who'd been stabbed in the back previously outside the Parsons Nose chip shop. A report came through the radio that a man was acting suspiciously in the railway goods yard just outside the city centre. We made our way there because we covered that area. The Zulu with Connor and Jon also said they were going. I tried to rush there because the first car that arrives usually deals and I didn't want to become embroiled in one of their self-initiated punch-ups.

By the time we arrived they'd already stopped a man and were searching him. They were putting the contents of his pockets on the bonnet of their car and were already winding him up. The man was just a young chap aged about 20. He'd been drinking at the local pub and was taking a shortcut through the goods yard. The PNC reported that he was not known to the police, so that was the end of it – or so I thought.

This guy was a perfect candidate for Connor to bully. Smaller than him, weaker, and a bit drunk. So Connor started to wind him up, 'Where's your mates, Billy? No mates?' he laughed, 'Do you live in a squat somewhere 'round here?' Pathetic really. Duncan and I knew that the bloke was in trouble.

He started to argue back telling them that he had his own flat and that he was a welder. Connor carried on and Jon chipped in as well. 'You dress like a tramp, mate, did you rob those clothes from the charity shop?' They were just trying to wind him up for their own pathetic egos.

The guy became angry and said to Connor, 'Fuck off, pencil dick,' which I found quite funny. Jon became incensed and pulled back his right arm and punched the man hard in the back of the head. As he was falling to the ground Connor lifted his foot back and kicked him in the side of his face. As soon as he hit the ground he began to have a fit. His body was convulsing and blood was coming out of his nose.

'You stupid fuckers!' I shouted. Connor went white as a sheet. Jon was starting to look very worried as well. This had never happened to them before. The man stopped convulsing and lay there perfectly still with his eyes shut. Connor reached down and felt his neck for a pulse. 'He doesn't have a pulse!' he exclaimed, 'he's fucking pegged it' (died). Connor stood up and began to cry like a baby, he knew that he was in deep shit. You could explain away a few cuts and bruises but not a dead body. His mind began to race and he imagined going to prison and being somebody's bitch.

When extremely traumatic events happen people usually lose their ability to think rationally. All Connor and Jon could think of doing was putting the body in the boot of their car and burying it somewhere. All Zulus have shovels in the back for clearing up after road accidents.

Duncan and I stood there speechless as Connor and Jon struggled to pick up the body. Connor was crying like a baby and Jon was completely silent. They struggled to drag the body 'round the back of the car. They had to put the body by the back of the car while they emptied out some traffic cones and shields from the boot and put it in the back seats. Connor had to stop halfway through to throw up and most of it landed on his doc martin boots.

I couldn't believe it. There's no way I was going to be part of this. I didn't like them both anyway and I'd done nothing wrong. I was going to have to shop them both in for murder. I looked over at Duncan and I could see he was thinking the same thing.

Connor and Jon picked the body up and swung it back to get enough leverage to get it into the boot. As it landed in the back with a loud thump the man immediately came to and screamed, 'Arrrgggghhh!' Connor staggered backwards and fell onto the ground into his own pool of sick. The man jumped out of the boot and ran off across the goods yard and out the entrance.

I began to laugh out loud, more out of relief than actually finding it funny; Duncan joined in. We drove off leaving Connor and Jon to reflect on what they'd learned during the incident – if anything.

After that I think they both calmed down a lot and stopped beating the shit out of people for no good reason.

∾ ∾

In the police we also dealt with many accidental deaths where people hung themselves. What some men do for sexual gratification is to tie a noose around their necks while they're having a wank. They often have porn mags in front of them or videos playing and pull down on the noose a bit which gives them a massive orgasm (so I'm told). It's due to the lack of blood flow to the brain which apparently enhances the feelings tremendously. Sometimes when they're wanking off they're wearing stockings and suspenders as well.

Unfortunately, it's very easy to pull down just a bit too hard and pass out, and of course death quickly follows. These people are then found and the police are in a difficult position. If the family see them like this they'll feel humiliated. But at the same time it wasn't really a suicide because the man wasn't trying to kill himself, just have a prize-winning wank. I did hear that many police officers covered up the porn mags for the sake of saving the man's family from humiliation, but then everybody thought he'd killed himself and had left no note behind.

I did have my own stash of porn mags when I was a teenager. It was the only way to find out about sex – well, that and watching Channel 4 art films which were a godsend. My first stash I got from the usual place, under my parents' bed. I used to borrow the odd one for medicinal purposes and then replace it a few days later.

When I was a paper boy I seemed to have some sort of unnatural talent for finding porn mags in the street. I used to be walking up the road and literally find them hanging out of bushes or lying on the ground. I was a lucky sod. The porn mags in the 1970s and 1980s were different from today's. The women didn't have Brazilians or the telly savalis, they had massively hairy fannys which looked like tropical rain forests. It was hard to see what they really looked like for all the hair.

Anyway, the second-worst sudden death I went to was of an elderly lady in Coventry. Her daughter and grandson had gone to make their weekly visit to her flat but couldn't get her to answer the door so they called the police.

When I attended I could see the look of concern on her daughter's face. I wish there was something I could've said to reassure her, but the vast majority of the time, when an elderly person hasn't been seen for a while it's usually because they're dead. It's one of those times where you wish you didn't have to be there, but you've a job to do.

I already knew that she was dead inside when I saw the papers and milk by the door. I forced entry by smashing the glass in the front door and turning the lock from the inside with my hand. I asked her daughter and grandson to stay outside. When I went in there was thick putrid smoke inside the flat. It smelled more like a roast dinner burning than the building being on fire. I just knew that this was not going to be pretty.

I went into the living room and could see the old dear had died while sitting up in a chair watching the telly. Her head had fallen forwards and landed in the electric fire which had two bars on full. She'd been there for a couple of days probably, so it's lucky the block of flats never went up in flames. Her head had got completely cooked and her face had melted and caved in. Huge purple blisters had developed all over the back of her head and her brains were sticking out. It was absolutely dreadful. I was breathing in all the smoke from her head cooking.

I had to crawl under her body to turn the power to the fire off so the flat didn't go up in flames. If that wasn't bad enough, I had to go outside and tell the woman that her mum was dead. She wanted to go in and see her but I told her that probably wasn't a good idea. I then suddenly remembered that a dead body has to be identified by a relative so we can confirm this is the right person. I had to let her daughter in to see her mum and identify her. She was absolutely distraught. Inconsolable, in fact.

I called the duty undertakers who arrived a short time later. I went down to meet them by their van and explained that they were going to have to pull her caved-in head out of the fire. The looks on their faces said it all. They didn't want to be there as much as me, but we all had a job to do. They zipped her up and before they carried her out and I took her daughter and grandson out of sight. Less experienced officers used to let the undertakers walk past the family with the dead body in a bag which of course would cause them to freak out.

After I did the paperwork and faxed it to the coroner I went back to the police station and had my dinner. Everyone asked about the dead body back at the canteen. It was just one of those common scenarios that people asked about. It was a bit of a relief to share the story with the others on the watch because you knew they'd always make light of it.

As horrible as it all was I wasn't overly shocked. I think this goes for most police officers because if you're crying yourself to sleep every night after seeing dead bodies or being in fights then you're in the wrong job.

        ✤ ✤

One thing that struck me when I joined the police was how the elderly are treated by different parts of the community. It hit home when I was called to attend a sudden death in Newland Road in Foleshill a few months into my service. An elderly Indian man had died in his sleep and we had to attend as a matter of course.

As I pulled into Newland Road I was shocked. There were literally hundreds of men, women and children standing in the street. The women were wailing and crying out loud and beating themselves in the chest. I thought to myself that this guy must've been somebody famous or an important part of the community for his loss to cause this much grief.

The house was crammed full of people. We had to wade through at least a hundred mourners to get up to the room where his body was. There were people all around his body wailing and crying. We got a family member to clear the room and we just gave the body a cursory check to make sure there were no signs of foul play. I asked the man's son who he was and he looked surprised, 'He is just a normal man,' he replied looking bemused, 'we do this whenever we lose somebody in our community.'

I left the house and it all began to make sense. In the British community when a person gets old their family usually sends them off to a flat somewhere or leaves them to rot in an old people's home. Their house and possessions are usually sold and after a few arguments the profit is split between them. This is even before they're dead.

Every death I dealt with involving an elderly person who died alone was a Caucasian British person. I never in my service dealt with an incident where an Asian or Chinese elderly person had been left on their own. They were always living in the house with their family and treated as a wise and respected member of the community.

Even though I dealt with many terrible deaths from babies to the elderly I was never once asked during my time in the police if I was OK or did I want to speak to anybody about what I'd seen. The worst thing ever was seeing a dead body, especially that of a young person and then going to have to inform the relatives. Even then though I was amazed to see the lack of knowledge police supervision had around this area.

A fundamental error is asking the same person who's seen the body to go and tell the deceased's family. It's 10 times easier to see a dead body at the scene of a car accident, for example, and not have to match that person with a family. From a trauma point of view, it's far easier to have one person deal with the scene and another see the relatives. But this mistake happens every day.

During 12 years I lost count of how many dead bodies I saw in total. On Red Watch, we'd go through spates of dealing with sudden deaths and then it'd go quiet. Winter was bad for elderly people. Strangely, you'd have thought that summer was when students felt most pressure, but often it was around Christmas when we used to have students commit suicide.

Perhaps they felt lonely or it was all too much for them. I had to deal with students who hung themselves, threw themselves off bridges and even one who stepped in front of a train. The guy completely disintegrated so the police officers had to walk for miles up the track with plastic bags putting bits of him in as they found them. Some parts of him were never found, I think they were carried away by foxes.

I always looked forward immensely to Christmas. When we were all growing up in my house we'd write our present list for Santa and post the letter off. Our stepdad John would decorate the front window with black electrical tape so it was divided into squares. He'd then spray on white foam in the shape of holly and stars. We'd have a nativity scene in the front window with a mini-baby Jesus and the donkey in the stable.

We had the Alpine man come around every week and there was always a buying frenzy as everyone in the street rushed up to buy every colour of pop going. We'd buy about 10 bottles and get about five pence back for our empties. He sold so many flavours: dandelion and burdock, ice cream soda, cola and every kind of 'ade going; cherry, pineapple, lemon, orange.

They must've been full of so many E numbers the kids would glow for weeks and we'd have multicoloured piss. The 10 bottles would last about two days in our house. My sisters and I'd keep running into the front room and swig out of the bottle so we didn't get caught carrying it in a glass. After two days my mum would find all the empties on the floor and come into the living room and cry out in anguish, 'Who drank all the pop?' But we just sat there with orange and green rings around our mouths looking innocent.

We'd always stay up late on Christmas eve so we could go to midnight mass and then have Christmas day free and clear to open presents and the grown-ups could have a few good drinks. We'd have loads of visitors all over Christmas and had lots of aunts and uncles so we'd have loads of selection boxes.

We'd wake up at the crack of dawn and find a huge bag of presents at the foot of our beds. Mum and John would always do us proud and get us all a bumper crop of pressies. The air would be filled with flying Christmas wrapping paper and you could hear the screams of delight when one of us would shout out what present we had, 'Great, its an Action Man', 'Brilliant! A Cabbage Patch Kid', or 'For fucks sake, socks and underpants.'

I didn't realise at the time but mum had to borrow money to pay for all the presents and then spend the rest of the year paying off the debt. I wish I'd have known because I wouldn't have wanted her to struggle just for the sake of buying presents.

A few years later, after we'd grown up and mum and John got divorced, Christmas lost its magic. It just seemed to be a let-down every year for me with the family living in different areas and busy getting on with their own lives.

I have been very down in my life, especially a while after I left the police and was unemployed and almost homeless. No matter how bad things got, though, I never once contemplated suicide. I knew that things would turn around for me and there were people who loved me no matter what was happening in my life.

The hardest sudden death I ever dealt with was whilst I was working as a sergeant at Stechford. I could cope with adult deaths but babies were a completely different matter altogether. The devastation the parents feel and the sheer tragedy of the loss of the person the mother has been carrying inside her for nine months and the life that could have been made it all the more dreadful.

As a police officer there are certain procedures that have to take place during a cot death. The incident has to be investigated in case of foul play so the blankets from the cot and the clothes the baby was wearing must be seized. Trying to explain this to the parents without saying that they're suspected of anything is very hard. The main reason for all of this, though, is that it all helps experts determine the causes of sudden infant death syndrome (SIDS).

I was called to a cot death at Birmingham Heartlands Hospital one afternoon and was absolutely dreading it. I already felt like crying as I pulled my car up to the hospital. I could feel the emotion welling up in my stomach and out of my eyes as tears but I kept forcing them back down. I didn't want to break down in front of anyone, especially when I was in uniform and supposed to be dealing with the incident. One of the mums had delivered a healthy baby but he'd died a couple of days later at home while he was in his cot one night. This is actually fairly common, and the causes of an apparently healthy baby suddenly dying are still being researched.

I went to an annexe near the hospital reception. The mum must've been about 24 and was sitting there cuddling her baby who was wrapped in a white cotton blanket. The baby's dad had left her when he found out she was pregnant. I was so upset I could hardly speak. I just nodded to the mum who was holding her dead baby close to her. The baby was beautiful and looked like he was just sleeping. The nurse was absolutely fantastic. She was sitting next to the mum chatting away, asking her all about the baby such as when he was born and how much he weighed. She said that she had her mum's eyes and nose and really did look like her.

She asked the mum if she wanted her to take a photo of them together since she hadn't got any photos of him yet. I felt another massive surge of emotion come up from my stomach; I just wanted to burst out crying but by sheer willpower managed to keep the tears from streaming from my eyes. I did all the paperwork and left. There was nothing I could do or say. I couldn't find the words. That day I realised that nurses really are angels.

I can't remember much about what happened afterwards. The pain and emotion came out some way, I think. Maybe doing boxing and grappling helped or maybe I just punched out the next person who came up to me and poked me in the chest when I was out at a job.

Holding in emotions such as anger, pain, jealousy or hatred is like holding poison inside your body. At some point it's going to either come out or cause you severe damage when it manifests as a disease. The effort it took to suppress the sadness and tears was huge. If we hold these things inside us and don't let them out then they have to find another way to escape. If you really don't want them to come out then you've to do things to prevent the pain such as drink, smoke or take drugs. It took several years for me to work out how to let the tears out and to understand that it was OK to cry and show emotions.

Shortly after the cot death I dealt with one terrible incident which was called an accident, but I felt that it was manslaughter.

A mother was leaving her house in a hurry in Stechford and the dad was inside doing stuff in the kitchen. The mum put her baby into the car seat in the car but her 3-year-old daughter wanted to come as well. The girl was jumping up and down and crying because she wanted to come but wasn't allowed. She shouted to her to go back into the house but didn't check to see that she had. Her mobile phone had gone off and she started chatting to a friend.

She was in a rush so got into her car and began to reverse off the drive while chatting away. She ran over something on the drive and a huge, sick feeling came over her. She dropped the phone down into the footwell still turned on and jumped out of the car with the engine still running. She'd run over and killed her beautiful little daughter. The father ran outside to see what the fuss was all about. You could hear his scream for miles around.

The woman's husband left her and she shortly afterwards had a nervous breakdown, no doubt caused by the guilt of what had happened.

I still wince when I see people chatting on their mobile phones when they're driving. At that moment they're choosing to make that call more important than their passengers' safety – and your safety if you happen to be crossing the road or driving nearby.

What I found most disturbing of all was when children died at the hands of the people who were supposed to be protecting them. The worst attack I'd seen against a child took place when I was working in the cell block at Stechford as a custody sergeant. A young mum who lived in one of the blocks of flats in Shard End had gone out one evening to get some heroin from a dealer who lived in the next street.

She left her 2-year-old boy, Miles, with her boyfriend who was called Dan. Dan was 24 and a heroin addict. He was jobless and survived on his dole check and the proceeds of any petty thefts he committed. He'd been arrested by the police a number of times for theft and possession of drugs but never been to prison.

Dan was sitting watching the telly and enjoying the feeling of the heroin he'd just scored coursing through his veins. It was 9 p.m. and he was slumped half asleep in his chair half watching TV. It was then that Miles began to cry. Miles didn't have his own bed, he slept on the floor in his mum's room, and if he was lucky he got to sleep on the mattress. Miles had wet himself and was becoming very distressed.

Dan tried to ignore the noise but he became more and more irate as Miles got louder and louder. Eventually, he could stand it no more. Dan got out of his chair in a rage and stormed into the bedroom. Miles was standing there in the doorway crying and rubbing the snot off the end of his nose.

Dan lifted his foot back and kicked Miles so hard he flew across the room and hit the opposite wall. He slid down and was dead before he reached the floor. Dan had kicked him so hard that he'd broken six of Mile's ribs, ruptured his kidneys, torn his spleen out, and burst his stomach open. I suppose at least it was a quick death. Dan went back to the living room and sat in his chair watching the telly.

Maybe half an hour later for some reason he thought that it would be a good idea to call an ambulance. He casually picked up his mobile phone and dialled 999. When the ambulance crew got there, it was clear that Miles was dead and how it had happened.

Daz from Red Watch went to the scene along with Insp. Ross. Dan was arrested on suspicion of murder and brought to the cell block where I was working. Daz told me the circumstances of the arrest. We didn't know at that time that he'd kicked Miles but the ambulance crew had reported severe injuries to him and so we knew that Dan had done something bad enough to kill him.

As Daz told me what had happened in front of Dan, Dan just stood there showing no emotion at all. He looked completely nonchalant as he heard that Miles was dead. I knew that I had to ensure that everything was done by the book because if there was a mistake his barrister could ask for the case to be thrown out.

I asked Dan if he'd understood what was said. He just looked at me, smiled and asked, 'Do you have a spare fag, boss?' Personally, I'd have liked to have beaten him to death with my bare hands and watch his face as I shouted, 'This is how it felt for Miles, you bastard.' Instead, I got him his cup of tea and cigarette and had him checked by the police doctor who confirmed he was high on something.

The police were at the flat when Mile's mum came back. She didn't know what had happened. She had her heroin on her when the police officer told her that she was under arrest for the murder of her son. She screamed so loud that half the neighbourhood came out to see what was happening.

I booked her in as well and had her placed under constant watch to ensure she didn't try to top herself (commit suicide). As far as we could see, if she'd left her little boy in the custody of a drugged-up criminal, what did she think was going to happen?

Dan was charged with murder. He managed to get a good barrister. The barrister managed to get the case pleaded down to manslaughter, and also explained that it was Dan who was the victim here and that he didn't know what he was doing. Mile's life was worth six years in prison for Dan – who was out in three.

In a strange way it may've been a blessing for poor Miles. With a heroin addict for a mum who left him to sleep on the floor I wonder what sort of future was in store for him. It's possible to turn your life around even with the worst possible upbringing, but I could only see a life of crime and drug addiction for Miles as well.

❧ ❧

Heroin addicts tend to die horrible deaths. After years of injecting, their body eventually rots from the inside out and the organs begin to fail. The veins collapse from being continually injected into, which is called thrombosis. Most of the heroin addicts I encountered are HIV positive and look like they're half dead already.

After long-term heroin use the heart lining becomes affected and abscesses appear all over the body. The cells that protect the liver become damaged causing disease and the pulmonary system is affected which often leads to pneumonia. Often, the addict reaches the point of no return when it's a just a matter of time before they die.

I attended one sudden death in a block of flats in Kitts Green near Stechford police station. The two PCs who attended were Daz and Owen who had about three years' service. Owen was a great worker and was always making good arrests. He absolutely hated being around dead bodies, though. They freaked him out completely but I don't really blame him for feeling that way. When Owen was near a dead body he'd turn white and hug the walls so he could stand as far away as possible from the body. The problem is that you're supposed to check the body for signs of foul play, and you can't do that from the other side of the room.

The man who'd died had been a heroin addict for quite a few years. He lived in a flat belonging to his parents, and his 7-year-old son lived there with them. It was tragic to see this little boy being orphaned because his dad chose to kill himself slowly with heroin. Most people who don't like themselves much only smoke or drink a lot; heroin use is of course even worse for you.

It took a few weeks for him to die. I wasn't sure of the exact cause but whatever it was caused him to vomit blood all over the room. When I went in with Daz and Owen it looked like the walls of an abattoir. Blood was splattered all over the walls and his duvet was plastered with blood and chunks of lung. Not a nice way to die.

Owen was hugging the back wall like his life depended on it. I didn't want to touch the body either. It was slumped in the bed half hanging out and half in. I had to put my latex gloves on and get Daz and Owen to help push it back onto the bed. As we did so the body let out a loud 'Ughhhh'. Owen screamed and fell backwards onto the floor.

When you move a body the trapped air can escape and it can either move slightly or make a sound as if they're still alive. Owen didn't know this and he was completely freaked out. I know I shouldn't have, but I just laughed and told him to get a grip.

We couldn't see any knives sticking out of his back or anything else suspicious (apart from the blood on the walls) so we called the undertaker to take the body away. I went out and said how sorry I was to his 7-year-old son and the dead man's parents and left. The parents just sat there in shock. I'm sure that none of this made sense to them. The only thing that bothered me was looking at his son's face. I don't think he understood why his dad had died and why he was going to be brought up by his grandparents.

❧ ❧

Police officers do often get a bum deal when it comes to large-scale deaths or when people get hit by trains. I don't know exactly why, but apparently it's down to us to pick up body parts off the ground when it happens. I've never seen it written anywhere that it's the police that have to do it. They just seem to be expected to pick up plastic bags and get on with it without complaining.

There was an airplane crash outside Birmingham in the 1990s and all 100 people who were in the plane died. When a plane hits the ground, it's travelling so fast that the clothes are literally ripped off the bodies of all of the passengers so they're naked. They don't advertise this fact because it's so distressing to the families of the victims.

When the plane crashed, teams of emergency services formed a rendezvous point (RVP). The paramedics couldn't do much until the firefighters made the scene safe. It was down to the police over the next few days to locate the bodies. They were spread over about a mile and there wasn't even a single body intact. The OSU had to walk around in pairs and put arms, legs, heads and torsos into plastic bags and take them to a refrigerated lorry so the coroner could try to match them all together.

I watched a video of the officers being interviewed a few years later as part of my sergeants' course. They'd been given some counselling but they were still very traumatised. Some had nervous breakdowns, some had developed cancers, some had divorced, and some just somehow managed to keep it together and crack on with their jobs.

To be honest, if I'd been sent to the scene, given a plastic bag and told to start picking up heads and arms I'd probably have said, 'Fuck off, you can sack me if you like but I'm not picking up pieces of dead people.' I know somebody has to do it, but I don't see why it has to be the police.

The police sense of humour surrounding deaths was very odd indeed. I think that it's shared by ambulance crews, doctors, nurses and firefighters. It's the only way some people can cope with the trauma of seeing dead bodies and the constant reminder of our own mortality.

The police method of dealing with it is to turn it all into one big joke. One of the first sudden deaths I went to was of an elderly old man who'd died in his flat during the summer. He hadn't been seen for a few weeks and was sitting on the sofa decomposing. Bluebottles had got in through the window and laid eggs in the recess that had developed in the man's eye sockets and now maggots were crawling about in there.

It was thought by the sergeants that it'd be a good idea to send me there to see how I coped. If I fell apart at the seams then they'd all know that I was not cut out to be a police officer because there'd be plenty more like that.

When I got there the two police officers dealing with it were laughing and joking. One had a Polaroid camera with him and insisted on being photographed sitting on the sofa with his arm 'round the corpse like they were two mates sitting about having a laugh.

I could understand it, I suppose. I didn't really take it that far when I was at sudden deaths, but if somebody made light of it I'd laugh along. The only other alternative was to sit there looking solemn and cry about it later on.

Death was used as part of the initiation ceremonies in the police. You'd either attend a gory sudden death or some sort of practical joke was set up to test your mettle. One standard joke was to double-bluff the probationer. He'd be told that he was to play a trick on somebody else on the watch.

We were to hide them in the slide-in fridge where the dead bodies were kept in the mortuary, cover them with a white sheet like the other corpses and take another new joiner there to see a dead body. When the door was opened and the slab brought out, the probationer was to jump out and scare the shit out of the victim.

It was all a ruse to get them into the fridge, though. Once they were slid in, you couldn't get out again unless the door was opened from the outside. The lights were switched off and you were left in the fridge with the other dead bodies. After a few minutes an arm would come out from under the sheet next to you and grab yours and a voice would say, 'It's bloody cold in here isn't it, mate?' You could hear the screams a mile off. The entire watch by this point would be standing outside the fridge. Hopefully, the probationer would see the funny side.

Sometimes though, the joke would backfire. In Greater Manchester Police Force, the graveyard joke was played on two young-in-service officers, one male and one female. They were sent to a local graveyard to investigate reports of somebody acting suspiciously. One of the watch hid behind a gravestone dressed in a gorilla suit and the rest of the watch watched from a distance.

The two officers arrived on a cold and foggy morning at about 3 a.m. It was pitch black apart from the light from their torches. As they got to the gravestone the policeman in the gorilla outfit jumped out at them. The two officers screamed and ran away as the watch laughed.

The female officer ran to a nearby wall and jumped over it. There was a 10-foot drop the other side and she landed hard, breaking her ankle. The male officer kept running and wasn't seen for the rest of the watch. He was eventually found at home shaking in his uniform and wasn't able to go back to work for the rest of the set of nights because his nerves were shot.

The inspector was busted down to sergeant and the sergeants were pushing Pandas as PCs by the next week. The female officer was paid several thousand pounds out of court for her injuries and never went back to work. It was meant as something funny, but it went horribly wrong.

We had something similar on Red Watch but our practical joke was far more creative. One of the sergeants got a mannequin from a local clothes shop and then a load of pig intestines and liver from the local butchers. They dressed up the mannequin in clothes and a wig and hid it in some bushes next to the River Sherbourne where it flows right through the city centre. The probationer who was sent was from the graduate entry scheme and so the watch supervision wanted to have a go at him before he was promoted above them.

At about 4 a.m. the entire watch hid in various locations around the scene and we heard the job being called in and given to the probationer. He was told that somebody had reported seeing a dead body. It was an anonymous call but had to be checked out nonetheless.

The probationer's name was Jason but everybody called him Kermit because he had big bulging eyes and so looked like Kermit the frog from the Muppets. Kermit walked to the scene but was useless, he was walking around the wrong area, but then some bright spark called over the radio that maybe the dog man should attend to help with the search.

It was genius. Makk the police dog turned up with his handler and began to search around. Makk's handler called Kermit over when he found the body after a few minutes of pretending to sniff around the area. He was in on the joke as well but wanted to make the search look realistic. Kermit took one look at the offal and began to heave. He went a whiter shade of pale. The controller on the radio told him to take a pulse to make sure he was dead. Kermit picked up the arm but it came out of the socket. He yelped out loud and dropped the arm to the ground. By now he was close to fainting.

As Kermit was thinking that this couldn't get any worse, Makk came off the lead, and being a police dog was partial to a bit of pork. He grabbed a mouthful of pig intestine and ran away along the riverbank with it in his mouth closely pursued by Kermit who was screaming, 'Come back, Makk, that's evidence'. We all jumped out laughing at Kermit. For a few seconds he stood there and then the realisation dawned on him.

The watch inspector was there and laughing the hardest. 'You absolute wanker,' said Kermit, but closely followed with 'Sir' – which was lucky for him. The control room sergeant was in on it of course and he'd told the force control room in Birmingham who were all listening and laughing as well. Kermit saw the funny side and no harm was done. It was a well-planned joke executed with military precision.

A few weeks later Makk's handler had his dog taken away from him. He'd dropped in the shit three times and was thrown off the dog unit. The first mistake was when for some crazy reason he helped arrest a drunken prisoner and put him in the dog cage in the back of his van and began to drive him to the police station in it.

Each dog van had two dog cages in the back. Makk was in one foaming at the mouth trying to bite chunks out of the prisoner. It became too much for him to bear, so when the van stopped at some lights the prisoner kicked the window in the back of the van, smashing it, and crawled out. Unfortunately for him, one of the shards of glass cut his scrotum open and as he landed on the road he looked up and his left testicle was stuck on the end of one of the shards. Nasty.

After that, force orders were updated to say that prisoners were not allowed to be transported in dog vans. It was a bit obvious to me but not to Makk's handler.

Later that set of nights there was a shout that a burglary was in progress in an office block just out of town. We were all in briefing at the time which indicated that the offenders knew what the watch crossover times were and were taking advantage of that knowledge.

There'd been a spate of commercial burglaries in Coventry and Red Watch were eager to catch the culprits. We all sped to the scene as soon as we were told the silent alarm had been activated. That gave us 10 minutes to surround the office before the bells started to sound.

Red Watch raced to the scene and covered every exit so escape of the burglars who were still inside was not possible. The force control room dispatched the dog van which arrived a few minutes later. Makk's handler tore around the corner in his dog van and screeched to a halt next to us. He ran to the back of the dog van and pulled the rear doors open to let the dog out. He then stood there silently for a few seconds staring into the van in disbelief. One of us shouted over, 'What's wrong, Gary?' He looked over to us and cried out, 'I've left the fucking dog back at home.' The dozy bastard had come to work and forgotten his pissing dog!

A week after that Gary was seen to be beating Makk over and over again with a leather whip by a PC on Red Watch who was a dog lover. She complained and Gary was kicked off the unit. He later transferred to a nice rural force up north somewhere where he could have a quiet life.

Strange really, no matter how horrible the incident I dealt with, rapes, murders, child abuse, I'd always go home and sleep like a baby. I still lived at my mum's house when I first joined the police. She'd always want to know what had happened during the day. My answer was always the same, 'Not much, Mum.'

Happy Birthday to Me – 5 June 1980

I'm going to America with my grandma, who has some redundancy money so is taking my cousin Gaynor and me. Her friend Jackie is coming as well. I tell my friends at school and they're all excited for me.

We fly over in an aeroplane. I've never been in one before. I get a log book so I can record how many miles I've flown. Gaynor and I are taken to the cockpit by the air hostess. We meet the pilots and the navigator who show us how the aeroplane works.

We stay at the Saint Moritz hotel at Miami beach. It's very nice and has a diner on the ground flo

or where we have breakfast. There's a swimming pool at the back of the hotel but I'm afraid of the water. I want to dive in from the side but am too scared. One of the guests shows me how and then I'm no longer scared. I do it again and again.

Gaynor and I have sunburn, our backs are covered in blisters and we're both crying. My grandma makes us eat sandwiches with tangerine segments in. I hate them.

We go to Disneyland and meet Mickey Mouse, Donald Duck and all the Disney characters. I eat hot dogs and popcorn but I don't like it because it has salt on it. I throw it away.

When I get back home we have to move house to Ranby Road in Hillfields. I hate it there. I have to sleep on a camp bed in the same room as Cheryl, Gina and Louise. They're all sleeping on a double bed together.

Worst of all, I have to move schools again. I'm very sad. Gina and I walk to St Mary's School with my mum and Louise in a pram. I sit in Mrs Priest's office, who's the headmistress. I start to cry and so does Gina.

Our teacher is Mr Bruce, he gives you the slipper if you talk in line. Every Friday before we go home he makes us sing the Peanuts song.

THE PEANUT VENDOR (El Manisero)
Don Azpiazu

In Cuba, each merry maid
Wakes up with this serenade
Peanuts! They're nice and hot
Peanuts! I sell a lot
If you haven't got bananas, don't be blue
Peanuts in a little bag are calling you.

(English words by Marion Sunshine and L. Wolfe Gilbert,
music and Spanish words by Moises Simons)

Year 11 – Sometimes the Bad Guys Wear Blue

Working at Alum Road was a very bad experience for me. The standard of police officers there I felt was generally very poor indeed. There were a few good bobbies there who stood out but at best the standard was average. There were more than a few police officers who were lazy and incompetent, mostly due to the fact that they'd spent years avoiding work and now were so out of touch that they didn't understand what do to, and even worse, didn't want to.

I think what had happened over the years was that the constables had gathered that the inspector wasn't really watching them and whether they worked hard or not they wouldn't be recognised either way. It can be hard to stay continually self-motivated if you're not even getting a thank you.

Another problem was that the force had been reorganised into operational command units. This was a good system for the public, but it meant that you now had a mix of local beat teams and response teams. The response teams provided 24-hour support, attended incidents and were on patrol all the time.

The local beat teams usually worked office hours and had a much slower pace of work. They'd visit victims of crime, take statements and make the odd arrest, but not that many. Most probationers were not joining the response teams but were put on the local beat teams. Instead of being thrown in at the deep end and learning how to be a police officer and learn the necessary skills at an intensive pace, their learning was very much retarded by being put on the beat teams.

The standard of knowledge of probationers dropped dramatically the day the OCU system was implemented. I firmly believed that all new joiners should be posted to the response team for at least a year so they understand the basics of being a police officer. I know that the training departments will cry out that they have to learn this stuff anyway, but it just isn't the same when you're working office hours on a beat team. You're not at the sharp end at all.

The sergeants at Alum Road were nice enough chaps but weren't particularly keen either. One was close to retirement and didn't give a shit, the other was always off playing rugby for the police so coming to work was a major inconvenience to him. Mac was another sergeant working there, the one who'd saved my bacon when the man with the axe had come towards me. I rarely saw Mac because of the shift pattern. Al was working there, the only keen supervisor out of five sergeants and one inspector.

Any watch or group of working people need a strong leader and that was what was missing at Alum Road. It was not a particular person's fault because most people are doing the best they can. I do know that if Insp. Ross had been in charge it would be a very different place but the current boss was just far too laid-back.

Supervising sub-standard police officers is an exhausting task. Every job they go to has to be checked to make sure they took effective action and every court file and other piece of paperwork must be closely checked for omissions and errors.

Once you got the measure of a police officer you'd know if they did a thorough job or if they cut corners. At Alum Road there was a core of officers who cut corners, slacked off, and who in my opinion were not worth paying in washers. Examples of their conduct was coming in late to work continually, attending jobs where people had been assaulted but not taking statements or making arrests. They'd continually be taking time off sick with a bad back. If there was a shout on the radio they'd never call up to say they were going.

It was a never-ending task and as the months wore on I became more and more ground-down. I suppose I could've left them to their own devices, but as a supervisor their work ethic reflected badly on me. I could've joined in and become a lazy bastard myself, but that isn't in my nature. Coming to work felt like a massive chore. My fellow sergeants were all on different shift patterns and the sense of camaraderie was lost. I suppose that there's deadwood in any occupation but my only real work experience apart from some labouring and warehouse work had been in the police.

While all this was going on I'd decided to study for the inspectors' exams, but when I looked at the inspector's role it became less and less attractive. They spent the entire tour of duty rushing around doing reviews of prisoners' detention in the cell block and of crime figures for their station and watch.

I studied very hard for the inspectors' exams and did four hours study per day for four months. You've to know everything in the sergeants' syllabus plus another very large chunk of law and procedure.

To my delight I passed the written exam, but a few months later failed the practical exam. I was gutted again because I'd seen a list of those who passed. Some of them I knew would make good inspectors, but I knew some were a disgrace as a sergeant, so how could the system not spot that?

As I became more dejected I began to wonder if I still wanted to be in the police. Another 18 years as a sergeant – no thanks. I thought that I may be able to make inspector if I passed the next year, but even that may not have satisfied me for long. I could apply to be a detective sergeant but there were a few problems with that. Many of the detectives had been bollocked by me when I worked in the cell block because they were cutting corners.

I didn't really rate Stechford CID and also the selection process was extremely nepotistic. Most of the appointments in there were based upon word-of-mouth invitation; your position was guaranteed before you'd even applied. I personally witnessed many hushed conversations in stairwells where it was decided who'd get in and who wouldn't. Some people were even asked to apply who hadn't considered it. I felt sorry for those who applied thinking that they had a decent chance of being accepted.

My sanity was saved when there was yet another reorganisation. It was the third superintendent we had in Stechford in 10 months and he wanted to make his mark (as they all do). This was one advantage of being moved. If you didn't like where you were, you could guarantee that you'd be moved in about 12 months by the next superintendent. I was moved over to Bordesley Green police station.

I remember the feelings of joy when at the end of my late shift I took the serial van from Stechford and drove it to Alum Road police station. I dragged my locker out and packed it in the van and swore never to go back there again. Working there was one of the lowest times of my police career.

I knew the inspector who was going to be in charge at Bordesley Green, Insp. Ross who was my boss at Stechford. I was overjoyed. Insp. Ross had very high standards and was a consummate professional. I didn't always agree with his ideas and methods but I did so nine times out of 10, and I'd have rather worked with him any day than any other inspector in Stechford.

We had four units at Bordesley Green and one crime team which Insp. Ross ran. The crime team was supposed to be proactive in our area swearing out warrants and taking the persistent offenders out of circulation. In reality, there were three good blokes on the team and two idle gits who stayed in smoking fags and reading books whenever possible.

One of the good blokes was Jerry, a really pretty boy who always had the latest aftershave and hair products on. The crime team all wore plainclothes but Jerry had to wear all the name brand stuff which was a bit of a waste because if you got into a fight or foot chase it would always end up torn and dirty.

Jerry had actually left the police once. He had three years service in and for some daft reason decided to become a painter and decorator and work with his dad. On his last week in the police his inspector had asked him to go to a job, but since he was leaving Jerry felt that he didn't have to do anything he didn't want to. He said to the inspector, 'You can stick that job up your arse,' and went home.

Three months later he applied to the police for his job back. He realised that painting walls wasn't as glamorous as he thought it would be. He had to go back to his old inspector and apologise for his behaviour. Silly arse. Whenever I've left a team or job I've always done my best to do so on a good note. You never know if you'll have to go back there one day, and word gets around very quickly in the police.

During this latest reorganisation all the sergeants were working different shifts so I'd often be working on my own which I found very lonely. I was in charge of a team of seven constables who were luckily a great bunch. On the whole they were enthusiastic, hard-working and reliable.

Because I'd been bullied so much as a constable I did my best to treat everyone fairly and also let them take responsibility for how they did a lot of their work. I found so many sergeants and inspectors wanted to hover over you all the time and question your every move, which was stifling.

The best part of the reorganisation was that I was in charge of my own beat. Beat 70 covered Birmingham Heartlands Hospital which is one of the biggest hospitals in the UK. It was a fantastic place to cover. My team and I developed a strong working relationship with the hospital's security team and some of the senior consultants working there.

I have enormous admiration for anyone who works in a hospital, from the cleaners to the senior management. Every hospital is a hive of activity 24/7 with emergencies coming in, packed waiting rooms and a never-ending list of performance targets and service-level agreements which have to be met. The staff at Birmingham Heartlands were superb.

I also began to work closely with the head of the hospital's security, a man called David. He ran a team of security guards who had to work a 24-hour-shift pattern. Due to very low wages he struggled desperately to find good people. Half of his team were complete wasters and the other half were fantastic, very professional and dedicated.

I knew how he felt because at Alum Road I had to supervise several deadbeats and it was a constant nightmare. You'd always worry that the bad apples would end up infecting the entire cart.

I was answerable for the crimes which took place on my beat so I felt personally responsible for making sure crime was as low as possible. We got to know the active criminals who lived on the beat or came over to commit crimes. We also started to make contact with people in the community.

This was one of the great things about the reorganisation that the current chief constable Edward Crew had brought in. For the first time ever, teams of police officers were responsible for their own areas. They were answerable to the local community and had to take into consideration the needs and concerns of those people who lived on their beat.

At that time I was still considering promotion and wanted to improve my police CV and find out more about how the force was run. I volunteered to join one of the force's operational committees. It was a committee to decide on police equipment and uniform and I felt that I could make a contribution to that. They met once a month.

It turned out to be a bit of a disappointment. There were about 20 members but only two of us were operational police officers. The rest were admin people, health and safety and senior management. The other police officer was a traffic PC on the motorcycle branch and all he wanted to do was get special kit for traffic officers. He'd ask for baseball caps to be made so that they could wear something on their heads when they were inspecting under lorries. The next month he was asking for special pouches for motorcycle officers (of which he was one) so they could carry their Casco baton on the side of their boots.

When they had to make a decision about a piece of equipment they'd turn around and have to ask me because most of them didn't understand what we did or how we did it. They'd often buy things that were inappropriate for us because we couldn't get in or out of the car wearing it. Until you've actually used the piece of equipment as part of your daily routine of getting in and out of cars, running and walking about for nine hours you don't know if it's going to be suitable.

For the committee to come to any decision would take months or even years. They'd been discussing stab-resistant vests and that item had been on the agenda for many years. They couldn't decide how much the vest needed to be stab-proof and how much bulletproof. You could have one or the other or a compromise which was a bit of both, but had to have less protection than one purely designed exclusively either for bullets or for knives.

It was pretty easy as far as I was concerned: look at how many of us were stabbed and how many were shot. I think we were more likely to be stabbed than shot so go with that, but it took years for a decision to be made. We were even taken to a large room to try the vests on but I was pulling my hair out. All the people trying the vests on were either senior police officers, health and safety or civilians. You needed to get the officers on the street to wear them when they also had all their belt kit and radio so you could see if it was easy to wear and easy to get in and out of cars with it on.

Due to the reorganisation we didn't see much of the inspector, which suited me fine. I was being paid a lot of money as a sergeant and it was great to be able to have more responsibility than ever before in my career. The difficult part for me was the loneliness. There were other sergeants working the same shift pattern as me but they were spaced out in five other stations. They rarely seemed to be out on patrol and there was only one of us ever designated as duty sergeant.

I did my best to establish relationships with them by driving over to their stations regularly, but when I did they just seemed wrapped up in their own workload and issues, which I can understand. I really did miss being out on patrol with Al and Mike and having someone to talk to as I worked.

The duty sergeant was basically responsible for supervising any incidents that happened out on the street so you'd spend a lot of time out in your car. The sorts of things you'd attend were anything serious such as robberies, missing children, serious assaults, armed robberies, sudden deaths and the like. I also always made a point of going to the cell block and helping the custody sergeant out if he was busy or needed a break.

The reorganisation meant that there was now a full-time staff of sergeants working at the cell block. It was a mix of those who wanted to stay off the street, and that was just about the only place to hide. The other half had upset the superintendent somehow and were sent down there for three years as a punishment.

One of the sergeants at Bordesley Green had been on duty when the superintendent paid a rare visit. Unfortunately, at the time most of the PCs were in the station and the superintendent was very annoyed because he felt that they should've been out on patrol. The next week he was pulled off the station and made to work in the cells for two years.

I always thought it strange that it was considered a punishment to work down there and how it made those that volunteered to do it feel. Either way, I knew what it was like to work in that hell-hole, and I was down there most days helping out and covering for anybody who wanted a break. I also had other reasons for going down there so often.

It was a lonely position working on your own beat. You couldn't get over-friendly with the PCs because you were their supervisor, at the end of the day. The other reason is that I wanted to keep my cell block skills sharp. You never knew when you were going to be working down there again either as punishment or cover. Some of the sergeants avoided it like the plague and I thought that they'd come unstuck if they ever found themselves down there again.

Out of all the jobs where you can fall foul of the police discipline code, the role where it's most likely to happen is that of custody sergeant. You can have a massive queue of angry and violent prisoners waiting to be booked in. Tired police officers, appropriate adults for juveniles, duty solicitors all waiting their turn to speak to you. You also have cells full of prisoners who need visiting and feeding, and detectives and constables who want to book their prisoners out for interviews or for fingerprinting and charging.

The rules and regulations surrounding each of those activities are stringent. If you break one, the only thing that's considered is your actions. You can't complain two months later in a discipline hearing or during a court trial that you were busy and had worked 12 hours without a break where nobody can see what it was like for you that day. As far as they can see, that one prisoner was the only person you had to deal with, they don't get to hear about the 20 other prisoners you had including the three fights and the one who gobbed in your face or the fact you dealt with five lawyers, three Bosnian interpreters, two dyslexic gippos and one prisoner on suicide watch.

There's also a huge amount of pressure brought to bear on the custody sergeant from other areas. It used to infuriate me when a PC would walk into the cell block and tell me that the inspector had decided that their prisoner was to be charged with this or that offence. It was like I was some sort of receptionist and was supposed to just nod and agree. The Police and Criminal Evidence Act is very clear on the fact that the custody sergeant decides if there's sufficient evidence to charge, *not* the inspector.

If there's any pressure brought to bear on the custody sergeant then the duty superintendent is supposed to be called to resolve the matter. In reality, the custody sergeant did often agree with the inspector's wishes, but sometimes they didn't. It was then down to the moral fibre of the custody sergeant whether or not he or she wanted to argue with the inspector.

Once when I was working in the cell block on a set of nights we had a prisoner come in who complained that he'd been assaulted by the arresting officer. The standard procedure is to log the complaint and call the police doctor who examines the prisoner for injuries and then the police officer.

There's no sweeping it under the carpet, because they'll only complain to their solicitor when they arrive or to the duty inspector at review time. This particular prisoner was a juvenile, which is a real pain because you're supposed to have an appropriate adult present when the doctor is there.

I went through all the procedures and called the watch inspector on nights. He turned up and listened to the story and then just left the cell block without speaking to the prisoner at all. I was shocked because he should've paid him a visit and at least explained that he could make an official complaint after he was charged (the usual procedure).

When the inspector left the cell block I was left in a situation. If there was any neglect, it would be me who was in trouble as the custody sergeant because the prisoners were my responsibility. I had to note that the duty inspector had been informed and attended the cell block. I left the entry as vague as possible, but it still had to go in.

Just before the end of the watch the duty inspector came back and read the custody sheet. 'You've stitched me!' he exclaimed. A 'stitch' means getting somebody else to take the fall or dropping them in the shit.

'I don't know what you mean, Sir,' I said, defending myself. 'I just put that you came and was informed about the allegation.' What was he expecting me to do exactly? He was not impressed and he did what he should've done in the first place. He went and spoke to the prisoner and explained the complaints procedure to him.

About an hour later the inspector phoned me in the block and told me that I wouldn't be working in there anymore. I asked if I'd made a mistake or if there was any reason for this, but he said that there wasn't. I was actually kicked out of the cell block, which as far as I know is the first time that had ever happened. If I'd known it was that easy, I'd have done it months before!

⊷ ⊶

During my time in the force I'd come across plenty of constables who I felt really didn't contribute anything at all. They didn't want to be in the job, did as little work as possible and were often off sick. They just talked constantly about how much they hated the job and that they were just staying in for the pension.

There were also a few who really let themselves and the police force down by committing crimes. You'd have thought that being police officers they'd know how to avoid detection, but in my experience police officers make the worst criminals going, they're just so bad at being bad.

One of the first unofficial lectures I received during my training was from the training PC in Coventry. He stood in front of all eight new recruits and told us about the quickest ways to get into trouble as a police officer. It was the three Ps apparently, which meant nothing to us. The three Ps stood for property, paperwork and PNC. PNC is the police national computer. Somebody at the back of the room shouted out, 'You missed the fourth P out mate, policewomen,' and we all laughed out loud.

It all came to pass, though. I lost count how many bobbies got into discipline trouble or sacked due to the above four Ps. I even got into a bit of trouble for my paperwork once.

I'll share a few stories with you now about some of the constables who did get into trouble and were eventually sacked or asked to leave.

I've called them the bad guys, but that's just a label I suppose. They were good guys who helped a lot of people like you during their service. Just at some point and for some reason they did a bad thing, got caught and paid the consequences.

During 12 years I can say I genuinely met about three bad cops. I mean by that corrupt cops who'd take bribes or commit crimes. Three out of thousands. I just want you to know how rare it actually is. It's standard practice for the media to ignore the good because it doesn't fit their profile of a story, and then sensationalise the odd one who does something bad.

Let's start with PNC. The police national computer is a massive nationwide database containing details of every person charged with a crime or who is currently wanted by the police. As a police officer you can request a check be made against a person to see if they're wanted or what their previous offences are.

If they're wanted for an offence you can arrest them, and if you know they have previous convictions (referred to as 'form') for a particular offence you've more information at your disposal. Technically, you cannot use their form as a reason to stop and search them, but of course that's the best reason to stop and search them before they come to steal your car or screw your home.

The PNC also contains the registered user of every vehicle in the UK. When a police officer stops a car they do a PNC check to see who the registered user is and then they ask the driver for their name and address. If the two don't match then they have grounds to ask you more questions about why you're driving it and if you're insured.

I didn't understand how a person could get into trouble for using the PNC until about two years into my service. I was at home when a relative of mine called. He said he was about to buy a car and wanted to know if it had ever been in a serious accident or written off. This information is held in the PNC. He didn't want to spend a few grand only to find out that it was a death trap. I knew that it was a bit dodgy to do this sort of check. We'd never been asked to sign any documentation or had the rules for using the PNC explained to us, but it didn't feel right to do a check so I politely declined.

A guy on my watch was not so shrewd. His uncle had driven into town and had an argument with another driver over a car parking space. The other driver gave him a mouthful and drove off to find another space. The PC's uncle was not happy about this and called his nephew and asked him for the name and address of the driver. Very stupidly, he agreed and the other driver was more than a bit shocked to receive a visit a few hours later from the guy he'd shouted at in the car park plus a few of his mates.

Luckily for him they just gave him some polite advice and drove away very happy with themselves for some reason. The other driver became very angry. It didn't take a detective to work out that these guys had somebody on the inside who'd got his address from the DVLA computer somehow.

He went into the police station to complain and a check was made to see who'd requested his details off the PNC. The PC was interviewed and admitted doing the check and giving the details to his uncle. He was disciplined for that and it was a black mark he carried on his record for the rest of his career.

Police officers' disciplinary records and any convictions have to be disclosed at court and the defending barrister or solicitor can use them to bring your integrity into question, which isn't good. You can also forget promotions or postings to traffic or the CID if you have a discipline record.

Paperwork is another area where it's very easy to get into trouble. I've seen so many constables get in trouble for late or missing paperwork, and then their sergeants for failing to supervise them properly.

You'd fall over if you saw how much paperwork is involved in just one simple arrest. Endless statements, crime files, court files, disclosure and non-disclosure items, evidence trails and so on. The list is endless. It's enough to put you off arresting a person at the very thought of spending the next five hours doing court files.

There are forms to fill in when you stop vehicles, search people, find property, drive your police car, use your baton or CS spray and any incidents you see or deal with. You even need to fill in a form when you have a shit (OK, maybe not that).

Even when you interview a prisoner and charge them you've to listen to the entire tape and either write out or type out a summary of the main points of the whole interview. If your interview took one hour it can take another six to listen to the tape and then write out the most relevant points. What a nightmare.

All paperwork and court files have deadlines and if you miss them you can be disciplined. A lot of the deadlines are there to make life easy for the admin people, so you'd have a small army of police officers sitting in the station doing paperwork when they wanted to be out on the streets catching bad people. It's madness.

To my knowledge, nothing has been done to alleviate the burden of paperwork for police officers. It's the sort of job where you're continually dumped upon and expected to just get on with it without complaining. The same goes for nurses and teachers. If you don't toe the line then you'll be disciplined, and if you speak out you get a black mark against you and you can forget promotion or attachments to squads.

When a crime is reported, a crime form has to be completed. This is for everything from a petty theft to a murder. The crime file is carbonated and the copies go off to various departments including statistics and the Home Office. When I was working at Little Park Street police station one of the chief inspectors in the admin department decided that all crime reports had to be faxed to his department within 45 minutes of being taken. So in effect if you took four or five crime reports in a tour of duty (which isn't uncommon), you'd have to rush back to the police station five times and stand in a queue for the fax machine so he'd have his copy.

Nobody questioned this madness. Some administrator decided that he wanted his copy in 45 minutes so uniformed officers are coming off the streets in droves to make his life easy. It used to get me down, especially when the sergeants were screaming at us to get the crime reports faxed in good time. I think I must've been one of the few people to question the sanity of some of the things that took place in the police. Worse still, you could be put on a charge if you didn't get back to the station in time to send the fax.

It was rarely the doing of the job of a police officer that would get me down. It was the petty rules and procedures whose only purpose seemed to me to be to make our job difficult and protracted. It was also the small army of ranking officers who wanted to catch you out and make an example of you.

One inspector at Little Park Street used to go to the police car park when his watch were out and check their private vehicles for worn tyres or cracked lenses. If he found anything wrong, he'd report them. He was universally hated (no surprise there). His name was Insp. Dean but he was referred to as 'Dogshit Dean' because nobody wanted to go near him.

There were some strange inspectors. Just because they had two pips on their shoulders didn't mean they had any interpersonal or management skills whatsoever. Green Watch had a newly-promoted inspector start with them. On the first briefing he introduced himself to the watch and said he was looking forward to working with them all. He then started to shout at all 20 of them, banged his fist on the table and screamed, 'But by God, if any of you cross me you'll regret the day you were born.' What a knobber. What on earth was he hoping to accomplish by saying something like that?

Another inspector would criticise his sergeants at every opportunity. His name was Merlin Pluto, so his parents must've been born with a sense of humour. I once asked one of his sergeants' team why he was called Pluto and he just replied, 'Because he's out in space.'

Merlin had a really annoying habit of using the phrase 'Blah, blah,

blah' when he was trying to explain something as if what he was saying was obvious to you. He'd say something like, 'They arrested him and took him to the cell block and blah, blah, blah.' I thought, 'And what? Was he charged, bailed, tickled or had his face painted in the cell? What the hell does "blah, blah, blah" mean?' Prat.

When his sergeants would submit paperwork to the superintendent, Insp. Pluto would put derogatory comments on it saying that the sergeant didn't know what he was talking about. He'd then pass it to the superintendent with the silly comments on. The job is hard enough without your colleagues having a go at you as well.

❧ ❧

I told you that I got into a great deal of debt when I was in the police. I was still paying it off as a sergeant. A police officer in debt is far more likely to do something wrong such as take a bribe. That's why government agencies such as MI5 will do a credit check on you when you apply to work for them. They don't want people who're susceptible to taking backhinders for some sensitive information.

We had a crime team at Little Park Street which targeted the serious criminals who lived in Coventry. The crime team had hired cars they changed every couple of weeks and were not makes that the police usually used. They'd use these cars to tail the active criminals. The team used surveillance-trained officers who were adept at following on foot or car and not being spotted. The trouble was that every time they changed their car, about a day later the villain they were covertly following would do U-turns in the road and wave at them as he drove past.

The crime team were baffled until a local druggie was arrested. He spoke to a detective that he informed for and told him something shocking. He'd heard that the team of villains had a police officer on the payroll and that this person was checking the backyard of the police station every day and passing the registrations to them.

There's something truly terrible about a police officer doing this sort of thing. They swear an oath to uphold justice and are given a huge amount of trust by the public. Betraying this trust is not only betraying this oath but also stabbing your colleagues in the back because we all get tarred with the same brush. It also puts officers in danger because their cover is blown and they don't even know it.

The observations team were now doing obs on the backyard of the police station instead of their targets. After a couple of days they saw a young WPC called Kirsty walking around the part of the yard which contained the crime unit's cars. She was writing down their registration marks – which could only be for one reason.

Kirsty was not the brightest of people. Everybody on the watch knew that she was in a lot of debt due to loans and credit cards. She made no secret of it for some reason. People should've got a bit suspicious when she started to book holidays abroad to exotic locations and then came into work driving a brand-new four-by-four. Silly cow.

She was questioned by the detective superintendent and folded under the pressure. She'd been approached by this villain who offered her large sums of cash to give her details of crime unit operations and car registrations.

Her locker and home were searched and copies of crime reports and court files were also found. She'd been copying these and giving the copies to the local villain, so he knew exactly as much as the police knew. She also had details of who'd given statements against him and where they lived. The repercussions could've been terrible.

For some reason, Kirsty was allowed the dignity of being permitted to resign rather than be sacked. I don't know why she was never prosecuted for any crimes. Perhaps she had some valuable information to swap in return for immunity.

Property was another hot potato. A police officer is constantly dealing with crime property taken from searches of people, vehicles or houses. Seized property can include money, high-value electrical goods or large quantities of drugs. If there's enough there and the opportunity arises it'd probably be easy enough to take some for yourself.

The two things that can stop you are, first, your morals around stealing, and second, what'll happen if you're caught. Police officers almost always go to prison for theft or other such offences. Things that Joe Average will get a caution for or perhaps a conditional discharge at magistrates' court a police officer will go to Crown Court for and get a prison sentence. I was always very methodical when I dealt with property. Making a note in my pocket notebook and ensuring that it was booked into the property computer and put in the safe or secure property room.

We often come into possession of forged notes in the police and have to fill in forged currency paperwork and book the note into crime property. I'd seized a forged 20-pound note once whilst out on foot patrol in town and put it into my pocket notebook to book into crime property when I got back to the station. I got very busy during that watch and by the end, I'd been to several incidents and completely forgotten about the note.

When I went down to the locker room in the basement to change I went to put my notebook in there and saw the forged note sticking out. I almost had a heart attack. I was off duty and could've left it in there until the next day and booked it in then, but you just never know. The bank could've phoned to get a reference number, and if the note wasn't in the safe at the station then it'd look like I'd stolen it. Even if it was found in my locker it'd still look as if something fishy was going on. Give a dog a bad name and all that. I went back to the front office and booked the note in. I knew I'd sleep well knowing that it was tucked away safely in the front office safe.

Property can get you into trouble either for not following procedures, or for stealing it. There was a smashing PC who used to work in the local beat team at Little Park Street. Toby was about 24 and very popular at the station, was respected in the city centre where he worked and well-known by many shop owners.

Toby was a single dad bringing up his 5-year-old son. I think his wife had left them both but I never asked for the story. He'd slid into a lot of debt and if he was anything like me, was wondering how the hell he was going to manage to crawl out of the hole he'd got himself into. The answer came when he arrested a prisoner for shoplifting and took him to the cell block. When he searched the prisoner's bag there was over 15,000 pounds in there, a shocking amount of cash.

News went all around the station, of course, because this amount of money was very much out of the ordinary. If it was me, I'd have called a supervisor or colleague and asked him to accompany me to book it into the safe so I had a witness. Just common sense to me, but it wasn't written anywhere that you had to have a witness. Maybe it should be.

Toby booked the cash into the crime property register because it was more than likely the proceeds of theft. When the safe was checked the cash wasn't there. All eyes pointed to Toby who was the last person to see it. Toby of course said that he'd put it into the safe. The safe keys are usually held by the person on duty in the front office, who didn't recall Toby asking for the safe keys that day.

A check of Toby's bank account showed a 15,000-pound deposit the next day. What a complete and total idiot. How could he think that he was going to get away with that? The problem was that he obviously didn't think, did he? He was so worried about the money he owed that when the money was in front of him he just took it.

Toby was charged with theft. He went to Crown Court and was sentenced to prison for 18 months. His little boy was without his dad for all that time, but luckily for Toby his own father was able to look after him or he'd have gone into foster care.

I saw Toby about two years later coming out of the probation office. He saw me and looked down at the ground and walked away. One stupid mistake had cost him his career and his freedom and 18 months of his son's life without his dad. Who'd want to employ a former police officer who'd served time for theft?

I've heard that prison is a terrible place for a former police officer to be in. You have to stay in the nonce wing for your own safety because if the inmates get to you, you're a dead man. The prison warders hate you as well because of what you've done. What a nightmare.

Mind you, I did steal something myself while I was a police officer. I was off duty one afternoon, had just finished a guitar lesson at my tutor's house in Cheylesmore in Coventry and was getting into my car. It was a terribly windy day, so bad in fact that a tree had blown over on the A45 and landed on a car killing the driver and his wife.

I slammed my car door shut, glad to be out of the wind and in the perceived safety of my Saab 900. I started the engine and looked up the road to make sure it was safe to pull out into the street. Just then I spotted a cat walking on the opposite side of the road. It caught my attention because it was struggling to walk up the road having to fight against the gale force winds. The poor little bugger was fighting for every step, but even worse was its coat. Somebody had shaved half of its coat off in various places so there were just tufts of hair sticking out and the rest of it was shaved to the skin.

I sat in the car and watched it struggle to walk up the road for a few minutes. I was hoping that it had an owner who'd come out of his house and carry it into the warmth, but it seemed to me to be a stray. How else could I account for it looking in such bad shape?

I'm not an animal lover at all but don't like to see animals suffer either. I turned my car around and drove up next to the cat and picked up the poor little bugger and looked into its eyes. They were full of mucous so it must've had very bad conjunctivitis. Poor sod. I carried it into my car and put it on the passenger's seat, took it home and gave it a tin of tuna which it devoured. I thought I'd keep it for a day and then take it to the vet's who'd treat its eyes and then get it a good home.

I was on late shift that day at Little Park Street so I left the cat at home in the warmth and went to work. On parade, the sergeant read out briefing and added an entry at the end. He said, 'Can you all be on the lookout for a Blue Saab partial reg. H 754? The driver of this car stole a cat today from Cheylesmore Road. He just grabbed it from outside the owner's house and drove away with it in his car. The owner ran up the road after the car but only got a partial registration.'

I sat there and gulped hard. That was the first half of my car registration. I'd nicked some poor old dear's cat. Pissing hell. I pretended to write down the registration and the next morning I handed it into a local vet's along with the owner's details. I said I'd spotted it from a photograph on a lamp post. I didn't think I'd have got into any trouble for taking it because I thought it was a stray, but I don't think I'd ever have lived down the humiliation.

The last way to get into trouble is with policewomen. I always thought that was a bit of a strange one. How could going out with a policewoman lead to a discipline charge or worse?

One thing I didn't like about being in the police is people getting to know about your private life. If you were living with or going out with another police officer then the things that happened between you would always seem to be known by everybody else. For this reason I never did date a policewoman. I wanted my life outside the police to be separate from inside.

Everybody seemed to know everybody else's business on the watch. Who was sleeping with whom, who was having an affair and even how much the divorced dads were paying to the CSA. If any female officers joined the watch the lads would ask, 'What's her form?' meaning who'd ridden her.

One WPC had been dating a guy on the watch for a few weeks. They both went out and got drunk one night and he talked her into having anal sex. He told his mate in confidence the next day while they were out in the car. He of course just told a couple of his mates 'in confidence' and before he knew it the entire station had heard the story.

Every time the poor girl went on the radio to call a job in or check a car somebody would squawk out on the air in a high-pitched voice, 'Me arse is in tatters, Sarge.' This went on for several months until she eventually left to work in another city. I'm sure her new watch knew about it before she even got there.

We'd often read a document called force orders or 'pinks' which came 'round the stations every two weeks. It contains details of who's moving to other teams, who's being promoted or demoted, and which vacancies are open to be applied for. If somebody was leaving on promotion we'd often get a phone call from the PCs at the station they were going to. The person would want to know if their new sergeant was OK or not. It was a sort of early warning system. We'd sit there on the phone giving a summary of our opinion of the person.

One of the guys I was in the police cadets with was George. He was a great laugh and was the life and soul of the party. It was a joy to have him on any course you were on because he'd be telling jokes and making everybody laugh and just being around him was fun. Something very strange happened to George when he had a drink, though. He was like Dr Jekyll and Mr Hyde. Something in his mind would flip and he'd become a wholly different person who was not so funny.

When we were in the police cadets one day he came in with his hand stitched together. He'd been out drinking over the weekend in Coventry city centre and as he walked past a shop with his mates, for no reason he punched his hand through the glass. He nearly severed an artery.

George's mates were very dodgy indeed. I met them a couple of times and they looked like druggies to me. I avoided them like the plague. I often wondered why he seemed to be one person at work and then a completely different person when he had a few drinks inside him.

When we were at police training centre at Bruche, George would go out on the Sunday evening. We had to have written permission to leave the training centre during the week at that time so Sunday was the only free night. I didn't go out with George after work because he was a loose cannon. He went out one Sunday night whilst at Bruche and saw an ambulance parked outside a house with the engine running. He was pissed as a fart and got inside and drove it away. He abandoned it a few streets away from the training centre and walked the rest of the way in.

Another Sunday evening he found a police traffic car outside a house with the keys in and engine running. He got into that and put the siren and horns on and drove it for about a mile before crashing into a wall and running away. Like I said, the guy was crazy. He'd be sitting in class the next day hung over and playing at being a police officer.

George came unstuck about three years later. He was living with a really nice girl whom I'd met once. Rose was from a well-to-do family, and I've no idea what she was doing roughing it with George.

One night the serial van was parked outside the Pink Parrot watching the drunken crowd spill out onto the street. George emerged with Rose and was recognised by a few people on the van. George must've been too drunk to see them because he turned to Rose and began to shout at her. A few seconds later he punched her hard in the face causing her to fall over to the ground crying. The police officers were shocked and ran out and rightly arrested George for assault.

When Rose was interviewed the next day it all came pouring out. George had been hitting her for quite some time. When he got up for early shift at 5 a.m. he'd wake poor Rose up and put a dog collar on her neck and make her sit in the dog basket while he got ready for work.

You could ask why the hell she agreed to do it, but maybe she was scared of what would happen if she didn't. Either way, George was charged with actual bodily harm and went to Crown Court. He was given a suspended sentence and sacked from the police. I never saw or heard from George again.

Dodgy behaviour happened at almost every rank, though. Superintendents have been disciplined and sacked as well as junior ranks. Even command team ranks' services have been dispensed with in the past.

We had a detective superintendent working at a station in Birmingham for a few months. There'd been a change in police procedures for the CID so that now senior officers with no CID experience were allowed to run the departments. It was of course a disaster. They were expected to run investigations of serious incidents and murder but had never done so as a detective constable or sergeant.

The training school had put together a course for them to learn some stuff but it was just woefully inadequate and a very bad idea. The detectives had to report to somebody who really didn't know what they were doing and who was bluffing away the best they could.

The detective superintendent in Birmingham took it upon himself to monitor everyone in the CID to make sure that everything was being done right. He'd check the time book to make sure everybody had booked in and out at the right times and checked every overtime claim. He was becoming a royal pain in the arse.

After a few months somebody found out that he'd been putting in dodgy overtime claims himself for quite some time. He was claiming double time for working days off when on those days he was supposed to be at work anyway. I don't know how he was found out but he'd basically taken over five grand worth of overtime that he wasn't entitled to.

In fact, that probably answers my question. If a person gets that greedy with the expenses then they're going to bring some attention to themselves. He was thrown out of the CID and busted down to inspector for his troubles. He should've been done in for theft as far as I was concerned.

We did have a running phrase in the CID, 'The time book never lies.' The time book was used to book on and off duty and it formed the basis of your overtime. There was a certain amount of flexibility so that some people were booked on duty by their mates before they'd actually appeared at work and some were signed off work a few hours after they'd actually left.

If any senior officers used to question the amount of overtime we put in we'd just look at them in disgust and say, 'The time book never lies, boss.'

~ ~

A few years into my service the police service came under the scrutiny of the Home Office. They began to measure us and release performance figures. This is fine of course, but the things they were measuring were a bit odd.

The first performance target was how long it took us to arrive at an incident. Chief constables had to answer to the Home Office about incident response times. Now we were expected to drive like bats out of hell to get to jobs so we could meet service-level agreements or SLAs. All the management jargon was new to us. Of course, nobody directly asked us to speed or to take risks but there are many ways of exerting overt pressure on people. The radio controllers became obsessed about our telling them the second we arrived at jobs.

The craziness was beyond me. Nobody seemed to care about what you did when you got there, just that you got there quickly. The fast-response drivers would be sent along with a Panda car. The fast-response car would arrive and give a TA (time of arrival) but sit outside parked there doing nothing and drive away when the Panda arrived.

One by-product of all of this was the walkers on patrol were pulled back into cars so that there were more Pandas available to meet the response times. No more foot patrols, I'm afraid. If the police area missed targets the Home Office kicked the chief constable's butt. He kicked the superintendents' who kicked the inspectors' who kicked the sergeants' who kicked ours.

The performance figures didn't matter whether you lived in the middle of the countryside or in a city. So for a fight for example, you had four minutes to get there even if you drove a diesel Panda and it was 10 miles across the countryside. It wasn't the figures that troubled me but the fact that everyone busted a gut to achieve them without question.

The next thing that was measured was detections. Of course, I do agree that the police should be accountable, but it's what we were measured for and how the figures were manipulated that seemed to me to be insane. Now we were no longer allowed to caution shoplifters at the scene. If an 11-year-old took a penny chew from the local corner shop we couldn't take her home to be punished by her parents. She had to be arrested, interviewed, cautioned and fingerprinted which is basically at least five hours worth of work. Crime detections went up by over 200 per cent which was great, but crime also doubled overnight because petty offences were now all being put on crime reports. Everybody on the watch became confused as to what we were doing. We were no longer allowed to use our discretion at incidents.

It was also decided that violent crime was too high so we had to do something to bring down the numbers of violent incidents. How can you do that? Most are committed by drunken people and how can you stop violent people getting drunk? It was then that what I consider to be one of the biggest betrayals to the public took place. There's a crime known as actual bodily harm or ABH. This is when a person assaults you or injures you in some way and it acts as a deterrent to stop violent people taking their anger out on you.

It was decided by the Home Office that the definition of ABH would change. Now you had to have a serious injury or cut to qualify. What this means to you is that if I feel like it I can walk up to you and punch you hard in the face or ribs so long as I don't break the skin. I can cause as much bruising as I like and there's not a damn thing the police will do about it.

One day we were filling in crime reports, taking statements and arresting offenders for ABH, the next we were advising people that there was nothing we could do and that they should consider suing the offender. Members of the public would sit there in disbelief as we told them this and then left their house. The offence of ABH was now considered common assault and not down to the police to deal with so you wouldn't be arrested. So if you feel really angry why not punch a politician and then tell them that you're not happy?

I merely give you all these examples to highlight the fact that figures can be made to show almost anything you like, and while police forces are becoming more obsessed about producing favourable figures the real job of policing is being seriously neglected. The police forces release figures and statistics to the public in their yearly report. I personally have never read the yearly report and don't know anyone who has. The report is almost meaningless anyway because figures are fudged and are not a true reflection of what's happening.

If you believe what you read in the police reports you want your head examined. Statistics can be made to prove anything and it was Benjamin Disraeli who said, 'There are three lies. Lies, damn lies, and statistics.' I have a feeling that all statisticians employed by the police and Home Office have to read the book *Damn Lies and Statistics* by Joel Best and *How to Lie with Statistics* by Darrell Huff.

The police are here to first and foremost prevent crime and public disorder. Speeding to low-priority jobs and fobbing victims of crime off for the sake of figures is not what Robert Peel had in mind when he formed the first police force in the 1800s. Peel set out the principles which the first police service were to stand by. The first one was: 'The basic mission for which the police exist is to prevent crime and disorder.' He never mentioned anything about getting there fast and doing nothing constructive when you arrive.

Politicians and senior police officers can speak all the waffle and jargon they like. The bottom line is that you want your property and your family to be safe when at home or when you go out somewhere. In countries like Italy entire families go into the town centre for a meal and a bit of shopping in the evenings and there's no fear that they're going to be attacked by drunken yobs. Looking at figures to tell you that your local station has hit targets set by some random Home Office person who lives in London somewhere probably holds no interest whatsoever for you (I'm guessing).

My point is that police corruption takes on many forms. The numbers of 'bad' police officers are tiny and as soon as they're found out they're arrested or sacked. The tens of thousands of heroes never get a mention for the amazing things they do, it's just expected of them day in and day out. Of far more pressing concern is how the wool is being pulled over your eyes without you even realising it (until now, that is). It's a shame when so much effort is put into producing friendly figures for a public who probably don't even read them. All for the sake of winning votes.

◈ ◈

Every police force is run by a group of senior officers and a couple of civilians who're in charge of finance and admin. They're all chief constable, deputy chief constable and assistant chief constable rank. To get this high you almost always join the police from university and are put on an accelerated promotion system so you're fast-tracked to the top.

The West Midlands Police top brass call themselves the 'Command Team'. You don't really have anything to do with them unless you're a superintendent. We did experience the fallout from their decisions, though. They'd meet up regularly in a room and come up with ideas about how we could do things 'better', a concept which always baffled me. How can a person who's completely disconnected from what is actually happening day to day for police officers make decisions which make our job better and things better for the public?

Our command team once hired a top management consultant and paid him a small fortune to come up with a slogan to put on walls on every police station in the West Midlands. The slogan was supposed to motivate us all and improve morale. After many weeks of brainstorming and meetings the slogan was created.

The slogan that was put up on every wall of every station was 'Right First Time – Every Time'. I think that caused more offence than anything else I ever saw while I was in the force. What the bloody hell did it mean and what pea-brain thinks that having things like that pasted on walls is going to make a jot of difference? As a police officer you're going to be in situations that require you to make a judgement call. You make the best decision you can based upon the information you have and keeping people's safety in mind. Guess what? You may get it wrong sometimes.

That consultant must be making a fortune still because 10 years later I saw exactly the same slogan used by LloydsTSB. It was pasted all over the walls at their branches behind the counters. Sometimes I think I've gone insane, you know.

Visits from the chief constable to police stations were rare events. He occasionally made what he thought was a surprise visit to a police station but we'd always have a phone call at least an hour before he was due to arrive. It must be the job of somebody in his office to check his diary and phone the relevant superintendent to warn him.

The idea was that people didn't want the chief to see what was really happening. Whenever we found out he was coming the entire station would be cleaned up and everybody would leave the station for the time he was there. Out of sight out of mind and all that. It must be a bit like when the Queen comes to visit a place. She probably thinks that the whole of the UK smells like fresh paint and the public all walk around carrying Union Jacks with them.

The chief came to visit us at Little Park Street once but we'd already been given notice. It was an especially rare visit because it was the start of nights. We'd arranged with the control room sergeant to send out a back-up call as soon as he walked into the briefing room so he could see us but not ask us any questions. Right on time, he walked in and opened his mouth but the back-up call went out and so we all ran past him and screeched out of the backyard for good effect.

Of course, I realise now that it might've been a good idea to stay and answer his questions, but our supervision didn't want that at all. We could've told him straight but experience showed me that when a senior officer asks for the truth, often they don't really mean it at all. It's a bit like when your misses asks, 'Do I look fat in this?' Only an idiot would say 'Yes you do, love.'

One of our former chief constables had a nickname that was not particularly flattering. He was called BIFFO. I don't know who told him that he had a nickname but he was anxious to find out what it stood for. Every chief constable has a civilian driver and this chief pestered his driver for days to find out what it stood for. The driver rightly just claimed ignorance and said he didn't know what he was talking about. For days the chief pressed him telling him that he wouldn't mind, 'honest'. Eventually, he cracked and told him that BIFFO stood for 'Big Ignorant Fat Fucker from Oldbury'. The driver never worked for the police again.

The next sucker to give an honest answer was a potential high-flyer in the police called Pete. Pete was well-respected because he was a good police officer and knew what it was like to be out on the streets. He'd have had empathy as a senior officer which is what he'd probably have become as part of the accelerated promotion scheme.

Some complete bonehead of a senior officer decided that we should buy 2-litre diesels as pursuit cars. This was before turbo diesels, so as you can imagine, they were just about suitable for towing a caravan and not much more. The Panda drivers in their 1.3 Maestros were now beating the 2-litre diesel Peugeot 405s to jobs which was very embarrassing. Local car thieves were driving past them and laughing.

Pete was asked to do a report on the suitability of police vehicles and he presented his findings to the station superintendent. He gave the facts and evidenced them and was fair and impartial when he stated that the vehicles were woefully inadequate for the job they were supposed to perform. The superintendent flew into a rage. He told a baffled Pete that he'd never work at his station again – and he never did. Pete had to work from another station from that day on and his place on the accelerated promotion scheme was cancelled.

It was exactly the same at Stechford. Our superintendent there was known as the 'Laffin assassin' because he'd always be smiling when he spoke to you, but if he took a dislike to you your career was pretty much over. Time and time again he'd banish sergeants to the cell block for years or pull them into his office for a bollocking. I realise now what it was all about. Before we all were reorganised he was in a very senior position and in charge of three other superintendents and three stations. Now he was just in charge of one. He knew that he was never going any further in his career and was a very angry man.

One day when I was called into his office for a chat, I was on edge already. A member of the public had written the superintendent a letter complaining about me. I'd arrested a man from a stolen car outside his house. I was trying to handcuff the prisoner and the man came out of his house and started shouting at me that his drive was being blocked.

He could see that I was trying to arrest somebody and I was on my own but he continued to insist that I move the stolen car. I put the prisoner into my car but there was no way I could remove the stolen one. I was on my own and it had come to rest at the bottom of a steep hill. It just couldn't be pushed out of the way. I told the man that I'd get a transporter to take it away and it would take about 20 minutes.

The man wasn't having any of it and went back into his house shouting to himself. I wouldn't have minded but he didn't have a car of his own so he didn't need the stolen car moved for any reason at all. What a complete prat. The man wrote a letter saying I was rude but it was ridiculous because he said that I shouldn't even be in the police because I was too 'short in stature'. Any boss worth his salt would've laughed at it, but not this one.

The superintendent began to shout at me and said that I should've pushed it out of the way. The thing is that force orders are very clear. Stolen cars must only be moved by professional car towing companies. I can't physically push cars up hills, I had a prisoner in my car, and it wasn't causing an obstruction. All this didn't concern the superintendent though.

I tried to explain what had happened but he shouted even louder and his face went bright red. 'That's it,' I thought, 'I'm in the cell block tomorrow.' He then stopped shouting and said, 'How dare you call me obtuse?' I was completely bemused by this comment, 'I didn't,' I replied. I didn't admit it to him, but I didn't even know what that word meant and had to go and look it up in a dictionary after I left his office. I had to laugh to myself because he was the most obtuse man I'd ever met.

He must've realised that he was obtuse for him to imagine somebody else accusing him of being so. I ended up apologising and was excused. I avoided him like the plague from then on. I knew he was a very sad man inside that uniform and probably a very difficult man for his wife and kids to get along with. Even his fellow superintendent and chief inspector didn't like him. It was a well-known fact in Stechford at that time that the senior officers hated each other – they never spoke to each other.

Soon afterwards, the superintendent was replaced with somebody far nicer. Our superintendent was sent to police HQ in Lloyd House and given a nice boring desk job where he could do no more harm. I saw him one last time a while later in a lift in Lloyd House. I asked him if he was enjoying his new role but he just looked back at me and said, 'No, I hate it.' It was all I could do not to say, 'Serves you right, you obtuse cunt.'

He'd ruined the careers of a few really good police officers during his time and I'm glad he was sent out to pasture. When he left Stechford not one of his 200 staff said goodbye or wished him the best.

෴ ෴

When I think of how police management waste money I shake my head in disbelief. If they ran companies like they ran their stations they'd go bust in one year. Every superintendent is given a budget for the year which has to cover overtime, operations, and special incidents such as investigating murders. I don't think they're given any formal training in how to manage these large sums of money so what tends to happen is that the money is hoarded right up to the end of the financial year.

Everyone is constantly told, 'There's no overtime,' so you know if you get a prisoner near the end of a tour of duty you won't be paid to deal with him. As the year end approaches there's lots of money left in the pot which has to be spent or the money the superintendent will be given next year will be less. They don't get any awards for having money left over to spend.

Every March at every station I worked at there'd be a huge amount of overtime money available and police officers would flock to it like flies round shit (myself included). It was like manna from heaven to us. We'd do something called 'high-visibility policing' which I think was another management term. It just meant that we walked around some of the areas with reflective jackets on so that everybody could see us. I couldn't actually see what benefit this had for the community, but of course I was broke and needed extra money so I joined in.

We also had a command team road show going on where the current team of senior officers was going to various locations around the West Midlands and holding open forums where police officers could ask them questions about what was happening in the force. There was another huge amount of reorganising going on and surveys had revealed that police morale was at an all-time low.

The thing was that the only people free to attend were usually on a day off. Staffing levels in the police are usually pretty thin, so to take Pandas off the streets to attend a conference is just not possible. If it's your day off you're probably not going to want to leave your wife and kids at home and go back to work to attend a conference and not get paid.

The superintendents were all panicking that nobody was going to turn up to the conference and so made us an offer. They'd use the overtime budget to pay those on their days off to attend the conference. They didn't want the command team to arrive in their area and have nobody attend. Tens of thousands of pounds were spent paying off-duty police officers to attend the conferences all over the force. I personally thought that it was a waste of taxpayers' money but there was not much I could do. I never went.

✌ ✍

There was one officer at Little Park Street who was always landing himself in trouble, but you couldn't help but like him. Reggie was very much old school, heaven knows when he joined the job but some of us thought it was decades ago and somebody forgot to tell him he could retire. Reggie was older than God's dog and had more years service than anyone could count. He like a few others had joined Coventry City Police Force before it was joined with the West Midlands Police Force.

Reggie stood 5' 10" tall, had scruffy greasy greying black hair. The skin on his face was always peeling and flaking away; I think it was psoriasis. He had a huge bushy moustache and long goatee like something the villain out of a Sherlock Holmes movie would wear. You'd often see him sitting at his desk in the front office twisting his moustache.

Reggie had worked in the front office since long before I'd been in the job which was several years at Little Park Street. He couldn't go out on patrol because he'd lost a leg in a motorbike accident some years before. How he'd managed to keep his job with only one leg I'll never know. I'd seen police officers with far less serious injuries and medical problems dismissed from service.

Reggie was a very intelligent man and spoke impeccable English. He was extremely articulate so many of the jokes he'd tell involved metaphor or other plays on words which of course if you were working class with just about one 'O' level went over your head.

I liked Reggie a lot. He was a very incisive character and if you treated him OK then he was OK with you. Some of the younger-in-service officers tried to treat him like a front office lackie occasionally and received a verbal slap from Reggie for their efforts.

Reggie's standards didn't stop at just police officers though, members of the public attend the police station all day long 24/7. Often, they come in shouting and demanding things as if they own you because they pay council tax. Reggie would never stand being talked down to. If I had one leg and was still in the job I probably would've kept my head down but not Reggie.

One day a rich couple came into the station to complain about a noisy neighbour. Reggie rightly told them that the environmental health office had to deal with this because they had the equipment to measure the noise and the powers to take the offenders to court. The man became irate and demanded that Reggie send the police to his house immediately, 'I pay your wages,' said the man indignantly. Reggie didn't bat an eyelid, instead he reached into his pocket and pulled out a shiny new 10-pence piece. He flicked it across the counter at them and turned away saying, 'Here's your money back, now fuck off.'

Thirty minutes later Reggie was in the superintendent's office. Mick (the superintendent) had known Reggie for many years; in fact, they'd joined the service together. Reggie took a bollocking and left. There was not much you can do to punish a man with one leg who works in the front office already.

A few weeks later a German couple came into the front office. Coventry attracts quite a lot of tourists because of the cathedral which was bombed during the Second World War. (You can hear the punch line already, can't you?) People come from all over the world to see the ruins. The German couple asked Reggie for directions to the cathedral. Reggie wasn't about to help the Germans find it again, so with a deadpan face he told them, 'You had no problems finding it during the war did you?'

Reggie found himself in the superintendent's office yet again. This time he was punished by being made to stand by the barrier to the police station's rear yard. Car parking was a major headache at Little Park Street all the time I was there. Everybody felt they had a divine right to park in the yard. Of course, uniformed police cars and CID cars should be there, but after that it was just a fight for spaces.

Police officers in the admin team who needed to use their personal vehicles for enquiries wanted to park there. Police management who felt that they were more important than everybody else wanted to park there and the top admin civvies wanted a space as well. The result was chaos with cars abandoned all over the place. The net result of course was that uniformed police vehicles were constantly being blocked in so they couldn't get out to emergency situations. Stickers were eventually issued so you could put a nasty sticker on people's windscreens, as if that made a difference. It was a nightmare.

Reggie was put on the barrier to stop people sneaking into the station and dumping their cars there. He was the perfect candidate actually, because he didn't care what people thought about him and he was personally backed up by the superintendent so if anybody had a problem they should go and speak to him about it. I'm not sure if paying a police officer over 30 grand a year to stand by a car park barrier is a good use of public funds, but there you go. For a few months the rear yard was a safe place to be.

Eventually, Reggie was sent to the control room for some crazy reason. He hadn't been on the streets for years and now he was thrust into a massively high-pressure role and working a horrible shift system deciding who went to which job. It must've been a ploy by the superintendent to get rid of him. The control room is a very stressful job and it can make you crack after a while.

It worked, because Reggie started to turn up to work drunk and shortly afterwards it came as no surprise to hear that he'd been arrested for drink driving and his services were no longer required by the West Midlands Police. It was a sad way to see such a great character finish his service.

Happy Birthday to Me – 5 June 1981

My stepdad John takes me to karate lessons; he says I need to toughen up a bit. We go to Stoke Park School for the lesson and I'm very scared. The teacher is a black belt and he beats everybody up. There are lots of beginners there. We also go to another karate club in Wyken called Black Sun karate club. I like it there. The instructor is called Andy and he's really kind. He shows me how to kick and punch; it's really hard but I keep going anyway. I want to be a black belt like him one day.

I start at big school. It's called Cardinal Wiseman Roman Catholic School. The girls go to the school next to us so we don't really see them. They even go home in different buses from ours. All the teachers are very strict, some of them hit us and shake us in the class and make people cry.

There's a dwarf boy in our class and everyone laughs at him. One boy picks him up during break, hangs him on the coat peg in the changing room and leaves him there. Another boy smells of piss so we all keep away from him. Another boy has a massive head so we all call him pin-head.

Some of the boys can't read or write very well so they're sent to the special learning unit. They're all called retarded by the other boys.

Every Monday I have to queue for my dinner tickets. We can't afford school dinners so I get tickets to pay for my dinners. There are hundreds of boys who have to queue for the tickets. Some of them sell their dinner tickets for 20 pence and keep the money instead of eating.

I'm 11 years old.

Year 12 – All Good Things

I mentioned before that things in the police are always changing. A few months after Insp. Ross started with us he left for a post as detective inspector in CID. I laughed to myself thinking that he'd be ruffling a few feathers over in the CID office at Stechford.

Our new inspector was Insp. Tubbs. I hadn't had any dealings with him but I knew he used to run Green Watch at Stechford and I didn't rate them as highly as Red Watch. I was worried that he was going to be a lazy git and that the standard of the station would slip a bit. When he arrived though, I was proved wrong. He was a smashing bloke and we got on really well over the coming months. When he came on duty he was often duty stick (duty inspector) so was busy doing reviews or dealing with other matters. He did have a different approach from that of Insp. Ross but I did warm to him more because he was more approachable.

Insp. Tubbs came to depend on me as his right-hand man. He knew me pretty well by then and understood how I worked and that I had very high standards. There was only one problem really: I was becoming very tired of being a police officer. It had been my dream since I was a little boy which I'd fulfilled.

I looked into the future and could see the next 18 years of my career. I may make inspector or possibly superintendent but I didn't see this as a realistic possibility. The new structure of the force meant that there were far too many superintendents already and the people who were doing the police MBA were favoured.

I couldn't imagine being a sergeant for the rest of my career. I love a challenge and the only change I could make was either into the CID (which I'd done already) or firearms which to me meant 99 per cent boredom and 1 per cent sheer terror as we dealt with armed criminals.

The firearms team in the West Midlands Police had a good reputation for being professional and well-trained. When they'd first been formed it was a bit of a disaster because it was just ex-army people who'd had a bit of handgun training. There was a couple of people accidentally killed during operations. They shot a young child while he was asleep in bed and then also shot a pregnant woman. You can't blame the officers, who simply were not trained adequately and thrown into life-threatening situations almost immediately.

After a massive review took place the selection and training process changed and the firearms team became a very effective unit. There was the odd hiccup such as when one of the teams was driving back from the firing range in a serial van. All the guns are kept in a Kevlar bag for safety but it was a hot day so somebody decided to drive with the van door held open. As they went around a bend the bag slid out onto the road but nobody noticed.

About an hour later a nice little old lady went into her local station and handed the bag over. The firearms team were back at HQ in a state of panic. A bag of 15 semi-automatic pistols was missing and if they ended up on the streets they'd be used in murders and armed robberies.

Luckily for them, the PC in the front office was 'on side', meaning he was a good bloke and knew the score. He phoned one of his mates who was in the firearms team who came and collected the bag very quietly. I hope they bought him a beer or two for that. If the PC had told his sergeant, that would've been the end of a few careers.

Another reason to not join the firearms team was that everybody who joins has to spend a year working at the airport before joining the unit. I couldn't think of anything worse than walking endlessly around Birmingham international airport carrying a gun. I'd probably end up shooting myself to relieve the boredom. Police usually carry an MP5 carbine which is a small submachine gun. The automatic facility is disabled so you've to press the trigger each time you want a round to be fired. I could only see one reason for wanting to join firearms, and that was the fact you wanted to shoot somebody. Why else would you want to carry a gun?

Something in my career had to change, but I couldn't see what to do. I'd fallen into the trap many police officers do. I felt that my only skills were as a police officer so what else could I do? I was also still heavily in debt and just about scraping by. I was frightened that if I left I'd go bankrupt or that no company would want me because my skills would not be transferable.

When I joined the police the standards were very high. You had to have some qualifications and pass entrance exams and be at a certain level of literacy. This is because you're taking statements from witnesses and preparing court files which are going to be picked apart by lawyers. If you can't even spell or construct a proper sentence, what hope do you have of putting together a statement of witness?

Slowly, the level of police wages compared to inflation dropped. Now you could earn more working in a factory than working in the police. The applications for the police dwindled and so did the standards. Entrance standards were dropped so that even if you had a police caution you could now apply. I began to see probationers join the service who had major problems with their English grammar. I'm not saying that it's a bad thing in itself, but a person can go on courses to improve their English and they're usually free to attend.

Crime files were being handed to me to sign which were disgraceful, full of spelling mistakes and missing evidence. One example is crimes of public disorder. The Queen is considered to be the victim on behalf of the general public so we put 'Regina' on the file. One day a probationer handed me a file and for the victim he'd put 'Vagina'!

Due to the lower wages, new recruits began opting out of the police pension scheme. This caused a massive danger for existing police officers because it's the current officers paying into it that pays for the ones who've retired.

The more experienced officers seemed to be dwindling and something very dangerous began to happen. Less experienced officers began to tutor the new probationers. One day I was in the backyard and I saw two officers leaving the station on patrol. The driver had just about 12 months service and the passenger had only just joined. It was a recipe for disaster.

It was the cry of the bitter and twisted PC, but I began to think, 'This isn't the job I joined.' With the new organisational structure, the shifts had been decimated. All policing was done on sectors now so out of every team only two would be designated as response officers. The others would be on sector duties.

I'm not saying that sectorisation was a bad thing. It put many office dwellers back where they belonged, in uniform and on the streets which is better for the public. I just began to feel that I didn't belong to a team anymore. I knew in my heart that my passion in the job had all but disappeared but I felt that there was nothing much else I could do. Who'd want an ex-police sergeant and what possible use could I be to their business?

I felt it was time to see Rich B. again. He was very generous with his time for me and patient enough to see that I had a lot of fear in me. I think he could see something of himself in me and maybe got a good feeling inside about helping others like I did while I was in the police.

When I went to see Rich at his home he was busy in a conference call with the management of one of his companies. They were buying another company and it was a very big step for him and his business. His personal assistant Michelle met me at the door to his mansion and took me through to his library. Michelle was about 26 and had jet black hair going all the way down to her waist. She had a fantastic figure and deep blue eyes.

If I could've chosen a PA it'd have been her. I didn't care if she was useless but knowing Rich she'd have been shit-hot. I found out later that she had an MBA and a PhD and spoke Japanese, and I was still trying to understand how to speak English. She came back a minute later with a nice mug of coffee and said Rich would be out in a minute or two.

I looked around the massive room which was wall to wall with books. Rich B. was a voracious reader and had read every book on the shelves. They were all personal development books, books on running companies, financial awareness, property investment, and many of what Rich called 'books of wisdom' including the Bible, and religious texts from Islam, Judaism, Buddhism and Hinduism.

Rich B. had a saying which he'd often repeated to me. It was from a man called Eric Hoffer who said, 'In a time of drastic change it is the learners who inherit the future. The learned usually find themselves equipped to live in a world that no longer exists.' He didn't rate degrees or university education much at all; as far as he was concerned it was just a system which rewarded people for how much they could regurgitate during exams.

My attention came back into the room when Rich strolled in. He was smiling and carrying a mug of freshly-brewed coffee. 'You look pretty chirpy,' I said. 'It's all very exciting,' beamed Rich, 'the company is expanding now and I want to make sure the team is all on the same page. But you didn't come to hear about that, did you?' he added as he sank into his comfy armchair. 'I do like to hear about it,' I exclaimed, 'but a lot of it is over my head.'

I didn't want to waste his time so I got down to the problem. 'I've had enough of being in the police now, Rich, but I don't know what I can do. I'm still paying off my debts which are very large and I'm worried about leaving the safety of the job, I have 12 years pension behind me.' 'Understandable,' said Rich nodding, 'so you've another 18 years left to work before you qualify for the pension then?' I nodded. 'So do you really want to spend another 18 years of your life in a job you no longer want to be in for the sake of a promise of a low monthly payout?' I now started to shake my head. I felt weak for even asking the question now but I was already there.

'Do you know how they catch monkeys in the jungle?' asked Rich. 'Funnily enough, no,' I laughed, 'they never covered that at police training centre.' Rich took a sip of his coffee, cleared his throat and said, 'Well, it's a very interesting subject and you should know about it.' He was trying to hide the grin on his face as he said, 'The hunters slice a coconut in half and put a peeled orange inside and bind the coconut back together with vine. They bore a small hole in the top big enough for a monkey's hand to fit in and suspend it from a tree just off the ground.'

I sat there nodding politely wondering what on earth Rich was on about. He looked me directly in the eye and said, 'When the monkey smells the orange it climbs down from the tree and puts its hand in the hole, but when it makes a fist around the orange it can't pull its hand out. The monkey starts to struggle and scream as the hunter approaches, but it doesn't occur to the monkey to let go of the orange so it can get its hand out and run to safety up the tree.'

I sat there processing what he was saying and working out how it applied to me. Eventually, the penny dropped and I asked, 'So I'm the monkey and the orange is the police pension then?' Rich nodded, 'Go on,' he said. I mumbled reluctantly, 'If I let go of the pension I'll be free.' 'Well done,' said Rich, 'there's no guarantee that everything will go well for you in the future, but if you want to be free you have let go of the very thing that would enslave you. Remember that winners play to win and losers play not to lose.'

I knew he was right. There was no point in arguing with him because he was living the type of life I wanted for myself. Rich could see I was taking it all in but he still said, 'A regular salary is more addictive than crack cocaine, Paul. Some people go their whole lives and are never able to shake free of their addiction to their monthly pay cheque.'

He got up and walked over to one of his shelves, came back with a copy of the Bible and began to read from it. He read, ' "Do not store up for yourselves treasures on earth, where moth and rust destroy, and where thieves break in and steal. But store up for yourselves treasures in heaven, where neither moth nor rust destroys, and where thieves do not break in or steal; for where your treasure is, there your heart will be also." That is from Matthew 6:19-21, Paul.'

I didn't really want to hear anything from the Bible because I'd had so much of it rammed down my throat at school and church. 'To be honest, I don't really believe in Christianity or heaven, Rich,' I said. Rich put his Bible down. 'I'm not a religious person either, Paul, and I don't go to church. What he is saying is that every material thing you cling to will eventually turn to dust or be taken from you. Heaven is actually a state of pure love, bliss and connection and not some place in the clouds you go to when you die.'

I sat and contemplated over what Rich was telling me. He could see that I was pondering over what he'd said. 'All the terrible things you may be imagining that will happen will probably not. Even if you did end up broke, so what?' Rich and I were interrupted by Michelle saying that he was needed on another conference call. Rich said, 'I'll be back in a minute, mate. Go for it, you can't fail and you can never be hurt.'

Rich finished his call and accompanied me to my car. He was going for a walk around the grounds of his house which he often did to clear his mind when he had a lot of things to think about. I started my car engine up and wound my window down to say goodbye.

Rich rested his arm on the roof of my car and leaned into my window. He looked around the inside of my shitty police car and then right at me and said, 'As you make your journey through life, opportunities will present themselves to you and they will be either gained or lost depending upon one thing. This is the thing that locks people in the same daily grind day after day, week after week, month after month and year after year. Everybody knows they could leave their job for one they really want, start their own business, write the book, go to college or even ask the person they fancy out for a drink, but one thing prevents you. I call it the YBWI programme.'

I sat there absorbing what he was telling me. I felt that this was a pivotal moment in my life. Rich then said, 'Every time you think about doing something you really want to you run the "Yes, But What If" programme in your mind and imagine lots of crap happening to you and things going wrong so you just put up with a crappy life instead because at least it is living. I don't know why people don't imagine lots of great things happening instead.'

I heard a shout from Rich's front door. One of his team was jumping up and down smiling and waving to him; he cupped his hands around his mouth and shouted over, 'The deal has just gone through, Mr Rich: you've just made three million quid!'

Rich looked back at me and smiled. 'You see,' he grinned, 'I could've looked at this deal and imagined lots of crap happening like it falling through or me going bust again, but I chose to face my fears and imagine lots of great things happening instead, and blow me down they did. When you choose to face your fears head on you'll pass through them and realise that they never existed. Those who run away from their fears are cursed to live an ordinary life.

'So many people reach the end of their lives and feel the bitter pain of regret. They look back and wonder what could have been. The businesses never started, the holidays never taken, relationships never experienced, cars never driven, and the time never spent. When you look back will you know deep down that you gave it your very best, everything you had, because if you did you'll have lived a life beyond most people's wildest expectations?'

Rich tapped his hand on the roof of my car twice and walked off towards the woods. He never looked back, he didn't believe in it.

I began to feel the emotion and tears. I bit down onto my lip so I could feel something apart from the surge of emotion gathering in my stomach and welling up towards my tear ducts. The 'Yes But What If' programme had been running my entire life. I had dreams and goals but whenever I thought about moving towards them I started to imagine it all going tits up for me and began to feel very fearful.

I knew from what Bernard and Rich were saying that it was time to let Paul the police officer die and I felt sad, as if it was the end of a relationship, but it had run its course and now was the time to let it go. I was overwhelmed with feelings of sadness and grief. It was similar to the end of my romantic relationships or when I was promoted. I'd been here before, and I knew that everything would turn out OK.

There were two Pauls: Paul the policeman, and the real Paul, and I'd forgotten who I really was. The real me hates to see other people hurt or in distress; I want to go and help them and when they were sad I felt part of their sadness inside me as if it was my own. My mum said that I was a very sensitive and caring boy when I was growing up, but a person like that simply cannot last in the police.

I'd become lost and couldn't feel much of anything anymore – all the things that had been part of who I was had been suppressed so far down that I couldn't access the feelings. I couldn't even find a tear when my dad was buried. When I saw a hypnotherapist a few years later she told me that I'd been brainwashed by the police. I suppose they were doing their best to prepare me for what I was going to face, but the effect of changing who I really was had an impact on who I was outside the police as well.

I'd become more and more discontented in the police. Have you ever worn an itchy jumper or other piece of clothing that just seemed to irritate you? It fits and you could wear it, but you just wouldn't feel comfortable in it. That was what being in the police was for me.

My team was great, my boss was great, but it just didn't *feel* right. Hard to put into words but I felt irritated and itchy. I hadn't yet started reading personal development books so I didn't understand about values and personal goals. All I knew was that I was very unhappy. I also hated nights with a vengeance. Working from 10 p.m. till 7 a.m. and then driving home was horrible. I was on my own for the entire shift apart from the visits I made to the cell block just for a bit of company.

On nights, I began to go into the inspector's office in Bordesley Green at about 4 a.m. to put my feet up and get some shut-eye. I'd turn the radio up full blast in case there was a shout but was just dog-tired. Once I had my feet up on the inspector's desk and was leaning back falling asleep in the chair. The chair fell backwards and I banged my head off the locker behind me splitting my damn head open.

I was really annoyed. I had to get a lift to hospital and get the split in my head glued back together. It was obvious to everybody that I'd fallen asleep but they all just laughed. I did think to myself though that if I'd been caught napping on camera I'd have been in big trouble with the chief constable.

I was so tired by 7 a.m. that I'd always start to doze off in my car driving back home along the A45. It was a long straight road and I'd frequently wake up in a panic. I'd probably only closed my eyes for a second but that would be enough to crash.

When I joined the job I never really came across police sleeping on the job much. I did spend a week of nights with a WPC who used to park up at about 3 a.m. and close her eyes. It was really frustrating for me because I was so keen to start with. I guess it was hard for her because I wasn't allowed to drive the Panda car yet and she was up all day with her baby daughter.

Apart from the odd catnap there wasn't really much sleeping at all on the job or not at least with the PCs I worked with. I did hear of a couple of constables who were caught on CCTV sleeping and it ended up in the news and the local papers which looked very bad for them. If you're going to have a kip you need to pick somewhere miles away from the possibility of being caught.

My team at Bordesley Green were a good bunch and I enjoyed working with them. As time went on I became less uptight as a sergeant and far more relaxed. I still expected jobs to be dealt with professionally but I gave my team more and more slack. If they wanted time off here and there I just let them have it. If they worked two hours extra I gave them four hours off in return. As far as I was concerned there were very few perks to the job so if I could make life a bit easier then that's a good thing.

We had a new guy join the team and we got on great from the very start. Mark Thompson had come from the observation team. He'd spent three years doing covert observations from flats or vans disguised to look like builders' or plumbers' vans. They had false backs in them so it looked like tools and bits of rubbish were inside but really it was two plainclothes police officers with cameras and video recorders.

I wouldn't have fancied it myself because it's boring and you've to piss and shit in a bucket in the back of the van because it's supposed to be empty. If you've ever followed me after I've used the bog you just know you wouldn't want to be in the back of the van when I go. I'd have thought Mark would've been a bit pissed off at having to get back in uniform but he was very keen. He was an advanced driver and loved to chase cars. Not my cup of tea, but horses for courses.

Mark was studying part-time at college to become a qualified Microsoft IT engineer. I'd been on a course to build computers and was interested in IT as well. We began to have a lot of chats about what it'd be like working in the IT field. It was early 2000 and the IT industry was booming. I'd chatted to a couple of friends whom I went to school with. They weren't that academic at school but they were earning more than the chief constable for doing basic IT support in London. It was staggering: at the time the chief constable was on 60 grand and they were on over 70 grand, just for fixing computers and installing software.

I started to read the IT magazines with Mark and we could see salaries of over 70 grand which seemed amazing to us. Even as a superintendent I could never dream of making that sort of money. What's more is that my mates were not working shifts or being told what to do. They were all running limited companies as well and paying hardly any tax.

Mark and I decided that IT was the way to go. I began studying more and looking around to see what jobs were on offer. Although all my experience was in the police I cobbled together a CV. I had no real IT experience but that didn't seem to matter. I had a couple of qualifications and was almost through the first year of a masters degree in IT for management.

A few months later I spotted a job with a company which looked wonderful. They only recruited graduates and had an amazing internal training system that gave you a great grounding in technical and project management skills. I could progress rapidly in that company I thought, so I applied. The company was called Pink Elephant (not the car parks) and were based in Reading.

I had two interviews and got on really well with the people there. They came back with an offer of 19 grand which was over 10 grand less than I was currently earning. I was still over 26 grand in debt and already falling behind with more payments. I had an old nail of a car still and no savings and was behind with my mortgage payments. The job offer was in Reading which meant I'd have to stay there all week in a bed-sit.

I knew I had to leave, and if I worked hard and had the right attitude I knew that I'd surpass the police salary very quickly. I had enough about me to pass a business law degree, the sergeants' and inspectors' exams and the CID exams. As far as I was concerned, my attitude and work ethic would be more than enough to be successful in whatever I chose to do.

I did the only sane thing and accepted the job.

I called the station superintendent who I got along well with and told him. He asked me to come over for a chat because he was shocked to hear I was leaving. We had a nice talk and he said he'd be sorry to see me go. He said he saw me as a diamond in the rough which I took as a great compliment. He said that if I ever decided to come back I was always welcome. I'd have to be a PC and push a Panda 'round some shit-hole but I was welcome back nonetheless. I thought, 'I'd rather eat my foot than do that again,' but I thanked him anyway.

My watch were coming off earlies so I phoned them from Stechford and told them not to go home until I'd been to see them. We all got together in a spare office and I told them that I didn't want to be in the police anymore. I didn't see my career going anywhere, and I didn't want to be a sergeant for the next 18 years of my life. They were shocked to hear the news. One told me I was making a mistake and I'd be back but another one piped up and thanked me for all my help and support over the last 18 months. I felt my eyes welling up so thanked them all and left for home.

As I left the room one of the WPCs on the team, Judith, stopped to chat with me. 'You jammy git,' she said, 'I wish I was leaving.' I had to laugh to myself. What was jammy about resigning and taking an 11 grand pay cut when I already couldn't afford to pay my massive debts? I just smiled and walked off. You'd be amazed how many people have called me lucky since. That's just about the stupidest thing you can say to another person along with the tired old favourite, 'Well, it's alright for you.' It would be like me saying it to Rich B.

News travels fast in the police so when I came back to work two days later everybody knew. Some people were supportive and others told me how lucky I was to be leaving. I was still baffled at these sort of comments. It was as if they thought my name had been pulled out of a lottery draw or something.

I went down to the cell block to see my mate who worked down there and I was approached by a PC I hadn't seen before. He uttered the classic line I'd heard hundreds of times over the years by police officers, 'I'd leave if it wasn't for the pension'. I was a bit surprised because he looked quite young. 'How much service do you have?' I asked. 'Two years,' he replied. I nearly fell over. This guy was going to stay in the job for another 28 years just for the pension. It was the most pathetic thing I'd ever heard, but like I said, I've heard that tired old excuse many times during my service and I still hear it now when I chat to police officers.

I'd seen many officers retire and when they do most of them have to find more work because they still have a mortgage, loans or children at university. I've seen a lot of them do some things that seem to me to be humiliating like taking menial jobs as civilians working for the police. Some come back as cell block strikers giving the prisoners tea and doing visits.

One sergeant left to have a triple heart bypass and then came back as a radio operator on one-third of his police wages. He had three times the stress due to the high-pressure environment, was working shifts and had to answer to a civvie for his performance. I can't imagine what goes through their minds.

If the pension is that good why aren't they all retiring and enjoying their lives? The answer of course is that they're trying to live on two-thirds of what they couldn't afford to live on before they left. They had no savings or other investments so they had to continue to work.

As I was working my last month's notice police morale dropped again. It was when we all found out that the tactics of the complaints and discipline department had changed. They became proactive and for the first time started to actually try to catch police officers out. They began to put hidden cameras in break rooms to see if they could catch you taking more than an hour's dinner and started to engineer scenarios to see if you'd follow police procedures.

A special 'shop a cop' line was set up which caused dismay in the force. Now you were being encouraged to grass your mates up and the assistant chief constable who came up with it must've been very happy with himself. The message it sent out to the police and general public was that police corruption is so rife that now we have to have a dedicated line to handle it. I was very upset at this action. Of course, if there's an officer committing crimes or doing something serious then they should be dealt with, but to start encouraging you to shop your mates seemed to me to be a complete disgrace.

I think I fell victim to a complaints set-up one set of earlies. If a police officer was ever involved in a road traffic accident (RTA) then it had to be dealt with by a sergeant. At about 7:20 one morning a call came over the radio that a PC had had a crash on the way to work and was in Birmingham Heartlands Hospital getting checked out for injuries.

I went there and got the guy's details. He was about 25 years and still in his civvy clothing because he hadn't made it to work yet. He was a bit shaken up or so he said and had just been seen by the doctor who said he had no injuries, just a bit of soreness around his neck. As I spoke to the PC I could smell alcohol on his breath. I asked him if he'd had a drink and he said he'd driven home just after the crash at 6:30 a.m. and had a quick drink to calm his nerves.

That seemed very strange to me. That a PC on the way to work would have a bump and then go home, have a drink and then drive to hospital and call in to report it. Something didn't feel right to me but I couldn't put my finger on it. The way he was speaking to me reminded me of the scenario situations I'd been through at police training centre and for my sergeants' exams where you're dealing with an actor who's pretending to be reporting something to you.

If a person is in hospital, by law you've to ask the doctor if it's medically safe for you to demand a specimen of breath from the driver. The doctor said it was fine and I got a breath kit dropped over to where I was by the Zulu. As soon as he blew it registered that he'd been drinking but was not over the limit.

I told the PC that he was all clear and then from behind me a curtain was parted and a uniformed sergeant emerged. He said that he was the officer's supervisor and would give him a lift home because he could have the rest of the day off to recover. I just stood there amazed. How the bloody hell could this guy be hiding behind the curtain while all this was going on?

I came to the conclusion that it was a pathetic attempt by complaints to see if I'd not bother to breathalyse the PC. If I hadn't, then I reckon I'd have either been arrested or at least disciplined and possibly sacked.

Shortly afterwards, another officer was disciplined when he was caught by a hidden camera taking too long for his refreshment break during nights. He'd fallen asleep in a chair for two hours and was severely reprimanded. His wife had been ill and he was looking after the baby every day when he got back from nights and was literally exhausted. Rather than go sick like many would have, he still went into work.

I felt angry because I'd only just asked for the use of a hidden camera for an elderly woman who lived on my beat who was being constantly harassed for money by some local youths and I was told that there were none available. Now I knew where they all were: hidden in police canteens trying to catch people out sleeping or by recording their conversations.

We all took to checking our police cars for hidden transmitters, and conversations became very guarded. You never knew when you were going to be recorded. I'd love to have hidden one in HQ and got some dirt on the senior officers and used it against them to see how *they* liked it.

∽ ∾

I worked my last set of nights with Mark. He'd been very down and in a moment of distress gone to the superintendent's office and told him to stick his job; he was shaking and crying at the same time. I knew that he was not in a good place so I gave him a week's gardening leave (unofficial time off). During that period he had time to clear his mind and decided that he wanted to leave the police as well, so he applied for the same company I was joining. He was accepted and put his notice in.

We had a blast on this set of nights. It reminded me of the old days. We'd chase cars and bad guys and have a fight and throw them into the cells and rush out to another burglary or fight and do the same thing again. It was heaven.

Halfway through nights I nipped down the cell block to cover the sergeant who wanted to go and eat his sandwiches. Most of the time you had to eat standing up there, and usually while you were booking in prisoners. I thought it was disgusting that you were just left down there for an entire tour of duty without even being given a 30-minute lunch break.

It was pretty quiet and about 2 a.m. I was behind the booking-in desk and there were three watch PCs there having a quick cup of tea. Suddenly we heard a car horn sounding over and over again. At first we thought it was a car alarm in the public car park which is just next to the cell block directly outside the front office.

It went on for a minute or so, so two of the PCs, Dave and Daz, went outside to see what was happening. Two minutes later all hell broke loose. Daz and Dave banged on the door that leads from the cells to the front office. Prisoners were never usually brought in that way unless they'd come in with their solicitor by appointment. I unlocked the door and saw Daz and Dave wrestling with a prisoner.

He was a big bloke at 6' 2", dressed in smart trousers and a white shirt. He had spiked black hair and smelled of expensive aftershave and alcohol. Clearly, he'd been on a night out and I was guessing he wasn't a local resident because he actually looked half decent. He was violent and was struggling with Dave and Daz. He wasn't punching anybody, but his arms were all over the place as he tried to get away. Looking at his eyes he'd obviously been taking drugs of some sort because they were rolling back in his head.

We dragged him into the holding area and he began to calm down a bit. We sat him on a bench and I went behind the booking-in desk. I started the custody record and he jumped up and started throwing his arms in the air. The guy was extremely strong, but the problem with the cell block is that people can't get in to help you. You've to either get to the buzzer or use the keys, and if you're fighting you simply can't do it.

He started to throw punches at Daz. We could've tried to get him onto the ground and handcuff him but he was so big and strong and the drugs would've prevented him from feeling pain so I didn't think that would work. I shouted, 'Gas him, Daz,' which meant to use his CS spray. Not a wise move in the cells, because even though the spray would hit him, most of it actually bounces off and affects everyone else as well. I couldn't see any other way of subduing this guy. He was as strong as an ox and we had no help.

Daz gave the man a blast of CS and he fell to the floor and started writhing around like a dying fly with his hands over his face, squirming around on the floor screaming out in pain. It was as if somebody had thrown acid in his face. Sometimes CS doesn't work on people, but not in this instance. He went down like a sack of spuds.

Unfortunately, it affected all of us and Daz and Dave lost their vision and snot started dribbling down their noses. The only thing to do when you've been gassed is let fresh air blow over your face to disperse the particles. The worst thing you can do is wash with water or rub your eyes, which just aggravates it.

I opened the exit door to let Daz and Dave have some air. My eyes were streaming but I could see. By this time the prisoner had run down the corridor and was throwing up. Great streams of snot were coming down his nose and he was covered in sick. At least he'd calmed down, though.

We all took him into his cell and then I made a huge rookie mistake: we searched him but it was a cursory search. Just a quick check of his pockets and taking his valuables, laces and belt. We were all suffering with the effects of the spray and I wanted to get some air.

Daz told me what had happened so I could fill in the custody record. The person sounding a horn was a young lady in her car in the car park outside the front office. She'd been on a first date with this man and they'd been for a drink. He'd had a few too many so she offered to drive him home. When they got outside his house he tried it on with her going in for a kiss and a feel of her tits.

She tried to push him off but he started to force himself on her. He'd taken various drugs and had become incomprehensible. She drove off with him still trying to grope her and managed to make it to the police station. He was still trying to get on top of her outside the police station, and as she pressed the horn he jumped over her and bit her on her cheek. She was sobbing uncontrollably and in a state of shock by the time Daz and Dave had got to her.

To be honest, if I'd known that, I'd have knocked some of his teeth down his throat in the cell. It would've stopped him biting any more women. I knew Daz and Dave very well and they'd have backed me up.

A couple of hours later I went to check the man in the cell. He was sleeping off the drugs and booze, but next to him was a huge block of cannabis, bigger than one of those massive chocolate bars you get at the duty free shop in the airport. I couldn't believe it, I was absolutely gutted. I'd missed it during the search, as he must've had it down his trousers somewhere. We could've had him for possession with intent to supply, but now he could say that it wasn't his and was in the cell when he got there.

I never made such stupid mistakes so I was extremely angry at myself. Finding that on him may well have got him a few months inside and God knows he deserved it. If that had been my daughter I'd have gone to court when he appeared because they read out your address there. I'd have paid him a visit and beat him so bad his mother wouldn't have recognised him. Fucker.

He went to court for actual bodily harm (ABH) and simple possession. He got a conditional discharge.

On my second-last night I was in the cells with Mark sorting out some paperwork. The outside buzzer sounded, indicating that there was a prisoner to be brought in. When you press the buzzer it allowed the officers and prisoner into a holding area. Once you close the outside door you can then be buzzed into the actual cell block and booking-in area.

The two police officers came in with their prisoner. I saw a problem to start with because the pair of them had handcuffed him with his hands to the front, which is a big mistake because the prisoner can still lash out with his arms or put them over your neck and choke you from behind.

The prisoner stood at about 6' 2" tall. He wasn't too stocky but towered over both policemen. He looked like he was in his early 20s but his skin was pale and pallid which indicated to me a regular diet of greasy food and dehydration, the classic symptoms of being a chav. He stank of alcohol and had been taking heaven knows what drugs. He was struggling and swearing and kicking out at whoever was in range. When prisoners are like this you can't ask them any questions so you just put them into a cell, search them and lock them in for a few hours to cool off.

Mark and I helped grab hold of the prisoner who by this time was fighting like a good 'un. We got him into the cell at the very end of the row. I was cursing because of the fact that his hands were in front of him so searching him was very difficult. We pushed him down onto the bench in his cell and tried to remove his shoes and belt so he couldn't hang himself. He kept kicking out so it was a real struggle.

Suddenly, he stood up. I was directly in front of him but I always made it a point to stand at an angle so I never got kicked in the knackers. He brought his head back preparing to head-butt me right on the nose. 'Cheeky bastard,' I thought. I was doing my best to search him and let him have a kip for a bit and here he was trying to spoil my boyish good looks. The attempt was pathetic because he brought his head so far back that I could see it coming a mile off. The best head-butts just begin from a normal position.

I moved my head to the left which is known as a slip in boxing and his head missed me completely. As he brought his head back for a second attempt I sank a right uppercut into his chin. His bottom lip burst open and blood began to gush from his mouth. His knees buckled from under him and he was knocked out and fell back unconscious onto the bench. He was only out for a few seconds but the blow had seemed to pacify him.

The inside of the cell did look like a bloodbath though. The lips are red because there's an awful lot of blood flowing through them. I'd hit him so hard that his upper tooth had gone through his lower lip and out of the skin underneath. I looked down at my hand and there was a big chunk of my knuckle hanging off by a little flap of skin. Bastard. I had to go to Heartlands Hospital for a tetanus injection. He had to go and get his mouth sewn back together.

The next day he made an official complaint against me. He was interviewed by complaints and discipline that same day because of the seriousness of his injury. Ten minutes into the interview he told the inspector from complaints that he'd tried to head-butt me and missed so

I punched him. They stopped the interview and never bothered to speak to me at all. I did respect him for at least telling the truth. He could've said it was unprovoked.

Two days later my right hand turned black and green puss began to ooze from the tooth-shaped gash in my hand. I went to Coventry and Warwickshire Hospital at 11 p.m. I'm really glad I didn't wait until the next day. They took one look at it and paged the specialist. He took a good look at my hand and said that it was infected with bacteria. All the bacteria had entered my bloodstream where the man's tooth had gone into my fist. He drew a line around the part of my hand that was black and said that if it went past my wrist they'd have to amputate my hand. It was my right hand as well, and I do all my favourite things with it. If it went past my elbow I'd lose my arm.

I was gutted. The doctor told me that the human mouth is one of the dirtiest places in the world. It's full of hundreds of different types of bacteria. That dirty bastard probably hadn't been brushing his teeth either and had a kebab that night from some greasy mobile van.

I was admitted and put on a drip. I just lay in the hospital bed and watched the line on my hand praying that the black poison didn't go past it. Two days later I'd responded well to the antibiotics and was discharged. I still have the scar on my hand to remind me of my last set of nights in the police.

I went on a bit of gardening leave for my last three weeks. My inspector gave me the wink so I stayed at home and enjoyed some free holiday time. I did a lot of studying for some IT exams I wanted to pass to help me in my new career.

I had a leaving do with my team and another one with my fellow sergeants and inspector from Bordesley Green. We all hugged goodbye and shook hands and promised to keep in touch. We met up one or two more times but eventually lost contact.

I was called to police HQ at Lloyd House to see the assistant chief constable. I wanted to see the chief but he was away. In my resignation I'd been very positive and thanked all my colleagues for the time I'd served. I thanked the station superintendent who I thought was doing a great job and thanked the chief constable for the changes he'd made.

Overall, I think putting more of us on the beat and out of the squads was a good thing. I think giving sergeants their own beats was a good thing and giving the sergeants more responsibility was also very good. It wasn't perfect, but I did enjoy having my own beat to look after and my own team.

I explained to the ACC that I didn't feel that my career was going anywhere so it was time to leave. She'd clearly been on the accelerated promotion programme and came out with all the management gobbledegook about 'downsizing', whatever that means. She said that in her experience the best people float to the top, which again is complete drivel. 'Turds and deadwood also float,' I thought but didn't say anything.

Happy Birthday to Me – 5 June 1982

I pass my Yellow Belt in Karate and run home to tell mum and John. I'm so happy. I do a talk at school about karate and all the bullys stay away from me now.

Karate is hard. There're no other children my age so I spar with the grown-ups all the time. I keep getting bruises and my knuckles are sore because we have to do press-ups on them all the time to toughen them up.

We're living in Catherine Street now with John. We only have three bedrooms and there are five of us so I have to share a room with Gina and Louise who sleep in the same bed.

John works in a factory and Mum works nights in an old people's home. Mum has to leave for work at 9:30 every night so she can walk to work. When she gets home she has to get us all ready for school. She sleeps for three hours and then has to get Louise and then get dinner ready for all of us.

The Secure Homes man comes every week and mum gives him money so he can pay our bills for us.

I'm 12 years old.

Epilogue

The day I left the police I felt a different man: it was literally an overnight transformation. I felt like a huge weight had fallen from my shoulders. It felt like I'd been an asthmatic for 12 years and now for the first time in a long while I could finally breathe. I felt so happy deep down inside. I can't find the words for the relief and happiness I felt to have left. It wasn't the leaving that did it but the message I'd sent to myself that I was in charge of my own life, I was the boss and could choose to do what I wanted to do. Life had changed from black-and-white into colour.

I didn't know what the future would hold for me but for the first time in my life I felt like it was I calling the shots and I was in charge of my own destiny.

At the end of my last tour of duty I put all of my kit into my locker as usual. Handcuffs, CS spray, pocket book, baton and my uniform. It was the last time I'd ever wear it. I'd always imagined that I'd spend my entire working life as a police officer but instead it was only 12 years.

As I walked out of the station for the last time my mind drifted back to the most memorable times I'd experienced. The highs were the great camaraderie on Red Watch at Little Park Street and Stechford, my time in the CID, passing my law degree, sergeants', detectives' and inspectors' exams. I'd worked with some brilliant people who were a joy to spend eight hours with every day, a third of my life for 12 years, in fact.

I'd worked with some brilliant police supervisors including Insp. Ross and my fellow sergeants Al and Mick at Stechford. I'd helped to arrest and imprison hundreds of bad people and felt that I'd made a difference to the people in the areas I worked in.

The lows were the bullying by Jed, my few days with that ignoramus Jay, the endless walking around the city centre on my own in the early hours of the morning and worst of all, the cover-up when Dale was beaten unconscious during the ill-conceived toilet operation.

I'd been in love, broken hearts and had my heart broken. I'd been relatively well-off and then fallen into the most dreadful amount of debt I thought possible. I had yet to face up to the prospect of managing my way out of that.

I opened the door of my old battered Saab 900 and sank heavily into the driver's seat. I turned the key, reversed out of the cramped rear yard at Bordesley Green and into Bordesley Green Road. I drove towards the A45 and homewards with a heavy heart. Maybe I was doing the wrong thing and would come to bitterly regret leaving the police. All I knew was that I'd have gone insane if I'd stayed.

I remembered a story Rich B. had told me one day. He said that there was a man standing in a bar having a pint and his dog was sitting next to him whining. Another man came into the bar and stood near to him having a pint himself. After a while he began to wonder why the dog was continually whining. He said to the owner, 'Why is your dog whining so loud, mate?' The owner said, 'It's because he's sitting on a nail that's sticking out of the floorboards.' The man was a bit bemused by this and asked, 'Well, why doesn't he get off the nail then?' and the reply came, 'Because it isn't sharp enough.'

I'd heard a huge number of police officers bitch and whine about their job. They hated it, they weren't being paid enough, it wasn't fair, they weren't getting a promotion and so on. And yet very few would bother their arses to do anything about it. When you dared to suggest that they leave and do something they enjoyed, the excuses would come pouring out about bills to pay, security, pension. All very sad reasons to do something you hate for the rest of your working life. It all comes down to the fact that the nail they were on was not sharp enough.

I'd love to tell you that after I left the police everything was plain sailing. That I went from strength to strength and made loads of money and lived happily ever after. I had some major challenges after I left the police. Some were financial, some with my career and business and some with my personal life. The things I went through over the next six years made what I dealt with in the police look like a picnic. I had a couple of jobs, was made redundant, started my own company, and then almost went bankrupt. I also had a nervous breakdown. All that stuff is a book in itself.

I'm doing great now. I own my own IT training company and a publishing company which is great fun and both are doing well. I make more money than I could ever have dreamed of making as a police officer and live in a wonderful house that I never thought I'd be able to afford, but more importantly, I'm happier than ever.

Sometimes people ask me if I regret leaving and I have to laugh. Eighteen more years of an endless stream of earlies, lates and nights working for a different boss every 12 months and the only thing to look forward to is retiring broke and tired aged 49 and to die of a heart attack a couple of years later. No thanks. I'd rather take my chances.

All I can say is that most of the things I worried about happening to me when I left the police never happened. There have been some very tough times, but due mostly to my decision to run my own business and working out how to do it without going bust.

I enjoyed my time in the police. I learned a lot about life while I was in there and had some great experiences. It also changed me as a person, some ways for the better but in many ways for the worse. I'd joined the job as a boy and became a man. I'd seen and done things that many people will never see or do in their lives and probably wouldn't want to.

I'd always done my best under very difficult circumstances. The police got their money's worth out of me and then some.

I became very confident and self-assured. I learned how to react in an emergency and how to be a team player and lead a team. I also became unable to express my emotions and how I was feeling. I became judgemental and dismissive of other people whom I labelled 'wasters' or 'chavs'.

Paul the policeman took six years and a lot of counselling, reading and soul-searching to die. I realised that I joined the police to go out and catch bad people and keep the public safe from harm, because if I saved enough people, then somehow I would save myself.

≈ ≈

Thank you so much for reading *The Good Guys Wear Blue*. I have put a hidden chapter on the page below as a 'Thank You' for buying my book. I hope you enjoy it.

www.goodguyswearblue.com/hiddenchapter.htm